W9-DFZ-567

Anthems, Sonnets, and Chants

Anthems, Sonnets, and Chants

Recovering the African American
Poetry of the 1930s

JON WOODSON

THE OHIO STATE UNIVERSITY PRESS • COLUMBUS

Copyright © 2011 by The Ohio State University.
All rights reserved.

Library of Congress Cataloging-in-Publication Data
Woodson, Jon.
Anthems, sonnets, and chants : recovering the African American poetry of the 1930s
/ Jon Woodson.
    p. cm.
Includes bibliographical references and index.
ISBN-13: 978-0-8142-1146-5 (cloth : alk. paper)
ISBN-10: 0-8142-1146-1 (cloth : alk. paper)
ISBN-13: 978-0-8142-9245-7 (cd)
    1. American poetry—African American authors—History and criticism. 2. Depres-
sions—1929—United States. 3. Existentialism in literature. 4. Racism in literature. 5.
Italo-Ethiopian War, 1935–1936—Influence. I. Title.
PS153.N5W66 2011
811'5209896073—dc22
                                        2010022344

This book is available in the following editions:
Cloth (ISBN 978-0-8142-1146-5)
CD-ROM (ISBN 978-0-8142-9245-7)

Cover design by Laurence Nozik
Text design by Jennifer Shoffey Forsythe
Type set in Adobe Minion Pro
Printed by Thomson-Shore, Inc.

The paper used in this publication meets the minimum requirements of the American
National Standard for Information Sciences—Permanence of Paper for Printed Library
Materials. ANSI Z39.48-1992.

9 8 7 6 5 4 3 2 1

FOR LYNN CURRIER SMITH WOODSON

Contents

Acknowledgments

My thanks to Dorcas Haller—professor, librarian, and chair of the Library
Department at the Community College of Rhode Island—for finding
the books that I could not find. Carol Doreski sent me many invaluable
books. I thank Alicia Catlos for digitally transcribing the unpublished
anthology of thirties poems which I assembled as an important part
of my research. I am deeply grateful for Amritjit Singh's longstanding
interest in my work. Without the help of Jean Currie Church, chief
librarian of the Moorland-Spingarn Research Center at Howard University, this project would not have been possible. Two grants from the
Howard University–Sponsored Faculty Research Program in the Social
Sciences, Humanities, and Education greatly furthered my research and
writing.

The students of my African American Poetry classes and of my
graduate seminars at Howard University were instrumental in helping
me develop my understanding of African American poetry and in
locating poems that would otherwise never have come to light. Libraries
that were generous include the Arthur and Elizabeth Schlesinger Library
on the History of Women in America (at Harvard University's Radcliffe
Institute for Advanced Study), the Marcus Christian Collection (at the
University of New Orleans), and the John Hay Library (at Brown University). My affiliate privileges at the Johns Hopkins University's Milton
S. Eisenhower Library are greatly appreciated.

I am deeply obliged to the anonymous reader, whose patient, per-
severing, and discerning comments about my earlier drafts helped
shape the final form of this book. I am also indebted to the anonymous
reviewer of the final draft of the manuscript and acknowledge the many

benefits of that reading. The guidance and support of Sandy Crooms, my editor at The Ohio State University Press, immeasurably sustained me while I wrote this book.

List of Abbreviations

AHD   *American Heritage Dictionary*

AJT   "Bibliography T Entries: Toynbee, Arnold J." *The Encyclo-
        pedia of the Lutheran Church* (3 vols.). Ed. J. H. Bodensiek.
        Philadelphia: 1965. 24 October 2004 http://home.comcast.
        net/~shuv/t_biblio.html.

AYL   *As You Like It.* William Shakespeare

BW   "Amos 'n' Andy in Person—Black and White?"
        Accessed 29 July 2003 http://216.239.53.104/
        search?q+cache:dFhWa1LGydsJ:www.midcoast.com/~lizmcl/
        aa11

DP   "Documentary Photography as a Medium." 13 July 2009.
        http://xroads.virginia.edu/~UG99/brady/doc.html.

DV   Redmond, Eugene. *Drumvoices: The Mission of Afro-American
        Poetry: A Critical History.* Garden City: Anchor Press, 1976.

EA   "Blacks in the Great Depression." *Encyclopedia Africana.*
        Accessed 22 July 2007 http://www.africana.com/articles/tt-644.
        htm.

KJV   *King James Version,* the Bible.

MAPS   *Anthology of Modern American Poetry.* Ed. Cary Nelson. New
        York: Oxford, 2000. Online journal. Web.

NRSV   *New Revised Standard Version,* the Bible. 1989.

PAA   *Propaganda and Aesthetics: The Literary Politics of
        Afro-American Magazines in the Twentieth Century.* Abby
        Arthur Johnson and R. M. Johnson. Amherst: University of
        Massachusetts Press, 1979.

SP   *Selected Poems of Claude McKay.* New York: Harvest, 1953.

VFHR *Voices from the Harlem Renaissance.* Ed. Nathan Irvin Huggins.
New York: Oxford University Press, 1976.

VS "Victorian Seedlings of the Twentieth Century." Accessed
22 July 2007 http://www.yale.edu/ynhti/curriculum/
units/1982/4/82.04.05.x.html.

Introduction

Literary recovery is a response to some mode of marginalization. In the case of the black American poetry of the thirties, there were three directly marginalizing factors: racism, history, and ideology. As Wahneema Lubiano has shown, racism presents a particularly difficult obstacle: "Afro-Americanists have often interpreted [African American] texts as if the relationship of a text to its production was an always already known quantity that could be referred to as a casually explicit or implicit reflection of the racism of the dominant culture. Such references suggest that racism operates always under a set of conditions that anyone could recognize. . . . For most of the period between its publication in 1937 and the early 1970s, for example, Zora Neale Hurston's *Their Eyes Were Watching God* was excluded by the movers and shakers of the Harlem Renaissance and then by Richard Wright's agenda. Now it is taken for granted that Hurston is part of the Afro-American tradition" (434).

In addition to racism, there were the exigencies of history. Writing in 1940, Langston Hughes suggested that the economic crash in the fall of 1929 marked the end of the Harlem Renaissance, for from that point on, "We were no longer in vogue, we Negroes" (*The Big Sea* 334). We now read Hughes's words from a perspective so totalized and immersed in the elaborate mythology of the Harlem Renaissance that it is barely possible to register the disturbing disposition of Hughes's discourse. Some sense of the unease is, however, detectable in the semantic shifts

1

that the phrase has undergone. Alain Locke had already written of a "fad" for "Negro things" in "Art or Propaganda?" (312). In its final form, the title of David Levering Lewis's book, *When Harlem Was in Vogue,* periodized the brief moment with a metonymic substitution of place for people. These shifting subject positions point to the question of whether or not, following the crash of 1929, the Negro and black cultural productions were to be allowed to revert to their devastating former position in American culture, or whether the interval of interest in the Negro and in Negro things marked a stage of social progress in an evolutionary process. The theorists of the Harlem Renaissance had hoped to construct a program of artistic production that would lead to social progress. In 1931, James Weldon Johnson wrote, "A people may become great through many means, but there is only one measure by which its greatness is recognized and acknowledged. The final measure of the greatness of all peoples is the amount and standard of the literature and art they have produced. The world does not know that a people is great until that people produces great literature and art. No people that has produced great literature and art has ever been looked upon by the world as inferior" (281). Then, with the crash of 1929, history intruded and wrecked the Negro's advance to greatness. It was with a historical metaphor that Alain Locke acknowledged that the Harlem Renaissance period had been traumatically set apart from the Great Depression; in 1938, he wrote, "In self-extenuation, may I say that as early as 1927 I said . . . 'Remember, the Renaissance was followed by the Reformation'" ("Jingo, Counter-Jingo and Us" 9). In other words, in the African American culture of the 1930s there existed a discourse that registered a perceptible break between the social triumphs of the 1920s and the setbacks of the 1930s. The reformation that Locke looked to as a succession to the Harlem Renaissance was the new culture ushered into the decade of the 1930s by a series of social catastrophes. The reformation was but a transitional stage in an ongoing evolutionary process, not a period unto itself, and in the end Locke saw that the process would lead to "great universalized art" (*PAA* 103). My argument is that *Harlem* and *renaissance* have subsequently come to signal the discursive construct of the Harlem Renaissance as a uniformity of space, time, and form that were never historical and material realities: most of the writers had left Harlem by 1932 (Bremer, "Home" 3). Joyce W. Warren has observed that "African American literary critics . . . have generally approached periodization by separating black literature from conventional divisions of white writers and identifying African American periods (the Harlem Renaissance, for example, instead of modernism)" (x). In contrast to the idealizing semiotics of a "Harlem Renaissance," Harlem writing was the work of a handful of moderately productive writers. The literature of the succeeding years lacked any such semiotic definitiveness; very few periods in African American literary history have been identified and named. Thus, "modern" texts that were not attributed to the Harlem period were easily dismissed and lost, since they lacked the aura of abundance and high accomplishment afforded by an association with the *Harlem Renaissance.*

The third factor, ideology, confronted the black poets of the thirties with critical discourses that defined the centers and the peripheries of African American literature. Perhaps the major component in the development of black literary discourse at the time was the magisterial *The Negro Caravan* anthology of 1941, edited by Sterling A. Brown, Arthur P. Davis, and Ulysses Lee. Deborah Barnes describes the anthology in this way:

The 1941 publication of *The Negro Caravan*—the first comprehensive anthology of African American literature—democratized American literature and, thus, actualized Brown's and Davis's discursive goals. . . . According to the "Preface," the 1082 page volume was designed to meet three specific goals set out by its editors . . . (1) to present a body of artistically valid writing by American Negro authors, (2) to present a truthful mosaic of Negro character and experience in America, and (3) to collect in one volume certain key literary works that have greatly influenced the thinking of American Negroes, and to a lesser degree, that of Americans as a whole (*Caravan* v). The editors incorporated previously excluded or ignored materials, especially those linking Negroes to their slave past and their so-called "primitive folkways"—"truths" most upwardly mobile Blacks were anxious to forget—to create and preserve "a more accurate and revealing story of the Negro writer than has ever been told before" (v). Thus, in addition to a general fare of short stories, poetry, prose, and drama, *The Negro Caravan* includes "unique," culturally relevant selections, such as folk literature, fugitive slave narratives, speeches, pamphlets, letters, journalism, as well as the earliest novels never before anthologized. Importantly, and innovatively, *The Negro Caravan's* canon of Negro writing reflects the breadth of the Negro's full discursive range. Even more significantly, the editors' inclusion of vernacular discourses authenticate and legitimize traditionally disparaged forms of ethnic expression and communication. Devised to introduce, instruct, and enculturate its readers to the vast world of Negro discourse from a Negro's point of view, *The Negro Caravan* transcends mere bibliography by including cultural, historical, and literary interpretations of its selected works. Each of the eight genre sections is prefaced by a still useful historical and critical introduction. Similarly, each author's work is heralded by bio-bibliographic notes. Moreover, the inclusion of "a chronology of events in American history and literature that have significant pertinence to the writings of American Negroes, as well as a chronology of the history and literature of Negroes," renders the anthology's comprehensiveness and pedagogic influence indisputable and, likewise, revolutionary. *The Negro Caravan's* enlarged scope—its work songs, spirituals, blues, and folk sermons, that is, its vernacular cultural artifacts—ensured a more "democratic" representation of Negroes within the text than segregation or Black middle-class strivings allowed beyond it. Hoping to be useful "not only to students of American literature, but also to students of American social history," the editors enforced a measure of literary equality. They write in the Preface, [The anthology] presents the literary record of America's largest minority group, and in doing so it sheds light upon American culture and minority problems. It pieces out a mosaic more representative than is to be found in any other single volume. Many classes of Negroes, from many sections, undergoing many sorts of experiences, are shown in this mosaic." (vi)

While some aspects of *The Negro Caravan* are tremendously progressive, other aspects are equally erosive. The editors worked with the attitude that their anthology was set in opposition to the misaligned desires of a socially retrograde black bourgeoisie:

> Writers belonging to the "we are just like you school"—as Davis called the proponents of "raceless" literature in his anthology *The New Negro Renaissance*—employed counter-discourses designed to undermine racist exclusion by proving their author's mimesis of white aesthetics and domestic values, specifically those advocating middle-class respectability and materialism. The "best-foot-forward school's" writing which "in no wise pointed to Negro authorship" (*Renaissance* 70) eschewed the vernacular-authentic aspects of Negro culture according to Davis and Brown—consequently, alienating itself from the Black masses and, thus, from realistic cultural representation. Embarrassed by Black folk idioms and "primitive" folkways, "old guard" writers—in discourses tempered generally for the tastes of white readers—were quick to note their assimilation to the "raceless" mainstream and, more significantly, their estrangement from Negro "low life." (Barnes 990)

These concepts are particularly relevant to the poetry of the thirties in Sterling Brown's *Negro Poetry and Drama* (1937), the seventh volume in Alain Locke's Bronze Booklet series of adult education pamphlets for the Associates in Negro Folk Education. In the "Summary" of that publication, Sterling Brown makes clear his opinion of poetry in the thirties:

Contemporary Negro poets are too diverse to be grouped into schools. Certain chief tendencies, however, are apparent. More than Alberry Whitman, Dunbar, and Braithwaite, the contemporary poets, even when writing subjective lyrics, are more frankly personal, less restrained, and as a general rule, less conventional. They have been influenced by modern American poetry, of course, as their elders were by post-Victorian [poetry], but one of the cardinal lessons of modern poetry is that the poet should express his own view of life in his own way. It has been pointed out, however, that "bookishness" still prevails, that the so-called new poetry revival has left many versifiers untouched. Secondly, more than the older poets who hesitantly advanced defenses of the Negro, the contemporary Negro poet is more assured, more self-reliant. He seems less taken in by American hypocrisy and expresses his protest now with irony, now with anger, seldom with humility. The poets who have taken folk-types and folk-life for their province no longer accept the stereotyped view of the traditional dialect writers, nor, lapsing into gentility, do they flinch from an honest portrayal of folk life. Their laughter has more irony in it than buffoonery. They are ready to see the tragic as well as the pitiful. They are much closer to the true folk product than to the minstrel song.

It is not at all advanced that the contemporary poetry of the American Negro is to be ranked with the best of modern poetry. Too many talented writers have stopped suddenly after their first, sometimes successful gropings. The Negro audience is naturally small, and that part devoted to poetry, much smaller. Few Negro poets have the requisite time for maturing, for mastering technique, for observation of the world and themselves. Negro poets have left uncultivated many fields opened by modern poetry. Many still confine their models to the masters they learned about in school, to the Victorians, and the pre-Raphaelites. Almost as frequently they have been unaware of the finer uses of tradition. The reading world seems to be ready for a true interpretation of Negro life from within, and poets with a dramatic ability have before them an important task. And the world has always been ready for the poet who in his own manner reveals his deepest thoughts and feelings. What it means to be a Negro in the modern world is a revelation much needed in poetry. But the Negro poet must write so that whosoever touches his book touches a man. Too often, like other minor poets, he has written so that whosoever touches his book touches the books of other and greater poets. (127–29)

Following the division established between the bookish poets and the "poets who have taken folk-types and folk-life for their province," *The Negro Caravan* published poets of the social realist group, while the poets of the "romantic" group were not included and in effect were thereafter overlooked by literary critics and scholars. In *The Negro Caravan*, Brown, Davis, and Lee did not so much select the African American canon as theorize the critical lens that prevailed over the reception of African American literature for many years to come. Thus, Deborah Barnes states that "[Brown and Davis] lived to see accurate, racially subjective depictions of African American perspectives increase and gain authority in mainstream discourses" (995). When it came down to actually publishing poems from the 1930s, the editors of *The Negro Caravan* included six poems by Sterling Brown (taking up eleven pages), four poems by Frank Marshall Davis (six pages), Melvin B. Tolson's award-winning "Dark Symphony" (three and a half pages), two poems by Owen Dodson (one page), Richard Wright's "I Have Seen Black Hands" (two pages), five poems by Robert Hayden (four and a half pages), and Margaret Walker's "For My People" (two pages). While all of this work bypasses the Victorians (and the pre-Raphaelites, whom Sterling Brown so criticizes in the "Summary" discussed above), the poems are instead merely rooted in the work of Whitman and Sandburg, with a few digression into imagism, albeit an imagism heavily shaded by the despondent satire of *The Spoon River Anthology.* "For My People" is particularly derivative; it recapitulates the stylistic mechanization and social horror of Carl Sandburg's *The People, Yes*. Sandburg's poem first questions its audience, only then to alienate it. When one turns away from the exhausting rhetoric of *The People, Yes*, one also rejects the image of society that it proposes. It offers us, on the one hand, an unacceptable status quo of oppression and victimization and, on the other hand, a revolution for and by a nameless, boundless, philistine multitude (Reed 208). As the "Summary" demonstrates, Brown does not make great claims for the aesthetic accomplishments of those poets in the 1930s who pursued social realist subjects and styles. Rather, the editors of *The Negro Caravan* were far more concerned with establishing and advancing a program of racially subjective folk-oriented literature (Barnes 995).

Much might be said about the merits and demerits of the racially subjective folk-oriented approach to literature, particularly because in many respects its influence continues to dominate much of contemporary literary and critical activity, while its contradictions and blind spots have never been entirely recognized or resolved. This study is not directed toward the decentering of the folk-oriented discourse of that undertaking and instead turns aside to consider the cultural function of the poetry of the 1930s without being persuaded by the aesthetic and ideological assessments of the critics at the time. In order to approach the poetry with a better grasp of its relationship to the discourses of the period, I place the poetry in relation to the crises that affected the lives of African Americans directly—the Great Depression;

the existential-identity crisis; and the Italo-Ethiopian War, with its threat of race war. One measure of this thematic approach through cultural discourses is to take stock of these crises by studying the poetry presented in *The Negro Caravan*. Through its valorization of racially subjective folk-oriented literature, the anthology is grounded in the recognition of the centrality of what I am calling the existential-identity crisis. At the same time, the mode in which the anthology historicizes African American culture places the poets in an idealized space outside of historical reality; the anthology includes no poetry that addresses the material realities of the period. *The Negro Caravan*'s "American Scene" entry for 1929 offers "Collapse of the New York stock market, followed by business depression" (1075), but the "Negro World" entries between 1930 and 1940 list novels by Hughes, Hurston, Fauset, and others, and a few major events, such as the first Scottsboro trials and the Harlem race riots. Even Tolson's "Dark Symphony," the only poem that can be said to incorporate historic events, erects heroic action and "inauthentic collective representation" (Reed 208) within the sublimated space of its symphony in an unresolved transcendence of the contemporary crises. Similarly, the implied historical narrative of Walker's "For My People" ordains its utopian end to history without conceptualizing the change of consciousness that is required to make possible such a social outcome: the poem depicts a black collectivity in a static culture. My study does discuss works by some of the poets included in *The Negro Caravan* (for example, Hughes, Dodson, and Wright); however, the works in which they confront the three crises under discussion are not included in *The Negro Caravan*. Thus, even when I take up poets who were included in *The Negro Caravan*, it is necessary to recover other texts by Hughes, Dodson, Tolson, and Wright.

The stock market crash of 1929 and the Great Depression that followed intervened in the cultural maturation of the New Negro movement, disrupting to a considerable degree the movement's cultural capital and displacing its program of social progress through art. Millions of people needed food, clothing, and shelter after the collapse of the American economic system. Black poets reacted to the new conditions indirectly, for there are few poems that address the crash or the Great Depression thematically; rather, the effects of the crash and the Great Depression form the background to themes that arise from the new conditions. In 1937 Eugene Holmes stated at the Second American Writers' Congress that "there has scarcely been any poetry—a few wilderness cries from Langston Hughes, Sterling Brown and Richard Wright, and with only one or two new names, like Owen Dodson and Frank Davis" (177). Holmes's dismissal of the black poets of the 1930s was but one of the several voices that established the truism that the Great Depression ushered in a time of poetic bankruptcy. One of the chief reasons for recovering the poetic work of this controversial and opaque decade is to disprove the truism that this period was a time of artistic inarticulacy and mediocrity for African Americans.

Ideology, the third factor contributing to the forgetting of black poets of the thirties, came into play in the political discourses that contextualized and shaped a larger understanding of that decade. Gloria Hull identifies the main thrust of the treatment of thirties poetry when she comments that "Hughes' 1930s poems are usually deemed inferior" to his nonpolitical poetry (quoted in Duffy 201). More broadly, in *New Deal Modernism: American Literature and the Invention of the Welfare State,* Michael Szalay addresses the forgetting and the recovery of thirties writing as the conflict between a dominant conservative culture and relatively powerless radical intellectuals:

> Without doubt, the most impressive new scholarship on the thirties and forties—from Alan Wald's *The Revolutionary Imagination* (1983), through Cary Nelson's *Repression and Recovery* (1989), Paula Rabinowitz's *Labor and Desire* (1991), James Bloom's *Left Letters* (1992), Barbara Foley's *Radical Representations* (1993), Alan Filreis's *Modernism from Right to Left* (1994), and Constance Coiner's *Better Red* (1995) to Michael Denning's *Cultural Front* (1997)—has explored comprehensively the often conflicted corporate identities that operated on the left of the period. These critics have tended to understand literary politics by mobilizing increasingly refined distinctions between conservative and radical, Stalinist and Trotskyist, fellow traveler and Popular Front moderate, and, most recently, between a "cultural front" and mainstream communism and liberalism. Understanding the politics of the era through impressively involved research, this body of scholarship faithfully reproduces and negotiates the often agonized constellation of political identities available to the radical writer of the time. Yet precisely because of the scruple for historical detail these critics have brought to their work, their otherwise excellent scholarship has operated within some very discernible parameters. In part because the distinctions among different political groups of the era seem crucial to these critics, their work has tended— with one exception, we will see—to "recover" the traditional protocols of literary biography as much as the literature of heretofore neglected writers. Hoping to compensate for a tradition of cold war criticism that whitewashed the impact of thirties radicalism, most of these critics believe that the most intelligent political accounts of the literature of the thirties and forties were made during the thirties and forties. (16–17)

In addition to the texts that Szalay lists, numerous cultural studies approaches are "dedicated to recovering and reevaluating repressed or forgotten, largely leftist or politically progressive poetry from the first half of the century" (Chasar).[1] Szalay's approach to the New Deal is salutary in that he refashions the assumptions that have been applied to this period. This revisionist tendency needs to be continued to the point where critics abandon their conventional dependence on the politics of the Left as a means to analyze the vast cultural production of this virtually neglected period and also in order that they may see past the ancillary categorizations that limit and preordain the investigation of an underappreciated but considerable body of literary production.

To avoid falling prey to the errors inherent in arbitrary periodization, I have situated my investigation of poetry as "social text" around three distinct "historical crises" (DuPlessis 26). However, the periodization of the thirties was not arbitrary; many of those who experienced these crises saw them as breaks in history that signaled a new historical period. I have interpreted poems by capitalizing on the ability of social philology[2] to resolve the apparent disconnectedness of "mixed methodologies," which seem questionable when associated with the notion that the poem is autotelic,[3] bracketed off from the world. Social philology uses the outside as if it were inside the language, so what appears to be an eclectic methodology is not that at all. Rather than thinking of the theories used in this study (Kittler's discourse networks [poststructuralist media theory], film theory, interart theory, semantic analysis, Virilio's dromomatics, psychoanalysis, and McGann and Bornstein's materialism) as *other* modes of literary analysis, here they are considered extensions of the *"interconnection of the work's elements"* (Dewanto "Periphery"; emphasis added). The relationship within social philology between "outside" and "inside" is further described by Maria Damon: *"Equal attention to the outlying context surrounding poetry's production, distribution, and reception, and to its inner workings will reveal how mutually imbricated, constitutive, and reflective these are"* (687; emphasis added). Thus, situated dialectically to the idea of the autotelic poem, "social philology" is not a "mixed methodology" despite the eclectic appearance it gains from its complex theoretical resourcefulness and diverse methodological inclusions.

The first chapter presents three long poems that confront the African American experience of the crash and the Great Depression—the watershed events of the thirties. Of the three poets discussed in the first chapter, Richard Wright is the only canonical figure, though he holds this status as a novelist and writer of short stories. But Wright published a dozen poems in leftist journals before he published fiction, and his antilynching poems, "Between the World and Me" and "I Have Seen Black Hands," have become anthology pieces—with the latter included in *The Negro Caravan*. His most

ambitious poem, "Transcontinental," has received no previous critical attention. The parallel neglect of Langston Hughes's radical poetry from the thirties perhaps suggests that the absolutism that characterizes Wright's third
period has similarly inhibited investigation. While ideologically predictable, "Transcontinental" is a stylistic departure from Wright's better known
poems: it is a surrealistic tour de force that uses revolutionary zeal to successfully unite, on the one hand, popular culture, American myth, and contemporary tensions between individual angst and unrest and, on the other
hand, longings for a collective destiny. "Transcontinental" turns out to be
Wright's most sophisticated and resourceful poem.

In contrast to the celebrated career of Richard Wright, Welborn Victor
Jenkins was nearly erased from literary history; little is known of his life,
and his work might have been entirely forgotten if not for one vague (but
sufficient) mention in Eugene Redmond's *Drumvoices*. Redmond was aware
of Jenkins thanks to the list of thirties poets that Sterling Brown provided
in *Negro Poetry and Drama*. This study's presentation and discussion of
"Trumpet in the New Moon" is my most significant recovery of a forgotten
work. Not only is "Trumpet" a poem of impressive length but also it is thematically rich, poetically innovative, and intellectually original. While Jenkins was praised in Sterling Brown's *Negro Poetry and Drama*, the length of
his poem perhaps prevented him from being included in *The Negro Caravan*,
an omission that no doubt played a major role in his being silenced.

Owen Dodson was another of the social realist poets whom Sterling
Brown listed in his 1937 pamphlet. He is represented in *The Negro Caravan*
by the small and diffuse "Cradle Song" ("Aluminum birds flying with fear /
will scream to you waking" [lines 7–8]), and a backward-looking ode to the
two white women who founded Spelman College. Thus, Dodson's sequence
of four sonnets, "Negro History," is yet another recovery that restores a
neglected master poet to attention, and one suspects that it was Dodson's use
of the sonnet that kept "Negro History" out of the anthology. The long poem
is a privileged modernist genre, where scope, transcendence, dynamism, and
difficulty, not length, are the determining factors of a poem's achievement.
As Lynn Keller indicates:

> I don't wish to quibble how long is long, a particularly fruitless activ-
> ity given that the scale of a poem as literary/cultural practice cannot
> necessarily be corelated simply to its scale as an object. After all, "The
> Waste Land," a central modernist long poem, has only 434 lines, and
> works like Gwendolyn Brook's "Anniad," or John Ashbery's "A Wave" or
> "Self-Portrait in a Convex Mirror," while far from being book-length,
> certainly have the heft of long poems. In some contexts, the complexity

of a poem's intent and conception, as well as its length. Relative to other works in a poet's *oeuvre,* might better determine whether it should be considered as a long poem than the number of pages it occupies. . . . (Keller 20–21)

Like many of the African American poets from the thirties, Dodson was a poet without a book. One characteristic common to the works of these so-called magazine poets is an impressive compression of theme, atmosphere, emotion, and memory. Dodson's "Negro History" is indeed the breathtaking distillation of his vision of an imperiled people who are held in suspension at a point of historical extremity and trial.

Cornel West has observed that African Americans entered modernity with the provision that they were things. In conflict with such insupportable repression was the emancipatory notion that "the project of the self—of an identity that one 'works on' for one's entire life—is itself the cornerstone of modernity" (Kimmel). Chapter 2 examines the need for *self-fashioning* (the development of identities), a need that arose in opposition to the existential obliteration of the African American by the ever-increasing persuasiveness of technological media. In the 1930s, radio, magazines, and films reinforced the inferiority of the black American in compelling and powerful ways, and a largely unrecognized body of poetry responded to this negative identity. The chapter takes the many sonnets published by African American poets in the thirties as the sign of the self-in-process. In order to examine the various subject positions available to African Americans in the thirties, I have assembled the sonnets into a metatext that treats the work of multiple authors as though they are the work of one author of a sonnet sequence: this collectivizing move liberates the poems to be read culturally and pro-duces revealing insights into the zeitgeist. While many studies deal with the "sonnetized" body, the treatment of the African American body in connec-tion with the sonnet opens a new chapter in literary and cultural analysis. In "Toward the Black Interior," Elizabeth Alexander states that

the black body has been misrepresented, absented, distorted, rendered invisible, exaggerated, made monstrous in the Western visual imagina-tion and in the world of art. The visual art world hegemony is very, very white. Black people have always made art and always imagined and understood ourselves to be other than monstrous stereotype. Therefore, the "real" black figure is a very different thing from the imagined one, and versions of what that "realness" looks like will frequently contradict each other. How do we understand "reality" when official narratives deny what our bodies know? (6–7)

The black body is not commonly associated with the sonnet (a few essays on Claude McKay being the exception, though they are more concerned with the body as body rather than the sonnet as body). Even Alexander, in her discussion of Brooks's turn to the sonnet in the 1940s, observes that "the sonnet is a 'little room,' and Brooks reveals the equivalent of painted tableaux in her sonnets" (6). Nor has the considerable extent to which black poets in the thirties published sonnets been previously realized. The chapter moves to a new understanding of the sonnet, beyond the framing of the sonnet as "the body of the sonnet—a privilege-soaked, white-identified form" (Palatnik) to the absorption of the sonnet into the black literary imagination where it became a component of new identities and new psychosocial potentialities. The thirties was simultaneously a time of social constraint and sociocultural richness—for African Americans as well as for whites—making available a wealth of materials for the construction of new individual, social, and collective identities. Broadly speaking, African Americans were successful in resisting the effects of the crisis in capitalism and the resulting social crises that were visited upon African Americans even as they were increasingly unable to compete for a share of the dwindling stock of national resources. The chapter examines the materials that African American poets used when constructing new identities through sonnets. The literary record provides evidence of the transformation of abjection, trauma, and inarticulacy into personhood, autonomy, and vocal citizenship.

The third chapter presents the body of poetry that addresses two topics that most Americans have forgotten—the Italo-Ethiopian War (1934–36) and the concept of race war. In the thirties Oswald Spengler's *Decline of the West* (1918) was a highly influential book, and part of its influence was that it disseminated the possibility of a war between races in which the white race was exterminated. The association of the fascist invasion of Ethiopia with race war was an inflammatory mixture for the African Americans of the thirties, so when it spilled over into poetic expression, it produced a stirring body of poetry. The interpretations layered onto this unique historical event ranged from labeling it a legal lynching to viewing it as the prelude to the end of the world. The chapter follows the drama of African Americans who assumed a variety of traumatic postures—warrior, victim, monster, citizen, and revolutionary—while taking note of the complex mixture of forces that these events directed toward African Americans.

While it is true that there were relatively few volumes of poetry published by African Americans in the thirties, no critic has dealt with the totality of what is known to exist. Several volumes have never come under discussion, presumably because they do not express a suitably social realist politics. In the body of work that is denigrated as romantic and escapist, the inner-directed gaze supposedly represents the counter movement to a communal polarity; but where individual expression and idealized art make themselves felt as discourses, they must be taken into account as legitimate discourses of the period. In other cases, important anthologies and volumes of poetry have been lost to literary history, and by recovering them, as I have in a few cases in this study, a fuller account of the culture has been made available. Generally, there is a tension between interiority and exteriority in the black poetry of the 1930s: the black intellectuals who dominated the interpretive discourses of the 1930s valorized exteriority, while black culture heedlessly and inexorably plunged into interiority. This dichotomy has barely been recognized, and where it has been, it has not been taken up as a topic for cultural analysis. One of the few exceptions is Elizabeth Alexander's *The Black Interior*, in which the binary emerges not as the opposition of the interior and the exterior but rather as the contradiction of the real and the dream:

If black people in the mainstream imaginary exist as fixed properties deemed "real," what is possible in the space we might call surreal? [Nto-zake] Shange powerfully suggests that the contagion of racism seeps into the intimate realms of the subconscious and affects how black people ourselves see and imagine who we are. Indeed, by writing a book of dream poems I learned that race, gender, class, sexuality—our social identities—exist and have been "always already" constructed in the dream space, even when they are constructed outside of a racist impetus. I imagined that in dream space I was a somehow "neutral" self, but found no such neutrality there. Yet social identity in unfettered dream space need not be seen as a constraint but rather as a way of imagining the racial self unfettered, racialized but not delimited. What I am calling dream space is to my mind the great hopeful space of African American creativity. Imagining a racial future in the black interior that we are constrained to imagine, outside of the parameters of how we are seen in this culture, is the zone where I am interested in African American creativity. "The black interior" is not an inscrutable zone, nor colonial fantasy. Rather, I see it as inner space in which black artists have found selves that go far, far beyond the limited expectations and definitions of what black is, isn't, or should be.

As black people we have been bound by mainstream constructions of our "real," and we have bound ourselves with expectations that we counter those false realities. (6)

This subject position that is "racialized but not delimited" had been anticipated by Sterling Brown and Arthur Davis in the thirties, as Deborah Barnes points out. The editors of *The Negro Caravan* had constructed their own version of the *insubordination* of the bluesman, an insubordination that dissented from the prevailing stereotypes of blacks: "In short, [Arthur P.] Davis asks Negroes to acknowledge their interpretive agency and autonomy. He wants them to replace self-alienating, stereotypic perceptions of the Black experience with their own; that is, he wants them to apprehend and evaluate their world from *a subjective perspective*—whatever that is—rather than swallowing whole received knowledge which denigrates Negroes" (992; emphasis added). Whereas the bluesman carries his insubordination into violence toward the community or toward the self as a form of resistance, black intellectuals of the thirties still longed for the "emancipatory" authenticity of the folk form. Thus, *The Negro Caravan* is freighted with folk texts and modern re-creations of folk-rooted insubordination. But Elizabeth Alexander' theorization represents a further advance in which there is a recognition of the problematic anchoring of the racial "real": "Many black viewers are looking for 'positive imagery,' and while we often need those images, the power of the wish places constraints on what a black artist might feel free to envision and find in that subconscious space" (7–8). To the extent that I have been able, I have attempted to follow the delineation of the struggle between the inner and outer worlds, a study made all the more difficult by the contemporary intellectual culture, which does not condone the search for the consistent, integrated self. This study, then, takes pains to recover the chthonic discourses of negative identity from which the African American poetry of the 1930s emerged.

1

The Crash of 1929 and the Great Depression

THREE LONG POEMS

THREE JEREMIADS

> Prophecy is the individualizing of the revolutionary impulse . . . and is
> geared to the future.
> —Northrop Frye, *The Great Code*

The three poems discussed in this chapter—Wright's surrealist montage, Dodson's sonnet sequence, and Jenkins's Whitmanesque catalog—are representative texts through which black poets have given literary form to the crash and the Great Depression. These poems might seem to have little else in common. However, all three poems center their discourses on the proposition that a sociocultural failure of ethics produced the Great Depression. When we look past the poems' differences in forms and discourses, we see that a common concern with ethics aligns all three texts through the language and thought of the American jeremiad. In *The American Jeremiad,* Sacvan Bercovitch observes that the European jeremiad, a lament over the ways of the world (7), was modified in America to convey the myth of a uniquely American mission: "The question in these latter-day jeremiads, as in their seventeenth century precursors, was never 'Who are we?' but, almost in deliberate evasion of that question, the old prophetic refrain: 'When is our errand to be fulfilled? How long, O Lord, how long?'" (Bercovitch 11). Applying Bercovitch's ideas to African American rhetoric, David Howard-Pitney in *The Afro-American Jeremiad* proposes that "the complete rhetorical structure of the American jeremiad has three elements: citing the promise; criticism of present declension, or retrogression from the promise; and a resolving *prophesy* that society will shortly complete its mission and redeem the promise" (8; emphasis in original). Howard-Pitney contributes the insight that African Americans see themselves as "a chosen people within a chosen people" (15) and as such have adopted the jeremiad and extended it as "a prime form of black social rhetoric and ideology well into the twentieth century" (15). Howard-Pitney notes that "the American jeremiad has been frequently adapted for the purposes of black protest and propaganda" so that it "characteristically addresses *two* American chosen peoples—black and white—whose millennial destinies, while distinct, are also inextricably entwined"(11). What Bercovitch calls a "litany of hope" (11) would seem well adapted to the needs of an incompletely emancipated minority group that is faced with the two-fold catastrophe of racial oppression and the Great Depression's rampant unemployment.

Given these twin calamities, African Americans felt the need both to describe their deteriorating and insupportable socioeconomic situation and to invoke themes of imminent social, political, and economic emancipation. It is immediately apparent that the problematic presented by the black poets' jeremiad represents a complex set of responses to social problems and aesthetic concerns. While for African Americans, the conditions under which they were forced to live in *normal* times represented grave weaknesses in the American social fabric, the crisis of the Great Depression and the contingent exacerbation of their social, economic, and political problems presented the prospect of a type of social failure hitherto unforeseen and unimaginable. Bercovitch suggests something of the gravity of this situation in his more general comments on the symbol of America (as it pertains to the construction of the American civil religion [*Afro-American Jeremiad* 195 n.6]): "The symbol of America magnified the culture into a cosmic totality: Hence the euphoria of its adherents. But the same process of magnification carried a dangerous correlative: if America failed, then the cosmos itself—the laws of man, nature, and history, the very basis of heroism, insight, and hope—had failed as well" (*American Jeremiad* 190). Thus, the theme of ethical failure results from a concern with cosmic failure: the poets' attempts to assign the crisis an identifiable cause, to place the crisis in a historical framework, and to determine the manner in which the crisis might be resolved foregrounded American society's latent social failures. All three poets viewed the Great Depression as a further development of the pervasive crisis of the black community.

In "Transcontinental," Richard Wright renders into poetry the black revolutionary sublime; Wright is faithful to the form of the American jeremiad to a remarkable degree, though given the pervasive biblical intertextuality of his poem, we might have expected this to be so. Wright has cast his poem into a primary concern with the controlling device in the discourse of the American jeremiad, what Bercovitch calls "the symbol of America" (176): "Of all symbols of identity, only *America* has united nationality and universality, civic and spiritual selfhood, secular and redemptive history, the country's past and paradise to be, in a single synthetic ideal" (176). The concern with revolutionary politics in Wright's poem reduces America's promise to three one-line refrains ("America who built this dream . . . [7] America who owns this wonderland . . . [15] America America why turn your face away"[25]) and describes the America of the golfing and cocktail-drinking ruling class. Wright's narrator is another, less abstract, manifestation of the failure of the promise: the man who cannot thumb a ride, the man who is literally left out in the cold and going nowhere. This critique is implicit. Wright's narrator knows of the promise only through movies and only as a class-restricted, capitalistic mode of distribution.

If the American jeremiad consists of promise, criticism, and prophecy, Wright's revolutionary joyride is the jeremiadic prophecy, whereby Wright foresees the imminent redistribution of the wealth of the leisure class. Having reached a platform from which he may effectively address his audience, Wright enunciates the promise portion of the jeremiad as the uprising of those wretched proletarians who form the American soviets. Wright's treatment of the jeremiad represents a major departure from the American jeremiad in that he foresees an overthrow of the American system. Bercovitch points out that in the conventional jeremiad, "the revelation of America serves to blight, and ultimately to preclude, the possibility of fundamental social change. To condemn the profane is to commit oneself to a spiritual ideal. To condemn 'false America' as profane is to express one's faith in a national ideology. In effect, it is to transform what might have been a search for moral or social alternatives into a call for cultural revitalization" (179). Wright is, above all, calling in his prophecy for moral and social alternatives of the most far-reaching kind: "America, America / Plains sprout collective farms" (lines 240–41). America will still be America, but it must undergo a radical alteration in order to fulfill the American promise. Wright is trapped in "jeremiadic ambiguities" (Bercovitch 183), so he does not reject the symbol of America; instead, he maintains a vestige of investment in the very American myth that he has set out to analyze and destroy.

Dodson's "Negro History: A Sonnet Sequence" departs from the complete rhetorical structure of the American jeremiad chiefly by restricting the address to African Americans. Dodson embraces what Howard-Pitney refers to as the black nationalistic posture that directed blacks to a redemption and salvation apart from the dominant white culture (15). Though the first three sonnets are addressed to black people in three distinct historical experiences—the Middle Passage, slavery, and Reconstruction—the historical remove of the addresses suggests that the 1930s reader, to whom the entire sequence is directed, is not assumed to be exclusively black. (Because the poem was published in *New Masses* in 1936, the poem in fact reached a wide audience.) The speaker of the first sonnet addresses his fellow slave using the collective "we." The second sonnet presents a pair of speeches that suggests a more complicated diegesis. In the octave the first voice is distinguished from the narrator through the use of quotation marks: the first speaker addresses the slaves as "you." The narrator's rejoinder castigates the first speaker as much for the separation manifested by the use of the second person as for the objectionable tenor of what is being asserted by the person that the narrator calls "this worshipper of dying" (line 9). In the twelfth line, the narrator again takes up the collective "we," where the narrator says "we will mend." In the third sonnet, "Post Emancipation," the speaker's voice is indistinguishable from the group's voice. It is only in the fourth sonnet, "Harlem," that the narrator assumes the previously unsanctioned second-person voice to direct a commanding denunciation *to a contemporary black audience*. Dodson's sonnet sequence, then, is a highly compressed jeremiad. The first three sonnets cite the promise and suggest that the very survival of Africans in the face of an excess of dangers constitutes the collective African American version of the American promise: in Dodson's jeremiad the promise for African Americans is that they are sustained by a future strength—"the hope that we will mend / The patches of these transitory years / With swords, with hate, in spite of frequent tears" ("Past and Future" lines 12–14). The theme of death is foremost among the narrator's concerns; through the first two sonnets, the poems' burden is to demonstrate the African American's heroic rejection of death. In the third sonnet, there is a more considered presentation of the promise, and it is striking to notice that Dodson has not only reified the promise but also dramatized its specific inefficacy: "The parchment that declared that we are free / is now collecting dust in some dark spot, / Despite the promise and the certainty / we thought its words would give, but gave them not" ("Post Emancipation" lines 10–13). "Harlem," the fourth sonnet, combines a further criticism of the present decline from the former heroic posture and the prophecy of a coming redemption. The rebuke is occasioned by black people's willingness to believe that they have somehow fulfilled the promise by assuming the role of the exotic Other. Dodson's narrator denounces the role of African Americans as the "deep, dark flower of the west" ("Harlem" line 1). The narrator urges them to assume another posture: in the concluding lines, the narrator shows that history "reveals the fears / The copper petals must be conscious of / If they would hold their life" (lines 12–14). The second half of the final line presents the redemption of the promise in the new era's brutal terms: "Grow strong or starve." The phrase is a paraphrase and a revision of a famous poem by Langston Hughes, and as such, Dodson's version is a denunciation of the entire project of the so-called Harlem Renaissance. In Hughes's brash and confident poem "I, Too," the American Negro who states in the concluding line that "I, too, am America" (line 18) says from his place in the kitchen, "But I laugh / And eat well, / And grow strong" (lines 5–7).

At issue in "Negro History" is the Harlem Renaissance's discourse of becoming: according to the New Negro movement, the Negro is "ready"— ripe, mature, full grown, and adult. Dodson wishes to intervene in this discourse and to have an end to its ambiguities and evasions. We can recognize that in Dodson's poem the New Negro movement's comedic discourse of growth, in which the fates of all Americans are intertwined, has been replaced with an alternative vision wherein the ambiguous banishment of the Negro to the kitchen (paradoxically, a sure prelude to freedom and inclusion) is at once an indulgent invitation and the enforcement of racial stigmas. Dodson's "Harlem" implies that the New Negro in Hughes's "I, Too" has been sent to eat in the kitchen *like a child,* and thus, childishly and fantastically, the New Negro sits in the kitchen eating heartily and boasting of his gathering strength. The New Negro's uncertain prospects for social advancement have been abrogated by the economic strictures of the Depression. The discourse of both/and (laugh-eat-grow has become in "Harlem" a matter of the conditional—either/or (either grow or starve). African Americans have no choice but to return to the former promise of survival, and the optimistic ending of Hughes's poem, in which the (New) Negro embodies America's promise, has been replaced with the Darwinian injunction to "Grow strong or starve" (line 14).

The most disturbing aspect of Dodson's conclusion is the separation of eating from growing strong: while Hughes's poem represents the imposition of a natural order, the taking of strength from food, Dodson suggests that strength is not contingent on food but on some other means of nourishment. The strength that Dodson invokes in his critiques of Hughes's poem is all the more effective for its rejection of food for strength; in Dodson's version, once black people have become strong, they will find a means to eat. The symbolism of growth frames "Negro History." From the nursing mother of "On the Slave Ship" to the flower, pollen, stamen, and petal described in "Harlem," the seed and the fruit are at issue. The "seed" is prophesied in

"Post Emancipation"—"the seed / Of Freedom" (lines 8–9)—but the seed is a future state, and the document that provides for it "is now collecting dust in some dark spot" (line 10).

We can neatly encapsulate the tension between the New Negro discourse of growth and Dodson's altered discourse of "grow strong or starve" by reading the word "Negro" as soundplay—Ne-*grow*. In Dodson's version, a choice must be made: the contradictory pleasures of the kitchen (the complex that involves such symptoms as "double consciousness," "black and blue," "we wear the mask") are no longer on the table, so to speak, and the Negro must either perish or resolve to persist. The sonnet sequence is an eloquent, acute demand that the Negro people answer the call of their history and produce the fruit that comes at the end of the cycle of growth: to *starve* is not a viable possibility. Neither is starvation a necessity, for the historical arc has been a path from inarticulacy to the articulacy of the jeremiad— and we see that discourse itself is Dodson's theme. The Negroes in Dodson's sequence begin inarticulately with "pounding," "groaning," and the "chant [of] agonizing songs" ("On the Slave Ship" lines 8–11), and in the person of Dodson, their discourse reaches its acme with the crisp and premonitory rhetoric of "grow strong or starve."

Welborn Victor Jenkins's *Trumpet in the New Moon* is couched in the rhetoric of the biblical prophet, though Jenkins chose to quote Psalm 81 in the title rather than to quote Jeremiah. So close was Jenkins to the tradition of the American jeremiad that he utilized its terminology; in framing his presentation of the promise, Jenkins calls it a promise:

> I saw that nation spreading toward the westward.
> Horace Greely gave good advice to the young men—
> St. Louis, Kansas City, Denver, San Francisco
> Took form and grew like mushrooms in the night.
> New Orleans, child of the Mississippi, basking in the
>   rich cotton fields of the Delta,
> Glanced proudly at the rising suns of Promise and Fulfillment.
> (lines 46–51)

At line 104, the poem begins a detailed depiction of "A Break in conduct" (line 107) that enacts Bercovitch's "retrogression from the promise." Like Wright's "Transcontinental," *Trumpet in the New Moon* is addressed to a personified "America," though Jenkins never moves away from this form of address to assume the various distances and intimacies so characteristic of Wright's poem. The prophetic section of *Trumpet in the New Moon* commences with line 410: "God hasten the day when 'Be American' / Shall carry the selfsame

Inspiration / To call forth all the heroism and nobility / That lie dormant in the human spirit" (lines 410–13). Despite the use of the jeremiadic discourse in *Trumpet in the New Moon,* the poem foregrounds a psalmic discourse of group unity acquired through "the metaphor of the individual" (*The Great Code* 90). The centrality of the psalmic discourse in Jenkins's poem elides the actual use of "you," and the poem is addressed to a heroic American "I." This device is used most effectively in the Charles Lindbergh section, where the aviator is an "I" who only becomes a separate "he" once the popular culture bestows fame and gold on him (lines 186–87), an act of separation that violates and repudiates the original collective American soul. The jeremiadic discourse is thus weakened and the device of deriving prophetic authority by the imposition of unpopular views (the need for morality, humility, obedience, and other virtues) (*The Great Code* 126) is moderated by affirming the centrality of the potential heroism of the American individual, the Lindbergian essence of symbolic America.

In the final analysis, even Jenkins, a poet who rejects the solutions offered by the Left, is a social revolutionary, though certainly not in Third Period terms. Poetry did not respond uniformly to the crash and the Great Depression. Instead, black poets made a number of revolutionary attempts to revive American democracy through the master discourses of the American culture. Like the prophets of the Old Testament, the black poets of the thirties derived their authority from the unpopularity of their messages, a stance that was natural given the sundered social margins from which those declarations were made.

RICHARD WRIGHT, "TRANSCONTINENTAL" (1936)

Richard Wright, a member of the Communist Party of the United States of America from 1932 to 1944, was one of the most prominent African American poets of the 1930s, despite his having written and published a mere dozen poems. Wright's combination of racial and proletarian characteristics were warmly received by certain elements of leftist culture. The only leftist African American poet who rivaled Wright's importance was Langston Hughes, but Hughes was not—in terms of Third Period convictions—a model revolutionary writer. Though Langston Hughes had been an advocate of radical causes for several years before the crash, the (economic) collapse of the Harlem Renaissance, and the subsequent interest of many American writers and intellectuals in the politics of the Left, Hughes had received a college education and patronage by wealthy sponsors. He did not join the Communist Party. Wright, a self-educated black poet who migrated from the Deep South to Chicago's slums, presented impeccable proletarian credentials. He also demonstrated a fervent commitment to the Communist program and an ability to write effectively in the service of his newfound cause. Economic hardship and racial oppression befell Richard Wright, forcing him to a new recognition of his place in the world and inspiring him to search for a means to relieve the suffering that he saw around him. The story of Richard Wright's transformation into a revolutionary poet is particularly illuminating. Wright was what his friend and colleague Horace Cayton called a "clear case": "His was a total exposure to the callousness and cruelty of the closed society" (Hill 208). Eugene Redmond gives this précis of Wright's tumultuous early career: "He joined the Communist party in the thirties and remained as a member until 1944. His poetry, coupled with calls for unity between Blacks and whites, was published in various journals and news organs of the period: *International Literature, New Masses, Anvil, Midland,* and *Left*" (*Drumvoices* 224).

The poetry that Wright and Hughes wrote was often sloganized, abstract, and breathlessly fanatical. Both poets lacked the formal, emotional, and imaginative resources of Vladimir Mayakovsky, "the poet of communism," who carried into early Soviet writing the experimental techniques of the prerevolutionary cubo-futurism, a movement with which he had been aligned before becoming a Communist. Wright and Hughes also suffer in comparison to the complex and resourceful surrealism of Louis Aragon. Hughes translated Mayakovsky while living in the Soviet Union in 1933, and Wright patterned what is his "longest and perhaps most ambitious poem" (Fabre 131) on Aragon's "Red Front." (It seems likely that Hughes's poem "Waldorf Astoria" is also derived from Aragon's influential long poem "Red Front.") Both Hughes and Wright fell victim to the limitations of the realistic aesthetics that circumscribed American political poetry in the 1930s. Even though they sought new social realities, Hughes and Wright were limited in their ways of extending that search into literature, and their works often have a banal ring to them, while poems by Aragon and Mayakovsky still hold up (largely because of their verbal pyrotechnics). Nevertheless, the poems that Hughes, Wright, Frank Marshall Davis, Welborn Victor Jenkins, and Melvin B. Tolson wrote in the 1930s were marked departures from what the majority of their black contemporaries were writing. Critics have called Wright's poems "protest poems" (Redmond 223); Dan McCall opines that "[agitprop] poetry has nothing to recommend it other than revolutionary enthusiasm" (47). However, Wright's poems are ones of dissent and struggle, not protest. James Scully states that "by rights we should distinguish dissident poetry from protest poetry. Most protest poetry is conceptually shallow. . . . Dissident poetry, however, does not respect boundaries between private and public, self and other. . . . It is a poetry that talks back, that would act as part of the world, not simply as a mirror of it" (5). Whatever else Hughes and Wright may be faulted for, their poems give voice to the resurgent Other; their works move beyond their own culture-bound sensibilities and contemplate social realities with an eye toward advocating—even engineering—specific radical readjustments.

Views of Richard Wright as a realist and a naturalist have given way to readings that account for previously overlooked elements of his work. It is said that Wright is "not so much naturalistic as hallucinatory, dream-like, and poetic" (Dickstein 380), a reading first broached by Morris Dickstein and reiterated by Hakutani, who follows Dickstein's lead in seeing that *Native Son* is greatly affected by "Wright's affinity to Dostoyevsky" (16). The hallucinatory character of Wright's prose may also be traced to his poetry, especially to "Transcontinental." That Wright based "Transcontinental" on Aragon's "Red Front" indicates Wright's commitment to risk taking, experimentation, and advancing beyond the restricted forms typical of proletarian poetry. Proletarian writing was supposed to be simple, realistic, precise, socially useful, and factual. It was supposed to avoid individual responses, lyricism, emotion, and eccentricities (Pells 176). Aragon's poem has none of these proletarian attributes. The poem is a collage that gives a sarcastic description of Maxim's restaurant in 1931 (Caws 40). The poem is complex in discourse, disorienting, provocative, and cruel. Aragon's poem was notorious, for in France it had provoked what was called "L'Affaire Aragon," and the poet was brought to court because the poem was interpreted by some as a call to anarchy (Caws 12 n.12). In 1933, Wright read e. e. cummings's translation of "Red Front" in *Contempo*. Eugene Miller has suggested that Wright may have been open to surrealist innovations because Wright could have appropriated surrealist techniques without risking political transgressions. The surrealists called themselves Marxists and saw their work as revolutionary literature (Miller, *Voice* 78). Moreover, Wright connected surrealism to African American culture, and he stated in his memoir that surrealism helped him to clarify the hallucinatory mode of langue used by his mystically religious grandmother and by blues singers (Miller, *Voice* 79). Wright wrote "Transcontinental" in 1935 and dedicated it to Aragon (Miller, *Voice* 78). *International Literature* published the six-page poem in January 1936. One critic has called it "the longest and perhaps the most ambitions [poem] he ever wrote" (Fabre 131).

Eugene Miller has observed that Aragon's poem is not obviously surrealistic (78), and Ruhle has confirmed that his poetry "was never so firmly committed to the Surrealist model as that of their teacher and mentor Breton" (*Literature and Revolution* 359). Since the conclusion might simply be that

Wright's "Transcontinental" is not surrealistic, it is necessary to establish more exactly the nature of Aragon's poem. Mary Douglas, in a discussion of jokes, has characterized the surrealist movement as "passionate frivolity" ("Jokes" 292) that has had wide cultural implications and has shaped the categories in which modern experience is structured. Surrealism, then, is not so much a style made up of strange juxtapositions as it is a valorization of "freedom from limitations of any kind" (Caws 43) by means of violating social conventions. André Breton framed the surrealist conception of freedom with his second surrealist manifesto, published in 1930: "The simplest act of Surrealism consists of going into the street gun in hand and blindly shooting into the crowd for as long as one cares to" (Ruhle 359). Matthews adds that "beneath his apparent frivolity in the surrealist poems of *La Grande Gaite* (1929) lies a sense of responsibility, often masked by a vulgarity it would be a mistake to consider gratuitous. . . . Deliberately offensive language hides in Aragon's work a deep concern, of which the search . . . for the purity of love is indicative" (34–5).

Though Wright acknowledges Aragon's "Red Front" by the name and title at the top of his poem, "Transcontinental" is a highly original text, for Wright situates his poem within specifically American cultural conditions, and he employs formal devices and rhetorical techniques that are not present in Aragon's poem. Chief among these devices is the use of the Hollywood film as form, as subject, and as a familiarizing discourse. The opening stanza of the poem alludes to screenplay, montage, newsreel, and drama:

> [Through] trembling waves of roadside heat
> We see the cool green of golf courses
> Long red awnings catching sunshine
> Slender rainbows curved above spirals of water
> Swaying hammocks slung between trees—
> Like in the movies. . . .

The opening five lines are suspended above the situational, anchoring, ingratiating simile "Like in the movies," as though the suave voice of the narrator could continue describing the alluring scene forever. "Like in the movies" abruptly forces a descent from the capitalist sublime of the visual imagery, distancing the reader with cinematic context that has been layered over the initially contextless opening hallucination. By juxtaposing the scene and the simile, Wright prompts the reader to ask: why am I being told about this beautiful place? Once readers have been prompted to consider the scene as though it is a scenario in a movie, readers may hear the voice simultaneously as the dramatizing, inflated voiceover of a newsreel reporter and as the more prosaic voice of a screenwriter who is merely reciting words. "Like in the movies"—both voices place the reader in a movie theater and deny the reader the opportunity to identify with the scene's drama.

American popular film played an important role in Wright's imagination and contributed to the discourses of his longer works of fiction. A movie theater is the setting for one of the most evocative episodes in *The Man Who Lived Underground*, a novella published in 1938. Early in Wright's acclaimed novel *Native Son* (1940) the thuggish teenage protagonist Bigger Thomas and his gang attend a movie, and Bigger—in the original and uncensored version of the text—masturbates while watching a newsreel in which the young woman that he later murders is presented to society at a debutante ball. Bigger's pornographic excursion to the movies illustrates that the newsreels and popular films of the 1930s provided the have-nots with images of the luxurious lives of the haves: "Thomas grows up on the dross of a glamorized popular culture he can see but never have, look at but never touch" (Szalay 253). "Transcontinental" shows that Wright's concern with the American popular film goes back to his poetry, where popular film is a controlling element of his harrowing depiction of apocalyptic revolution.

In the 1930s the motion picture was the most important form of entertainment available to the American people. A more realistic style of acting and the increased use of sound (and later, color) coincided with the social conditions of the New Deal era and the studios' resistance to censorship between 1930 and 1934. Production Code began active enforcement of a ban on interracial marriage and applied other conservative social standards. These factors influenced the development of new genres of film: the screwball comedy, the spectacular musical, the western, the detective film, the horror film, and the gangster film. The Depression had shaken some of the oldest American cultural myths, such as the myth that hard work and perseverance would bring success. People did not know what to believe in. Some men and women in politics and the media saw it as their duty to revitalize and refashion America's cultural mythology. Direct portrayals of the Great Depression rarely appeared in movies; usually, filmmakers represented the Depression by "structuring absences" (Schatz 83), though films such as *My Man Godfrey* (1936), *Wild Boys of the Road* (1933), *Hallelujah, I'm a Bum* (1933), and *Mr. Deeds Goes to Town* (1936) did offer undisguised portrayals of the Depression. Robert Sklar states that

> in the first half decade of the Great Depression, . . . the movies called into question sexual propriety, social decorum and the institutions of law and order. The founding of the Breen Office in 1934 seriously curtailed the permissible range and depth of Hollywood films for years to come. . . .

> The movie moguls gave up their adversarial stance because they suddenly found greater opportunities for profit and prestige in supporting traditional American culture, in themselves becoming its guardians. (175)

The American movie in the thirties was a highly contested cultural site, and it is no wonder that Wright sought to situate his poem within the discourse of the popular film. In Wright's texts, movies reinforce popular myths and moral economic values. While genres of social order (like the gangster film) and genres of social integration (like the screwball comedy) may have helped viewers think about class, gender, individuality, and crime, movies rarely addressed racial themes.

"Transcontinental," Wright's surrealistic "movie" poem, is a proletarian comedy. First, we are shown scenes of haute bourgeois luxury. In Wright's comedic fantasy of American political revolution, displacements and reversals result from questions in the first three stanzas: "America who built this dream . . ." (line 7); "America who owns this wonderland . . ." (line 15); "America America America why turn your face away. . . ." (line 23). The lines are impressionistically punctuated and the derelict mode of Wright's inquisition establishes a rhetorical progression that carries away everything that it opposes. This outcome is, however, not readily apparent, for the first stanza modulates the luxury into a lament: the scenes of luxury and leisure are but reminders of a time when the proletarian-revolutionary "we" who are standing on the highway "used to get paychecks."

The Great Depression is graphically depicted in the poem through the postures that the enounced (the speakers selected inside the work) assume: in the tenth line of the long fourth section of the poem, they have "begging thumbs" (line 33). Several lines further down, the poet describes their reduced circumstances in grim detail: they have the hot sun on their backs, their stomachs growl with hunger, and when they sleep on the streets at night, their hips rest on the unforgiving pavement. In the concluding lines of the fourth section, Wright again briefly presents their poverty—their "empty dinner pails" (line 94) and "the tight-lipped mother and the bare meal-can" (line 95). Presumably, it was not necessary for Wright to provide more than a few of these images; his readers would have been familiar with these images already. The poem is not so much invested in depicting the ravages of deprivation as it is in providing a look at the transformation of the characters' circumstances. And when Wright does present the Great Depression's most salient image, the bread line, it is subordinated to the highway—"See the bread-lines winding winding winding long as our road" (line 157). Since the road is where Wright's poem situates his regime change, the bread line takes on the meaning of progressive change and agency. Similarly, the word *crash* is given a new meaning when it is surrealistically reinscribed as the wish-fulfilling climax of a revolutionary cartoon:

> O for the minute
> The joyous minute
> The minute of the hour of the day
> When the tumbling white ball of our anger
> Rolling down the cold hill of our lives
> Swelling like a moving mass of snow
> Shall crash
> Shall explode at the bottom of our patience Thundering
> HALT
> You shall not pass our begging thumbs
> America is ours
> This car is commandeered
> (lines 24–35)

In order to approach "Transcontinental" as a comedy, it is necessary to frame it within a theory of comedy. In *Semiotics of the Comic*,[1] Peter Marteinson argues that "the comic will be shown to be an instinctive response to an epistemological problem resulting from the 'undesirable' realization that several truth categories operate in social being" (3).

Marteinson's theory allows values to be assigned to the "comedic" components of Wright's poem. Wright satirizes the wealthy (bankers, brokers, and businessmen) in the opening stanzas of the poem. In his opinion, and in the view of many others at the time, the wealthy caused the Depression. The wealthy created chaotic social conditions, and they responded to those conditions irresponsibly and amorally. Wright makes evident their awkward social position by describing their "close-up" responses, their "glazed faces" (line 19), their tight lips (line 22) when in public, and their private laughter (line 11). The conflict, then, is between the antisocial motivations of the powerful bourgeoisie and the impoverishment of the powerless, disorganized masses. The hero's social identity is structured by a dialectical social identity—hobo and worker—assigned from two opposing perspectives determined by class. By *worker*, Wright indicates that the unemployed hitchhikers are to be understood to be the revolutionary proletariat. At first the bourgeoisie are able to laugh at the worker-hobos while speeding past them in luxurious automobiles, but once the workers have commandeered the automobile—transforming the symbol of class privilege into the reified *revolution*—it is the revolutionaries who eject the wealthy and laugh.

The Hollywood film that most closely parallels the comedic scenario of "Transcontinental" is *It Happened One Night* (1934), a screwball comedy that was one of the most popular films of the era. Due to a series of reversals, the hero (a newspaperman) and the heroine (an heiress)—a mismatched and constantly bickering pair—are reduced to thumbing a ride to New York, and they are picked up and driven to a roadside stop for lunch. When the driver makes off with the protagonists' suitcases, the newspaperman runs desperately behind the car. In the next scene, the newspaperman returns driving the car: he tells his traveling companion, a spoiled rich girl that he calls "Brat," that he gave the man a black eye for the car. Though the newspaperman wears a few scrapes, there is no explanation about how the exchange was accomplished. The car having been miraculously "commandeered," the blithe couple drives off—with all of their former animosities forgotten in the wake of their righteous indignation.

Wright's poem takes a plotless approach to the revolution that it narrates, so the elements of what Marteinson calls *illusion* and *discovery*—the features that would take up the majority of the screen time in a movie—are reduced to mere gestures in "Transcontinental." In *It Happened One Night*, the illusion and discovery phase is the long narration of the heroine's trip from Florida to New Jersey. As she moves north, she descends the social scale, losing her wealth and social status: she is forced to hitchhike, ride in a stolen car, and eat stolen carrots. In "Transcontinental" the illusion phase is represented by the brief and indistinct struggle over the steering wheel, a struggle that Wright signifies through roughly forty lines of pseudodialogue (lines 37–81).

Wright's poetic model, Aragon's "Red Front," consists of four sections. The first two dwell on the absurdities of the bourgeoisie, and even the third section, in which the revolution begins, devotes many lines to the possessions of the enemy class. It is only in the final section that they lose their statues, finery, and attitudes, so that Aragon's much longer poem is more heavily invested in mocking the bourgeoisie than is Wright's poem. Rather than waiting until the end of the comedy for the discovery of the hero's true identity, the disclosure that the pathetic, perishing hobo is a robust, cacophonous revolutionary comes very close to the beginning of "Transcontinental," in line 36, where the "car" is commandeered. And here is the crucial factor in Wright's comedy: in the movies, the comedy aims to deflate antisocial agents in effigy: in *It Happened One Night*, the mockery of wealth climaxes when the absurd groom flies in an autogiro to his lavish wedding only to find that his betrothed has run off with a newspaperman. For Wright, the deflation must be carried out directly on actual class enemies. Wright presents a surrealistic enactment of "justifiable" mass murder. In Wright's dreamlike carnival of death, countless racially motley underdogs speed across America in an apocalyptic clown car to run down their oppressors.

Having established the contrast between the "wonderland" (line 15) and the "hot highways" (line 17) on which the displaced and dispossessed wander, the poem juxtaposes two disparate circumstances. The anger of the proletarian masses is compared to an avalanche rolling down "the cold hill of our lives" (line 28). However, although the effect of this "tumbling while ball" (line 27) is to smash the status quo, it does so by bringing to a halt the automobile of American capitalism. Wright recalls Old Testament rhetoric by making the verbs "crash" (line 30), "explode" (line 31), and "HALT" (line 32) conditional to the uniform application of "shall" (lines 31, 32), an effect that is reminiscent of the syntax and parallelism of Psalmic poetry (for instance, "Surely goodness and mercy *shall* follow me all the days of my life, / and I *shall* dwell in the house of the Lord my whole life long" [*NRSV* Psalm 23; emphases added]). The cascade of images is at once surrealistic and cinematically "realistic" in that it is within the power of movies to picture such impossible eventualities, thereby rendering them in a sense realizable. But since what Wright presents is "like in the movies" (line 6), the revolution is accomplished in the same way that insurmountable obstacles are routinely overcome in the movies. If a giant ape climbs a skyscraper in pursuit of a femme fatale in *King Kong*, and if young men with no prospects become wealthy and powerful in *Scarface*, what might not be accomplished within cinematic *unreality*? In Wright's cinematic text, the mythic historicity of biblical subtext supports the unreality of events. "*America America America why turn your face away*" (line 32), alludes to Armageddon: "Nevertheless Josiah *would not turn his face from him*, but disguised himself, that he might fight with him, and hearkened not unto the words of Necho from the mouth of God, and came to fight in the valley of Megiddo" (*KJV* 2 Chronicles 35:22; emphasis added).

Wright uses Judeo-Christian myth to frame the climax of the class war, indicating the ambivalent, polyvalent character of his thought: here he encapsulates the theme of social identity in the refusal of the bourgeoisie to recognize his humanity. He also locates the class struggle within the framework of biblical eschatological myth as a subtype of (African) American folklore. African American Marxists who steered more closely to Communist Party ideology maintained an unsympathetic attitude toward African American Christianity, so in "Blacks Turn Red," Eugene Gordon could state that "the automobile, the newspaper, the radio, and the motion picture have carried knowledge to the backwoods, and the church, with its mumbo-jumbo superstitions, has retreated, mouthing curses" (238). Gordon's view—a dialectical construction of modernity that saw technology and media as having rendered irrelevant the folkway of religion—was not uncommon among radical intellectuals. J. Edward Arbor in *The Crisis*, in 1935 acrimoniously gives a similar opinion: "Perhaps if the Negro put less faith and vigor into worshipping the Lord and devoted more of his energy toward solving the substantial and complex problems that face him, he would gain a few of the blessings he waits to be showered upon him by the heavenly hand" (111). Neither Gordon nor Arbor made a distinction between the church and Christianity. Both saw the religious enterprise as a continuum of outward social forms and ideologies. Wright was not as condemnatory in his approach to the black church: "While Wright dismisses Christianity as useless for black people's freedom and independence, he values the black church in the city because it enhances their community life" (Hakutani 111). In "Transcontinental" the discourse of Judeo-Christian religion represents the power of collective myth, and the revolution that Wright delineates is an exchange of one communality for another. Rather than seeing modernity as a liberating force as do Gordon and Arbor, Wright's understanding of modernity lies in his own experience of its power to dehumanize, to isolate, and to nullify.

Thus, it is ironic that Wright has chosen the automobile—one of the most prevalent reifications of modernity—as the site of the struggle for mass emancipation. In contrast to the hallucinatory exchange of roles that occurs through the trope of an avalanche that intervenes in "the joyous minute" (line 25), Wright presents American totality through the trope of the automobile. In a comedic reversal, the speaker declares, "This car is commandeered" (line 35). The automobile has a powerful totemic presence in the movies. The protagonist of the gangster movie *Scarface* is closely identified with his armored car's bulletproof glass and steel body, for example. The automobile offers a compressed space in which to depict the Armageddon of class war. It is also one of the most pronounced factors through which modernity isolates, disrupts, and depersonalizes. Wright's poetic moviemaking depends on a deep intertextuality between social realism and the Bible. In the poem's subtext, the realism of industrial commodities, "Packards Pierce Arrows / Lincolns La Salles Reos Chryslers" (lines 20–1), is layered over mythically inflected wordplay—*commandeer* compresses *Communist Manifesto*. The word *commandeer* not only suggests seizure for public use through its literal meaning but also occurs in the lexicon adjacent to *commandment,* thereby suggesting the inexorable power of the Ten Commandments. The commandeered car is the *Ark* of the Covenant, reminding us of how the Hebrews carried the Ten Commandments throughout years of wandering in the desert. Wright makes the masses—the We, who hitchhike in the "roadside heat" (line 1)— analogous to the biblical wanderers. Thus, Wright refashions the bourgeois American car into the *ark of the Communist Manifesto*, which will exist in the new order brought about by a revolutionary Armageddon. In *The Great*

Code, Northrop Frye describes the ark as the sign of "the end of all cyclical movements and the coming of a final separation between apocalyptic and demonic worlds" (177).

Wright's use of the car as the vehicle by which the revolution is disseminated is surrealist, for it is the car's dreamlike and polymorphous qualities that allow it to accommodate the multitudes of "WOORKERSWOORKERS" (line 91) who are invited to "pile in" (line 92). Wright's fantasy represents the victory of desire over reality. The workers (no longer merely *workers*) are metamorphosed into WOORKERSWOORKERS by the comedic order of the revolution, which Wright presents as essentially a matter of garnering a sufficient quantity of laughter: those who once owned the "silvery crescendos of laughter" (line 11) now moan (line 176), and in the new order, "The world is laughing The world is laughing" (line 203). The laughter of the new proletarian order is the laughter produced "in order to judge the position that gives meaning" (Kristeva 182). Thus, it is the laughter of the mass audience that has been radicalized and is now aware of itself as a class; it is the laughter of the workers in revolt. Wright rejects bourgeois laughter's fundamental ugliness, and allows his monologic construction of bourgeois consciousness into the poem only as parody. Bourgeois consciousness is no longer to speak for itself through its novels, operas, and dramas: bourgeois discourse is stripped to the cognitively dissonant wheedling of a woman in the back seat of a luxury automobile (lines 67–69).

Having commandeered the car, Wright presents a series of uninspired caricatures of the upper class through a radical and comedic revision of social identity. When the (Negro) hobo is beside the road, his physical circumstances enforce his social identity, for he is motionless outside of the speeding car. The wealthy drivers enforce the social codes not only by driving past the hitchhiking hobo but also by refusing to meet his gaze—thus refusing social interaction and in effect determining that his social identity is a negative identity. Here the specifics of his place on the highway have made him invisible, immobile, and silent. Because the hobo is outside of the car, he is beyond the reach of social discourse, for his social identity—an *outsider*—removes him from the social whole. But once the hobo has climbed into the car, a new type of social identity comes into effect, for suddenly the mode of social exchange is face-to-face. Wright presents the bourgeoisie as cartoon characters, and this is very much a limiting device that robs "Transcontinental" of the more evocative and detailed portraiture that Aragon accomplishes through his more literarily self-conscious, lingering, and capacious satire. Wright's decision to situate his attack within a "movie," nevertheless, rings true. We can rationalize and justify Wright's caricatures of the idle rich by recognizing that he does not depend on the presupposition of direct familiarity with the bourgeoisie (in contrast to Aragon's method of allowing us to hear their voices); rather, Wright approaches the bourgeoisie through the remove of their semiotics in the discourse of the Hollywood movie and by allowing the hero-worker to feel the presence of the idle rich as antagonists. That is, Aragon goes among the wealthy and reports on them in intimate detail, though, of course, satirically. Wright reaffirms the depiction of the rich that the mass audience has gained through movies: he only transvalues what the masses have seen, and he does this by placing the mass audience within a movie reinscribed as revolutionary comedy.

The Hollywood movie was designed to extract from the mass audience a consensual, conspiratorial laughter. As movies presented the rich, social differences could be bridged through laughter, a laughter not of rejection, contempt, or disgust, but of sympathy and affection: it is laughter that arrives "in order to put ourselves out of judgment's reach, in some surreality where everything is equal" (Kristeva, *Desire* 182). The "surreality" of the screwball comedy made the rich merely amusing—thus it made them seem harmless. In "Transcontinental" Wright follows Aragon by withdrawing that amused sympathy. The proletariat's laughter is not the laughter of a leisurely mass audience; it is the black laughter of moral exhaustion, where no sympathy remains for the wealthy, and the masses inflict a bloody and thorough revenge upon their class enemies. Wright insists that once the world has been freed of the bourgeoisie, the world will laugh (lines 185–201). However, Wright's imaginative powers are limited, and the liberated masses really do not laugh. Under the new social conditions, they pursue appropriately banal, collective, proletarian entertainments: socialist baseball leagues spring up, and accounts of the revolution written by formerly outcast proletarian authors are utopian best sellers.

Wright's automobile—the conveyance of the revolution—stands in marked contrast to the train, which assumes that function in Aragon's "Red Front." Moreover, the railroad helped disseminate the Bolshevik revolution, so Aragon's use of this trope is not definitively surrealist, nor is it especially imaginative. Wright perhaps rejected Aragon's use of the train because of its associations with the old order in the semiotics of the Great Depression: the railroad was the chief means by which the unemployed moved about the country, and riding aboard freight trains was comfortless and dangerous. The automobile, the semiotic opposite of the freight train, was associated with escape from the effects of the Depression, and going for a drive in a car was as popular as going to the movies. Sales of gas and oil increased during the Depression, and oil companies were profitable. Hobos hopping freight trains became one of the stereotypical images of the Great Depression; thus, the American railroad was an inappropriate sign for revolutionary emancipation. The contrast between the car and the railroad is tacit in *It Happened*

One Night. When the newspaperman blissfully drives to retrieve his beloved, he is forced to stop at a crossing to let a train go past, and he joyously salutes first a lone hobo atop a box car, then a group of hobos in the door of another car. The contrast between the freedom and jubilation expressed by the driver is contrasted with the expressions of the men on the train. The latter seem either lonely or overwhelmed by unwelcome company. Their futures are determined, deprived, and precarious.

Wright's automobile is problematic, then, in several ways. The private car was the antithesis of the railroad train, and the car was also a reaffirmation of individual identity. The car operated consistently as a sign of wealth and social power. In selecting the car as the vehicle for the revolution, Wright reinforced all of these associations, and he did so because, to some degree, he was unwilling to abandon private individuality if doing so meant being swallowed up by the collective consciousness of the masses. In his presentation, Wright seems to have constructed a position between the two extremes, a type of public individuality that "would try to put some of that meaning back" (Fabre 120).

Wright's presentation of the revolution in terms of the discourse of the movies is easy to trace. The speeding car is an overwhelmingly prevalent feature of the early gangster films. The gangsters (like the proletariat) begin as weak, impoverished men who desire power and notoriety. In *Little Caesar* these desires are voiced as the protagonist's desire to "be somebody." The attainment of an identity is achieved through ruthlessness, an unhesitating willingness to kill and to take—to commandeer—but its signs of this identity are an automobile, clothes, and an office. In *Scarface* the car itself suffices as a status symbol. When Little Caesar is recognized by the policeman slinking alone through the dark streets at the end of the movie, the policeman shouts, "Halt," much as the masses shout "HALT" (line 32) to stop the cars of bourgeois America in Wright's poem. When Little Caesar does not immediately surrender, the sergeant reaches for a "chopper," a Thompson machine gun. In "Transcontinental" the chopper is disguised and rendered through metonymy—"All right *chop* us into little pieces" (line 46). Ironically, once the revolutionaries are in the car with the bourgeoisie, the Marxists take up their defensive justifications in the tough guy dialect of the gangsters—"You say we're robbers / So what" (lines 41–42). The comedy in this revision is that Wright has also cast the bourgeoisie as gangsters who need to be eliminated: like the alienated, sociopathic gangsters of the movies, the bourgeoisie are beyond rehabilitation and must be gunned down without hesitation. Yet, the workers have adopted the voice of the gangsters (the *comedic* device used by the protagonist in *It Happened One Night* to rid himself of a blackmailer), and the workers reply to the derogatory accusations of the bourgeoisie in the language of movie gangsters.

The workers/gangsters are allowed to speak first; when we hear the voices of the bourgeoisie, their words issue from the imaginations of the workers. The bourgeoisie is present only as a ventriloquized other during the struggle for the steering wheel of the stationary automobile. When the voices of the bourgeoisie are allowed to be heard in a passage not prefaced with "you say," we must continue to suspect that their voices are mediated by the workers' imaginations, for what the bourgeoisie utter is little more than what the workers must assume is the authentic racial discourse of the bourgeoisie: "But dear America's a free country / Did you say Negroes / Oh I don't mean NEEEGRROOOES / after all / Isn't there a limit to everything" (lines 54–58).

The parody of privilege was a common feature of thirties movies: though we seldom meet the upper class in the gangster films, there are sufficient hints, if only in the social-climbing of the gangsters, to allow viewers some access to the upper-class social stratum. Though "Transcontinental" is concerned with the expansion of justice, the bourgeoisie and the gangsters share the same fate of being gunned down in the streets. Once the conflict has been racialized, the car is used to redress racial injustices. The revolution heads south, and after the car destroys the capitalist government ("congressmen Fascist flesh sticking to our tires" [line 126]), it slams into a lynch mob—"Plunging the radiator into the lynch-mob / Giving no warning" (lines 131–32). In Wright's poem the alienated individual assumes the posture of the movie gangster in order to enact his aggressive campaign of revenge. The gangster type is usually read as an anarchic individual battling a disordered society (Sklar 181), with the question of the final resolution remaining in the hands of the audience, who were charged by messages from the studios at the opening of these movies to take action in the face of government inaction.

The final result of Wright's revolution is not the Faustian-Dionysian tragedy that the unhinged assassin-on-the-make enacts in the gangster film but the comic reversal accomplished in the screwball comedy: social order is restored as in gangster movies, not by the removal of the gangster but by the removal of an offending social class. In the screwball comedy, the lives of the rich are exposed so that the audience comes to recognize them as funny, lovable, and harmless (Sklar 188). Schatz observes that "by restructuring the fast-paced upper-crust romance, the screwball comedy dominated the Depression-era screen comedy and provided that period's most significant and engaging social commentary" (151). Meanwhile, "The screwball comedies by and large celebrated the sanctity of marriage, class distinctions and the domination of women by men" (Sklar 188). Similarly, Wright resolves his poem in a successful courtship after overcoming social obstacles to such a resolution by using gangsterish violence.

In "Transcontinental" the wealthy are callous, racist, and corrupt, while the workers are joyous and loving. The workers' victory is one of laughter. It results in social integration through the screwball comedy, where things are not what they seem, where reversals bring about community cooperation and utopian harmony. In its final episode of specific dramatic action, Wright's poem embraces the dominated/dominating female, a character that is one of the hallmarks of the screwball comedy genre, by elevating Pocahontas as an emblem of collectivization: "Bring her from her hiding place Let the sun kiss her eyes / Drape her in a shawl of red wool / Tuck her in beside us / Our arms shall thaw the long cold of her shoulders" (lines 219–21). Having brought its "Red" bride into the car, the revolution achieves its final phase, described in depersonalized and abstract action: "rolling over tiles of red logic" (line 218), collective farms sprout up, prisons empty, and justice thunders. Wright urges the "forgotten Men" (line 208) to bring out from her hiding place Pocahontas, and here it is possible to recognize the Indian bride as a comedic heroine who is the sign of public individuality—thus Pocahontas mediates the abstract and the subjective. She is historical (and mythic), the protagonist of another romantic comedy (a comedy with a happy ending), and she is abstract in her capacity to symbolize the merging of the races in "maternal, semiotic processes" (Kristeva, *Desire* 136). Seated in the car beside the African American wheelman, Pocahontas is the matrix of the future, the essence of "AmericaAmericaAmerica" (line 248)—the poem's glossolalic, fugue-like final line—the surreal engenderer of the fetal mass individual of the revolution gestating in the maternal womb.

OWEN DODSON, "NEGRO HISTORY" (1936)

One of the most conceptually ambitious poems written by an African American poet in the thirties was Owen Dodson's "Negro History: A Sonnet Sequence," published in *New Masses* on April 14, 1936. In *Sorrow Is the Only Faithful One: The Life of Owen Dodson,* James V. Hatch relates the strange account of Dodson's becoming a published poet. Dodson's diffident reaction to a poem by Keats provoked his English instructor at Bates College, Professor Robert George Berkelman, to direct Dodson to "write a sonnet every week and bring it to me each Monday . . . until you write one as fine as Keats, or until you graduate, whichever comes first" (Hatch 27). Under Berkelman's direction, Dodson wrote sonnets from 1932 until 1936, and in his senior year he published a collection of eight of them in a chapbook titled *Jungle Stars*. Subsequently, these poems were published in *The Crisis* and *New Masses,* though Hatch does not explain how Dodson's work came to appear in radical publications. Hatch concludes this account by relating that after Dodson published his eight sonnets, Berkelman informed the young poet that Dodson had made a grave error in choosing the Shakespearean sonnet as a form in which to write about slavery—a subject too fiery for the cool, formalized sonnet. (The sonnet is further discussed in chapter 2.) Berkelman further informed Dodson that because content and form go together, the subject of slavery required "a kind of Walt Whitman style" (Hatch 29). (In the thirties a style of poetry that blended elements from Walt Whitman [paratactic and parallel line structures] and Carl Sandburg [a less lyrical voice that Whitman's] became de rigueur for a number of black poets, including Sterling Brown, Frank Marshall Davis, Richard Wright, Welborn Victor Jenkins, and Margaret Walker, though Dodson never did adopt the Whitman-Sandburg manner.) In later years Dodson dismissed his sonnets as vitiated from a lack of writing experience, life experience, and in-depth reading, given that he had not even read Frederick Douglass's *Narrative*. Despite Dodson's statement that "Negro History" is nearly valueless because "it was all imaginary" (Hatch 29), the sequence tackles the trans-Atlantic transportation of slaves, a subject one encounters only rarely in African American poetry prior to Robert Hayden's "Middle Passage" (1962).

Ignoring Berkelman's opinion about the racial nature of form and conetnt in poetry, Dodson used a number of innovations to make the sonnet a more resonant instrument. Dodson superseded the restricted emotional range of the sonnet by extending the lyric into a sonnet sequence that carried the theme into a more analytical and discursively resourceful handling than was possible in the solitary sonnet. Dodson had taken as his mainstay Keats's "extravagant and sensuous wordplay" (Hanson "Byron on Keats"), compounding and concentrating the effects of allusions, synecdoches, and puns, so that (as I will show) his four sonnets attain a wide span of associative meanings. As it announces its historiographic purpose, the "Negro History" sequence reaches toward historical consciousness, where as Marx has it the "vision of the past turns [historical individuals] toward the future, . . . kindles the hope that justice will yet come and happiness is behind the mountain they are climbing" (Schmidt 3). In these ways Dodson's "Negro History" bears the stamp of the documentary and historicizing forms that characterized much of the cultural production of the iconoclastic period in which Dodson wrote his poems (Browder 2). Yet on close examination, Dodson's sequence does not cohere with Marxist ideology. And though his four sonnets appear to conform to the conventions of the sonnet form, Dodson invented a technique that transforms and extends the form's semantic possibilities.

"Negro History" deserves a place in a discussion of long poems on the Crash and the Great Depression because the long poem is not only a formal but also an intellectual construct. The long poem expresses the will to grapple with the largest possible questions and to encompass or create a world (Shepherd). Dodson's meditation on the phases of black identity construction takes as its subject the struggle to build a new type of humanity and a new society. In "Negro History" the formal, antimodernist surface is deceptive, for Dodson overrides the archaisms of the form with collagelike and interart techniques. In their *New Masses* printing, the left margin contains subtitles set in italic type that serve as explanatory frames for the poems: "*On the Slave Ship*," "*Past and Future*," "*Post Emancipation*," and "*Harlem*." This presentation suggests in both form and content the influence of the "documentary imagination" that was the hallmark of New Deal art—particularly mural cycles with historical themes, although these complex historical murals had appeared before the crash.[2] Boardman Robinson's *The History of Trade* [*Commerce*] had been painted in 1929 and placed in the Kaufman Department Store in Pittsburg in 1930. The ten panels, painted in the style of Thomas Hart Benton, depicted episodes such as "The Portuguese in India— The Fifteenth Century," "The English in China—The Seventeenth Century," and "Slave Traders in America—The Eighteenth Century" (Potter 2). K. A. Marling characterizes this treatment of the past as a "smooth, unbroken flow of events" that provides the viewer with a sense of stability derived from the feeling that "the sequence can and will continue ad infinitum" (quoted in Staples 35).

Notably, "Negro History" periodizes history as Negro history, not as American history. The four sonnets treat four aspects of Negro history; however, the sonnets are not equal in transparency and exigency. "On the Slave Ship" takes up the signal collective experience of the transportation of millions of Africans across the Atlantic Ocean—voyages that occurred many times over hundreds of years. In order for the Middle Passage to be thought of as a historical period, Dodson's periodicity must construct a paradoxically *egoistic* and *collective-simultaneous* handling of time in which many other things must happen during the *period* of individual acts of transportation. In "On the Slave Ship," this disparity is demonstrated by the narrator's address to a collective "We" while also by measuring the span of the historical period of waiting and suffering against "the last / Black exile" (lines 3–4). "Past and Future" presents an eventless and impersonal debate between religious otherworldliness and rebellion that may also be thought to have extended over a long period of time, perhaps the entire span of Negro history. Emancipation was a historical event, though by assigning his third sonnet to "Post Emancipation," Dodson addressed his poem to another long period of time without limiting his periodization to events, historical figures, or a narrative: the sonnet summarizes the failure of Reconstruction and the imposition of

Jim Crow. Finally, the mysterious fourth sonnet, "Harlem," seems to suggest that the crash of 1929 ended the relative social progress initiated by the brief and recent phase of black migration out of the South for industrial work in the North. In contrast to the abstraction of the preceding sonnets, "Harlem" names a specific location (which may also be read as a period of time), yet its botanical imagery and premonitory tone present considerable difficulties of interpretation.

Thus, Owen Dodson's sonnet sequence, "Negro History," through an explicitly Negro historical panorama composed of four discrete, sequential episodes or historical moments, reinscribes the cultural nationalism promoted by the New Deal. Dodson's panoramic-modular approach to the depiction of historical imagery parallels that used in many of the 1,100 public murals commissioned by the government's Section of Fine Arts during the New Deal. Many of the more ambitious murals depicted narrative scenes in sequential order. For example, the *Plants of the World* mural (1938) at the Field Museum in Chicago consists of eighteen panels. *The Story of Natural Drugs* (1937); at the University of Chicago Medical Center, consists of two large murals that are meant to be read chronologically from top to bottom. Similarly, the historical narrative in Dodson's poem implies a linear progression that brings the reader from Africa to Harlem in four monumental stages. Harlem, thus, not only is a resonant geographic location in space but also embodies the final historical epoch in the narrative of the American Negro. Dodson's struggle to bring order to this sweeping sociohistorical idea and his desperate ideological conviction resulted in a highly compressed sequence of four sonnets—a sequence whose emotional timbre is at once nervous, lyrical, and repressed.

Keats, according to James V. Hatch, is the source of Dodson's conception of the poetics of the sonnet. However, it is Claude McKay—as a contemporary literary progenitor and as a militant radical—that Dodson's sequence interrogates. The "boys" (line 2) and "girls" (line 4) of "Harlem" are synonymous with "The wine-flushed, bold-eyed *boys* and even the *girls*" of McKay's sonnet, "The Harlem Dancer" (*SP* 61; emphasis added). Because he strips away McKay's romantic handling of these figures, the implication remains that Dodson finds fault with the depiction of McKay's lascivious and degenerate youths: McKay's sonnet serves as an example of the tendency of the sonnet tradition to overwhelm the poet, as McKay gives in to the lengthy and lyrical depiction of a subject that is not worthy of such elaborate and costly treatment—the result of the so-called ideology of form that inhabits the sonnet. McKay and Dodson are equally subject to the influence of Keats's intricate wordplay. McKay enriches his textures with a musical style that is "between sense and nonsense, between *language* and *rhythm*" (Kristeva,

Desire 135) so that his sonnets repeatedly play off of such musical-semiotic pairings as dim/mad, ancient/sciences (*SP* "Africa" 40); gaze/gauze, self/ falsely, (*HS* "The Harlem Dancer" 42), and sinks/king (*SP* "America" 59). Such phonic uses of "sound-symbolism" are subjective, and they provide no unchanging or intrinsic meanings; only the contexts create semantic meanings for the music (Dicking 83). The synthesis of sound and sense in Keats's work perhaps reached its limit when the sound motifs "echo the sense of the poem, as in the repetition of s-n-t in Keats's "Sonnet on the Sonnet" (Logan 213). Dodson, in his more completely realized *anagrammatic* language play, has developed this technique beyond motifs of sound-symbolism so that in his sequence the words *interrelate* in ways that are definitional, systematic, and contextualizing.

In Dodson's four sonnets, his high degree of formal and thematic unity yields two systems of anagrams that enact the meanings of his poem so that his textual recombinations eschew musical nonsense and achieve semantic intersection. Through these semantic intersections, Dodson created a new poetic device—the *dialectical anagram*—that sets in opposition pairs of words that contain an anagrammed relationship in addition to a dialectical semantic discourse. The motivation for this figure may be that Dodson was influenced by a comment that Spengler made about the quality of "form-language": "The more nearly a Culture approaches the noon culmination of its being, the more virile, austere, controlled, intense the form-language it has secured for itself, the more assured its sense of its own power, the clearer its lineaments" (*Decline* vol. 1 107).

In "Negro History" there are two sets of dialectical anagrams. The first set operates within the four sonnets. "On the Slave Ship" primarily depends on the dialectical anagram that transposes "times" (line 2) into "smites" (line 4). "Past and Future" transposes "damn" (line 1) into "mend" (line 12). "Post Emancipation" transforms "hope" (line 1) into "echo" (line 13). "Harlem" changes "easy" (line 3) into "ex-ray" (line 10). A secondary set of dialectical anagrams operates among the sonnets—"lives" (1) / "shrivel" (sonnet 4), "dies" (sonnet 1) / "seed" (sonnet 3), "source" (sonnet 1) / "curse" (sonnet 2), "freedom" [doom] (sonnet 3) / "mood" (sonnet 3), and "groaning" (sonnet 1) / "grow" (sonnet 4). All of these varyingly associative relationships are dependent on a more succinct transposition that defines what Dodson is doing with language, namely the "swords" (line 28) and "words" (lines 40, 41) anagram that spans the final line of the second sonnet and the twelfth and thirteenth lines of the third sonnet. The swords/words conversion alludes to Edward Bulwer-Lytton's aphorism from his play *Richelieu; or, The Conspiracy* (1839)—"The pen is mightier than the sword." Because Dodson ends the sonnet sequence with "grow strong or starve," his swords/words figure also extends to another saying: "Beat your plowshares into swords, and your pruning hooks into spears: let the weak say 'I am strong'" (*KJV* Joel 3:10). The implication of these conjoined aphorisms in the context of the poem is that Dodson casts doubt upon the efficacy of promises, and this is asserted in the surface text: "Distrust all words that echo to the stars." (line 41). In other words, Dodson only brings up the Bulwer-Lytton aphorism to dismiss it with the aphorism from the book of Joel. To paraphrase the sense of the swords/words anagram, Dodson posits that the sword is mightier than the word and that the present historical period is a time in which it is best to take up arms.

Dodson's time/smite anagram opens the poem to wordplay that I will designate the Spenglerian level of the poem because it derives from Oswald Spengler's *The Decline of the West* (1918). In a sense, this Spenglerian level is announced by the title of the poem—"Negro History"—though the implications are not at first obvious. In contrast to Marxism,[3] time is a manifest force in Oswald Spengler's historiography":

> The central theme in *The Decline of the West* is that all higher cultures go through a life cycle analogous to that of an organic evolution, from birth to maturation, and to inevitable decline. Spengler used the analogy of four seasons: the spring (birth and infancy), summer (youth), fall (maturity), and winter (old age and decay). . . . Spengler found eight [great cultures] which are self-contained and have a distinctive "soul" or "style." . . . Each of these units has an identical life-cycle lasting some thousand years. (Liukkonen "Oswald Spengler." Web)

Spengler insists that Time is not an abstraction: "'Time' is no abstract phrase, but a name for the actuality of Irreversibility. Here there is only forward, never back" (*Decline* vol. 2 102). The thrust of "On the Slave Ship" becomes readily apparent only in comparison to its countertext, the thesis of the *Communist Manifesto*: "Workers of the world, unite and fight. You have nothing to lose but your chains, and a world to win." Dodson plays with Marx's trope in the near homonym change (14) / chains (30), which emphasizes the futility of hope; Dodson's phrase "Distrust all words that echo to the stars" (line 41) applies as much to Marx as it does to Lincoln.

It is clear that "Negro History" is couched in an ethical premise derived from Oswald Spengler. As Clare Corbould has observed, "The idea that civilizations come and go, rise and fall, was popular among black Americans because it meant that they could not only rewrite the past but also imagine and hope for a better future, one different from that bound to emerge from dominant histories of the day. . . . Drawing heavily on Oswald Spengler's popular *The Decline of the West*, the first volume of which was translated in into English in 1918, black historians foretold an end to Western civilization" (65). Dodson suggests the title of Spengler's book in line 43—"deep, dark flower of the west," which invites us to extract *lower* from *flower* (with the sense of *going down, Untergang*) as the German title *Der Untergang des Abenlandes* has it. Oswald is heard indistinctly throughout the third and fourth sonnets in the assonance and alliteration of *dust, distrust, walls, petal's, petals, hold,* and *shallow* (line 53), which approximates an anagram of *Oswald. Splinters* in line five sounds roughly like *Spengler.* If the title, "Negro History," is read as an ideologically specific proposition, the concept of Negro history conforms with Herderian romantic nationalism but is well beyond the concerns of Third Period communism. Spengler's system of world history, which is not directly descriptive of Negro history, which only takes in vastly larger historical structures, is not directly descriptive of Negro history, though *Decline* describes a mechanism that allows Dodson to find a conceptual niche within the temporal and intellectual vastness of world history for his minuscule study of Negro history in poetry. Keith Stimely summarized Spengler's world-historical system[4] in these terms:

> Human history is the cyclical record of the rise and fall of unrelated High Cultures. These Cultures are in reality super life-forms, that is, they are organic in nature, and like all organisms must pass through the phases of birth-life-death. Though separate entities in themselves, all High Cultures experience parallel development, and events and phases in any one find their corresponding events and phases in the others. It is possible from the vantage point of the twentieth century to glean from the past the meaning of cyclic history, and thus to predict the decline and fall of the West. (2)

"Negro History: A Sonnet Sequence" recapitulates the central concepts of Spengler's world-historical system, though since this is done at the figurative and lexical levels of his poem, Dodson offers a more cryptic than literal presentation. The word most closely associated with Spengler's historiography is *doom*; Neil McInnes states that "Spengler provided a doomsday scenario regarding the future of civilization. . . . The Untergang he was prophesying did not mean a smash-up: 'The idea of catastrophe is not implied in the word.' It meant rather fulfillment (*Vollendung*); as Lewis Mumford said, 'The title whispered the soothing words downfall, *doom,* death'" (quoted in McInnes, "Oswald Spengler Reconsidered"; emphasis added). Uncharacteristically, Dodson's sequence creates a musical anagram with "doom" and "*mood*" in line 4 of "Post Emancipation." Yet, the music of "doom" and "mood" plays unsatisfactorily against the dialectical anagrams that otherwise dominate the word play in "Negro history." It is tempting to add "freedom" (Post-Emancipation, line 6) to this reading, where "freedom" stands as the antithesis of "doom," while also affirming the Spenglerian idea that freedom is illusory: "Universal human rights, freedom, and equality are literature and abstraction and not facts" (Spengler, *Decline* vol. 2 183).

Another important Spenglerian concept is the "seasonal life cycle of civilizations,"[5] and this is alluded to by the four sonnets that stand for the four seasons. Since Dodson assumed that the Great Depression was a further sign that the West was in its autumnal phase, he chose to refer to this decline by means of a rich lexicon of decomposition, using words such as "season" (line 16), "autumn" (line 25), "fall" (line 5), "died" (line 36), "dies" (line 4), "death" (lines 1, 16, 25), "dying" (line 23), "rotting" (line 53), "rancid" (line 12), and "shrivels" (line 46). Spengler's system describes two kinds of time, so Dodson replied with a rich temporal lexicon, including the words "time" (line 14), "times" (line 2), "future" (line 15), "forecasting" (line 25), "years" (line 27), "yet" (line 19), "when" (line 42), "till" (line 35), "centuries" (line 35), "eons" (line 35), "destines" (line 14), "fate" (line 14), "transitory" (line 27), "delay" (line 16), "passed" (line 1), "anew" (line 47), "never" (line 7), "wait" (line 13), "end" (line 24), "frequent" (line 28), and "past" (line 15). In "Negro History" Dodson pairs *time* with *smite*. *Smite* is a word heavy with associations. It occurs 125 times in the Old Testament and appears in five of the Bible's books: Genesis, Deuteronomy, Samuel, Zechariah, and Numbers. The biblical story that best corresponds to Dodson's concept of Negro history is the story of the Jewish people's captivity in Egypt, especially when Yaweh tells Moses in Exodus 3:20, "And I will stretch out my hand, and smite Egypt with all my wonders which I will do in the midst thereof: and after that he will let you go." (*KJV*). In "Negro History" Dodson subverts the lack of agency that characterizes the original narrative, since Yahweh delivers the enslaved Hebrews who are not called upon to resist the Egyptians: the time/smite anagram seems to suggest a parallel delivery that does not require action from the enslaved African Americans.

However, the redress that is to come about through the potential agency of the "black exile[s]" (line 4) must occur in some future period of time that exists beyond the four sonnets of Dodson's sequence, for "Negro History" completes its recapitulation of Negro history with the speaker continuing to turn his attention and his intelligence *toward the past*. Yahweh's promise takes the form of "I will," whereas the slaves in Dodson's sequence must content themselves with the polyvalence of smite/might—with the comic/tragic double meaning of *might* as either "physical or bodily strength" (*AHD*) or "the past tense of may" (*AHD*), the latter definition suggesting conditionality (and the possibility of failure). At the same time, the first two sonnets reinforce the assertion of some immaterial promise of emancipation in the insistent repetitions of "will sleep" (line 2), "will come" (line 12), and "will come" (line 13) in "On the Slave Ship" and of "will come" (line 18) and "will mend" (line 22) in "Past and Future." Thus, Dodson creates tension between metaphysical predetermination and human effort. The poem turns on the word *reign*—a homonym of rain in line 13, which the desperate Africans look to for relief from their misery. The *reign* to which Dodson looks is the Roman phase of Spengler's historical morphology: "During 'autumn,' life becomes dominated by materialist, instead of artistic and religious, concerns, and by purely rational and mechanical, instead of dream-like and imaginative, thinking. . . . This is the transition to the era of 'Civilization' (again, used in a technical sense). The realm is falling back into barbarism, the only thing that counts being brute force" (Chin 2007). In keeping with the requirements of this violent phase of history, Dodson's sequence ends with an analogous endorsement of violence, "Grow strong or starve"—a parodic rejection of the ambivalence of Hughes's "I, Too" (1925): "I am the darker brother. / They send me to eat in the kitchen / When company comes, / But I laugh / And eat well, / and grow strong."

In Hughes's poem, "I, Too," the implications of "the darker brother's" strength, for Hughes's "darker brother" speaks as one who represents the Negro masses—who are in Hughes's poem orphans who are sent into the kitchen and self-assured and optimistic. By contrast, in the enounced of "Harlem," the individual has been merged into a "you" ("Together you must silence winds that blew" [line 47]) that the speaker charges with carrying out the collective action of taking the strength depicted by Hughes and using it as a means to action. In Dodson's poem, it is clear that without direct and timely action, the moment will be lost and the gathered strength will come to nothing. "Harlem" considers the danger of failure: the strength of the New Negro movement may be wasted. Dodson's empirical and emulative wordplay opens up *wary* in line three of "Harlem" to a reading of the word as "war-y," so that the embedded word *war* is emphasized, and the meaning shifts to "warlike"—"be war-y"—an exhortation not to wage class war but to adopt the stance of the warrior. Dodson wrote this passage in the shadow of Spengler's description of the shift to a new historical phase of the decline of America: according to Spengler, "The civilization phase concludes with the Age of Caesarism. . . . The advent of the Caesars marks the return of Authority and Duty, of Honor and 'Blood,' and the end of democracy. With this arrives the 'imperialistic' stage of civilization, in which the Caesars with their bands of followers battle each other for control of the earth. The great masses are uncomprehending and uncaring" (Stimely 2). *Wary,* derived from "to perceive, to watch out for" (*AHD*), intimates the same advice given in line 14, where "be conscious" is an emphatic echo of "be wary." Dodson delivers his opinion of the Harlem movement in "Harlem" through the pun on "veins" in the twelfth line: "Within the petal's veins, reveals the fears"— namely, that the "renaissance" was *in vain* unless African Americans adopt a new resolve.

Much of "Harlem," the final sonnet in the sequence, is derived from the opening paragraphs of volume 2 of *The Decline of the West*. The opening line of the sonnet, "Harlem—deep, dark flower of the west"—takes up the substance and mood of the opening sentence, "Regard the flowers at eventide as, one after the other, they close in the setting sun" (4). Dodson's association of flowers, darkness, and the west suggests the similar associations of Spengler's text. The fear that Dodson refers to in line 12, "Within the petal's veins, reveals the fears," is introduced in the second sentence of the opening paragraph: "Strange is the feeling that then presses in upon you a feeling of enigmatic fear in the presence of this blind dreamlike earth-bound existence" (3). Dodson's introduction of the x-ray machine in line 10, "Remember that the x-ray of the years," is the most original element of his sonnet. is the most original element of his sonnet. Spengler looks at his specimens with another machine—the microscope: "The seeds of a flowering plant show, under the microscope, two sheath-leaves which form and protect the young plant that is presently to turn towards the light, with its organs of the life-cycle and of reproduction, and in addition a third, which contains the future root and tells us that the plant is destined irrevocably to become once again part of a landscape" (4). This passage provides the suggestions that generate the unaccountable materials that belong to the fourth sonnet, namely stamens, pollen, petals, petal's veins. Several lines later, Spengler makes clear why Dodson associates these plant forms with the boys and girls of Harlem: "Sense and object, I and thou, cause and effect, thing and property each of these is a tension between discretes, and when the state pregnantly called "détente" appears, then at once fatigue, and presently sleep, set in for the microcosmic side of life. *A human being asleep, discharged of all tensions, is leading only a plantlike existence*" (4; emphasis added).

In the thirties the x-ray marked a more recent advance in the powers of scientific observation than the microscope. In the thirties, pulmonary tuberculosis took more lives than any other contagious disease. There was no cure for tuberculosis in the thirties, but the "public health community was already successfully linking x-ray technology to the control of tuberculosis" (Curtin 48–9). Dodson's handling of the x-ray machine is couched within the medical discourse of disease detection, and as such it is a symbol of the Spenglerian world-historical gaze with which Dodson's poem analyzes the Harlem phase of Negro history. Also, the x-ray looks beneath the skin, and thus it dissolves the importance of race. Spengler was not interested in race as it was understood in America in the thirties: "Thereby the cosmic-plantlike side of life, of Being, is invested with a character of duration. This I call race" (*Decline* vol. 1 113). Dodson's skepticism would seem to have extended far enough that the unconventional notion of a "Negro history"—in the America of the thirties, black Americans officially had no officially recognized history—ultimately serves to deconstruct the racial essentialism that might have been thought to give them a history. Dodson's thesis asserts that in the philosophy of history described in *The Decline of the West,* there is no admissability for such a concept as Negro history: black Americans either become world-historical actors or cease to exist.

The Great Depression is Dodson's x-ray machine. In "*Harlem,*" Dodson reifies his break with Hughes's romantic, cultural, nationalist discourse by *medicalizing* his nationalist-realist analysis and by equipping the Spengler-inflected speaker in the poem with the latest scientific diagnostic device, the Roentgen X-ray machine. With the new technological perspective that "the ex-ray of the years" (line 10) provides, Dodson's persona diagnoses the pulmonary tubercular condition of the racial lungs—the "deep, dark flower[s] of the west"—and directly observes and measures the "rotting of the shallow halls / Within the petal's veins" (lines 11–12). Through his "ex-ray" trope, Dodson indicts Americans for their social failures. Since the counteranagram of *ex-ray* is *easy,* the associations revolve around dis-ease and Spengler's animal-plant analogy. The historical x-ray shows the diseases in the social body, specifically the diseases within the bodies of black Americans: black Americans are passive, plantlike, and they are tubercular. The theme of American social failure is depicted in the "rotting of the shallow halls" (line 53), for in the thirties it was common knowledge that the "hallowed hall" was Carpenter's Hall, where the Founding Fathers signed the Declaration of Independence. So to say that the hall is "shallow" and "rotting" is to reveal the ill health of American culture. In the third sonnet, Dodson deprecates the Emancipation Proclamation: "The parchment that declared that we were free / Is now collecting dust in some dark spot" (lines 37–8). This statement depicts American racial hypocrisy as a "dark spot" of infection—a dark spot that might appear on an x-ray film.

Through an intricate series of tropes, Dodson rests his analysis of Harlem on "x-rays" of Langston Hughes and other Harlem colleagues. It is possible to identify Harlem Renaissance poet Countee Cullen as one of the subjects of "Harlem," for "copper" (lines 8, 13) and "sun" (line 3) insinuate the title of Cullen's 1927 collection of poems, *Copper Sun.* Another prominent Harlem Renaissance figure, novelist Rudolph Fisher, is implicated through the fact that he was a medical doctor and an x-ray specialist, a rarity in the 1920s and 1930s. But Dodson's x-ray is designated an "ex-ray" (line 10) to emphasize that the Harlem Renaissance is forevermore passé. Because the (e)x-ray machine is a technological trope, the poet opposes order and rationalism to the irrationalism, exoticism, and primitivism of the Harlem Renaissance. Dodson's disgust with Harlem is also derived from Spengler, who argues that in the autumnal phase of civilization, there is always to be found, so to speak, a New York and a Harlem: "But the relief of hard, intensive brain-work by its opposite conscious and practiced fooling of intellectual tension by the bodily tension of sport, of bodily tension by the sensual training after 'pleasure' and the spiritual straining after the 'excitements' of betting and competitions, of the pure logic of the day's work by a consciously enjoyed mysticism all this is common to the world-cities of all the Civilizations. *Cinema, Expressionism, Theosophy, boxing contests, nigger dances, poker, and racing—one can find it all in Rome*" (*Decline* vol. 2 103; emphasis added). Dodson articulates a harsh new meaning of the Cullen-Hughes debate between "art for art's sake" and "racial art"; the Depression forced a shift in the debate. The discourses of the twenties that depended on the dyad of culture/politics were reinscribed by Dodson as the dialectic of survival/death. The Great Depression silenced the laughter of Hughes's "darker brother." The unemployment rate for black men was as high as 50 percent in some major cities. The speaker in Hughes's poem assures the reader that African Americans have achieved social progress; the speaker in Dodson's sonnet rejects this claim.

Looking beyond "Harlem" to the three sonnets that precede it in the "Negro History" sequence, it is apparent that what Dodson means by "history" rather than a series of events, is a tension between "the heavy chains of servitude" ("Post Emancipation" line 2)—abjection, dehumanization, and chattel slavery—and emancipation. In the sonnet sequence, unidentified voices debate the wisdom of choosing either accommodation or resistance during this period of suffering. The militant interlocutor dismisses accommodation as "hopeless resignation" ("Past and Future" line 10). He urges his people to "distrust all words that echo to the stars" ("Post Emancipation" line 13), so that the day will come when they "will mend / The patches of these transitory years / With swords, with hate" ("Past and Future" lines 12–14). The political position of the speaker is presumably that of the poet: resistance is ineffective and dangerous until the proper time arrives. The resistance-accommodation dyad was evident in the thirties: the National Association for the Advancement of Colored People (NAACP) and the National Urban League (NUL) adopted gradualist positions while the Communist Party of the United States of America called for revolution. While Dodson did not assume the strident mode of Hughes, Wright, and Davis, all of whom embraced the revolutionary position, Dodson nonetheless challenged the black masses to "grow strong or starve"—suggesting that with the weakening of the capitalist system in the Depression, the *time* for movement, life, and individuation had finally come to pass. Dodson's sequence shows that he had absorbed the analogical form of Spengler's thought. In the final analysis, what Dodson presented was the notion that in the autumnal phase of Caesarism, black Americans must make the transition from "plants" to "animals," for as Spengler states, "Servitude and freedom—this is in last and deepest analysis the differentia by which we distinguish vegetable and animal existence" (*Decline* vol. 2 23). Dodson looks to the coming of "the force-men of the next centuries" (*Decline* vol. 1 37), and he aligns his sonnets with Spengler's admonition "I can only hope that men of the new generation may be moved by this book to devote themselves to technics instead of lyrics, the sea instead of the paint-brush, and politics instead of epistemology. Better they could not do" (*Decline* vol. 1 41).

WELBORN VICTOR JENKINS, TRUMPET IN THE NEW MOON (1934)

Jenkins's *Trumpet in the New Moon* is a 448-line free-verse sequence with a prosy and didactic tone that was derived more from Sandburg than from the meditative, prophetic, and celebratory lyricism of Whitman. At line 24, the poem begins to describe what are for Jenkins the significant and defining episodes of America's history. Lines 24 to 110 describe the discovery of the North American continent, the founding of the United States, and the chronicle of events leading up to the late 1920s. Lines 112 to 138 detail the exploitation of black labor. Lines 138 to 172 present Jenkins's discourse on African American labor, which Jenkins conceives of as "service." Lines 173 to 185 discuss patience. The nearly one hundred lines from 185 to 270 present the story of the aviator Charles Lindbergh. Lines 272 to 284 offer a discussion of racism and lynching. From line 285 to 305, the poem addresses the theme of historical decline, and the aura of Oswald Spengler's *The Decline of the West* seems to inform that section. Lines 306 to 351 exhort the nation to change its ways. Subsumed in that section is a brief presentation of the Scottsboro Boys case (lines 346–351). The poem crescendos after line 352 as the speaker describes the British model of nobility and heroism; this section celebrates nationalism and sacrifice. Searching even farther afield for models of fortitude and dedication, Jenkins invokes the Roman gladiators in lines 419 to 436. In lines 437 to 448, the poem concludes with the possibility of a national rebirth. Though failure is the subject of *Trumpet,* Jenkins does not appropriate the imagery of failure directly. He treats the Great Depression as a speech act that can be reversed through language; accordingly, he says, "Fail not has been your watch word" (line 239).

In *Trumpet in the New Moon,* the Whitmanian persona that the poet adopts is not so much the sign of the slippage of the real (Barnard 101) as it is the means to regain the world of *real things.* Jenkins's project revolves around the possibility of a vision of an authentic culture in the past that has been overshadowed by the infinitely replicated and adroitly meaningless productions of modern mass culture. Jenkins associates Whitman with the discourses of an authentic culture which the social artists of the 1930s were striving to reconstruct (Barnard 101). Whitman is above all the poet of work and the visualizer of the worker: while Whitman spoke as an individual, he also placed himself among the masses and within the community and the nation. Whitman's style provided Jenkins a vehicle for the assimilation of *the real:* the loose, organic form of the Whitmanian sequence allowed the introduction and consideration of an endless variety of themes. Jenkins embraced Whitman because Whitman was considered democracy's poet and spokesman. Jenkins proved to be a political and philosophical descendant of Walt Whitman. Though Jenkins's poetry does not match Whitman's lyricism and eloquence, Jenkins succeeded in assuming the voice and posture of the authoritative national poet.

Trumpet opens with a stern declaration addressed to the nation: "You have work to do, America— / You have work to be done / The goal which was set for you in the dreams of your founders / has not been realized" (lines 1–4). The word *work,* a fundamental word in Whitman's vocabulary, occurs many times in *Leaves of Grass,*[6] indicating the intricate intertextuality between *Trumpet* and *Leaves.* The passage of Whitman's that comes closest to Jenkins's opening occurs in "By Blue Ontario's Shore." The lines point to work that is yet to be done (one of the major themes of *Trumpet*): "The immortal poets of Asia and Europe have done their work and Pass'd to other spheres, / A work remains, the work of surpassing all they have done" ("By Blue Ontario's Shore" section 5, lines 3–4).

Whitman expresses concern that softness and civilization will lead to degeneracy and threaten America's prospects for survival. In Whitman's cultural critique, he urges his countrymen to take up *a work* as a means to avoid cultural decline and historical obliteration. Yet the work that Whitman recommends to future generations is not work and is not to be undertaken for its own sake. It is in the Sandburg corpus that work is the defining, authenticating activity of American culture: Chicago's identity is stripped to its work—it is nothing more or less than the "Hog Butcher for the world" ("Chicago" line 1). Whitman conflates the American builders with the *poets* of Asia and Europe. Whitmanian work is not labor, it is something approaching a *work of art:* "Our republic is, in performance, really enacting today the grandest arts, poems, etc., by beating up the wilderness into fertile farms, and in her railroads, ships, machinery, etc." ("Democratic Vistas" 494). While *Trumpets* also addresses the broader sweep of historical succession, Jenkins's poem does not warn against the abstract dangers of civilization; rather, *Trumpet* warns against the barbarism of the Great Depression and the oppressive racism of the unchallenged Jim Crow system. *Trumpet in the New Moon*—Jenkins's revision of Whitman—is a historical narrative that structures the American democratic experiment as an enterprise that begins with a golden age and thereafter suffers a series of lapses that endanger the nation's promise:

> The goal which was set for you in the dreams of your founders
> Has not been realized.
> You are off the trail, America—
> You are wandering in the Wilderness like the Israelites of old.
> You are worshipping strange gods, America—
> You have lost your first love and fallen
> from grace.
> In your early garb, I thought you beautiful.
> Your coon-skin cap, your leathern breeches, your brogans,
>   your axe and your flintlock were beautiful to me, America,
> Because your motives were pure.
> Then was your Love boundless,
> Then was your Hope boundless,
> Then was your Enthusiasm boundless
> Because
> Your faith was boundless.
> (lines 3–17)

In the conceptual structure that underlies *Trumpet in the New Moon,* the "Age of Gold is in the past and also in the future": "You were honor bright; and, at least your heart was right" (ln 23; Eliade, *Myth and Reality* 53). The debate about history that Jenkins engages by structuring his poem as a degenerating historical narrative does not in any way exempt his formulations from being provisional. For example, Frank Marshall Davis's "What Do You Want, America?" (a parody of Sandburg's "Chicago") proposes a counternarrative in which Jenkins's American Eden never existed. The first twenty lines of *Trumpet in the New Moon* establish, *as the major theme of the poem*, the proposition that *the golden age of American purity is in eclipse.*

At the outset, Jenkins establishes a crucial intertextuality between the Bible and *Trumpet in the New Moon*. Jenkins compares Americans to the Israelites. Both peoples have wandered in the wilderness and worshipped strange gods. Further, the title of the poem is taken from Psalms 81:3. Jenkins grounds his poem in the intertextuality between the American historical narrative and the Jewish historical narrative so that the Bible serves as a historiographic underpinning to his reading of American history. Jenkins's historiography follows the shape of biblical mythic narrative—"a repeating *mythos* of the apostasy and restoration of Israel. This gives us a narrative structure that is roughly U-shaped, the apostasy being followed by a descent into disaster and bondage, which in turn is followed by repentance, then by a rise through deliverance to a point more or less on the level from which the descent began" (Frye 168). Jenkins's historiography intersects the American historical narrative at the phase of the Great Depression, the specific instance of the nation in decline, and it equates the American people with the lost and wandering Hebrews. Thus, *Trumpet* departs from the tradition of the spirituals, a tradition in which slaves and sharecroppers identified themselves with the enslaved Israelites of the Bible. Jenkins's poem appropriates the Bible as an intertext to assist in the mythologizing of American history. The most striking feature of Jenkins's poem, then, is that he presents American history as the myth of an originally socially fused and spiritually homogenous people that comes in time to be afflicted with their adherence to individuality—a contradictory myth of fundamental social fragmentation. So carefully is this feature of the poem obscured beneath the rhetoric of Jenkins's argument and beneath the panoply of historical details, it is not readily apparent that Jenkins includes African Americans in his condemnatory dissertation on American history.

Hazel V. Carby has located two discourses that are particularly pertinent to the examination of Jenkins's poem: "ideologies of a romantic rural folk tradition" and "[representations of] the collective acts of a black community as signs for future collective acts of rebellion and liberation" (140). However, Jenkins's discourse is a departure from the discourse of *revolution* and the discourse of *romance,* for Jenkins's poem constructs an individual and original textual response to the historical conditions of the Depression. Yet Jenkins does not announce his program in terms that challenge these pervasive discourses. Instead, he approaches his subject tangentially by using a prophetic voice as rhetorical subterfuge while creating a complicated tragic-heroic national myth.

Jenkins's rapid and compressed narrative of American history proceeds conventionally, until his narratives reaches the beginning of industrial modernity and the rise of American national power at the conclusion of the First World War:

But now I thought I saw another shadow creeping
    over the epic canvass:
Unrest—The casting Adrift from the Moorings of Faith—
    "The Revolt of Youth"—Candor Run Riot—Morals Amuck—
A Break in conduct—A loss of Respect for many of the Ancient Virtues.
So what have you? I ask you, America—
What have you done? and what have you come upon?
Cynicism! Disillusionment! Night Clubs! "Legs" Diamond!
    "Speakies!" Capone! Joy Rides! "Whoopee!!!"
(102–111)

In Jenkins's view, one destructive attribute characterizes the modern sensibility: disillusionment. Jenkins writes, "Directly I thought I saw the bitter fruit of that 'Disillusionment'" (line 114). Disillusionment is the new factor that prevents Americans from doing the required work and that breeds a catalog of modern evils: "intolerance" (line 116); lynching ("the altars of Human Sacrifices," [line 119]); race riots ("Tulsa, Atlanta, Washington, Chicago," [line 124]); and hatred ("Who are they who drove the shaft of hate between / the working black and the working white?" [lines 128–29]). Jenkins's eccentric interpretation of American history aligned with the Southern Agrarians' reading of history. Responding to the crash of 1929 and the ensuing economic collapse, the Southern Agrarians published *I'll Take My Stand: The South and the Agrarian Tradition* in 1930. The Agrarians believed that the economic catastrophe was the result of industrialism, and they advocated a return to the older way of life: "They wished to recapture the virtues of the vanished past through a program that called for de-industrialization and the encouragement of widely diffused small property holdings as a basis for social stability and order" (Sutton 109). The Agrarians ignored the facts that the society that they idealized "had rested upon a system of human slavery" (Sutton 109) and that "the stable, cultured old order to which they looked back nostalgically never existed except in the realm of fantasy" (Sutton 109). Despite what sounds like a Marxist critique of class conflict in such lines as "Who are they who drove the shaft of hate between / the working black and the working white?" (line 126), Jenkins came to a similar advocacy of agrarian culture.

The pronouncedly un-Marxist interpretation of race relations that Jenkins develops in his long poem centers its discourse on the words *disillusionment* and *service*. Disillusionment is at the heart of Jenkins's analysis. Whereas the Marxists and the Southern Agrarians thought that racial problems resulted from the socioeconomic system, Jenkins believed that the problems started within the hearts of the ruling class. Whereas the Marxists saw capitalism as the producer of its own destruction, and the Agrarians traced the failure of capitalism to the rise of industrialism, Jenkins thought that the problems stemmed not from *systems* but rather from moral lapses brought about by the shocks of modern warfare. Jenkins's reading of history does not allow for a Marxist bifurcation of classes, in which the proletariat defeats its class enemies and creates a new type of society. Jenkins's perception that the ruling class suffered from *disillusionment* caused him to confront his contemporaries with the proposition that no single faction of society can save itself at the expense of another. Society succeeds or fails in its entirety. This proposition resembles Oswald Spengler's conception of civilization as a living organization. Jenkins was right to take disillusionment seriously; it ultimately contributed to the discourses of the thirties that helped to end the Depression. Disillusion recognizably entered American life during the First World War, and social analysts took it seriously as a social factor. From a psychoanalytic perspective, disillusion is considered dangerous, as "it is accompanied by . . . depression, despair, rage, or anxiety, and it results in self-fragmentation or self-dissolution" (Rotenberg 140). Hence, it follows that McKay characterized the Harlem rioters of 1935 as "disillusioned" (see chapter 3). In his "Negro History" sonnet sequence, Dodson grounds the second sonnet in "The disillusion of this life" (line 17). Yet Jenkins disagrees with the Agrarians, who, like the dialectical Marxists, were grounded in a systemic dialectic, one that opposed agrarianism with industrialism. In Jenkins's antidialectical discourse, the collapse of the capitalist economic system was the result of the willingness of highly placed individuals to violate moral and ethical codes that had long been in effect and had, throughout American history, been responsible for assuring the stability of society. Of course, both Jenkins and the Agrarians endorsed idealized views of the past; their visions of society were based on myth more than on history.

Jenkins saw interethnic, interclass *service* as the principle that organized and sustained traditional American society. Fundamental to this view is the proposition that American society was originally without contradictions, tensions, and contending factions, with each component serving the common good. In this view, divisions within the social whole do not arise out of inherent conflicts (such as competing class interests or the dehumanizing means of industrial production) but out of the willful and conscious decisions of individuals to separate themselves from the social collective. Antisocial actions, if they are to have consequences, must be performed by individuals with formidable social power who violate the social contract to benefit themselves: "You Masters who have exploited the black laborer for centuries, / Held us up as a constant threat to the white working-man, / causing him to despise us, / Causing him to consider us a perennial menace to his well-being— / Is the light worth the candle? / Does the end justify the means?" (lines 130–35).

In *Trumpet*, Jenkins does not recognize that he contradicts himself about slavery. The historical fact of slavery at times can be treated in various discourses as a signifier, the meaning of which is shifted according to various requirements so that slavery may in a sense disappear altogether, as it has in Jenkins's *Trumpet*. Hazel V. Carby has remarked upon "Selznick's liberal gesture in portraying blacks as peasants rather than as slaves" in *Gone with the Wind* (133). Slavery undergoes a similar disappearance in *Trumpet*, as Jenkins investigates the relation between blacks and whites, an investigation that leads to his revisory concept of *service*: "Sing of the service— / Remember the service" (lines 135–36). In privileging service, Jenkins ignores the textual productions of the black folk (work songs, spirituals, folk tales, blues, and slave narratives) that was so widely embraced by writers and intellectuals in the 1930s, so that Jenkikns disallows African Americans any unmediated oral responses to their *enslavement*. The performers of these vaunted musical and narrative forms are denied their own voices in *Trumpet*. Nevertheless, Jenkins's evocative and original treatment of service was of sufficient importance that Sterling Brown quoted it in *Negro Poetry and Drama*.

While the discourse of work (labor, unemployment, strikes, jobs) permeated every aspect of the culture of the thirties, there was no discernible discourse of *service*, as there had been under the feudal social system, where servants appeared often in the comedic movies of the thirties. Their performances are marked by a resistance to service and a willingness to refuse to be *servile*. For example, in the *Thin Man* movies, Beulah, the black servant, constantly grouses about her duties and disparages the bohemian behavior of her employers. The screwball comedy *My Man Godfrey* (1936) presents a racially neutral depiction of service. In the movie, a whimsical, upper-class architect masquerades as a "forgotten man" who is happy to work as a butler for an obnoxious wealthy family that is unable to keep servants. "Godfrey's" servant-as-trickster persona subverts his upper-class employers' anachronistic expectation that servants are servile. In the Great Chain of Being, even a king was the servant of God: while the serf owed fealty to the lord, the lord was bound to the serf by duty.

Szalay shows that in the thirties it was the discourse of work that was all pervasive, while there was little impetus to serve: for example, Szalay states that "the advantage of the salary form in particular, writers came to realize, was that it made the writer's ability to perform his or her work no longer dependent on the public's response to what labor did in fact produce" (68). In contrast to the universality of *work*, the word *service* appeared in the language primarily to express the condition of being "pressed into service." At other times, *service* was used as a rhetorical flourish—a substitution for the word *work*—in order to allow for some variation in the monotonous and pervasive discourse of work. Jenkins uses an older meaning of the word: the "pressed into service" cliché derives from impressment, which is defined as "compelling a person to serve in a military force" (AHD), while the other usages are derived from the meaning of service in the more neutral meaning of useful—"employment in duties or work for another" (AHD).

Service is a word related to preindustrial, premodern work, and in that premodern society the serfs were "the lowest feudal class in medieval Europe, bound to the land and owned by a lord" (AHD). Both *serf* and *service* are derived from *servus,* the Latin word for slave; thus, to be of service was to be in some sense a slave. The Southern Agrarians dedicated their program to resurrecting feudal society. The appeal of feudal society to the modern consciousness lay in the nostalgic feeling that this archaic form of social organization contained a more humanizing form of social relationships than did postindustrial modernity—that humanity would no longer be alienated from its work, and that individuals would be supported spiritually, culturally, and psychologically in ways that were no longer possible in modern society. This is a utopian view of society that parallels the utopian outcome sought by Marxists, the difference being that the Southern Agrarians' golden age was the feudal past, while the Marxist golden age was the worldwide dictatorship of the proletariat. Like the Agrarians, Jenkins believed that the solution to the economic and social crisis lay in the past. In order to support this belief, he had to revise the entire matrix of American social relations, for his thesis was that African Americans had served willingly as slaves and with "100% Loyalty" to their masters (line 163). In order to formulate a new understanding of the role of African Americans in American culture and history, Jenkins interrupts his admonitory presentation of service—a presentation that he develops over the course of nearly fifty lines (140–85)—to insert the narrative of Charles Lindbergh.

At the center of Jenkins's concern with service is the problem of alienation that arises in Marxism, where service is unalienated work, and Jenkins rejects Marx's Theory of Alienation—that capitalist workers have no autonomy: "Then, as now, a Black Face was a badge of Loyalty no one doubted. / Remember the Service!" (lines 166–68). Jenkins conceived of labor as service, and he opposed the Marxist thesis that in capitalist economies, even those economies based on slavery, there is inescapably "*antagonism between the proletariat and the bourgeoisie*" (Engels 110; emphasis in original); thus, alienation and antagonism arise under capitalism because "the work has ceased to be a part of the worker's nature" (Fromm, *Marx's Concept of Man* 47). In contrast to the Marxist view of labor, Jenkins's view revised the relevance of antagonism and assigned social alienation and racial prejudice to the dominant class. Jenkins is particularly concerned with the reaction of the white man to the problem of race relations: "You speak of the burdens— / You speak of the 'white man's burden' / But you speak patronizingly, / And you boast overweeningly— / The 'white man's burden!'" (lines 174–78). According to Jenkins, the white man claims to have dealt with his own alienation by assuming the social cost of the black man; thus, the white man views himself as the laborer. Not only has the black man ceased to be a laborer but his labor has vanished, leaving only the alienated white man.

Jenkins's presentation of racial labor has interesting implications with regard to one of the most challenging components of Marxist systemizing. Marxism, for all of its attempts to construct a scientific understanding of history, society, and the human condition, contains indefinable terms. Chief among these is *commodity fetishism*: "The object produced by labor, its product, now stands opposed to it as an *alien being,* as a *power independent* of the producer. The product of labor is labor which has been embodied in an object and turned into a physical thing; this product is an *objectification* of labor" (Marx quoted in Fromm, *Marx's Concept of Man* 47; emphases in the original). Daniel Tiffany states that "in effect, the commodity fetish is a split or double object, with material and phantasmic properties; it is an inert body haunted, or animated by the specter of human labor. This spectral dimension of the fetish has not been overlooked by critics. Michael Taussig, for example, has observed, 'Fetishism elucidates a certain quality of ghostliness in objects in the modern world and an uncertain quality of fluctuation between thinghood and spirit'" (6). It has always been possible to focus on the commodity and its component of human labor while repressing the fact of the existence of the human laborer: to paraphrase Blanchot, the slave/laborer is no one, he no longer has any relations with this world except as a burden (Tiffany 8). Race, then, is a structure of absence that renders the slave invisible. With the slave turned into a phantom, "the object of this [white man's] gaze always escapes visibility, or disappears as it becomes visible"—so that the phantom slave is subject to what Blanchot speaks of as "the gaze of Orpheus" (Tiffany 8, n.13). The white man, as Jenkins has depicted him, imagines that by virtue of being white he has performed the labor that has brought the commodity into existence, that he himself has assumed the burden of the labor. Jenkins is insistent that the black man's *service* must be remembered, because as the black man's labor comes into view, the false slave/phantom dichotomy becomes visible.

Jenkins denies that the slave ever was a phantom. Jenkins insists on the visibility of *service*, which is also the cryptic *surface* that he insists is all that is visible. This ahistorical, visible surface that Jenkins uses to present the slave/black as a uniformly laboring subject, and the strangely consistent black worker who inhabits Jenkins's historical panorama are fashioned to hide the phantom, the historical subject-in-process that is "a constantly changing subject whose identity is open to question" (Kristeva, *Desire* 147)—the *other* that Jenkins is determined to continue to repress. In Jenkins's system, the sign *slave/service* is affixed to the sign *master/service*. The creators of the white system of signs and the black system of signs refuse to look beyond the surfaces of their creations, for both systems of signs are systems of surfaces. Jenkins's complaint is that modernity interrupted this benign system of service/surface: to his horror the new system of race relations insisted on the *otherness* of the black man and established an inalterable system of stereotypes. The white man became a subject-in-process, while the black man remained a servant, as he always has been. Thus, Jenkins's system is based on types. The white man has exchanged the *heroic* type of feudalistic social relations for the *intolerant* type of modern social relations. When the white man makes movies like *Intolerance,* he views the black man as his own creation, and suddenly the black man is portrayed as lazy, sexually depraved, conniving, and arrogant.

The white man creates and enforces various forms of minstrelsy in order to establish and maintain these signs of otherness in the discourse of race relations. What Jenkins is saying is that the black man looks upon these signs of his spectrality, and nowhere does the black man recognize himself; yet Jenkins cannot understand that the black man is and has always been a phantom. Why? Because prior to modernity, nothing informed the black man of his spectrality. Through the medium of popular culture, the black man then looks at the creator of these discourses and does not recognize the creator: the white man is as much a phantom as is the black man.

Jenkins has constructed what Derrida calls "a messianic teleiopoesis" (235), an unrequited friendship. Despite the incompleteness of this type of relationship, Jenkins centers his poem on the "logic of gratitude" (Derrida 178), with no regard for the inappropriateness or the contradictory outcome of this strategy. Were there indeed a friendship of the type that Jenkins presents in his historical account, there would be one soul shared by two bodies: "The union of such friends, being truly perfect, leads them to lose any awareness of such *services,* to hate and to drive out from between them all terms of division and difference, such as good turn, duty, gratitude, request, thanks and the like" (Montaigne quoted in Derrida [178–79]; emphasis added). Thus, in being able to catalog a long list of instances of service, Jenkins demonstrates that the relationship was not that of friendship; rather, the services rendered were performed by an *other*. Ultimately, Jenkins allows us a view of the spectral nature of the black phantom, even though he intended to historicize a discourse of a racial relationships without pitting the "white self" against the "black other."

The Lindbergh section that follows the discussion of service etiologically replies to the white man's argument as Jenkins's narrator has given voice to it:

> But you speak patronizingly,
> And you boast overweeningly—
> The "white man's burden!"
> "A Negro should know his place"—
> "A Negro should be taught his place"—
> "A Negro should stay in his place"—
> The white man's burden!"
> (lines 176–83)

Jenkins answers the "white man's burden" argument by presenting what is for him modernity's finest example of the white man, the aviator Charles Lindbergh. In lines 184 to 218, Lindbergh's transatlantic flight of 1927 is a reification of the discourse of the messianic friend. The airplane, itself a product of modernity, is absented from the poem by an acutely dematerializing and romanticizing metonymy—"Sing of Wings!" (line 189). In line 111, Jenkins describes the flight as a hedonistic and antisocial joyride. Elsewhere, he puts his tongue into his cheek and refers to Lindbergh as "Norseman," "Youth Incarnate," "Lone Eagle," and "Manhood" so that Lindbergh is not a modern man accomplishing a technological feat *in a machine* but rather a primordial savior-god analogous to Attis or Osiris:

> Listen, I shall tell you a true story, America:
> There was a young Norseman came up from obscurity
> Upon wings.
> Sing, O Sing, of wings—and the dark earth—and
>   mountain crest—and stormy skies—
> Sing of Wings!
> He was intrepid; he was "American Youth Incarnate"
> Sing of "Youth Incarnate!"
> You saw him hover upon the shore of the Atlantic
> Like some "Lone Eagle" poised above the rocky promontory;
> And then you saw him point straight into the gloom
>   of the ocean, America,
> and the Night and a Silence like Death swallowed him up.
> "Flying Fool!" said some;
> "God keep his soul!" prayed some.
> The World held its breath, America—

The World had one thought, America:
Black water, angry—menacing—frightful—deep—
Black night, deep as all Eternity—
Loneliness sublime, infinite—
But Paris and Glory at least! America.
Glory for your Prowess, your Institutions,
Your undismayed and invincible Youth,
Your virile and intrepid Manhood,
Your courageous and Unquenchable Spirit!
Glory for the "Land of the Free and the Home of the Brave"—
A Land where a Rail-splitter may become a King!
Yet what have you Done, America—
(lines 184–212)

The Lindbergh "saga" introduces the subject of nobility into the poem, a theme that is fundamental to the value system of feudalism—and feudalism is central to the development of Jenkins's discourse of service. Similarly, Jenkins alludes to Abraham Lincoln as a king—"A Land where a Rail-splitter may become a King!" (line 211)—an indication of the degree to which the discourse of *Trumpet* flies in the face of the Whitmanian democratic aesthetic, the radicalism of Sandburg's poetics, and the characteristic social realism of the thirties. In Jenkins's narrative Lindbergh's feat is analogous to an ordeal in which death is temporarily conquered; at the end of Lindbergh's trial in the poem, Jenkins alludes to the tragic destruction of the hero. The poet construes Charles Lindbergh as the exemplary white man to further demonstrate the decline of the white man: Lindbergh's transatlantic flight is an instance of transcendent service, and the pilot is the exemplary, messianic, Christlike friend alluded to in the lines below. In contrast, the degenerate modern world sullies the meaning of Lindbergh's service by rewarding him with money and fame:

How have you rewarded him who pawned his life for your Glory?
Gold you gave him—yes;
Fame you gave him—yes;
But the Dregs in the Cup you gave him to Drink—
Sing of the Bitterness, the Wormwood and the Gall!
Go hide your head in Shame, America.
You speak of burdens;
But you speak condescendingly,
And you boast unbecomingly.
(lines 185–221)

At the end of the Lindbergh interlude, Jenkins takes up the anticrime discourse of the gangster movies that were popular in the 1930s. In the transitional line, "Think will you, of your underworld, America" (line 221), Jenkins refers to *Underworld* (1927), the first of the gangster movies, though the allusion is understated. However, the name of the protagonist of *Underworld*, Bull Weed,[7] is heard in the consonance and assonance of lines that cast crimes as infectious diseases:

Think, *will* you, of your underworld, America.
Ah! Here is the sore that is galling your *back;*
Here is the *ulcer* that is *eating* your vitals;
Here is the virus that is chilling your heart;
(lines 218–21)

Jenkins's treatment of the theme of crime situates *Trumpet* in relation to the important discourse of a resurgent concern with morality by censors and film studios. As I have shown, Richard Wright appropriated the gangster films' iconography to create a language of revolutionary emancipation: Wright's poetry uses the criminal's automobile, gun, dialect, and antibourgeois ethos to construct the persona of the militant revolutionary. In contrast, Jenkins (who was more concerned with religious morality and selfless sacrifice) uses the gangster film to depict the criminal nation brought to justice:

Stand forth before the Bar, America,
While I read from the Indictment;
While I enumerate your Transgressions;
While I prosecute before the Jury!
You have made of "Success" a fetish
(lines 227–31)

Though the narrative frame tacitly implicates the gangster movies, the charges against "America" are not the transgressions of gangsters, but the crimes of American business culture: the pursuit of success, materialism, prejudice, class hatred, injustice, and economic inequality. It is only after enumerating this list of crimes for thirty-one lines that Jenkins returns to the gangster theme:

Racketeers infest your streets;
Dealers in "hot goods" lurk on every corner.
Kidnappers drive a thriving business;
"Come-on" men and Crooks consort with Ward-heelers

and "Public Citizens."
Your children are abducted.
And you call high heaven to witness your sorrow;
(lines 261–67)

In *Trumpet*, Jenkins conflates business and organized crime; it was common for writers to do so in the thirties. Robert Warshow's 1948 essay in the *Partisan Review*, "The Gangster as Tragic Hero," theorized that "in the deeper layers of the modern consciousness, all means are unlawful . . . one is *punished* for success" (quoted in Maltby 1). Richard Pells refines the idea somewhat by stating that the gangster film "often functioned as a parody of the American dream . . . the criminal became a sort of psychopathic Horatio Alger embodying in himself the classic capitalist urge for wealth and success" (quoted in Maltby 1). Jenkins observed this "metaphorical relationship between crime and business" before Warshow and Pells (Maltby 3). Given that Jenkins argues in favor of social relations based on an idealized concept of totalized, other-directed service, he is hardly interested in distinguishing between the self-made business entrepreneur and the successful, organized gangster. The racketeer and the entrepreneur are equally guilty of antisocial practices. Thus, Jenkins treats the gangster only tangentially, never endowing his Bull Weeds with the powerfully attractive attributes that give gangsters an important place in American popular myth.

Jenkins never settles on a verdict, however. He defers justice because he has submerged the source of his legal discourse—the fictional lawyer-detective Perry Mason, who became "the most famous lawyer in the world" through books and films in the thirties. Pursuing his argument as if enacting a legal thriller in the Perry Mason style, Jenkins builds toward the climactic moment when he wittily, urbanely, and astonishingly unmasks the perpetrator (Robinson 1). In *Velvet Claws*, Perry Mason states his objective: "I take people who are in trouble and try to get them out of trouble" (Robinson 1). This position parallels the objective of *Trumpet*'s "lawyer" in lines 227 to 269. The poem, then, is less concerned with making a legal argument than with depicting the stock courtroom maneuverings of a legal thriller. Jenkins's disinterest in pursuing the trial motif by means of a logical strategy is demonstrated by his abandonment of the argument at its conclusion. Jenkins's narrator not only quits the courtroom but also breaks off his courtroom indictment of the American people. The narrator grandstands by indulging in a Perry Mason–like ruse: he gives a long catalog of infractions, injustices, crimes, contradictions, and violations before concluding with an anecdote that seems to be a non sequitur but ultimately is the linchpin of the argument. Like Perry Mason, the narrator sees "human nature with the shutters open" (Robinson 1).

This brief anecdote is about "an eminent foreigner" who lacks the tact to avoid bringing up the contradictory construction of race in American culture. The anecdote operates in an ironic mode to question how "so many octaroons and quadroons and mulattoes" could have been born without the complicity of white people (line 277). For broaching such a taboo topic, the foreigner is summarily driven from the country, though this is accomplished with genteel discretion: the foreigner "was told of a ship leaving port at a certain hour: / And that we were grieved he so soon must be going" (lines 281–82). The ten lines of the anecdote are one of the most effective passages in *Trumpet*. Jenkins has returned to the racial theme by using the brilliant interplay of the narrator's Perry Mason persona to introduce courtroom irony into an irrefutable indictment of sexual hypocrisy. Moreover, the passage introduces one of American culture's forbidden topics, the discourse of the sexual basis of racism.[8] Finally, the effectiveness of the anecdote is grounded in its form—it is a joke formed by the pattern of threes:

There was an eminent foreigner visited our Country
To observe and study our manners and customs.
Was told of certain Creeds and Laws and Restrictions
That held the two races in separate compartments.
Was told that the Noose and the Rack and Faggot
Are oftimes evoked to maintain these Restrictions.
The visitor listened in grave and respectful silence,
Then asked: "Whence so many octoroons and quadroons
    and mulattoes?"
Was told of a ship leaving port at a certain hour:
And that we were grieved he so soon must be going.

The social constraints of the superego[9] ("Creeds and Laws and Restrictions") are enforced by the violent social mechanisms ("the Noose and the Rack and the Faggot") of the more primitive features of the psyche. But the lawyer-trickster-narrator then delivers the punch line that brings the repressed sexual contents into social consciousness: "Whence so many octoroons and quadroons / and mulattoes?" (line 281). The delivery of the anecdote through the language of the insider—"our Country" (line 274) and "we were grieved" (line 283)—plays with the narrator's relationship to the "You" who the narrator "prosecute[d] before the jury" (line 333). In the anecdote, the narrator uses the "eminent foreigner" as an objective observer of American culture to deliver the punch line—a verdict that is not explicitly stated, though it is implied by the foreigner's question.

This passage shows remarkable artistry and restraint, for it is likely that Jenkins was thinking of Sigmund Freud and Carl Jung's visit to New York and

Massachusetts in 1909.[10] By concealing the psychoanalytic function of the eminent foreigner's revelation, Jenkins's jocular anecdote enacts the repression of the sexual content of race, thereby recapitulating Freud's psychoanalytic work on jokes (always indicative of repressed wishes) in *Jokes and Their Relation to the Unconscious* (1905). The anxiety that develops around the need to silence the foreigner reveals the dangerous nature of the truths foregrounded by his innocent questions. Thus, the psychoanalytic reading of "an eminent foreigner" gives rise to *an inner enemy,* namely, *the shadow* (see note 8), from which the white man flees by enacting horrifying, primitive, and futile deeds in a quest for purifying the self. The function of the foreigner is to violate an important taboo that structures American society but that is never consciously acknowledged. The narrator's joke at the expense of "America" is delivered as a shock: in order to maintain the illusion of purity, the personified nation is forced to seek a means to return conditions to their former status—repressed, racist, murderous, and soulless. The "eminent foreigner" is hustled aboard a departing ship: the barely hidden degree of haste with which he is sent on his way is humorous. Abandoning the courtroom at the point of having won his case against a malignant and unrepentant nation, Jenkins once more assumes the voice of an Old Testament prophet:

> Wake up, America!
> The black man is not your Real Burden.
> Your inconsistence, your Selfishness, your Indifference, your
>   materialism, your Intolerance, your descent from the Ancient Virtues,
> Make up your Real Burden.
> Buck up, America!
> And "Come out of the Wilderness
> Leaning on the Lord."
> Drop some of your Prejudice—
> Some of your Intolerance—
> Some of your Disdain for the Common Man, the Forgotten
>   Man, the Man Farthest Down.
> Discard some of your Scorn for the Darker Races;
> For the Darker Races will be living in their present habitat
> When Chicago, London and Berlin are one
> With Tyre, Sidon, Sodom, Gomorrah,
> And all the buried cities of the past.
> Gray beard Chinamen will be carrying burdens upon
>   their backs in their native fields
> When your civilization shall lie buried beneath the
>   rust and dust of forgotten centuries.

Unless
You shall change your ways, America,
And get yourself a new Religion
Based on Humane Co-operation
And Brotherly Love twixt Man and Man;
And unless
You shall strip your hearts of Intolerance,
And turn unto the ways of Justice and Love,
The germs of decay will proceed unrestrained;
And your paths will lead down to Confusion and Death.
(lines 281–312)

This warning is a complex syncretism of several discourses. "Come out of the Wilderness / Leaning on the Lord" alludes to Numbers 9:1 and John 13:23 respectively, though the wording that Jenkins offers is like nothing that exists in the Bible.[11] The lines that address the theme of intolerance and prejudice reiterate the NAACP's discourse of racial advancement.

In framing the consequences of continued racial divisiveness, the poem suggests that Jenkins had acquired a rudimentary familiarity with Oswald Spengler's theory of the cyclical ascent and descent of civilizations as it was formulated in *Decline of the West* (1918, 1922).[12] However, Jenkins's treatment of the theory is a considerable departure from Spengler's position. In place of Spengler's idea that cultures invariably decline given their inherently organic structure, Jenkins situates his approach to culture *prophetically*, with moral correctness being the crucial factor: just cultures survive, while external forces topple unjust cultures. Jenkins's focus on cultural morality anticipates the work of Arnold J. Toynbee (*A Study of History*, 1948), which contends that civilizations are destroyed from within but that decay can be reversed by creative new attempts to meet challenges *(SHV)*. Jenkins phrases the conceit of destruction similarly to T. S. Eliot's depiction of the fall of the great world cities in *The Waste Land*. Where Eliot's long poem is a concatenation of individual voices and personalities that the poet seeks to unify into a transcendent "voice of history itself" (Longenbach 208), Jenkins's performance is derived from popular culture: *Trumpet* is personal and it substitutes the sermon for the montage, whereas Eliot embraces the montage and programmatically strains toward impersonality. The realism and documentation that serve as the background to Jenkins's poem ensures that the personas through which he delivers his poem are more restrained in their theatricality—they merely imitate familiar stereotypes (the gangster, the lawyer, the southern patrician), don costumes, and always address the audience from center stage.

Eliot portrays successive historical ages through the form of a two-line catalog of five cities[13]—"Falling towers / Jerusalem Athens Alexandria / Vienna London / Unreal" (lines 374–77). This brief historical panorama is a prophecy delivered by Tiresias—Apollo's priest whose blindness ironically allows him to see the circularity of the rise and fall of cultures throughout history. Jenkins adopts a similar two-line catalog of ancient and modern cities:

> For the Darker Races will be living in their present habitat
> When Chicago, London and Berlin are one
> With Tyre, Sidon, Sodom, Gomorrah,
> And all the buried cities of the past.

For Spengler, the megalopolis is a prime symbol of every civilization, and he named Rome the classical megalopolis, Alexandria and Constantinople the Magian megalopolises, and London, Paris, Berlin, and New York "the giant cities of our own civilization" (Fennelly 51). A comparison of the two passages shows that Eliot repeats the names of two of Spengler's world cities, Alexandria and London, one ancient and one modern. Jenkins lists two of Spengler's modern cites, London and Berlin. That Jenkins only lists ancient cities that have biblical and prophetic connotations suggests the degree to which Jenkins's poem is grounded in the biblical discourse of the depravity of cities. Jenkins's cities are not exemplifications of culture but instead are cases of the moral failure of of urban life. His catalog names ancient cities that were destroyed in the Bible because of their embrace of perversity, wealth, and idolatry. Eliot, with his view encompassing only "falling towers" that are always already "unreal," sees only the rise and fall of the cities themselves. For Eliot, the cities may be "unreal" but they are necessary; they are triumphs of the human spirit. Jenkins seems indifferent to the loss of the cities. What is central for Jenkins is not the attainments of civilization but the perfection of man, and he defines man not as the builder of towers but rather as "the Man Farthest Down" (line 293). Having diagnosed a gangrenous racism at the core of America's rottenness, Jenkins bids Americans to save themselves by purging themselves of their racial affliction: "Discard some of your Scorn for the Darker Races" (line 294). In Jenkins's estimation, the problem is modernity itself:

> You shall change your ways, America,
> And get yourself a new Religion
> Based on Humane Co-operation
> And Brotherly Love twixt Man and Man;

And unless
You shall strip your hearts of Intolerance,
And turn unto the ways of Justice and Love,
The germs of decay will proceed unrestrained;
And your paths will lead down to Confusion and Death.
(lines 307–15)

Returning to the practice of using disease to describe the criminal underworld (lines 222–24), Jenkins medicalizes America's culture of racism through the trope of infection: "The germs of decay will proceed unrestrained" (line 314). Decay belongs to Spengler's vocabulary: "Each culture has its own new possibilities of self-expression which arise, ripen, *decay*, and never return" (quoted in Fennelly 31; emphasis added). Jenkins aligns his poem with the analogical discourse of Spengler's *Decline* as a "morphology of history" in which "each separate culture [is] a living organism which is born, grows, decays, and dies within the framework of a fixed and predictable life-cycle, just like any other living organism" (Fennelly 28). Thus, it is only a short step from Spengler's organicism to Jenkins's trope of America as a sick body: if the body becomes sick, it must be treated like any sick body. Either it is cured by modern medicine or it perishes because of neglect. Tomislav Sunić has traced Spengler's "biological" analogy to the discourse of eugenics. "Mankind," writes Spengler, should be viewed as either a "zoological concept or an empty word" (Sunić 61–2).

In contrast to the biological-social solutions of the discourse of eugenics, which seeks to ensure the health of the white race through the *discharge* or voiding of the black other, the counterargument of *Trumpet* revolves around the discharge of the disease of racism itself, and even the discharge of the eugenic model: Jenkins has rediagnosed the affliction, and he indicates that the affliction can be cured only by our realizing the true nature of the infectious agent that caused the decay of American civilization. Black Americans are not the infectious agent. Rather, unequal treatment of black Americans causes social and spiritual effects, criminal behavior and moral outrages. Therapeutic cultural change occurs through "discarding" ("Discard some of your scorn for the darker races" [line 307]), which corresponds to the biological analogy of discharging disease agents. *Scorn* intimates whipping (*score*) and burning (*scorch*). The "discard" of these activities may be interpreted as medically equivalent to the lancing of a boil. The passage makes a final assertion in line 315 that the "paths" (which social philology reads as pathological; pathology—caused by disease; disordered in behavior), thus the *pathogens* of intolerance, irreligion, inhumanity, and injustice, will "lead down to Confusion and Death" (line 315).

The "Wake up, America" passage (lines 284–315) has more the shape and tone of a sermon than of an Eliotic montage depicting the Spenglerian historiographical landscape. Jenkins uses a biblical vocabulary throughout his homilectic discourse, but the compression and combination of his signifiers frees them from reference to specific passages of the Bible. This compression provides his language with an authoritative tone that allows him to compound material from several discourses, while maintaining the illusion that he is employing an authentically biblical idiom. Such words as *paths, scorn,* and *confusion* belong to the vocabulary of the King James Bible, while *discard* does not. The concluding line of the "sermon" ("And your paths will lead down to Confusion and Death" [line 315]) strikes a gravely effective note of warning, and though it is suggestive of Isaiah 59:7 ("Their feet run into evil and they make haste to shed innocent blood; their [thoughts are] thoughts of iniquity; wasting and destruction [are] in their paths"), Jenkins's line lacks the specificity and urgency of Isaiah. If we go one step further and supply a congruent occurrence of *confusion* from Isaiah ("Behold they are all vanity; their works are nothing; their molten images are wind and confusion" [41:29]), we can see that Jenkins uses the word *confusion,* which Isaiah associates with *vanity,* to bolster *Trumpet's* more abstract language and more temperate tone.

The long concluding section of *Trumpet* consists of 132 lines; therein, the poem returns to the theme of chivalry. Jenkins's strategy is to turn the values of chivalry claimed by the South against the actual conduct of Southern culture. The verses construct an abstract/concrete dyad; on one side, the chivalric virtues—liberty, wisdom, justice, moderation (line 333)—and on the other side, historical occasions of intolerance—the Atlanta race riot (line 340) and the case of the Scottsboro Boys (line 342). Jenkins presents the concluding section as yet another sermon. It begins with an approximation of the Whitmanian voice:

> And now particularly to "white" America,
> And the sovereign commonwealths of Georgia and Alabama—
> I address myself to you:
> You are direct descendents of the men
> Who made the greatest contribution
> To the conserving forces of civilization
> This side of the crucified Jesus.
> (316–22)

What Jenkins offers to support his position is the "High English Chivalry" that the crew of the RMS *Titanic* demonstrated as the ship sank, an episode that Jenkins describes in forty-seven lines of compressed narrative (lines 352–99). Jenkins addresses the Southerners of English heritage with the proposition that this "Noble English Chivalry" is "the nearest approach to a redeeming perfection / Which has appeared on this earth" (325–26). Jenkins suggests that when "'Be American'" (line 411) is equated with the captain's command to "'Be British'" (line 400), an end will come to intolerance and injustice. Jenkins offers as a further example the comparison of the Roman gladiators to the American Negro soldiers (lines 419–436). The contrast is between the *despair* of the dying gladiators who are subservient to Roman tyranny and the *devotion* of the Negro soldiers who honor the democracy for which they sacrifice themselves. Comparing himself to "the Hebrew Harpist" (line 439), Jenkins ends the poem by declaring that the poem is the preparation for "the solemn Love-Feast of Brotherhood and Democracy" (line 448).

Jenkins designed his poem to shame white America into embracing what he calls "the heroism and nobility / That lie dormant in the human spirit" (lines 412–13). He treats this theme without irony, for his method is to take at face value the virtues claimed to be the sustenance of Southern culture. Jenkins gives only minimal attention to summoning instances of Southern barbarity. Instead, he focuses on the sinking of the *Titanic* as depicting a modern instance of chivalry. He wishes that the racists of Georgia and Alabama might rise to inhabit the values that they claimed to be theirs but that they were sorely missing:

> Look to "ATLANTA," America—
> Have you been Tolerant?
> Look to "SCOTTSBORO," America—
> Have you been Just?
> I am appealing to your Heart of Hearts, America—
> You can afford to be Just.
> I am appealing to the hearts of Georgians and Alabamians—
> You can afford to be fair.

Jenkins cast his moral argument in economic terms, speaking of what the racists can *afford* to do with regard to black Americans. The issue is interesting given the role of the Great Depression in determining social conditions. Here, Jenkins does not address the issue of material abundance; rather, he addresses heroism and nobility, which are dormant but abundant in the American spirit. This idea is markedly different from those of leftist figures such as Richard Wright, for whom "'the reality of the state' [was] the only mechanism for securing the Black body from the abrasions of history"

(Szalay 22). The abundance of brotherhood and democracy that Jenkins points toward in "Blow[ing] up the Trumpet of the New Moon" (line 441) has its source in individual agency, not in the state. Moreover, history is the memory of such instances of individual agency, not the impersonal tides of insurmountable forces: the captain of the *Titanic* gives voice to words that are historic, pointing others to their destined moments of historical superiority, moments when they might rise above the "Mediocrity" (line 408) of intolerance.

2

Existential Crisis

THE SONNET AND SELF-FASHIONING IN THE BLACK POETRY OF THE 1930S

> In the society that has come into existence since the Middle Ages, one can
> always avoid picking up a pen, but one cannot avoid being described, iden-
> tified, certified, and handled—like a text. Even in reaching out to become
> one's own "self," one reaches out for a text.
> —Illich and Sanders, *ABC: The Alphabetization of the Popular Mind*

> Largo: Cry pine!
>   I pierce you through for turpentine,
>   To heal the white man's wounds.
>   —David Cannon, "Black Labor Chant"

THE SONNET AS A MEDIUM FOR BLACK SELF-APPRECIATION

It is highly significant that the first chapter of this study includes a consideration of the jeremiad in the black poetry of the 1930s. An inescapable sociocultural stimulus—the American institutionalization of
lynching[1]—compelled black poets to assume the jeremiadic posture of
anger, repudiation, and despair through which they produced a literature
of agency, struggle, and dissent. In the 1930s lynching was, above all, a
cultural undertaking directed toward *the self-negation of the black person*
through ritualistic acts of terrorist violence and the dissemination of
such acts of violence, whether it was a severed and charred human head
thrown directly into a crowd of black villagers or the regular and impla-
cable publication in newspapers of photographs of the mutilated bodies

of black persons. So the black jeremiad came about as a counterdiscourse to the culturally empowered discourse of the negation of the black self through a semiotics of terror. To borrow a phrase from Arthur F. Marotti, lynching was a fundamental component that sustained the social order.

What I propose to examine in this chapter is the proposition that what Sterling Brown had categorized as "romantic escapes for the sensitive authors from depressing actualities" (*Negro Poetry and Drama* 126–27) was not a discourse situated in escape, antimodernity, or antirealism or the individualistic self-fashioning that Brown dreamed escapes were. To the contrary, the individualistic self-fashioning that Brown deemed escapes was yet another modernist discourse that has been heretofore unrecognized—a discourse that may be thought of as a type of *individualist self-fashioning* that operated in parallel to the generally acknowledged, valorized, and institutionalized discourse of collectivist *social realist self-fashioning*. Socialist self-fashioning has been made iconically familiar through murals, proletarian fiction, documentary journalism, and documentary photography and film.

Recent academic studies of selfhood, subjectivity, interiority, inwardness, and identity in Western literature have focused on the Renaissance. It is common to encounter such rhetorical-theoretical formulations as *Renaissance Self-Fashioning* (Greenblatt), *Renaissance Women: Constructions of Femininity in England* (Aughterson), "The Flexibility of the Self in Renaissance Literature" (Greene), *Betraying Our Selves: Forms of Self-Representation in Early Modern English Texts* (Dragstra), and so on. Feminist critics have recognized the blazon tendency in literature that enacts the unmaking of women in literary texts. Discussing sixteenth- and seventeenth-century love poetry, Moira Baker shows that "Philip Sidney's *Astrophel and Stella*, Fulke Greville's *Caelica*, and Robert Herrick's *Hesperides* offer a diverse sampling of Renaissance verse, and serve to illustrate a range of rhetorical stratagems for (dis)embodying female power and thus attempting to master it, textually, at least, if not sexually" (7). A related topic is resubjectivization in the neocolonial theory that describes women in Africa and the Caribbean.[2] Jenny Pinkus shows that another way in which self-fashioning is framed is in terms of the production of selves and the social psychology of selfhood discussed; according to Pinkus, social psychologists discuss selfhood as subject positions and positioning:

> Certain social groups are defined by the dominant orthodoxy as "other." One example is *women*, who within a male hegemonic system are variously defined in terms of whatever men are (which is valued positively) women are not; they are "other." In this way, the self/other binary intersects with others such as rational/emotional, culture/nature, public/

private and are seen to represent male/female respectively. Within this particular discourse women disappear, become invisible in the binary man/not (wo)man, and women do not have a positive identity but are constructed from a "position" of "lack" and "without male identity," the "absence of the phallus." ("Subject Positions and Positioning")

While the understanding of self-fashioning and, to a lesser extent, embodying/(dis)embodying are topics of considerable interest in certain fields of literary history, there is little to be seen on the self-fashioning of the black person in American culture, a culture in which the institutional abjection of the black person was a central feature. In the example above, while there is a passing mention of several groups that constitute "other[s]," the writer fluidly moves on to a heavily theorized presentation of female otherness and reconstruction without divulging the nature of the several "others" that have been passed over. The Harlem Renaissance has commanded a great deal of critical attention in studies of collective and individual projects of self-fashioning, without the term self-fashioning being applied by scholars. At the same time, the understanding of the movement has undergone a number of shifts as evolving social-aesthetic movements and critical methodologies (black aesthetic, black feminism, multiculturalism, new historicism, cultural studies, and neocolonialism) have affected how we consider the Harlem movement. Along with these shifts in methodology, many versions of self-fashioning have been produced, though the result of most of this work points in the direction of demonstrating the failure of the writers in the Harlem Renaissance movement to advance beyond the conceptual limitations of exotic primitivism and the hegemonies of class, sex, and intraracial color prejudice. In order to categorize those efforts at black self-fashioning in the thirties, I will return to the topic of subject positioning with the idea that the sonnets written by black poets in the thirties constitute a collective sonnet sequence that narrates black self-fashioning in the way that Davie and Harre describe the dynamism of developing social selves: "[Subjects] use the metaphor of an unfolding narrative, in which we may be constituted in one position or another, in one narrative or another within a story, or perhaps stand in multiple positions or negotiate new ones by 'refusing' the ones that have been articulated by posing alternatives" (quoted in Pinkus).

The overriding social condition of the black experience in the 1930s was the *white nullification of the black self*:

The Negro's inferiority was being engraved in every public edifice—railroad stations, court houses, theaters—with signs showing rear entrances for Negroes or kitchens in which Negroes might be served. Moreover, in every representation of the Negro, he was pictured as a gorilla dressed up like a man. His picture was never carried in the newspapers of the South . . . unless he had committed a crime. In the newspapers the Negro was described as burly or ape-like and even Negroes who looked like whites were represented in cartoons as black with gorilla features. All of this fitted into the stereotype which represented the Negro as subhuman or a beast without any human qualities. (Frazier 122–23)

It is important to contextualize this idea so that it addresses white self-fashioning through the control of the black self-image; the intersubjective dynamic inherent in this process should not be forgotten. Whereas, according to the new historicist narrative, the self-fashioning of the early modern (white) man was accomplished textually through the sonnet sequence and other forms of the lyric (one finds many discussions that are similar to Marotti's "'Love is Not Love': Elizabethan Sonnet Sequences and the Social Order"), in the 1930s the *textual absenting, canceling, and annihilation of the black self* were effected primarily through technology. It is nearly certain that the wide dissemination of photographs showing lynched black men and women was the most extreme attempt to undermine the black self. The nature of cultural communication changed during the 1930s as American culture became a culture of sight and sound: Doris Pieroth comments that "it is virtually impossible to overstate the importance of the movies in the life of the nation during the 1930s" (94). Other forms of the textual absenting of African Americans proliferated throughout the media folk culture of the thirties (the discourse network[3] of the 1930s), as radio, newsreels, movies, and photo-magazines shaped new modes of social interaction and extended and shaped social myths.

Thus, the 1934 box office triumph *Imitation of Life* stereotypically portrayed loyalty between the races (and loyalty especially from the black characters), black selflessness, blacks accepting their place, the commodification of black culture, and unending sacrifice and labor. Similarly, in the 1936 film *Showboat*, a black character effaces herself in the service of a white songstress while engaging in the commodification of black culture. The appearance of African Americans in the films of the thirties as set dressing (menial workers, porters, cooks, and laborers) was a common occurrence, and the roles often called for clownishly incompetent characters. Minstrel-oriented characters and local blackface comedy troupes were abundant on network radio during the first half of the thirties (BW). Thus, in terms of the new forms of culture that rapidly transformed the nature of American consciousness in the thirties, African Americans found themselves faced with an entirely new form of the white cultural gaze: while the new media often replicated preexisting myths, attitudes, and complexes, the new media disseminated racist content instantaneously, creating a new type of popular culture. In other words, the subjugation of black Americans was reinforced and amplified by technological means.

In response to this complex cultural attack on the black self, black Americans created a countertext in which they attempted the resubjectivization of the black self. This countertext took many forms (and to a large extent was *unconscious*). It may even be proposed that the antiracist, antilynching textuality of the 1930s consisted of a subjectivizing countertext, of which formal poetry constituted but one aspect. My thesis is that this body of poetry was of vital importance in the resubjectivization of African Americans, and that, to paraphrase Pinkus, African Americans used poetry to create new "subject positions" for themselves—subject positions in which they were valued as African Americans.

Psychologist K. R. Gergen states that "Persons of letters—including *poets*, historians, journalists, essayists, philosophers, novelists and the like— are of special interest for the study of the diachronic development of self- understanding. It is such groups in particular that have most effectively pushed forward the dialogue of self-construction" (76; emphasis added). Writing in 1966, Erik Erikson conflated periods of black literary production but nevertheless was able to suggest the role that African American literature had played in the formation of African American self-understanding and self-construction: "In a haunting way they [Du Bois, Baldwin, and Ellison] defend a latently existing but in some ways voiceless identity against the stereotypes which hide it. They are involved in a battle to reconquer for their people, but first of all (as writers must) for themselves . . . [reconquer] a 'surrendered identity.' . . . What is latent can become a living actuality, and thus a bridge from past to future" (297). Erikson's insistence on the latency of African American identity is suggestive. It points to the usefulness of examining black literary production in the 1930s for some indications of the nature of this process of individual and group self-formation. It may be suggested that there was a central role for poets in this activity of black self-construction during the Depression, given the paucity of historians, philosophers, and novelists who work along these lines: Gergen's insight further supports the centrality of the writings of the black poets whose works were routinely situated adjacent to journalism and essays in such journals as *The Crisis* and *Opportunity*. This chapter will, after some preliminary considerations, examine some of the sonnets written by black poets in the 1930s to uncover an African American narrative of self-formation.

Given the cultural power of racism as it was disseminated by the technological innovations of the discourse network of the 1930s, blacks were socially, politically, and technologically at a severe disadvantage. Nevertheless, it is important to introduce the idea that formal poetry—such as the work appearing in poetry collections, anthologies, and in journals like *The Crisis* and *Opportunity*—has a relationship to other cultural productions besides the blues and other folk forms, which are already considered central to our understanding of this period of history. Moreover, scholars already recognize the centrality of formal poetry in reshaping modern consciousness under the influence of romanticism and modernism. Thus, we should take seriously African American self-fashioning as a cultural production that offered a forcefully oppositional response to the white nullification of the black self. The difficulty here is that I am speaking of an incremental achievement, as poems changed the minds of individuals over a long period of time. It is impossible to measure this effect, though it is well established that, in similar terms, entire cultures came under the sway of romanticism and modernism. I am proposing that in another set of circumstances, African Americans came under the sway of the poetry of the 1930s, with some important social effects. However, because the poetry of the 1930s has never been adequately surveyed and analyzed, it is simply not known what effect it had on its readers. It is clear which historical events occurred (for example, there was not a socialist revolution in America during the 1930s, nor was there a black American expeditionary force sent to Ethiopia to combat the Fascists). But beyond *mythological* accounts of the period (for instance, totalizations of the New Deal, totalizations of Communist Party culture, or totalizations of documentary culture), it is difficult to determine what shaped the responses of individuals to the cultural environment. The cultural environment of the thirties has been interpreted along restricted ideological lines that have not served very well to illuminate the course of recent social history.

The sonnets of the thirties were exceptional sites for the appearance of the antilynching discourse. Furthermore, these sonnets have not been previously studied. There are many other components of the African American discourse of self-fashioning in the 1930s that deserve attention as components of a hypothetical antiracist countertext. Yet a qualification is in order, since the sonnet contains one of the most revelatory and resounding textualizations of the black self-in-process[4] (to use Julia Kristeva's particularly apt formulation [*Desire in Language* 140]). The goal, then, is to present a discussion of the sonnet as an important black cultural production in the 1930s.

I hope to show that I am not privileging the sonnet simply because it is a traditionally valorized literary genre. In their discussion of the postcolonial female African subject, Tadjo and Liking state that "once in a position to write, being able to say 'I' is by no means straightforward, which is why many of the pioneering texts take the form of a searching for self, or a creative self-affirmation, and why autobiography is such a significant literary paradigm" (quoted in Syrotinski 141). Similarly, in the 1920s the lyric poem became a malleable mode of textuality through which African Americans pursued a search for selfhood, and the sonnet especially attained ascendancy as it was adopted by some of the leading writers of the Harlem Renaissance. Sterling Brown included nine sonnets in *Southern Road* (1932), a volume that is generally associated with the modernist use of the black vernacular: "[*Southern Road* is] an enthusiastic immersion into and embrace of the Black South, especially its folk life, language, and lore—a relationship from which would come [Brown's] best-known work" (Tidwell 471). As I will show, it is symptomatic (and ironic) that Sterling Brown himself serves as an example of self-in-process through engagement with the sonnet. Tidwell and Genoways state that

> Brown's quest for a distinctive, engaging poetic voice began, as it did for most writers, with the self. According to archival sources containing his "apprentice" work, the young Brown was thoroughly steeped in late 19th-century Victorian poetry. For example, many of these early experiments clearly show an effort to gain formal mastery of the ballad, villanelle, ballade, hymn, and sonnet. Conceptually, Brown located his vision in an aesthetic that critic David Perkins, in another context, calls "the nineteenth century convention of personal utterance" (*A History of Modern Poetry* 5). By developing themes of unrequited love, anger, self-recrimination, beauty, and self-doubt, he focused much of this early work on feelings, as if the very cultivation of emotion was poetry's raison d'être. These and other Brown poems self-consciously courted "racelessness," symbolic expression, and the romantic excess that places emotion on a poetic pedestal. Although Brown preserved the best of these early poems in the "Vestiges" section of *Southern Road* and the "Remembrances" section of *No Hiding Place*, other poems reveal much about Brown's developing proficiency. (471; emphasis added)

For African American writers in the thirties, the sonnet was sufficiently a cultural paradigm that in 1935 one-third of the poems published in *Opportunity* were sonnets. Marcus Christian's anthology, *Poems from the Deep South* (1937), contained many sonnets, and even Dorothy West's radical literary journal, *Challenge*, published sonnets by Frank Yerby in 1937. The *Negro Voices* (1938) anthology contained thirteen sonnets. Many of those sonnets address political and social subjects, and they show the influence of Claude McKay. Among the group of the more familiar black poets writing in the 1930s, besides those mentioned above, Melvin Tolson and Georgia

Douglas Johnson published sonnets. Deborah F. Atwater relates that beginning in 1936, the *Pittsburgh Courier,* with a circulation of 200,000, relied on porters in sleeping cars to slip 100,000 papers a week into the South, where the *Courier* was unofficially banned. Once in circulation, each copy was passed from reader to reader, and the number of readers multiplied. Poetry was a regular feature of the *Pittsburgh Courier,* and its poems often were sonnets. As late as August 31, 1940, the features page carried, beneath comic strips and alongside astrology and columns about the card game contract bridge, three sonnets in the "Courier Verse" column—a love poem and a protest poem ("To My Son") by Lafayette M. Brumby and a love poem by Walter G. Arnold.

In contrast to George Berkelman's observation about the inappropriateness of the sonnet for black poetry, the sonnet figured commonly as a normative form for poetry published in African American periodicals in the 1930s. Michael Thurston's discussion of the sonnet illuminates Berkelman's perception of "the ideology of form"—the sonnet's supposed "cool" emotional tenor and Berkelman's consequent notion of the appropriateness of Whitman's style to the African American emancipatory cause (Hatch 29). Citing Davidson's work on Zukovsky, Thurston shows that there is a danger that the sonnet's "ideological saturation" threatens to overwhelm the poet with the form's traditional associations and critical frames (31). Thurston's discussion of sonnets by the radical poet Edwin Rolfe is particularly apropos in that Rolfe and Langston Hughes associated with each other during Hughes's visit to the battlefields of the Spanish civil war in 1937. Subsequently, Hughes wrote and published a few sonnets.

According to Thurston, Rolfe's appropriation of the sonnet is an example of "a complicated relationship that drew on the form's contractual expectations and accumulated power to attract and convince readers even as it aimed to dislodge those forms from the social structures that had, over the centuries, empowered them" (*Making Something Happen* 31). Thurston shows that radical poets subverted the sonnet by introducing "'unsuitable' thematic content" (31). By traducing the *familiarity* of the sonnet as a "culturally sanctioned discourse" (33)—a discourse that was so much a part of nineteenth- and early twentieth-century education (32)—radical poets invested the cultural capital of the sonnet in a political agenda. Finally, radical poets exploited the "multiplicity of traditions" (33) in which the sonnet had been used to take up political themes both covertly and directly—so that the disparity of form and content was "a potential resource for political poets to exploit (even though it presented a potential obstacle to the poet's immediate political aims)" (31). These comments suggest that the assessment made by George Berkelman underestimated the degree to which, given the ahistorical identity of the Negro at that time, the subversion of the sonnet usefully contributed to the subversion and reinscription of *American* history as Dodson went about writing "Negro History."

In *Applied Grammatology* Gregory L. Ulmer comments on the metaphoric nature of abstraction that "every abstract figure hides a sensible figure" (22), leading us to conclude that since the poet writes a *body of poetry*, and since each book contains a *body of text*, the sonnet is also a body. The sonnet, from its Petrarchan beginning, was traditionally associated with the body, and by extension, it was associated with what I am calling the body/self. Moira Baker, discussing the representation of women in early modern sonnet sequences, states in her concluding paragraph that

> the female body serves as the battleground on which Sidney contests with other poets to prove his own mastery of language and his control of woman. Nowhere is this as apparent as in his use of the *blazon,* which Nancy Vickers sees as a device of control ("Diana Described" 265–79). For Sidney, the act of praising the woman is an act of self-fashioning as he dismembers her body and divests it of its autonomy. Through his stylized fragmentation and reification of the female body, he asserts his subjectivity as a poet, manipulating and controlling her objectified person. (Baker 9)

Similarly, Gayle Whittier observes while discussing the sonnets in Shakespeare's *Romeo and Juliet* that "the inherited Petrarchan word becomes English flesh by declining from lyric freedom to tragic fact through a transaction that *sonnetizes the body,* diminishes the body of the sonnet, and scatters the terms of the *blazon du corps*" (27; my emphasis). When Wordswoth reshaped the sonnet, the possibilities of the form expanded to allow for the contemplation of political, moral, and social themes. With Toussaint L'Overture, the sonnet could address the spectacle of the black revolutionary body/self under the white sublimating gaze. Modern poets used the sonnet to protest, among other things, the First World War (Rupert Brookes) and racial oppression in America (Claude McKay). Yet, the modern sonnet retains the full range of its past developments and associations; thus, Robert Frost was able to produce "The Silken Tent" (1939), a fully modern sonnet that so preserved the forms of the sonnet's evolution that H. A. Maxson praised it for its flawless rendering of the sensuous presentation of the body of the beloved woman (103–6), the traditional treatment of the beloved and idealized woman in the *blazon au corps*. Similarly, the black poets of the thirties used the sonnet to record their reactions to new social stresses and new means of extending the process of self-fashioning. In order to see the innovations of the poets of the thirties, it is necessary to briefly examine the sonnet as it was positioned in the twenties.

The sonnet arrived in Harlem by virtue of several intervening discourses, including the revival and alteration of the sonnet by the British romantics, Rupert Brookes's and Siegfried Sassoon's exemplary protests of the First World War, and McKay's colonial British education. The common critical understanding of the sonnet as the signifier of an elite white discourse (for example, Palatnik labels the sonnet "Shakespeare's discourse") misunderstands how it was used in the 1920s and 1930s. The sonnet was at the time a popular form and was regularly a feature of middlebrow mass-circulation magazines (Thurston, *Making* 32). Edna St. Vincent Millay's volume of sonnets that she published during the nadir of the Great Depression in 1935 was a best seller. It sold an impressive 50,000 copies. While the body is certainly blazoned, reified, and imitated in the sonnets of the Harlem Renaissance, the presentation of embodiment is controversial: the work that resulted from the thirties was layered over the production of the twenties, which led to even more questions, the fundamental question being whether there was a discernible break between the Harlem Renaissance and the Great Depression. The question about the break between the two periods led in turn to further concerns. To what degree was such a break said to exist? How was such a break discerned by the poets? How did the poets who might have followed such a break comment on the poetry produced in the earlier period?

THE SURRENDERED IDENTITIES OF BLUES SUBJECTIVITY

With the above in mind, it remains to be determined what types of bodies existed in the cultural space of the thirties and what type of body the sonnet may thereby textualize. In *The Emotional Self,* Deborah Lupton shows that there are essentially two types of bodies in the modern period, the "Grotesque" Body/Self and the "Civilized" Body/Self. Lupton describes the open, or premodern, body in these terms:

> Early European accounts of foreign peoples were rich in the expression of revulsion for their bodily habits and appearance (Greenblatt, 1982: 2). In colonial discourses, the black man was typically represented as highly embodied, particularly sexually, and as infantile and emotional compared to the white man. . . . Bordo (1993: 910) points out how colonial and "scientific" writings on and illustrations of African women often drew attention to their similarity to wild animals, particularly monkeys,

in their supposed over-developed sexuality, reliance on instinctive drives and savagery. (81)

Lupton contributes the following discussion of the civilized body:

> By the nineteenth century, the "grotesque" body, the body whose bound-aries were not well contained, became viewed as a source of horror and disgust, particularly for members of the bourgeoisie. Disgust for "gro-tesque" bodies became a potent means by which the bourgeois sought to distinguish themselves from those they considered socially beneath them, who were marked out as "Other": as dirty, contaminating and repulsive because of their supposed lack of self-control over their bodies and their general deportment, including over their emotions. (83)

Using these observations, it is possible to identify the entire social construc-tion of the black self (or social imposition of black negative identity) with the grotesque body/self and to identify the construction of the white bour-geois subject with the civilized body/self. The folk blues can be said to have written the body/self of the black peasant (what Gussow calls the blues sub-ject), while the sonnet has written the body/self of the white subject—from Petrarch to Dante, Shakespeare, Millay, and Frost. The blues, a performative form of racialized folk poetry, is traditionally spontaneous, improvisational, and momentary. Consequently, it is "illegitimate," and it bears the sign of the abject subject who uses the blues to further declare his or her own insuf-ficiency. The poetic speaker within the song is self-described as "broken," "dirty," "devilish," "poor," "alone"—signs that the subject embodies the gro-tesque body/self. Conversely, the sonnet partakes of the semiotics of the per-fect closure of its textual surface; the sonnet's aesthetic resolution has the power to preserve the body from death. It encloses the subject in its fourteen lines of austere, flawless music. How, then, does the black performance of the sonnet relate to the view of the body as grotesque/idealized? When the black poet writes in the sonnet form to construct the self through *a body* of poetry, what contingencies come into play?

In *Drumvoices* (1976), Eugene Redmond reiterates Brown's overview of poetry in the 1930s as follows:

> Brown separates the poets writing in the thirties into "new realists" and "romantics." The word "romantic" seems to be analogous to "library" or "literary," and both are used to speak somewhat disparagingly of poets thus categorized. The "realists" and writers of protest included Welborn Victor Jenkins (*Trumpet in the New Moon,* 1934), Frank Marshall Davis

and [Richard] Wright. Among those concerned with "romantic escapes" were Alpheus Butler (*Make Way for Happiness*, 1932), J. Harvey L. Baxter (*That Which Concerneth Me*, 1934; *Sonnets for the Ethiopians and Other Poems*, 1936), Eve Lynn (*No Alabaster Box*, 1936), Marion Cuthbert (*April Grasses*, 1936) and Mae Cowdery (*We Lift Our Voices*, 1936). The romantics wrote about nature, delicacy, love and quaintness, and their work reflects more book learning than anything else. (*DV* 223)[5]

Because the discourse of social realist self-fashioning operated as a narrative that repressed, prohibited, and overshadowed other discourses through the control of critical media, it is necessary to retheorize our critical understanding of the poetry of the thirties and to closely examine texts that exist only as names in fleeting accounts of works published in the 1930s.

By embracing social realist self-fashioning, poets hoped to engage *the real* in order to effect social and political changes. Beneath the surface of this assertion, a great deal of myth-making has been carried out. The blues singer and the genre of the folk blues had been co-opted to serve the purpose of sociopolitical revolutionary art. Not only is this project fundamental to Sterling Brown's poetics but also it is a consistent feature of the leftist discourse of the 1930s. Indeed, the major leftist anthologies and scholarly journals of the period (such as *Negro, American Stuff*, and *Folk-Say*) included collections of blues lyrics.[6] The centrality of the blues in framing leftist discourses on race is further indicated by the general embrace of black folk music and the celebration of such nominally political folksingers as Huddie Ledbetter and Josh White as *bluesmen* within the vibrant leftist culture of the 1930s. In order to elevate the blues to such a level of importance, it had been necessary to treat the folk blues as the authentic expression of the black working class, while at the same time overlooking the unwavering investment in subjectivity of the folk blues. Ideological-aesthetic contradictions are an important feature of social realist self-fashioning: the blues attracted an audience among the black and white intelligentsia *because* it was a powerful expression of subjectivity, while at the same time the intelligentsia rejected the poetry of the published, literary, so-called romantic black poets at face value for indulging in subjectivity. Thus, because the blues was coded as a cultural production of black folk culture, leftist doctrine rendered the subjectivity of the blues singer invisible. On the other hand, because black poets writing bookish poetry were visible only by virtue of their supposed ideological deficiencies, their subjectivity was recognized and was coded as *escape* from the real. This distinction is helpful in framing my questions about the degree to which the blues is celebrated as *inarticulacy*—a description that prevents the emotional and existential expressivity of the blues as subjectivity from speaking to Marxists. Support for the idea of the invisibility of the subjectivity of the black peasantry is suggested by William Ian Miller's observation that when academics consider the world of people socially unlike them, they fall subject to an "upper-class sense that the richness of one's emotional life varies directly with one's education, refinement, and wealth" (15).

But while it was possible for Sterling Brown and other leftists of the 1930s to construe African American blues as proletarian and politically contestable, this was only made possible by the separation of the cultural production of the black peasantry from that of the black middle class. The view that cultural production may be placed on a continuum was not within the discourse of social realist self-fashioning that so decisively partitions the blues from the sonnet. Yet, these two modes of textuality are but two components of what is in effect the same project. In his revisory cultural study of the blues, *Seems Like Murder Here: Southern Violence and the Blues Tradition*, Adam Gussow shows that blues music is "an assertion of black selfhood and identity in the face of white violence" (5) and that the blues was a "way in which black southern blues people articulated their some-bodiness, insisted on their indelible individuality" (4–5). By reading blues as a means to selfhood and identity (a text incorporating self-in-process), Gussow broaches the view of the blues as a textuality invested in affect, that is, centered in developing the singer's emotinal identity. Along these lines, Adamson and Clark state that "what forms the human self, besides certain genetically inherited predispositions, is the nexus of human relationships in which the human individual is intensely engaged from birth (even prebirth) on. This engagement with others, which is the basis of the deeply social nature of human beings, is primarily of an emotional or affective nature" (5). It is possible to gain a further perspective of Brown's rejection of subjectivity, emotion, and interiority by considering Sylvan Tomkins's observation that "the belief in the reality or irreality of affect is a derivative of the socialization process . . . and there has been for the past two thousand years a recurrent polarity of ideology which centers upon the reality or irreality of human affect" (Adamson and Clark 6).

Brown's social realism is, then, a rejection of interiority, and as such it is perhaps a justifiable flight from the harsh realities of the Great Depression. This contradicts the prevailing view that Brown's poetry is "a poetry of motion, vocality, and subjectivity, conceiving agents and actors impinging themselves upon the cultural and psychic landscape" (Sanders xi). Often, subjectivity is invoked by those who do not really advocate a deep, complex, and contradictory experience of subjectivity, namely contemporary poststructuralists[7] who argue that the self is a social construction or a linguistic-textual formation.[8] Social realism was not positioned to embrace an emotionally based narrative of human agency. Slavoj Žižek has commented that the leftist project may be thought of as "the belief that humanity, as a collective subject, can actively intervene and somehow steer social development," and he opposes that belief to the "the notion of history as fate" (Mead 40). Thus, the collective subject (impersonal, generic, interchangeable) of the social realist project stands in marked contrast to the solitary individual (the bourgeois subject faced with uncertainty and internal division) who enacts what Brown denigrates as a romantic escape through the medium of lyric poetry.

Through the lens of social realism, Sterling Brown theorizes the popularization of the blues as a subset of the social realist/romantic escape dyad, although this is not explicitly established in his discussion. Brown chose to attack certain aspects of technological and popular modernity because they represent the bourgeois separation between individual and collective praxis. He was chiefly offended by the popularization of the Negro folk blues, which threatened to reduce the blues to an exotic means of escape for record buyers and radio audiences. In "The Blues as Folk-Poetry" (1930), Brown set forth one of the most authoritative interpretations of blues music in the 1930s, in effect authoring the master narrative for the reception of black folk art in the 1930s. Brown's article begins by listing the several ways in which modernity has served to distort, commoditize, and misconstrue the culture of the African American peasant. Because of the popularity of the blues, which had been disseminated by the radio, the phonograph, and troupes of various kinds of traveling performers, Brown laments that "it is becoming more and more difficult to tell which songs are truly folk and which are clever approximations" (*Folk-Say* 325). For Brown, authenticity is a matter of "imagery and attitude" (*Folk-Say* 325). Brown urges us to recognize the complexity of the blues, pointing out that "something of an introduction to folk life might result from the mere reading of blues titles" (*Folk-Say* 325). The "deep knowledge [that] would result from a close study of the songs themselves" (*Folk-Say* 325) indicates that, while "it would be foolhardy to say that everything is here, any more than in more sophisticated lyric poetry" (*Folk-Say* 325), nonetheless, "as documents about humanity they are invaluable" (*Folk-Say* 325–26).

William Stott points out that the phrase "human document" had an important meaning in the thirties; what is unique about a human document is "the glimpse it offers of an inner existence, a private self" (7):

> Human documents show man undergoing the perennial and unpreventable in experience, what happens to all men everywhere: death, work, chance, rapture, hurricane, and maddened dogs. . . . Social documentary,

on the other hand, shows man at grips with conditions neither perma-
nent nor necessary, conditions of a certain time and place: racial discrimination, police brutality, unemployment, the Depression, the planned
environment of the TVA, pollution, terrorism. One might say briefly that
a human document deals with natural phenomena, and social documentary with man-made. (20)

Not only does Brown treat the blues as a human document when it is actually
a social document but also he suggests that the blues is indelibly limited—
that there are significant social aporias, and that the blues may be defined
by those nullities with respect to what is contained in more sophisticated
poetry. We can get Brown's measure of the social limits of the blues and his
disinterest in subjective experience (affect and emotion) when he states that
"the diction of most of the Blues is immediately connected, as it should be,
with folk life" (*Folk-Say* 325) and that "[c]ottonfield parlance" (*Folk-Say* 326)
is in 'Makes me feel I'm on my las' go-round '" (*Folk-Say* 325). For Brown,
the tangible aspects of folk life—here, the *place*—overshadow the intangible
aspects of interiority. The singers standing in a cottonfield, and their diction may be shaped by the socioeconomic deprivations of their lives as black
agricultural peasants, but the theme of his blues text is not the cottonfield, as
Brown would have it, but their own feelings. The blues subjects focus on projecting themselves into that cottonfield (or out of that dreary cottonfield) in
order to locate themselves and to establish their identity. Brown constructs
and disseminates a sentimental and romantic version of the blues, of folk
life, and of the black experience in the South. Though Brown valorizes the
peasant and the blues, it is not really possible for him to do so adequately,
and often he merely registers the reduced subjectivity of his version of the
peasant. He comments, "There is a terseness, an inevitability of the images
dealing with suffering. Irony, stoicism, and bitterness are deeply but not
lingeringly expressed" (338). In order to present his proletarian, romantic
version of the blues, Brown downplays the psychological abyss of the cottonfield in which the peasant stands to sing his song. Brown invokes the
peasant's loneliness and rootlessness, but Brown offers no sense of the blues
as a phenomenology of the black self—no understanding of the blues as a
testimony to the unendurable life that is composed of backbreaking work,
social erasure, and the ever-present promise of arbitrary, horrifying torment
and brutal annihilation.

In briefly summarizing blues subjectivity, it is important to situate this
form of becoming in contrast to the subjectivity that Sterling Brown claimed
to have found there. Brown, himself possessing a bourgeois sublimated
consciousness, also analytically sublimates the consciousness of the blues

subject. The "terseness" that he finds there indicates the sublimation that he associates with blues subjectivity. He cleans up and resurrects the blues, though the chief characteristic of the blues is its unsublimated, "excremental" subjectivity. Brown and other interpreters of blues subjectivity (Gussow 206) refuse to acknowledge black-on-black violence as a component of black self-fashioning (or self-making). According to Gussow, "inflicting wounds on black bodies and finding in such violent acts a source of fierce expressive pleasure" is essential to blues subjectivity (200). This subjectivity is powerful because it accepts its excremental character-function. Blues subjects do not aspire to sublimation; they accept that they are the very stuff of death and defilement. In blues parlance, blues subjects embrace the "lowdown"; thus, as N. O. Brown has said, "archaic man retains the magic body of infancy" (297). In that realm of bodily fantasy and magic dirt, the blues subject revels in the infantile narcissism that may be heard throughout blues lyrics. The insufferable tension expressed in the blues is generated by the fact that the blues subject, rather than being totally freed by the acceptance of his or her excrementality and the subordination that follows, is still aware of being cast out and is plunged into self-regard and self-hatred, a sort of negative narcissism in which he or she is in love with a reflected image of horror. Thus, the blues subject recognizes on some level that sublimation has not occurred: as N. O. Brown has said (and this brings us around to Sterling Brown's point of view once more), "The irony is that sublimation activates the morbid animality (anality), and the higher form of life, civilization, reveals that lower form of life, the Yahoo. To rise above the body is to equate the body with excrement" (295). Gussow graphically describes the result of this form of self-in-process: "Blues culture was, among other things, the scene within which an indelible individuality denied by the white South (with its ritual imposition of "boy" and "girl") could be inscribed with the help of a weapon, or a distinctive wound: Razor-Totin' Jim, Razor-Cuttin' Fanny, Peg Leg Howell, Automatic Slim. Gender equality in such dealings was presumed" (204).

While during the 1930s the blues had been rendered intellectually, politically, and aesthetically germane, perhaps even a privileged literary genre within the frameworks of leftist critics, the sonnet was an invisible component of the literary history of the period. As a gauge of the recent reception of this work, we can consider Eugene Redmond's account of the 1930s, in which he states that "compared to the first three decades of the century, relatively little black poetry was published in book form between 1930 and 1960. In a 1935 article in *Opportunity*, Alain Locke lamented the low quality and quantity of post–Harlem Renaissance poetry: according to Locke, with the exception of Hughes and Cullen, most of the older poets were silent during the thirties" (*DV* 222). Countee Cullen had excelled at writing sonnets in the 1920s, and he continued to write them during the 1930s. Langston Hughes was a modernist who had experimented with a blues aesthetic in the 1920s, yet he wrote and published a few sonnets in the thirties. Addressing the developments in African American poetry in the 1930s, Redmond lists Frank Marshall Davis and Sterling Brown as new poets (*DV* 222–23). Davis was a poet of the modernist and experimental manner who eschewed the civilities of the sonnet. Brown published a few love sonnets, but his reputation does not rest on his sonnets. The same may be said about Countee Cullen, Helene Johnson, Claude McKay, James Weldon Johnson, and other Harlem Renaissance poets.

Redmond next identifies a subsequent group of poets who emerged in the 1930s—Robert Hayden, Melvin B. Tolson, Margaret Walker, and Richard Wright, among others (*DV* 223). Of those poets, only Tolson published sonnets in the thirties. Redmond continues his account by listing a second wave of "transitional" poets who supposedly appeared in the 1940s, a number of whom actually began publishing in the 1930s—Owen Dodson (who exclusively published sonnets); Gwendolyn Brooks (who came to write sonnets later but published none in the 1930s); and Pauli Murray (who wrote long, free-verse protest poems). Redmond next discusses Sterling Brown's review of poets. Of the protest poets whom Brown names "new realists" (Jenkins, Davis, and Wright), none wrote sonnets. A list of six "romantics" follows, many of whom published sonnets during the thirties.

ROMANTIC MODERNISM AND THE DOCUMENTARY TENDENCY

During the 1930s, African American poets created and published a considerable body of poems that, in the collectivist, leftist critical view, they had no mandate to write. This challenge to the centrality of the folk and collective subject suggests the emergence of a counteraesthetic, which gave expression to tendencies that were native to lived experience. This individualistic tendency was at that time repressed by leftist opinion-makers such as Sterling Brown and Richard Wright, who dismissed a considerable volume of the poetic output of African Americans in the 1930s, because it was deemed deficient by virtue of its romanticism. As a first step in reclaiming this poetry, I will review the nature of the romantic discourse. In "The Romance of Realism," John Koethe states that

> the central impulse of romanticism is, I take it, the affirmation of subjectivity. While this affirmation may, in concrete instances, be embodied in or disguised by a championing of individualism, the presentation of the

heroic, the picturesque, or the languorous, or the celebration of nature, the underlying movement of romanticism is a contestatory one, in which subjective consciousness seeks to ward off the annihilating effect of its objective setting, a context which is lifeless and inert. (725–26)

Koethe's argument challenges Sterling Brown's view that romanticism is necessarily a strategy of escape. (The theoretical assessment of the dyad realism/romanticism can be furthered by noting that realism is not itself an unassailable discourse, despite the opinions of Sterling Brown and other social realists. Roland Barthes suggested that literary realism referred first and foremost not to the real world but to a painted representation of the real world. He argued that while nineteenth-century representations of reality in fiction were modeled on painting, those in twentieth-century fiction were modeled on the theater. Twentieth-century fiction included an admixture of atmosphere and setting rather than descriptions of the social or topographical landscape [Robertson 198–99].)

We should also note that the 1930s is often considered to be a period during which the primary form of expression was documentary realism. This new form of realism so dominated the cultural production of the period that few artists were able to resist its influence. In *Documentary Expression and Thirties America,* William Stott discusses James Agee's *Let Us Now Praise Famous Men* as an exemplary and rare exception to the prevailing discourse of documentary realism. There are a number of problems with this view of the thirties, chiefly the tendency to ignore works that do not adhere to the documentary mode: Stott discusses Agees's book not because it is anti-documentary, but because superficially it has the form of a documentary, though it ultimately rejects the realist methodology. Texts that cannot easily accommodate the documentary mode are not given serious attention. Even the lyric poem was taken seriously only when it was aligned with the documentary tendency—as where Brown's poetry recapitulated the language and attitudes of black folk culture. And so this discussion began with Sterling Brown's statement about the blues that "as documents about humanity they are invaluable" (*Folk-Say* 326).

John Steadman Rice's discussion of romantic modernism offers a more specific account of the relationship of realism to the romanticism of black poets who wrote in the 1930s:

Romantic Modernism espouses and rests upon a *distinction between formal rationality and emotion, intuition, spirituality, and individual expressive freedom.* This distinction is reflected in the Romantic Modernist view of the appropriate relationship between the individual and society, which is predicated upon a distinction between a true self and a false self, with the latter understood in terms of the social roles that society imposes upon and demands of the individual. This societal imposition, in turn, is seen as a violation of the self's integrity and the individual's expressive freedom. Indeed, a "feeling of being violated by an inimical society . . . lies at the root of Romantic alienation," an alienation born of the Romantic Modernist's apprehensive "consciousness of the void beneath the conventional structures of reality." . . . This more positive strand of Romanticism is most clearly embodied in the American Transcendentalist movement of the early nineteenth century. . . . The assertion of the individual's will—the projection, as noted above, of that will onto the external world—was, of course, an abiding theme in Transcendentalist essays and poetry. Thoreau, for one, repeatedly stressed precisely this theme. For example, in *Civil Disobedience,* he baldly asserts that "the only obligation which I have a right to assume is to do at any time what I think is right." Emerson espoused precisely the same point even more succinctly: "The individual is the world." (Rice; Rice's emphasis)

Walt Whitman is the most widely acknowledged influence on the romantic modernism of the African American poetry of the thirties, and I have discussed in the first chapter the centrality of Whitman in Wellborn Victor Jenkins's *Trumpet.* Thus, in looking at the sonnets written by black poets in the thirties, we are also observing the poems' underlying Whitmanian discourse. Looking beyond the sonnet's formal façade, one encounters a core of romantic modernism. What Brown calls the adoption of romanticism by black poets in the 1930s is nothing less than their attempt to reformulate the nature of black subjectivity along the lines of the important features of bourgeois subjectivity in order to provide for an "ideal of the human agent who is able to remake himself by methodical and disciplined action" (Lupton 75). The "annihilating effect of its objective setting" (Koethe 726) presented the prospect of literal annihilation in the form of psychological abuse, which legally and socially denied food, shelter, security, and love to black people, and which was backed up by an unrelenting campaign of violence, terror, and murder.

In opposition to this insufferable Jim Crow culture, African American poets constructed a new mode of being-in-the-world that was complex, life-affirming, and healthy: these qualities were the heritage of the aesthetic, psychological, and philosophical experiments of the romantics, and they were of immediate use to the women and men of the 1930s. Chiefly of use was what Lupton speaks of as a conceptual tension that developed as a late phase of romanticism: "The modern subject . . . was not defined only by rational control but by this new power of self-expression and engagement with one's own nature and feelings. There was a continuing tension between the privileging of rationality and of free affective expression" (81). The precarious, paradoxical, and demanding nature of the project of modern subjectivity is described by Michelle Weinroth: "Unable to contemplate the outer world coherently, the modern subject lapses into maudlin nostalgia for the restoration of some prelapsarian unity" ("Kant"). This pattern raises a number of questions when applied to African American subjects. We might think that, given the ahistorical nature of their collective negative identity, African Americans would have difficulty invoking such golden ages as were invoked by modernist intellectuals and writers (Pound's Provencal and China, Eliot's and H. D.'s Greece, T. E. Hulme's Egypt, Yeats's Ireland, and Leo Froebenius's and D. H. Lawrence's Atlantis, to give a few examples). Yet this is not true, for E. Franklin Frazier refers to the black bourgeoisie's tendency to "escape into delusion" (188) as a means to "shield itself from the harsh economic and social realities of American life" (188). Frazier commented that "[some] seek an escape from their frustrations by developing, for example, a serious interest in Negro music—which the respectable black bourgeoisie often pretend to despise. In this way these intellectuals achieve some identification with the Negro masses and with the traditions of Negro life" (189–89). It is difficult to see this as anything other than a description of Sterling Brown, since Frazier and Brown were both on the faculty of Howard University, and Brown was famous for his expertise in and advocacy of black folk music. Frazier's comment, then, allows a rather precise deconstruction of Sterling Brown's realist/escapist dyad, disclosing that the realist term of the divide is no less determined by the forces contingent on the modern subject than those consigned to participate in a so-called romantic escape. The appropriation of the discourses of the modern body/self through revolutionary self-fashioning was a complex, contradictory, and poorly understood enterprise that nevertheless provided some African Americans with the means to negotiate the harrowing difficulties that they faced in America during the Great Depression.

THE SONNET PANTEXT: A NARRATIVE OF SELF-FORMATION

In *The Identity of Man*, Jacob Bronowski uses "Provide, Provide," Robert Frost's poem on the Great Depression, to map the aesthetic divide between the profound and the "shallow." Bronowski comes to the conclusion that "a profound poem is not an exercise in resolution, and does not teach us to opt for one kind of action rather than another. The knowledge that we get from it does not tell us how to act, but how to be. A poem tells us how to be human by identifying ourselves with others, and finding again their dilemmas in ourselves. What we learn from it is self-knowledge" (63). Bronowski's conclusion that "a poem informs us in a mode of knowledge that is many-valued" (65) is certainly nothing new in light of recent work on indeterminate theorizing. What Bronowski brings to this discussion is the observation that poetry is not a mode of language but a mode of knowledge. This view is regularly discounted, and it needs to be reestablished within the discussion of African American literature, for the concept is of great use. In the 1930s, aesthetic theories were divided between the discourse of social realism and its anti-discourse of romantic escape. They were conceived as two distinct modes of political behavior manifested as *language*. Bronowski reveals that the fallacy of viewing literature in terms of language (politics) and not as knowledge (being) is a common habit that produces a monoglossal conceptualization of literary truth in which literature is only justifiable as a precursor to action, performance, and agency—a requirement that diminshes our humanity. The African American sonnet served as a record of the collective knowledge of the African American consciousness as it "entertained new concepts of individuality and tried to rationalize new feelings of alienation and ostensibly to assign value to its new surrounding" (Sanders 11).

When taken together for the purposes of this study, the sonnets written by African Americans in the 1930s form an extended, multiauthored sonnet sequence. Jason R. Rudy comments that "through Cultural Studies, we can now imagine techniques of formal analysis that bring to literary texts the direct opposite of New Critical decontextualization. . . . Such a coupling of methodologies has the dual benefit of enlivening formal approaches to poetry and grounding work in cultural studies more firmly in textual evidence" (590). We can assemble the sonnets by African American poets of the 1930s into a *pantext* in order to use literary form as "a subtle [though] often neglected vehicle for [describing] broader cultural forces" (Rudy 590). Analogously, Nick Browne has argued that the U.S. television system is best approached through a notion of the "super-text" (Brunsdon "Television Studies"). The collective treatment of folk ballads is common, though the practice of studying works as an "assemblage" appears to be undertheorized. (This chapter borrows the method by which such writers as Paul Oliver [*The Meaning of the Blues*, 1953] and Adam Gussow [*Seems Like Murder Here: Blues and Southern Violence*, 2002] have compiled the individual and disparate lyrics of the blues into narrative discourses—into a *cultural studies approach*.) An African American sonnet pantext for the 1930s would involve arranging sonnets into a sequence or a cycle in the same way that sonnets by a single author deal with a single theme, situation, character, or narrative. Indeed, it is possible to read such a discursive assemblage as a collective record of the exploration of black modern subjectivity that existed under the unique conditions (the discourse network) of the 1930s. The various modes of individuality appropriated by black poets in the 1930s are indicative of the responses to the discourse network of racism. I aim to study these responses by examining the sonnets published during that decade.

One use of the sonnet pantext is the application of the "collectively-focused and quantitative methods" (Schweik 52) of social philology to interrogate the sonnet for the existential parameters of the crisis of identity.[9] Elizabeth Alexander writes that "the sonnet is a 'little room,' and [Gwendolyn] Brooks reveals the equivalent of painted tableaux in her sonnets. . . . She understands that any space can be sanctified, that space is what we have, and that if, as a poet, she makes space visible, manifest, then she is getting us closer to the inner lives of her poetic characters who tell us so much about black people in a very specific place and time" (6). In contrast to the secure room is the imperiled black body: "Regardless of the artist's intent, he or she is painting against a history of deformation and annihilation of the black body and is thus challenged with resisting or redirecting the current (though ancient) vogue for a stereotypical black realism" (Alexander 7). Often when the modern sonnet is not a room, it is a body, as seen in the conventions of the blazon. Thus, by determining which words appear most frequently in the sonnet pantext, we can examine the sonnet's body/room construction of interiority as an indication of existential polarity. By comparing the occurrences of the insecure black body to the occurrences of the secure room, it is possible to measure the existential polarity of the black sonnet pantext of the thirties. This pantext consists of a representative selection of thirty-three sonnets published in journals and collections by black poets in the thirties.

In the pantext, however, *body* is present only once and *room* twice. *Life* is the most frequent noun in the pantext, which suggests the importance of existential parameters (for example, self-reliance, being, truth). The nouns that appear most frequently, in descending order, are *heart, land, day,* and *man.* While these instances are suggestive, they do not point to the specific body/room question. The body only appears when it is examined metonymically in connection with phrases beginning with *my,* as shown in the selection below. In this way the sonnet pantext of the thirties reveals the existential formula of the ownership of the body:

"He cries, 'O, God, my very heart is sore'" (Toussaint)
"My heart is beating; life has lost its prime" (Auld)
"My tongue has been in cheek too long—and now" (Lilly)

"Weep no more tears my eyes but gently close" (Auld)
"Reluctantly, my dragging feet I turn" (Christian "Spring in the South")
"I extricate from my sore heart this thorn" (Lilly)
"Sackcloth against my heart for siring you" (Brooks)
"Today that ancient beam crushes my soul" (Twynham)
"What was denied my hungry heart at home" (Cullen)

Similarly, the room appears when phrases beginning with *in* are considered:

"In Mamre of the cold, cave-chambered dead" (Brooks)
"That holds me fettered like a beast in cage!" (Lilly)
"And as in great basilicas of old" (Hughes "Pennsylvania")
"Slaves lived within the dungeons there in Greece" (Dodson)
"To kill and plunder? Yet, in iron chains" (Christian "The Slave")
"Then in his room where none may hear or see" (Toussaint)
"Down in death's secret chamber no one cries" (Auld)
"In meagre courts and canyoned streets" (Twynham)
"In flowery nook, henceforth, a hallowed ground" (Townes)
"Caged in and stifled by the walls of earth" (Toussaint)
"Heaps not my roses in their vase of gray" (Rauth)
"My feet are free; my mind is in a pen" (Smalls)

Both selections indicate a high degree of existential crisis. And one further suspects that this is a reinscription of the sonnet itself pointing to the *heart-rending* experiences of black life, given the many emotionally contextualized uses of *heart*. Moreover, the adjectives *black* and *white* appear with relative frequency. It is clear by looking at the instances in which "the room" obtrudes that there is no sanctuary for the black body. Often when the spaces encountered in the sonnets are not unpleasant and confining, they are instead vast and threatening, as in Hughes's lines, "And back in space to where Time was begun" ("Search") or "Life rolls in waves he cannot understand" ("Ph.D."). These examples present a generalized sense of the depersonalizing nature of the American culture that affected the existentially exposed black Americans in the thirties.

I am approaching subject positions as instances of personal identity. Personal identity is the result of four factors: eudaemonism, self-actualization, personal responsibility, and universality (Waterman 29). In describing the development of individuality, Waterman emphasizes the importance of identity crises in this process, noting that "at least three types of information are considered when one is attempting to make identity-related decisions regarding goals, values, and beliefs. These are (a) personal potentials [eudaemonistic concerns], (b) the presence of models deemed worthy of emulation, and (c) the likely reactions of others to one's choices" (31). In the chart that appears on page 94, I have placed these three considerations along the horizontal axis. These identity-related materials come into play by virtue of the dramas, contests, forces, and stresses of actual life. Erik Erikson attempts to situate the struggle to form an identity within historical actualities,[10] observing that

> in discussing identity, as we now see, we cannot separate personal growth and communal change, nor can we separate . . . *the identity crisis* in individual life and contemporary crises in historical development because the two help to define each other and are truly relative to each other. In fact, the whole interplay between the psychological and the social, the developmental and the historical, for which identity formation is of prototypical significance, could be conceptualized only as a kind of *psychosocial relativity.* (Erikson, *Identity* 23; emphases added)

It is just such a crisis of identity that informs the sonnets by black poets of the 1930s that I have assembled as the sonnet pantext. (To address, if only superficially, Erikson's notion of the historical development of identity formation, it is generally agreed that certain types, or subject positions, were valorized in the thirties, such as the worker, the rugged individual, the hobo, the superhero, and the gangster-outlaw. What African Americans faced in their own identity crises must in some ways have been played out against the background of these widely recognized identities.)

Moreover, it is the poets themselves who recognized both the existential crisis of the thirties and a discernible break between the Harlem period and the Depression era. I have already given some indication of the poetic reception of this crisis in my discussion of Owen Dodson's historical imagination. Other poets sometimes experienced and expressed the crisis of identity formation more directly, as this sonnet by J. G. St. Clair Drake makes clear:

DEDICATION IN TIME OF CRISIS

The woe and calumny of cruel years
Heart-rending did not crush their spirits down;
And slavery's lash, evoking blood and tears
While still their cross, bore promise of a crown.
The spiteful glance, the scornful Nordic sneers—
The murderous pack that, snarling hemmed them round—

The crispy corpse that swung to fiendish cheers—
All failed to keep our fathers fetter bound.

We must not fail—the sons of men like these!
Nor cringe in terror bound by sickening fears.
The battle-axe with eager hands we seize;
Our day of destiny in glory nears!
Unborn, the future raises urgent pleas
That we fight on till victory appears.

Sonnets written by black American poets in the 1930s are responses to the racist discourse of negative identity. The sonnets thereby present the trajectory of the narrative of self-formation or self-in-process.

I have placed along the vertical axis of the table an extremely abstract rendition of subject positions. Jenny Pinkus observes that "[Davies and Harre] argue that central to acquiring a sense of self and interpreting the world from that perspective is the learning of the categories which include some and not others such as male/female, father/daughter, then participating in various discursive practices that allocate meaning to those categories. The self is then positioned in relation to the storylines that are articulated around those categories (for example as wife not husband, or good wife and not bad wife). Finally, they say one [recognizes] oneself as 'belonging' psychologically and emotionally to that position through adopting a commitment entailing a 'world-view' commensurate with that membership category" ("Subject Positions"). I am not so much interested in assigning the applicability of the familiar stereotypes to the sonnet pantext as determining the subject positions generated by past conditions in relation to the new types of subject positions under development in relation to the historical contingencies of the thirties.

For the purpose of this discussion, I have selected a representative group of thirty-three sonnets that appeared in *The Crisis, Opportunity,* and various anthologies during the 1930s. This is the collection that I have referred to as the African American sonnet pantext of the thirties. The discussion that follows relates to the chart and to the sonnets on the chart; it is my hope that the graphic presentation of the intersections of subject positions and materials for identity formation will clarify how these concepts may be seen in the sonnets under discussion. The terms used to define the subject positions and materials for identity formation are interchangeable with the other terms in the same cell. The sonnets have been assigned to the cells of the chart according to what possibilities existed in the society of the thirties; where there are blank cells, we may say that there is no corresponding social

TABLE 1. THE SONNET PANTEXT OF THE 1930s: SELECTED SONNETS PRESENTED AS EXAMPLES OF SELF-FASHIONING

SUBJECT POSITIONS	MATERIALS FOR IDENTITY FORMATION		
	1. eudaimonism; true self; self-discovery;	2. role models	3. expectations of others
a. super-ego; transcendental; invocational prophetic	"Foregather" "Search" "The Wine of Ecstasy"	"Cross Bearer"	
b. ego; mediational; social; individual	"Desert in Ethiopia" "Interview" "Museum Portrait" "Pennsylvanian Station" "Spring in the South" "Thoughts from a Train Window"	"Hampton Institute: (Gen. Armstrong)" "Henry Alexander Hunt" "To a Fallen Leader" "Vestis Virumque Cano"	"Achievement" "To France" "McDonogh Day" "Muse" "Ode" (Dodson) "Similies" "Sonnet" (Lilly) "Sonnet" (Prendergast) "Sonnet in Black" "St. Charles Ave." "This Is the Dream America"
c. id; abject; the insubordinate subject; the outcast	"Carnival Torch-Bearer" "The Octaroon" "Song of the Mulatto" "Torches"	"Ex-Slaves" "Ph.D"	"Jesters" "Southern Share -Cropper"

formation. Thus, there is no transcendental subject position for the expectation of others, meaning that in the black sonnet pantext of the 1930s there was no expression in poetry that anyone would assume a visionary context. The authors of sonnets include such well-known poets as Langston Hughes, Countee Cullen, and Owen Dodson and a number of lesser-known "magazine poets." I have divided these thirty-three poems into Waterman's three categories of information required for self-formation, so that thirteen of the poems relate to personal potential (eudaimonism),[11] seven to role models,[12] and thirteen to external expectations ("the likely reaction of others to one's choices" [Waterman 31]).[13] The substantial concern with eudaimonism that this breakdown reveals suggests the importance of self-discovery and self-assertion in the process of moving beyond the self-canceling formations of racialized negative identity: "The question here is whether a particular goal, value, or belief will be experienced as expressive of whom one genuinely is" (Waterman 31). Thus, as the poets explore the question of "who one genuinely is," they are unavoidably engaged with questions concerning the true nature of the African American self.

Of these thirteen eudaimonic sonnets, three assume the transcendental (invocational-prophetic) subject position, six assume the mediational subject position, and four the abject subject position. Individual invocational-prophetic subject positions are not socially acceptable (though support by groups for messianic conceptions is common); thus expressions of individual invocational-prophetic subject positions are rare in the sonnet pantext. Of the total of the thirty-three sonnets under consideration, the majority used the mode of an ego-mediational subjectivity. The minority of the poems adopt abject subject positions. These poems combine the subject position of the blues with the form of the sonnet. The abject subject position embraces the low (the rebellious social mode) as opposed to the high (the invocational-prophetic mode). In the embrace of the low, the discourse is one of *insubordination,*[14] which is described by Georges Bataille as "submission only to what is below" (Hollier 136–37). A third type of sonnet, one that is invested in mediational subjectivity, more often than not uses the first person. The speaker tends to be situated within bourgeois subjectivity, unlike the first-person speakers in poems that use abject subjectivity. It is apparent that an important part of the project of self-formation is a critique of older versions of the self, for the transition is described as a crisis, and nowhere is the crisis more evident than in the pain manifested in the sonnets evocative of abject subjectivity. These sonnets that speak from abject subject positions are often reformulations of material that traditionally belonged to the blues genre, and a number of them make direct reference to blues subjectivity.

SUBJECT POSITIONS:
FROM THE SUBLIME TO THE DEGRADED

The subject positions that black poets of the thirties utilized in their sonnets may also be correlated with psychological research on the identity formation of individual subjects. In general terms, the subject positions available to modern identities may be thought of as a hierarchy of possible narrative structures (Harris 153–54). At the top of the hierarchy is the subject position of the sublime, which often takes the form of a transcendental subjectivity; this subjectivity appears in poetry as the disembodied voice of an omniscient narrator (Fand 98). Below this level are the subjectivities of the social, the individual, and the abject: these categories roughly correspond to the three subject positions outlined in Freudian psychoanalysis. Thus, they derive from the superego (the social), the ego (the individual), and the abject (the id). In reading these sonnets collectively and categorically, I will be particularly interested in examining the delineations of the particular types of subjectivities that emerge as subjects-in-process (Kristeva 135). For example, where does the sublime space originate and in what form? How does the individual mediate the contradictions of societal and instinctual forces? To what degree is the black subject-in-process able to resist the racializing discourses of the dominant technological network?

The subject position that expresses the sublime or the infinite through a narrator with an exalted consciousness—the invocational-prophetic mode (Culler 166)—is present in a minority of the sonnets written by African American poets during the 1930s. The relation of this subject position to a narrative of transcendence may be thought of as an imaginative "lunge into the realm of infinitude" (Weinroth) by the speakers. In poetry, this is often accomplished without the narrative materials that are available in works of realistic fiction. A sonnet written in this mode succeeds when the poet assumes a visionary consciousness and encapsulates a transitory vignette—a *tableau vivant* viewed from on high. By leaping over the overwhelming social and material contingencies of the lower levels through transcendental subjectivity, the poet achieves the beneficial and therapeutic advantages of detachment, objectivity, and relief from the disruptions of emotional trauma, intellectual conflict, and indeterminism. Any number of subject positions are derived from the sublime, the chief one being that of the superman. The superman is the subject of Melvin Tolson's mystical-esoteric sonnet "The Wine of Ecstasy." Other poets' sonnets provide far more conventional and approachable conceptions of the sublime; their romantic, liberal, and aesthetic formulations fall within the limits of "ordinary" reality. Given the unique qualities of Tolson's sonnet, a detailed examination of it is justified.

In 1938 Melvin B. Tolson published "The Wine of Ecstasy" in the "important" anthology (Redmond 372) *Negro Voices,* edited by Washington, D.C. poet Beatrice M. Murphy. "The Wine of Ecstasy" has escaped attention by Tolson's critics, even by Joy Flasch, who wrote her doctoral dissertation on Tolson's poetry under his direct tutelage. Flasch's dissertation was published as the first book-length study of Tolson's work. The absence of any mention of "The Wine of Ecstasy" by Flasch suggests that Tolson, after publishing the sonnet, concealed its existence where possible. The errant sonnet does not appear in bibliographies of Tolson's publications. The significance of the suppression of this particular poem is that thematically it establishes a concern with religious mysticism,[15] a concern distant from his more characteristic and recognized interest in meticulously delineating the oppression of proletarians and racial minorities. Tolson's critics routinely associate him with Marxism and the black arts movement,[16] and while there has been mention of Tolson as a Marxist-Christian, this view has never been comprehensively explored. But even if we allow for a measure of Marxist-Christian religiosity on Tolson's part, there is a vast distance between the social activism of the Marxist-Christian position and the otherworldly mysticism described in "The Wine of Ecstasy." Prior to composing "The Wine of Ecstasy," Tolson had worked for several years on "A Gallery of Harlem Portraits," a Marxist epic of the Great Depression era (with pronounced echoes of *The Spoon River Anthology*) that he was never able to publish. Subsequently, Tolson sufficiently veiled his revolutionary politics and became a nationally recognized literary figure. His ascendancy was based on the prize-winning and widely anthologized "Dark Symphony" (1939),[17] a historically based protest poem in the manner of Carl Sandburg that concludes with a utopian crescendo reminiscent of the fervor of Margaret Walker's "For My People," though lacking her poem's turbulent and ruthless overthrow of the present political order.

But now to Tolson's sonnet. On close examination, "The Wine of Ecstasy" initially seems to be a resoundingly eccentric and ambiguous performance. A distinct departure from the sociopolitics of "Dark Symphony." Tolson's title presents one of the most widely disseminated formulas belonging to the Kabbalah, the coded permutations of language that make up the literary component of the system of Jewish mysticism. Philip S. Berg states that "the primary purpose of the Kabbalist is to obtain a direct mystical experience of reality" (*The Zohar* iv). Tolson's poem thus claims that he has succeeded in this visionary quest. In *The Holy Kabbalah: A Study of the Secret Tradition in Israel,* A. E. Waite's early and widely disseminated study of the occult and secret tradition in Judaism, Waite writes that there is a . . . *wine* reserved for the righteous from the creation of the world, and it is said to signify Hidden and Immemorial Mysteries which will be revealed in the age to come. . . . Isaac Myser sought to increase the significance by an indication that the word "wine" refers Kabbalistically to "the mysterious vitality and spiritual energy of created things," an opinion based on its investigation by Notarikon, for Wine = 70 = SOD, or secret. (169; emphasis added)

Waite played a vital role in the dissemination of esotericism into modernist literature,[18] and there are many indications that Tolson was familiar with his writings. It is likely that the above passage served as a source for the Kabbalistic lore in Tolson's sonnet. *Notarikon* is one of three methods of Kabbalistic exegesis whereby the Torah is treated as though it is written in a divine code.[19] The meaning of the coded level may be determined through a system of manipulations based on the equivalence of the Hebrew alphabet with the Hebrew numerals. Three techniques serve the process of the literal or practical Kabbalah: *gematria* (the conversion of Hebrew words into numbers, and then into other words of the same numbers); *notarikon* (a "shorthand" method of making new words by combining initial or final letters from several existing words); and *temura* (the transposition of letters by definite schemes). Waite, who disparages the practical Kabbalah, (9 n.2) inaccurately points out that the numerical equivalence of *wine* and *secret* is determined through *notarikon*. The device that makes this equivalence is *gematria*.

We also note that the formula as Waite presents it is not symmetrical, for he omits the Hebrew word for wine (*yayin*, 10 + 10 + 50 = 70). It would have been both more explicit and more accurate for Waite to have presented this Kabbalistic formula as *yayin* (wine) = 70 *sod* (secret). In Tolson's treatment of Waite's formula, he inserts the word *wine* prominently in his title, and he then constructs his poem—as shall be shown below—so that it reproduces the word *sod* through poetic wordplay, though the word's appearance is adeptly concealed. Any reader with basic familiarity with the lore of the Kabbalah would recognize that Tolson has established a key in his title, and such a reader would try to determine whether there are additional hidden meanings within the body of the poem. The text of Tolson's sonnet is as follows:

THE WINE OF ECSTASY

One night I drank the wine of ecstasy,
Drank till my soul throbbed with a verve sublime.

The incident became a memory
Set, like a jewel, in the ring of time.
I had not lived until that moment came:
I was a plodding thing of servile breed;
Today, tomorrow, naught can be the same,
And people marvel at my change of creed.

Now I can see how men have given all
An interlude of ecstasy to win,
Have left behind the virtues that appall,
Have scorned the status quo, the censor's din.
The opium of custom drugs the clod;
The wine of ecstasy makes man a god!
(Tolson 153)

It is immediately apparent that Tolson's efforts have produced a mediocre and unconvincing sonnet. While "The Wine of Ecstasy" is inescapably reminiscent of Claude McKay's celebrated sonnets, the impression is that Tolson's performance tends toward a parody rather than an imitation of McKay's work. Like The Curator of Tolson's *Harlem Gallery*, Tolson may be said "to dangle Socratic bait" (line 2784). It is well known that McKay's sonnets were grounded in "the sheer musical beauty of Keats's language, the luscious sensuousness of Keats's words" (Keegan). While Tolson has incorporated McKay's vocabulary into his sonnet, none of McKay's finesse is reflected in Tolson's heaving, end-stopped lines or in his indistinct imagery, and the degree to which Tolson's poem employs inversions and archaisms suggests that "The Wine of Ecstasy" is purposely flawed. Of McKay's sonnets, Tolson's "The Wine of Ecstasy" most closely resembles "I Know My Soul," from the 1922 volume, *Harlem Shadows*.

I KNOW MY SOUL

I plucked my soul out of its secret place,
And held it to the mirror of my eye,
To see it like a star against the sky,
A twitching body quivering in space,
A spark of passion shining on my face.
And I explored it to determine why
This awful key to my infinity
Conspires to rob me of sweet joy and grace.
And if the sign may not be fully read,

If I can comprehend but not control,
I need not gloom my days with futile dread,
Because I see a part and not the whole.
Contemplating the strange, I'm comforted
By this narcotic thought: I know my soul.
(McKay 46)

The soul is the subject of both sonnets. Tolson's experience of his soul's rapture—"a jewel in the ring of time"—is comparable to McKay's soul as "a twitching body quivering in space." In McKay's final line, there is a "narcotic thought" that Tolson echoes in his penultimate line as the "opium of custom [that] drugs," suggesting that Tolson's speaker can dispense with depressants and instead transcend habit and opinion by directly experiencing divinity. But what is perhaps the most interesting feature of these poems is that McKay's sonnet gives prominent position to the important word *secret* in its opening line. This word is, of course, absent from Tolson's poem; however, the motivation for the poem is to manifest the word *secret* as it appears in the Kabbalistic formula given above, *wine* = 70 = *secret*. Since Tolson's sonnet reproduces *wine* but not *secret*, it seems that Tolson writes this poem in order to complete the equation *wine* = *secret* by the surreptitious presentation of *sod*, the Hebrew word for *secret*. The word *secret* is reintroduced into Tolson's manipulations by McKay's intertext, where in the first line the soul is plucked "out of its *secret* place" (emphasis added).

Tolson's disappearance of McKay's "secret" is not his poem's only instance of intertextual wordplay. Tolson's use of *jewel* (jew-el) clearly points to his interest in Jewish mysticism. And the playful effect of his intertextual recapitulation of McKay's poem is heightened by Tolson's parody of McKay's allusion to the Marxist dictum that religion is the opium of the masses.[20] McKay says, "By this narcotic thought: I know my soul," to which Tolson ripostes, "The opium of custom drugs the clod." While Tolson sides with Marx by rejecting religion, Tolson does so here because he privileges the direct experience of transcendent unity over the indirect experiences of belief, faith, and hope. The pointedness and specificity of Tolson's attack on Claude McKay is further emphasized once we realize that to read Tolson as a one-dimensional poet is to severely underestimate him. Tolson provides the reader with a salient landmark for navigating his intricate sonnet by phonetically sounding out his detractor's name, Claude McKay, as "clod mak a" in lines 13 and 14: "The opium of custom drugs the *clod*; / The wine of ecstasy *mak*[es man] *a* god!" (This playful device is hardly unique, and as I will show below, Langston Hughes treats W. E. B. Du Bois similarly in one of his sonnets.) The use of sound to confirm the double meaning of a text was called by Tolson "sight, sound, and sense" and is discussed below in more detail.

Further examination of "The Wine of Ecstasy" shows that Tolson reformulated McKay's "secret" as the Hebrew word *sod,* which is aurally present throughout the poem. Tolson's sonnet employs the English sonnet's traditional pattern of rhymes; yet by means of a space between the eighth and ninth lines, he separates his poem into two stanzas and reminds us of the octave and sestet of an Italian sonnet. Though Italian sonnets are at times printed as two stanzas of seven lines, McKay's "I Know My Soul" has no such division. Tolson further emphasized this resemblance to an Italian sonnet by introducing a turn (a change in the argument that resolves the poem) in the ninth line, as in McKay's Italian sonnet: "And if the sign may not be fully read" (line 9). Anyone experienced in reading formal poetry will quickly conclude that by intermixing elements of the English and Italian sonnets, Tolson has produced a bungled synthesis in which the two forms of the sonnet are in conflict. Here again, Tolson follows McKay's lead, for McKay experimented with the synthesis of the sonnet forms, as Nilay Gandhi observes about McKay's "The Lynching":

> Its form is a striking variation on the Italian sonnet. Much of the Italian sonnet's aesthetic appeal is its ability to go slowly, cruise the reader through a description and then a calm conclusion, in contrast to the quick *abab* rhymes and epiphany of the final couplet (*gg*) in a Shakespearean (or the variant Spenserian) sonnet. Accordingly, the octave in this poem follows the traditional Italian form, rhyming *abbacddc.* The concluding sestet breaks form, rhyming *effegg.* The embedded third quatrain makes the poem mimic a Shakespearean sonnet (three quatrains and a couplet). Because of this formal duality, it might be difficult to call "The Lynching" Italian or Shakespearean; the key is the poetic pace—the reflective tone is more indicative of an Italian sonnet and so the poem can be primarily characterized as such. It largely follows the Italian rhyme scheme but has Shakespearean organization. (Gandhi)

For Gandhi, McKay's sonnet makes its point by means of the formal experiment: "Lynching becomes not only accepted but natural. This is why McKay breaks the Italian form. The added quatrain and lengthened pauses have us pensively consider the descriptions. The couplet is a way of saying nothing that preceded it makes sense" (Gandhi). In contrast, Tolson's combination of the two major forms of the sonnet is not justifiable as a poetic expression of cosmic consciousness. However, like McKay, Tolson has also usefully exploited the formal synthesis.

In "The Wine of Ecstasy," the use of the concluding couplet contradicts the octave-sestet development of the sonnet so that there is a pronounced cessation at the end of the twelfth line, "Have scorned the status quo, the censor's din." The abruptness with which the concluding couplet follows is emphatic, and the lines add little more to the poem than unconvincing declarative bombast and the thudding reverberation of *clod* and *god*. Yet in this emphatic conjunction is to be found the entire point of Tolson's intentionally halting exercise: in concluding with the "od" of *sod*, Tolson has presented the reader with the word *sod* through an indirect combination of sounds. The components s and -od of sod are not contingent in the concluding heroic couplet, but the rhyme of clod and god as end rhymes emphasizes the importance of the -od sound.The poem begins with *s* sounds— as in *ecstasy, soul, sublime, incident,* and *set*; thus, *s* sounds predominate throughout the first four lines. Beginning in the fifth line, there are a number of *o*'s. The sixth line contains *plodding*—a rhyme for *clod* and *god*. Moreover, the fifth line signals the replication of the letter *d* as a final letter in *breed, creed, behind, scorned, clod,* and *god*. Finally, there is a parallel pattern in the concluding couplet that suggests that the close approach of "drugs the clod" to the disclosure of *sod* [drug*s* the cl*od*] is echoed in the final line by "makes man a god" [make*s* man a g*od*]. To summarize, the elemental components of the word *sod* occur in "The Wine of Ecstasy" ten times—in lines 1, 2, 6, 7, 10, 12, 13, and 14. An interrupted presentation of *sod*—where other letters come between the s-o-d—occurs twice in lines 12 and 13, with the letters presented in the proper order to spell *sod* all four times; the letters also follow the proper order in the fourteenth line. In this manner Tolson presents the word sod as sight. *Sod* is sounded three times in Tolson's sonnet in the sense that when the poem is read aloud, the word sod is heard among the other sounds the poem delivers.

If McKay's poem is used as an experimental control—a poem in which the poet has no interest in the word *sod*—the letters that compose *sod* occur only four times (lines 4, 9, 11, and 13) and only once in the proper order, a marked contrast to the ten occurrences in the proper order in Tolson's poem. It is also clear that the *od* sound is present only once, in the fourth line of McKay's poem ("body . . . space"), and not in such a way that it may be combined to produce *sod,* since it is in partially reversed order, and the *s* occurs only as *sp*. Thus, Tolson's sonnet functions at the level of the practical Kabbalah more so than at the level of formal poetry. While the poem suffers as a sonnet, it succeeds as a Kabbalistic cipher. At the same time, the features that degrade Tolson's performance formally are those features of the poem that serve as aids to its Kabbalistic level, for the formal disruptions call attention to the patterns that reveal the code.

The source from which the theory behind Tolson's sonnet originates is the *Book of Splendor,* also known as *The Zohar.* Section 68 states that "'Wine makes glad the heart of man' (Psalms 104:15).[21] This is the wine of the Torah, for the numerical value of the letters of the word *yayin* [wine] (10 + 10 + 50) is the same as the letters of *sod* [secret] (60 + 6 + 4)" (Berg 34). In Jewish mysticism, the man who is transformed by the mystical "wine" of the Torah is the zaddik, the enlightened saint. Thus, the burden of Tolson's sonnet is his claim to have attained mystical enlightenment (*Yechidah*, union with the Absolute) and to have become a zaddik. The poem confirms that he has become a zaddik through another cipher. Six lines of the poem contain a number of occurrences of the letters *l* and *v*, the predominant example being in the second line—"Drank till my soul throbbed with a verve sublime"—which contains four *l*'s and two *v*'s. This effect of superabundance is echoed by the eleventh line with its three *l*'s and two *v*'s. The *l* and *v* cipher also occurs in lines 5 ("lived"), 6 ("servile"), 8 ("marvel"), 9 ("given all"), and 11 ("Have left behind the virtues that appall"). In all, there are ten occurrences of the *l* and *v* cipher in Tolson's sonnet. *L* and *v* are the Hebrew letters *lamed* and *vau*, and since the Hebrew numbers and letters are interchangeable, the number 36 is written as *lv*.

The number 36 is, in a sense, the most important number in the lore of the Kabbalah. The lore surrounding the number 36 goes back four thousand years to Sumerian civilization, in which groups of thirty-six judges heard matters of law. Throughout the body of his published poetry, Tolson repeatedly alludes to the so-called inner circle of humanity, or, as they are called in occultism, "those who know." Allusions to the phrase "those who know" were worked into "The Man from Halicarnassus" and *Libretto for the Republic of Liberia*. In *Harlem Gallery* Tolson writes, "Who knows, without no, / the archimedean pit and pith of a man?" (lines 55–56). In *Kabbalah* Z'ev Halevi explained that "those who know" was a traditional name for Kabbalists in ancient times (29). This usage is further supported by the fact that in two of his poems, "The Man from Halicarnassus" and *Harlem Gallery*, Tolson uses variant forms of the word, *qabala* and *cabala*,[22] respectively. "Those who know" are called the zaddikim in the Hasidic tradition, a tradition that he refers to directly in *Harlem Gallery*: "Hideho's joy was Hasidic" (line 3372). The traditions surrounding the zaddikim were borrowed by Tolson who applied them to himself. The following discussion of the zaddikim is very helpful in explaining how Tolson viewed himself and the activity of writing poetry:

> We also have the concept of thirty-six *tzadikim* whose existence sustains the world from one generation to another. In this age-old tradition, it is not a body of people who are in touch with one another; each one is alone and for the most part does not have any idea about himself or the others. They simply do not know who they are or what they're doing.

> The important thing is that, from the point of view of divine justice, the world cannot continue to exist except if there be a certain number of persons who justify its existence. As an archetype, we have the story of Abraham and the destruction of Sodom and Gomorrah. The question is: Why should any place that is full of wickedness be allowed to perpetuate itself? And the answer is that a minimal number of righteous persons can compensate for the evil of the many and check the course of retribution. Thus if there were not a certain number of *Tzadikim* who justify the continued existence of the world, the world would be destroyed like Sodom, like the world at the time of the Flood. Therefore there is the tradition of the thirty-six persons whose existence on earth in every generation, whether they know it or not, keeps the world from being annihilated. (Steinsaltz 100)

Tolson's assertion that he was a zaddik was his indirect way of indicating that he was involved in the Gurdjieff movement, an important component in American intellectual life beginning in 1924.[23] While accounts of the Harlem Renaissance submit that Jean Toomer lectured on Gurdjieff's system to Harlem writers in 1925 and 1926, the lectures were actually conducted by A. R. Orage and C. Daly King, figures far more advanced in the Gurdjieff work than Toomer. As a graduate student at Columbia University from 1931 to 1932 and the author of the thesis "The Harlem Group of Negro Writers" (1940), Tolson encountered a large number of Gurdjieff's followers. He also encountered an American version of the phonetic Kabbalah, a form of esoteric writing employed by the psychologist and mystery writer and Gurdjieff group leader, C. Daly King. Tolson referred to King's method as "[the] three S's of Parnassus" (Flasch 48)—"sight, sound, and sense," implying that he had invented it. King first presented the phonetic Kabbalah in *Beyond Behaviorism* (1927)—a Gurdjieffian treatise on "conscious evolution" that masqueraded as Buddhist thought. Tolson intended his spurious sonnet to be a purposeful mistake, a parallel to C. Daly King's naming his detective novels "obelists"—*Obelists at Sea* (1933) and *Obelists Fly High* (1935). Tolson writes always in the mode of Gurdjieff's *legominisms*—coded texts that use deliberate imprecision ("lawful inexactitudes") to force the reader to follow a pattern, only to interrupt the pattern with something that is both obviously wrong and contains some wisdom or insight. This technique alerts readers that they will be forced *to look beneath the surface of what is written*. Here is Gurdjieff's description of "lawful inexactitudes" from *Beelzebub's Tales*:

> In all of the productions which we shall intentionally create on the basis of this Law [of Sevenfoldness], for the purpose of transmitting to remote generations, we shall intentionally introduce certain *lawful inexactitudes,*

and to these lawful inexactitudes we shall place, by means available to us, the contents of some true knowledge or other which is already in the possession of men of the present time.

In any case, for the interpretation itself, or, as may be said, for the "*key*" to those inexactitudes in that great Law, we shall further make in our productions something like a Legominism, and we shall secure its transmission from generation to generation through initiates of a special kind, whom we shall call initiates of art. (Gurdjieff, "Art" 51–52; emphases added)

C. Daly King used the phonetic cabala to write his obelist series of detective novels, and many of Gurdjieff's students adopted this technique. Here is Tolson's presentation of the rules for reading the "sight, sound, and sense" code, which he uses in his epic, *Harlem Gallery:* "contrives the triple-rhyming oblong leaf / of the metaphor-maker of Naishapur; / fashions the undulant mold / of the cyma reversa" (lines 4035–63). In this passage Tolson indicates that his hidden words may appear reversed, may be present only as sound, or may appear through intermittent, complex patterns. Using C. Daly King's system of phonetic repetition, Tolson has created yet another hidden level in his sonnet in which he has inserted the name of his teacher, *Daly King.* Other names that appear are [Jean] *Toomer* in lines 7 and 13; *A. R. Orage* in line 12; *P. D. Ouspensky* in lines 13 and 14; and *Gurdjieff* in lines 13 and 11 (*drugs* read in reverse combined with *left*).

Our view of Tolson's early poems has to be revised, for even his unpublished manuscript of the early 1930s, *A Gallery of Harlem Portraits,* was freighted with esoteric content. Since he could not comfortably insert it in the plainspoken, proletarian poems of the *Portraits,* he concocted improbable names and turned the table of contents into a cabalistic text.[24] Thus, the sonnet "The Wine of Ecstasy," rather than being an early esoteric exercise, comes after Tolson had written a considerable body of coded poetry. Tolson positions himself as a zaddik primarily because by claiming enlightenment he could place himself in the highest rank of individuality, beyond all social, cultural, intellectual, and biological limitations: "Those who attain enlightenment become liberated, released from the attachment to suffering and limitation of any kind. They are absolutely free, and extraordinarily awakened" (Ullman xv).

The textual strategy for erecting this subject position has involved surmounting an inferior subject position so that here Tolson surpasses Claude McKay's romantic genius as a self-originating subject (Strathausen 141): McKay's subject is trapped in paradox and unable to observe the totality of the world. Tolson indicates through the esoteric coding of his sonnet that he has surpassed the limits of his former self; simultaneously, he uses parody to indicate that he has outgrown the limitations of subjective literature. Finally, it must be noted that Tolson's mysticism did not lead him into an inner-directed style of life. Rather, Tolson's predilection for extroversion and engagement was acknowledged in a recent film, *The Great Debaters* (2008), which portrayed Tolson as a radical involved in the clandestine unionizing of Texas farm workers in the early 1930s. His colleague Wallace Thurman commented in his novel *Infants of the Spring,*, in shockingly frank terms, on the connection between the esoteric doctrine of the superman that Tolson expressed in his sonnet "The Wine of Ecstasy" and Tolson's radical political activities: "It is mass movements that bring forth individuals. I don't care about stray darkies getting lynched, but I do care about people who will fight for a principle. And if out of a wholesale allegiance to Communism the Negro could develop just a half dozen men who were really and truly outstanding the result would be worth the effort" (*Infants* 218–19).

LANGSTON HUGHES'S HANDBOOK ON EUDAIMONISM

Langston Hughes published three sonnets in the 1930s: "Pennsylvania Station" (1932), "Ph. D." (1932), and "Search" (1937). Hughes worked out an existential and ontological credo across the span of his three-sonnet sequence; in combination, the sequence expounds a modern treatment of becoming or self-fashioning. Thus, Hughes's three sonnets compose a sequence that is a handbook on eudaemonism. Hughes's sonnets reveal a derivation not so much from the romantic modernism of Walt Whitman as from Ralph Waldo Emerson, for the sonnets are couched in an expressly Emersonian vocabulary. For Emerson, *range* is a key word, appearing in nearly all of his essays.[25] The word *range* figures in "Search" ("To seek the sun that ranges far beyond" [line 2]) and in "Ph.D." ("And quite beyond his Ph.D.'s small range" [line 14]). Similarly, the word *search* appears in both "Search" and "Pennsylvania Station" (where it has two appearances).

Emerson's individualism was situated in the idea of searching. For Emerson, searching was a generative activity throughout his years as a writer.[26] Rather than being informed solely by collective discourses, Hughes's poetry was also influenced by romantic modernism, and his sonnets are expressions of Emerson's liberating individualism. While this finding seems on the surface out of place (especially given Hughes's association with the Communist Party in the 1930s), in truth Hughes was a complex, experimental, and eclectic personality. Added to this is the cultural centrality of Emerson in the 1930s. Bliss Perry, in the Vanexem Lectures at Princeton in 1931, noted that "more books have been written about Emerson in the last five years than in any five years since his death" (11), and he detected a rising interest in Emerson (136). In the 1930s Emersonian individualism was most powerfully reformulated and advanced by John Dewey in *Individualism Old and New* (1930), which developed a view of individualism in the wake of the stock market crash of 1929 that framed what he saw as the increasing corporatization of social life fostered by neoliberal economic policies: "The tremendous disruption occasioned by the Great Depression left many Americans asking 'what happened?' The incredible insecurity and impoverishment that subsequently followed made the revaluation of rugged individualism not only a welcome philosophical exercise, but an urgent one" (Willet "Individualism").

In the table of subject positions and materials for identity formation, Hughes's "Pennsylvania Station" sonnet intersects eudaemonistic materials for identity formation and the mediational subject position.

PENNSYLVANIA STATION

The Pennsylvania Station in New York
Is like some vast basilica of old
That towers above the terror of the dark
As bulwark and protection to the soul.
Now people who are hurrying alone
And those who come in crowds from far away
Pass through this great concourse of steel and stone
To trains, or else from trains out into day.
And as in great basilicas of old
The search was ever for a dream of God,
So here the search is still within each soul
Some seed to find to root in earthly sod,
Some seed to find that sprouts a holy tree
To glorify the earth—and you—and me.

"Pennsylvania Station" locates the speaker within a specific modern artifact, though this is done somewhat distantly, as the speaker foregoes presenting the self as a lyric "I," preferring to remain behind the scenes until the concluding "me." The sonnet is particularly interesting in that it begins by comparing the train station, completed in 1910, to "some vast basilica of old," so that one at first suspects that the burden of the poem will be to present the terminal of a modern transportation system through a realistic description. Conventional wisdom suggests that vast public spaces threaten individuality—that individuals, in effect, become dehumanized by overwhelming structures. This is not the case in Hughes's poem. On the contrary, the poem quickly dispenses with the material world. The train station's secular origin—it was in fact designed in imitation of a Roman bath—becomes spiritual through reference to sacred architecture. Simultaneously, the station transitions backward into history. This twofold action reveals that Hughes's omniscient, disembodied narrator is relegated neither to the historical present nor to materiality, for the transcendent trajectory of the poem locates the speaker within the "soul" (line 4). The lofty *public interior* of the train station, whose marble-sheathed main waiting room was 150 feet high, becomes a part of each individual who enters the public space, transforming it into a *private interior*. Not only is the subject position of the narrator outside of historical time but also the narrator is capable of projecting each traveler into a direct experience of his or her own interior vastness. The speaker is powerful enough to transform a collective public space into a site of transcendence, an interior psychological event: "so here the search is still within each soul" (line 11).

"Pennsylvania Station" is a hymn to the subject-in-process. The individual searches for "some seed" (line 13) that will bring into the world a new quotient of being, "To glorify the earth—and you—and me" (line 14). Thus, the train station becomes an emblem of the sublime, and even though the modern subject is dangerously close to losing his or her soul in the rushing crowd that the poem describes, the train station inadvertently conducts modern subjects into the experience of the ineffable and the mythical. The speaker uses the growth of a "holy tree" (line 13) to symbolize the attainment of individualism. Certainly, the elevation of the train station to a house of worship and subsequently to a place of mystical experience occurs within the psyche of the speaker. The speaker, though, assumes a Whitmanian posture that allows him to extend his private sublimation of the train station to all who pass through, though it is not realistic to assume that anyone who passes through the station attains the speaker's level of perception. Rather, we have access to this experience through the magical space of the sonnet itself, thanks to the way that sonnets have operated traditionally as portals of access to intellectual immortality: "The subject of the image, once chosen, is abstracted from the world of nature and yoked to a conceptual scheme. Its natural properties are wholly subordinated to its place in the allegory, and are never regained. When . . . Guillaume de Lorris . . . makes his rose the *sanctum sanctorum* of courtly love, it gives up its being as a natural flower and becomes . . . the life-less and undying symbol of an idea" (Lever 4).

Like de Lorris, Hughes uses the conventions of the sonnet to portray subjectivity in a manner that disguises the sublimated fantasy that is the essence of the poem; thus, the discourse of monumentality that the poem presents on a number of levels must be rejected:

Architecture represents this silent, homologous, gravitational mass that absorbs every meaningful production. The monument and the pyramid are where they are to cover up a place, to fill a void: the one left by death. Death must not appear, it must not take place. Death comes with time as the unknown bourne of the future. It is the other of everything known; it threatens the meaning of discourses. Death is hence irreducibly heterogeneous to homologies; it is not assimilable. The death wish, whose action Freud recognized whenever a return to the inanimate could be noted, whenever difference was denied, wears the elusive face of this expanding homology that causes the place of the Other to be imported into the Same. One plays dead so that death will not come. So nothing will happen and time will not take place. (Hollier 36)

Thus, "Pennsylvania Station" narrates the sublimation of excremental man. The fantasy encapsulated in the poem is that the dead monument of the train station transcends death: by the act of being engulfed within the monument, the subject is protected by the monumental and immortal body which is then further sublimated by the monumental body of the sonnet.

"Pennsylvania Station" is particularly interesting in that it helps us to see that the mechanism of sublimation equates the monumentality of the train station with the monumentality of the sonnet, a feature that might have otherwise remained outside of the reader's consciousness. The poem also acknowledges the sublimating character of the process, for it names "the terror of the dark" (line 3) against which the subject requires protection. Thus, the poem presents a fantasy in which the building-as-body engulfs the basilica and endows the subject with monumentality; it is through the magic textuality of the sonnet that the subject is able to attain monumentality. Of course, as Bataille, Laing, and Brown tirelessly argued, the monument/sonnet has only the capacity to preserve the dead/abstract form of the tomb/poem. Discussing Bataille's view of architecture, Hollier observes that "one of the labyrinth's most subtle (treacherous) detours leads one to believe it is possible to get out, even making one desire to do so. Sublimation is a false exit that is an integral part of its economy" (73).

THE BLACK PEASANT

It should not be surprising that the African American poetry of the 1930s often utilizes the subject position of the black peasant. In Marcus Christian's sonnet "Carnival Torch-Bearer" (*Opportunity*, Feb. 1938: 45), this familiar figure is placed at the intersection of eudaemonism and abjection.

CARNIVAL TORCH-BEARER

In nondescript clothes and run-down, broken shoes,
His small, dark face unnaturally lean,
He walks the brightly lighted avenues
With smoking, flaming torch of kerosene.
He lights the way for one more King tonight,
Just as his dark forbears have always done
From Caesar to some lesser ones in might—
Tomorrow night will be a different one.
What are a thousand years but one tomorrow?
What are five hundred years but one long night?
None sees his face, pinched hard by want and sorrow,
Although he carries in his hands a light.
Lighting a dream, he dreams another dream
Of dives on Poydras Street where bright lights gleam.

One of the most accomplished and perceptive black poets working in the 1930s, Marcus Christian wrote highly original sonnets that are situated in an intellectual version of bourgeois subjectivity. Though his poems suggest an investment in a transcendental-romantic modernism reminiscent of Hughes's sonnets, Christian's poems are anti-Marxist contemplations of historical determinism. Christian addressed a number of sonnets to the theme of the "man farthest down," the figure that Adam Gussow calls "the blues subject"—the slave, the agricultural peasant, or the urban proletarian. Marcus Christian was a social realist with a determination to voice his political concerns in sophisticated, complex, and challenging poems. Whereas Sterling Brown presents his black folk subjects through dialect and in forms that approximate those of folksongs, Christian experimented with social realist aesthetics in order to frame the black peasant in a broader context, at times reaching for a Spenglerian temporal vastness and at other times reaching for a cosmic grasp of causality.[27] Though he often wrote in the sonnet form, Christian employed a diction that confirms the influence of modernist aesthetics, and his writing shows few remnants of the romantic or the archaic.

Christian's peasant comes under the gaze of a Spenglerian narrator in a manner reminiscent of Owen Dodson's prophetic treatment of the Harlem underclass in his sonnet cycle, "Negro History," with the difference that in Christian's poem the peasant has not yet escaped from working the southern land. Except for the decisive shift in rhetorical register effected by *nondescript*, the poem's opening line echoes the familiar posture of the blues subject, who candidly refers to what would have been obvious to his immediate audience, the fact that he was "broken-down," "a broke man" (Paul Oliver 57), "broken and hungry" (Oliver 44) with "shoes [that] ain't got no bottom, feets standin' on the ground" (Oliver 57). The blues subject willingly comes under the gaze of his onlookers because he can look forward to gaining their sympathy; perhaps they have suffered similar indignities. Not so in the case of the carnival torchbearer: Christian's narrator allows the torchbearer neither to address the audience directly nor to come voluntarily before his onlookers. The omniscient speaker seizes upon the carnival torchbearer and subjects him to an objective historical analysis. The effect is metonymic; the man himself becomes nondescript. Though the sonnet supplies realistic details of a traditional Mardi Gras celebration in New Orleans, the language points to its function as a conveyer of semiotic multiplicity: "His small, dark face unnaturally lean" (line 2) inescapably alludes to Caesar's iconic description of Cassius in act 1, scene 2 of Shakespeare's *Julius Caesar*: "Yond Cassius has a lean and hungry look; / He thinks too much: such men are dangerous." The contrast between the nameless torchbearer and the named Cassius cannot be more indicative. Yet the poem enforces this reading by mentioning Caesar in the seventh line, where the secularized and degenerate celebration of the beginning of Lent in carnival is semantically elevated by the historicizing discourse of the narrator in the second quatrain:

He lights the way for one more King tonight,
Just as his dark forbears have always done
From Caesar to some lesser ones in might—
Tomorrow night will be a different one.
("Carnival Torch Bearer" lines 5–8)

Christian's reference to Cassius and Caesar raises the issue of revolutionary violence (if we assume that Christian grounded his poem in Marxism): "Rene Girard observes that *Julius Caesar* is Shakespeare's deconstruction of the mythology of revolution. The modern world, still gripped by dreams of regenerative violence, has yet, Girard contends, to catch up with Shakespeare" (Leithart). For Christian's narrator, Shakespeare's Cassius does not so much indicate a condemnation of revolution as an incitement to revolt. The peasant torchbearer refuses to take up the revolutionary role. Down through the ages, the oppressed classes' political inaction has made it possible for kings to rule. The narrator's chief distinction is that he is able to see the peasant, for, despite the illumination provided by the torchbearer himself, he remains otherwise *historically* invisible. The word *light* is used in the poem five times, and the torch appears in the title and in line four, so the narrator is inexorably connected to this pervading light. In contrast, the peasant wears a darkness on his face (line 2). This darkness surrounds him in the form of historical ages that mark his political and social irrelevance and impotence: "What are a thousand years but one tomorrow? / What are five hundred years but one long night? (lines 9–10).

At this point, it is apparent that the handling of time has itself become a subject within the poem, and (as I have said in connection with Owen Dodson's "Negro History") *time* as a metaphysical abstraction is not a Marxist concern. It was the philosopher of history Oswald Spengler who addressed the form of time within historical dynamism:

> Spengler was convinced . . . that the dynamics of decadence could be fairly well predicted, provided that exact historical data were available. Just as the biology of human beings generates a well-defined life span, resulting ultimately in biological death, so does each culture possess its own aging "data," normally lasting no longer than a thousand years— a period, separating its spring from its eventual historical antithesis, the winter, or civilization. The estimate of a thousand years before the decline of culture sets in, corresponds to Spengler's certitude that, after that period, each society has to face self-destruction. For example, after the fall of Rome, the rebirth of European culture started anew in the ninth century with the Carolingian dynasty. After the painful process of growth, self-assertiveness, and maturation, one thousand years later, in the twentieth century, cultural life in Europe is coming to its definite historical close. (Sunić 51)

The centrality of time in Christian's sonnet is not the only theme that points to Christian's interest in Spengler's philosophy of history; in *The Decline of the West*, one of Spengler's cultural-historical stages is *Caesarism:*

> By the term "Caesarism" I mean that kind of government which, irrespective of any constitutional formulation that it may have, is in its inward self a return to thorough formlessness. It does not matter that Augustus in Rome, and Huang Ti in China, Amasis in Egypt and Alp Arslan in Baghdad disguised their position under antique forms. The spirit of these forms was dead, and so all institutions, however carefully maintained, were thenceforth destitute of all meaning and weight. Real importance centered in the wholly personal power exercised by the Caesar. (vol. 2 431)

Spengler's Caesarism also incorporated the peasant in rather specific terms, so it is possible not only to evaluate Christian's use of time and his use of

Caesar, but also to relate the sharecropper, around whom time and the political order revolve, to the scene that Christian depicts in his sonnet about carnival. Spengler states: "With the formed state having finished its course, high history also lays itself down weary to sleep. Man becomes a plant again adhering to the soil, dumb and enduring. The timeless village and the 'eternal' peasant reappear, begetting children and burying seed in Mother Earth. . . . Men live from hand to mouth, with petty thrifts and petty fortunes and endure" (vol. 2 435). The expansion of these themes in Christian's poems points away from Marxism and toward Christian's alignment of the Great Depression with Spengler's prediction of the collapse of Western civilization: "Civilizations are the most external and artificial states of which a species of developed humanity is capable. They are a conclusion, the thing-become succeeding the thing becoming, death following life, rigidity following expansion, intellectual age and the stone-built, petrifying world-city following mother-earth and the spiritual childhood of Doric and Gothic. They are an end, irrevocable, yet by inward necessity reached again and again" (vol. 1 31).

Christian does not present the black peasant as a subject-in-process. There is no corresponding progressive historical frame in which the peasant operates: Oswald Spengler describes no matrix on which the peasant can attain bourgeois subjectivity. The peasant is subjugated to the decline of his civilization. Thus, in the final line of the poem Christian shows the torch-bearer retreating into a dive ("a disreputable or run-down bar or nightclub" [*AHD*]). Spengler's *Decline* outlines "a new kind of primitivism" as the historical stage that corresponds to the peasant's descent into the *dive*. *Dive* can be "a nearly vertical descent at an accelerated speed through water or space" (*AHD*). It is also possible to metaphorically dive (descend) through time. The figure in Christian's sonnet retreats into the primitive future, where he will seek the end of both selfhood and the process of becoming.

In *The Psychology of Individualism*, Alan Waterman argues that identity-related decisions are partially made in relation to role models: identity does not develop through carefully looking at oneself, but rather, at least in part, through actually performing an identity role (Cober). These role models can be derived from subject positions that are transcendental, mediational, or abject. I have shown that even though Tolson's sonnet "The Wine of Ecstasy" was a transcendental poem, he used a coded subtext to name the esoteric teachers who were his role models, thus demonstrating the centrality of role models in Tolson's identity formation. In the African American sonnet pantext of the 1930s, a number of factors influence how we read sonnets that hold up role models—the most salient factor being that white poets (by publishing in African American publications in the 1930s) have inserted texts into the African American literary discourse of the thirties at the intersection of mediational subject positions and role models. It is not possible to ascertain whether it would have been known that such writers as Isabel Fiske Conant, Leonard Twynham, Carolyn Hazard, Kathleen Sutton, and others who regularly published in *Crisis* and *Opportunity* were white poets. I suspect Conant and Hazard were sufficiently famous that their race was known to many readers; in other cases, the assumption must have been that the poets were black. Since there are major differences in how the black and white poets of the 1930s treat the central themes, it is important to at least acknowledge that race is a factor.

One example of the imposition of a role model by a white poet is a sonnet published in *Opportunity* in 1937, "Hampton Institute (Remembering General Armstrong)" by Isabel Fiske Conant, a popular poet, social activist, and philanthropist of the twenties and thirties. Conant's sonnet intervenes in favor of General Samuel C. Armstrong, the founder and president of the Hampton Normal and Agricultural Institute for the education and training of young African American men. Maurice O. Wallace states that "General Armstrong exemplified the very abstract disembodiment and disciplinary individualism that had come to idealistically define the social and political preconditions of (white) American masculinity" (101). Through his influence on Booker T. Washington, Armstrong did influence the development of a particular cast of black masculinity: "It was that—Armstrong's capacity to domesticate the masculine—which Washington sought to emulate: 'I have observed that those who have accomplished the greatest results are those who "keep under the body"; are those who never grow excited or lose self-control, but are always calm, self-possessed, patient and polite' [*Up from Slavery*, 182]" (102). Wallace labels Washington's masculine subject position a "eunuchistic, if still manfully rugged, ideal" (105). African American sonnets that present mediational role models are relatively rare in the pantext of the 1930s; thus, intervention by white poets was potentially all the more consequential. Only toward the end of the decade were there elegiac sonnets addressed to James Weldon Johnson and Henry Alexander Hunt. The two living figures who inspired sonnets were Marian Anderson and Haile Selassie.[28] Anderson's historic concert on the steps of the Lincoln Memorial in 1939 was a turning point in racial relations, so it is not surprising that Anderson became the subject of poems; similarly, the uniqueness of Selassie's position on the world stage as a black head of state lent him an aura that was in a few cases translated into sonnets.

Henry Alexander Hunt, the subject of an elegiac sonnet by George A. Townes, stood in marked contrast to the repressed, quasi-military subject position that Isabel Fiske Conant ascribed to General Armstrong. Hunt, a member of President Franklin D. Roosevelt's "Black Cabinet,"[29] had worked his way to national prominence through his commitment to educational efforts among black southern farmers: "In spite of various economic adversities and certain social controls not favorable to black southern farmers during almost a half century before 1938, Hunt had some successes in his attempts to help a large group of 'forgotten' farmers turn their labor into assets for themselves" (Bellamy 464). In attempting to convey something of the force of Hunt's individualism, Bellamy states that

> Hunt's personality and his determination must be considered as large factors in any attempt to measure the degree of his success as a leader. His understanding of the "real problems" of the region in which he worked during some of the most fruitful years of his life, his sympathy with rural black people, and his ability to convey to them important practical instruction and information in a convincing way were essential attributes of the man. Hunt was a very able and useful man whose leadership was a major force in helping to change the course of the agricultural story of the South. (479)

Townes wrote a very rough sonnet in tribute to Hunt, but it is a unique social and cultural document. The sonnet is formally inconsistent, with the first quatrain following the Italian pattern of the sonnet and the second quatrain taking up the English pattern. The poem also has an irregular appearance due to indentations that are not systematic. There is a turn at the ninth line as would follow from the Italian pattern, while the rhymes of the sestet follow the English pattern, though without any sense of a turn or recapitulation in the final couplet. While poets often take such liberties in sonnets, Townes's poem exhibits none of the qualities of stylistic innovation that encourage the reader to overlook formal deficiencies. The sonnet also uses a number of archaisms of diction.

HENRY ALEXANDER HUNT

Mid classic shades with genial friends and true.
Where cheerful, welcome duties brought no moil,
    He planted his life-tree in friendly soil;
    And piercing deep, its fibers lusty grew.
Then came a summons that he set himself
    Anew, in doubtful, distant, native earth,
That offered him nor recompense, nor pelf—
    Mere privilege to serve a land in dearth.

This fruit of golden deeds his life-tree bore:
The humble sheep and lanky lambs he fed;
Made pastures bloom on arid lands of yore;
    And stony glance and wanton insult led
To change in rev'rence, ere he lay him down
In flowery nook, henceforth, a hallowed ground.
(*Opportunity,* Dec. 1939: 358)

Townes's casual approach to composition may be attributed to the influence of his model, Joaquin Miller's[30] hodgepodge of neoromantic postures, "In Classic Shades." Townes borrows from Miller's poem the phrase "in classic shades" and further borrows "I sat me down," though Townes changes the lines to "Mid classic shades" and "he lay him down." Miller's poem is a strange model for "Henry Alexander Hunt," given its jingoist subject and its handling of race. "In Classic Shades" relates an occurrence that takes place in Italy. An American tourist is despondent due to loneliness. In a café he finds that the waiter is a black man of severe countenance, and the speaker is daunted by the waiter's fearsome demeanor to such a degree that he refers to the waiter as Hannibal. "The Carthaginian general Hannibal (247–182 BCE) was one of the greagtest military leaders in history. His most famous campaign took place during the second Punic War (218–202), when he caught the Romans off guard by crossing the Alps [into Italy]" (Lendering "Hannibal"). By calling the black waiter "Hannibal," Miller's speaker characterizes the waiter as an African invader of Italy. The speaker is an American, an outsider; he projects his own otherness onto the waiter so as to cast the waiter as the outsider.

    Finally, in despair the speaker tells the waiter that he cannot understand the waiter's Italian, whereupon in a sudden reversal the waiter reveals himself to be the stereotypical Negro who knows his place. The waiter fawns over Miller's American tourist:

His black face brightened as I spake;
He bowed; he wagged his woolly head;
He showed his shining teeth, and said,
"Sah, if you please, dose tables heah
Am consecrate to lager beer;
And, sah, what will you have to take?"

Relieved to have arrived at a familiar social arrangement in a foreign country, the speaker then orders the waiter—now characterized as "that colored cuss"—to bring him two cocktails, which presumably they partake of in some type of unequal fellowship: the matter of social equality would not seem to enter into the arrangement, since the waiter's speech reassigns him to a socially inferior position. The waiter, now that it is determined that he is merely an American Negro, is assigned to bringing the drinks, and the socially dominant speaker, having defeated Hannibal, revives the "classic" arrangement by paying for the drinks:

> Not that I loved that colored cuss
> Nay! he had awed me all too much
> But I sprang forth, and with a clutch
> I grasped his hand, and holding thus,
> Cried, "Bring my country's drink for two!"

> For oh! that speech of Saxon sound
> To me was as a fountain found
> In wastes, and thrilled me through and
> through.

> On Rousseau's isle, in Rousseau's shade,
> Two pink and spicy drinks were made,
> In classic shades, on classic ground,
> We stirred two cocktails round and round.

The speaker has taken his revenge on the black waiter, who discomforted a white man by demonstrating his superior abilities to speak Italian and to function adequately outside of the United States. Townes's allusion to this racist poem makes sense only if we consider Henry Alexander Hunt the role model who replaces "Hannibal." There is some ambiguity on this point, since it is originally Miller's waiter who wears the uncompromising stare, while in Townes's sonnet it is the white people who disapprove of the efforts of black people to improve their economic and social status: "And stony glance and wanton insult led / To change in rev'rence." However, when read independently of the Miller intertext, Townes's point is direct and forthright: Henry Alexander Hunt's life was uncompromisingly directed toward the social improvement of black people, and his example is to be followed.

THE ABJECT SUBJECT POSITIONS

"Ph.D.," the third poem in Hughes's three-sonnet sequence, was published in *Opportunity* in 1932. The poem combines eudaemonistic materials for identity formation and the abject subject position.

PH.D.

> He never was a silly little boy
> Who whispered in the class or threw spit balls,
> Or pulled the hair of silly little girls,
> Or disobeyed in any way the laws
> That made the school a place of decent order
> Where books were read and sums were proven true
> And paper maps that showed the land and water
> Were held up as the real wide world to you.
> Always, he kept his eyes upon his books:
> And now he has grown to be a man
> He is surprised that everywhere he looks
> Life rolls in waves he cannot understand,
> And all the human world is vast and strange—
> And quite beyond his Ph.D.'s small range.

The contradictions that Dewey exposed in his study of American individualism are very much a part of Hughes's treatment of the protagonist in this poem: Hughes's application of Emersonian individualism in "Ph.D." is an exercise in the construction of an other, a black scholar with an advanced degree. This poem was modeled after the satirical portraits of individuals in *The Spoon River Anthology* (1915). Edgar Lee Masters's subjects, townspeople—always examples of existential failure—take a regret-filled approach to their lives, so that *never* (with fifty occurrences in the text) is a customary word in the vocabulary of *Spoon River*'s characters. Hughes's "Ph.D." is similarly generated from the word *never,* and is comparable to Masters's "'Ace' Shaw":

"ACE" SHAW

> I never saw any difference
> Between playing cards for money
> And selling real estate,
> Practicing law, banking, or anything else.
> For everything is chance.
> Nevertheless
> Seest thou a man diligent in business?
> He shall stand before Kings!
> (*Spoon River Anthology* 45)

One important distinction between "Ph.D." and "'Ace' Shaw" is that Masters gives speech to the dead, while Hughes denies autonomous speech to a living character. The anonymity of the doctorate-holding protagonist is, however, illusory, for the poem is a mocking description of Hughes's Harlem Renaissance adversary, W. E .B. Du Bois, PhD. Du Bois had a reputation for being arrogant, puritanical, condescending, and uncompromising (Kellner, *Harlem Renaissance* 106), and Du Bois disapproved of Hughes, one of the antagonistic and provocative avant gardists of the Harlem Renaissance movement. Hughes had been a devoted follower of Du Bois and had dedicated poems to him as well as echoing the title of *The Souls of Black Folk* (1903) in the title of his collection of short stories *The Ways of White Folks* (1928). Du Bois's unfavorable comments on *Fire!!!* (1926), the literary magazine that presented the work of the younger Harlem writers, sparked a Hughes-Du Bois contretemps. In his autobiography Hughes comments that "Dr. Du Bois in the *Crisis* roasted it" (*The Big Sea*, quoted in *VFHR* 379).

If we assume that Hughes's race-neutral sonnet is directed at a black PhD, the title of the poem—"Ph.D."—is itself adequate to identify Du Bois as the subject, for at that time black PhDs were rare. Hughes has not made the subject of his sonnet ambiguous, however. In the first line, the soundplay of *boy* points directly to Du Bois. Moreover, the importance of the sound *boy* is further emphasized by the poem's failure to supply a complementary end rhyme for boy—for the unrhyming *girl* occupies the complementary position in the third line. Additionally, in line with the boy/Du Bois rhyme, other sonic elements of Du Bois's full name (William Edward Burghardt) make prominent appearances in the poem : silly/William, book/Burg, and hair/hardt.

Hughes used his confrontation with Du Bois as a means of conducting his own search for his true self. Du Bois's *The Souls of Black Folk* (1903) was an important document in the resubjectivization of the American black person. The form of the subject that Du Bois described was a divided and tormented double-consciousness, in which, under the white gaze, the black people had no choice but to see themselves as they were seen: their images were reflected back to them by the discourse network. At the time, Du Bois's resubjectivization through double-consciousness was relatively effective because it made available a subjectivity that was complex, flexible, and emancipatory. Double-consciousness made the acquisition of self-formational resources far more life affirming than did blues subjectivity (submission only to what is socially below bourgeois subjectivity: crime, sex, noise, violence, and ecstasy) and Booker T. Washington's program of accommodation to second-class citizenship (which at least was a form of participation-in-exclusion). The problem with Du Bois's insistence on double-consciousness was that it erected and materialized categories where they were not wanted. Du Bois had made a fundamental mistake in naming his psychic apparatus *double-consciousness,* for what Du Bois described by that phrase is Lacan's process of self-identity: "To achieve self-identity, the subject must identify himself with the imaginary other, he must alienate himself—put his identity outside himself, so to speak, into the image of his double" (Žižek 104). In contrast, Emerson saw the subject as "from the start free of the temptation to see the connection between self and other . . . as a mutually implicating puzzle or detective story . . . for him, illuminated moments of power or self-reliance authenticate us, even in our aloneness, with a clarity that shines through our meeting with others" (Mikics 3). Though Hughes does not explicitly mention Du Bois in his sonnet, and though Hughes does not challenge double-consciousness, he provides a scheme that allows us to identify his rejection of Du Bois and thereby allow us to recover Hughes's description of the evolution of black subjectivity. (And by overlaying this reading of "Ph.D." with readings of Hughes's other two sonnets, we can recover a more detailed delineation of the new form of black subjectivity.)

Hughes presents double-consciousness as an absence—a missing part of his childhood self: "He never was a silly little boy." (line 1). Hughes's formula registers Du Bois's double-consciousness as the subjective experience of shame under the gaze of the white Other; because the little boy was ashamed of his racial (bodily) difference, he defended himself against his shame by internalizing the "decent order" (punishment) of the school, thereby deforming his character and predisposing him to serious pursuits. Through these defensive mechanisms (repression and reaction formation), he created a rigidly disciplined world over which he exercised control—he was a successful neurotic. His bodily shame later motivates him to propound a social theory based on a projection of his distorted view of reality, and it is this distorted view of life—the PhD's books, sums, and maps, that Hughes attacks. Again, the sonnet both compresses and exaggerates certain aspects of Hughes's subtext. Hughes does not elaborate much after providing a picture of the PhD's limitations; accordingly, *The Spoon River Anthology,* with its failed townspeople revealing their regrets from the grave, casts the shadow of its influence over Hughes's poem. By presenting this portrait of the PhD/ Du Bois, Hughes suggests that the alternative course would have been the refusal of shame (and its resultant double-consciousness) and the embrace of Emersonian individualism in the form of "a dream of individual power set against . . . conformity . . . [a dream of] vitalism, which emphasizes the development of an instinctive or spontaneous moral life rather than one imposed from without" (Mikics 1–2).

Having identified the sonnet "Ph.D." as a satirical treatment of Du Bois, it is evident that Hughes's enterprise is what I have framed above as the familiar process of self-fashioning that Stephen Greenblatt has described: "Self-fashioning is achieved in relation to something perceived as alien, strange or hostile. This threatening Other . . . must be discovered or invented in order to be attacked and destroyed" (quoted in Dyche 6). Hughes's disparaging treatment of Du Bois's bourgeois subjectivity is a counterdiscourse in which Hughes advocates the validity of raw, unmediated experience over and above the *textual* approach to reality that Hughes extends to Du Bois: "paper maps that showed the land and water / were held up as the real wide world to you" (lines 7–8). The sonnet form that Hughes has chosen to frame his analysis of Du Bois's "small range" (line 14) is itself a text that provides only a small range; the question arises as to whether the sonnet's presentation is in itself yet another aspect of the ironic treatment that Hughes accords Du Bois in the process of Hughes's romantic self-fashioning at the expense of Du Bois's mode of operating situationally within language. In other words, are the sonnet's textual diminutiveness and formal uniformity to be read as an analogue to Du Bois's allegedly stunted scope?

Hughes opened the door for ambiguity by using romantic materials when constructing his own subject position. He chose not only to work within the form of the English sonnet but also to echo (in the twelfth and thirteenth lines) Shelley's "The everlasting universe of things / Flows through the mind, and rolls its rapid waves" (lines 1–2); Hughes wrote, "Life rolls in waves he cannot understand, / And all the human world is vast and strange." Hughes has linked his poem to Shelley's first-hand description of a visit to Mont Blanc; thus, Hughes's speaker formulates his subjectivity out of Shelley's text, while disparaging Du Bois for a similar dependence on texts. Thus, where Hughes might have been expected to situate his speaker within modernist or social realist subjectivity, he has instead resorted to the resources of nineteenth-century British romanticism when critiquing Du Bois.

Hughes's sonnet operates by means of subterfuge. He appears to address himself to the problem of empirical knowledge in the modern era, as though he wishes to show that the type of agency represented by the PhD is the wrong method of self-construction. He has, however, shifted his critique from dissatisfaction with the discourse of scholarly inquiry to his dislike of a particular type of character (the archetypal pedant), and of even a particular person (Du Bois). In doing so he has set up the hierarchical discourse of romantic subjectivity over and against the discourse of Du Bois's sociology, but he has not allowed sociology to emerge into the discourse of the poem. Consciously or not, he endorses popular culture's stereotypical depiction of intellectuals as unimpressive figures. Hughes wins this sham contest by reducing his argument to an ad hominem attack. Hughes ridicules the

PhD's way of being-in-the-world because, as Hughes's speaker depicts him, the scholar attempts to deal with the world through repression, reducing experience to inadequate maps. The title of the poem, "Ph.D.," is an abbreviation of *doctor of philosophy*; by abbreviating the name of the degree, Hughes removes *doctor* and *philosophy* from the poem, figuratively reducing the scholar's capacity for transcendence. Hughes leads us to assume that the speaker's character is expansive, realistic, and playful, while the PhD is contractive, axiomatic, and serious.

Alfred Adler defines a character trait as "the appearance of some specific mode of expression on the part of an individual who is attempting to adjust himself to the world in which he lives. Character is a social concept. We can speak of a character trait only when we consider the relationship of an individual to his environment. . . . It is the behavior pattern according to which his striving for significance is elaborated in the terms of his social feeling" (133). In his section *of Understanding Human Nature* on "Pedants and Men of Principle," Adler's description of the pedant matches the character of Hughes's PhD. Adler grounds the motivation for the pedant's character in feelings of insecurity, commenting that "these overconscientious individuals are moved by an unchecked vanity and a boundless desire to rule" (210). Thus, even though Hughes acknowledges the "terrors of the dark" in "Pennsylvania Station," he does not admit the scholar's need for psychological protection through the construction of a defensive type of character. It is striking to recognize that "Ph.D." blames the PhD's character on himself, as though his character resulted from his own decisions rather than as unconscious responses to his social and cultural surroundings: the prosecutorial speaker is quick to inform us that "he never was a silly little boy," as though that was his choice. What is missing from the enunciation, though covertly present in the enounced subtext, is Hughes's treatment of Du Bois as a race man. Du Bois gained his prominence by analyzing race, and this prominence elicits from the sonnet's speaker an Oedipal response: the demotion of the *father* (W. E. B. Du Bois) by the *son* (Hughes) is a "necessary" component of individuation. Hughes's ability to negotiate his own racial crisis was, by Hughes's admission, largely due to Du Bois's literary and personal example. However, once Hughes reached the point in his career where he became a rival, it was necessary that he strike a blow against his predecessor in the process of eventually surpassing him, which he was ultimately able to do, eventually becoming a figure of greater fame. This pattern is visible in Owen Dodson's "Negro History" sonnet sequence that I have discussed in the first chapter. In "Past and Future" and "Post Emancipation," Dodson criticizes the black leaders who have preceded his own self-in-process. In "Harlem" Dodson singles out Langston Hughes for a demotion similar to that which

Hughes applied to Du Bois. Barely discernible in the background of Dodson's less sublimated sequence are his role models, the shadowy "force-men[31] of the next centuries" (*Decline* vol. 1 37) that rule the imagination from the past.

As Hughes develops the theme of self-construction across his three-sonnet sequence, he makes individuation a matter of size: the PhD's discourse is obviated because it is "abbreviated," not because it is ideologically unjustifiable. Both "Pennsylvania Station" and "Search" are treatments of the outside reality as internalized infinities, and as such they dismiss the manifold difficulties of modern disorder, complexity, and conflict. Hughes uses the finite/infinite dyad to portray the quest for modern subjectivity, through the finite/infinite dyad, and as Hughes depicts this process, the plunge into limitlessness is not dangerous. However, Hughes does not plunge into the modern sublime so much as retreat into various habits of mind in which the romantic masquerades as the modern. Thus, in Hughes's incomplete grasp of this trope, transcendence is not real.

Hughes's strategy of avoidance is a common response to the demands of modernity. László Moholy-Nagy, the pioneering modernist theorist and suprematist-constructivist photographer, invented modernist positionality by experimenting with point of view—"bird's eye views, worm's eye views, extreme close-ups, asymmetrical compositions, clipped heads and torsos, emphasized shadows" (Makovsky 146). Yet his daughter, Hattula, was distressed that she could not locate her own bourgeois subjectivity within her father's photographs and films of their family. It was not her father's style to establish a panoramic setting for filmed action: Hattula Moholy-Nagy states, "Oh, if only he had shifted the camera . . . and let us see the rest of the room . . . the artwork and furniture in our London living room" (Makovsky 146). By comparison with Hughes's treatment of setting, this example shows us the degree to which Hughes's approach is comfortably and familiarly contextualized according to premodern conventions for narrative and perspective.

Hughes's speaker defines his own subjectivity negatively through the abjection of the scholar rather than leaping beyond the scholar's bourgeois subjectivity: Hughes shows us the furniture. In the folk blues, the speaker conventionally assumes the abject subject position and speaks of his difficult life. Were the PhD allowed to speak for himself, presumably, what Adler calls his "unchecked vanity" (210) would block any such perception of his inadequacies. Hughes satirizes those inadequacies, as though the smallness of the PhD's interiority is sufficient to condemn him. The disguised substitution of the dyad of transcendent idealism/scientific materialism for the dyad of bourgeois/proletarian occurs because the speaker refuses to make it clear that he has situated his discourse in proletarian revolutionary terms so that he can denigrate the PhD's bourgeois subjectivity. We are shown the PhD from the point of view of a narrator who seems to speak from above, when in truth it speaks from below—in the manner of the proletarian sublime—which is an instance of what Bataille calls *subordination,* submission only to what is below (Hollier 136–37). Of course, Hughes's poetic output in the 1930s was not limited to the three sonnets that he wrote, and in fact during that period not only was he prolific but also he wrote for three widely different audiences—the political left, the black underclass, and a segment of the middle class. (Hughes's middle-class readership encountered his poems in African American periodicals.)

THE INDIVIDUAL AND THE EXPECTATIONS OF OTHERS

One of the most explored locations for identity formation in the African American sonnet pantext of the thirties was the intersection of mediational subject positions and the expectations of others. This category may in part account for the tendency toward the creation of a collective identity, and thus it represents the area in which individual, social and cultural efforts of African Americans were being expended in opposition to the Jim Crow culture that so methodically oppressed them through governance, social discrimination, media propaganda, and terrorism. Few possibilities existed for the creation and dissemination of effective role models, so there are few poems in that category. While there were a number of poems that describe bourgeois subjects who struggle to discover themselves, these concerns were perhaps too rarified and abstract for the times: the imposition of leftist anti-individualism throughout the creative writing of the thirties and the general deemphasis of individualism in the culture of the Depression contributed to the tendency for poets to write in advocacy of the expectations of others. Marcus Christian's sonnet "McDonogh Day in New Orleans" was printed in *Opportunity* in June of 1934 and reprinted in the *New York Herald Tribune* on Sunday, June 17, 1934.

MCDONOGH DAY IN NEW ORLEANS

The cotton blouse you wear, your mother said,
 After a day of toil, "I guess I'll buy it";
For ribbons on your head and blouse she paid
 Two-bits a yard—as if you would deny it!
And nights, after a day of kitchen toil,
 She stitched your re-made skirt of serge—once blue—

Weary of eye, beneath a lamp of oil:
    McDonogh would be proud of her and you.

Next, came white "creepers" and white stockings, too—
    They almost asked her blood when they were sold;
Like some dark princess, to the school go you,
    With blue larkspur and yellow marigold;
But few would know—or even guess this fact:
    How dear comes beauty when a skin is black.

John McDonogh owned enslaved Africans and had educated a handful of his slaves, granted them manumission, and helped them establish a model community at McDonoghville. His intent was to prepare them for a new life in Liberia. In 1842, eighty of his former slaves left New Orleans for Liberia in a ship provided by the American Colonization Society. Upon his death in 1850, McDonogh left half his estate to New Orleans and half to Baltimore for the education of poor children in those cities, no matter their ethnicity. For many years, students from the public school system of New Orleans would gather in Lafayette Park each May to pay homage to John McDonogh. The event was called McDonogh Day. In these segregated ceremonies, white students would be the first to lay their flowers at the McDonogh statue, the first to sing songs, and the first to receive the keys of the city from the mayor. Black students waited in the hot sun while the white students performed their ceremonies. Black students could only begin after the white students had finished (McDonogh Neighborhood Snapshot).

Christian's moving and perceptive sonnet, reprinted and then anthologized many times, succeeds because of its meticulous blend of the intimate and the distinguished: the sympathetic speaker addresses the schoolgirl from a godlike vantage point and yet is concerned with accounting for every component that contributes to her makeshift appearance. The speaker is that Other who has the highest of expectations, perhaps the superego, and the reader is privy to the pleasure that this remote being feels as it catalogs the fulfillment of those lofty expectations. The speaker's measured tone, however, belies the social horror of the occasion and installs in the sonnet an extreme tension between the text's surface (with its fleeting indulgences in balladic lilt, romantic imagery, and restrained lyricism) and the drive of the poet to register a firm though reticent protest. Because Christian is so effective in bringing the reader close to the schoolgirl, the reader enters unaware into his conspiracy. Christian exposes the ritualistic humiliation of the black schoolchildren, yet he keeps secret from them the reality of their position.

One of the most innovative aspects of this sonnet is that the speaker addresses the schoolgirl without irony on behalf of John McDonogh—"McDonogh would be proud of her and you" (line 8). This device brings the speaker ambiguously close to McDonogh himself so that McDonogh becomes the indirect speaker, the superego, and the uncontradicted benefactor of the schoolchildren who celebrate him sincerely, though they are forced by their social circumstance to do so in a markedly unfair manner. The poet's refusal to deal with this situation by employing irony places the efforts of the mother and the daughter within a framework of ethical individualism (self-acceptance, self-esteem, a sense of personal identity, and self-actualization) that elevates them above their barbaric surroundings. Ultimately, Christian's sonnet addresses the theme of shame: racial shame was a fundamental component of black life under the Jim Crow system. In the face of the shame-generating experience of McDonogh Day and through the narrator's attentive and appreciative recounting of the mother's preparations for her daughter, the reader is privy to the daughter's experience of the event. Her unambiguous assumption of personal beauty thus reinforces her self-worth, belonging, and personal identity.

Finally, we see that a second innovation results from the sonnet's refusal of irony: the sonnet is an antiblazon—a variation on the blazon, which is a type of love poem that praises a woman or a man item by item. Often the blazon partitions the body into metaphors. Gayle Whittier states that "the *blason* . . . removes the woman from the human realm, which is, after all, the Platonic lover's aim" (33). In the most famous antiblazon, Shakespeare's "Sonnet 130," the speaker seems to forego conventions for a more realistic depiction of the "dark lady." Jeremy Braddock states that "the dark lady sonnets are often considered—as a whole, and particularly in certain poems, such as 'Sonnet 130'—to be working against the blazon tradition inherited from the Italian Renaissance poets. Demonstrating the failure of figurative language to account for an adequate experience of the described subject, anti-blazon poems are seen to refuse or frustrate the metonymic mode of praise, as employed by Petrarch. Yet as in the blazon tradition, the dark lady sonnets repeatedly anatomize their subject" (1257–58). Christian's antiblazon has reflexively reworked Shakespeare's "Sonnet 130" just as the mother in Christian's poem has reworked "the re-made skirt of serge—once blue" (line 6). In "McDonogh Day in New Orleans," the love-object is a schoolgirl, so the speaker's gaze does not directly glimpse her body and instead describes her clothes. The clothes that substitute for the parts of the body are not described metaphorically ("cheeks like roses," "lips like rubies") but in terms of the labor that was required to produce each item of clothing. Since the traditional blazon originated in the (white) patriarchal sexual discourse as a device of control that dismembers the woman's body and divests it of its autonomy (Vickers, quoted in Baker "Uncanny" 4), it is clear that Christian's sonnet privileges the abjected binaries of the patriarchal discourse); thus, the mother represents action, culture, and reason. Overcoming the negative factors of poverty, exhaustion, and hedonism, the toiling mother finds a way to dress her daughter adequately for McDonogh Day. In re-dressing the daughter through selfless "toil" (lines 2, 5), the mother *labors* to bring into being her daughter's subjectivity. *Labor* is socially and psychologically transformative. By the end of the catalog, instead of having a portrait of the traditionally idealized and dehumanized woman who is loved from afar, Christian's sonnet presents an intimate portrait of an ordinary African American schoolgirl, a person who usually would be accorded little social worth but is here treated reverentially as an embodiment of grace and esteem. Christian's sonnet troubles many waters, for it disorders the motifs of white child/black child, boy/girl, and princess/pickaninny. And as I have shown, Christian deliberately engages these themes through the sonnet tradition and under black and white patriarchal gazes.

The conjunction of abject subject positions and the expectation of others was a highly active category in American culture during the thirties. In keeping with the negative character of what was being directed at black people at this time by texts in this category, black poets published relatively few sonnets in the mode that describes abject subject positions and the expectations of others. At the same time, it is useful to see that black poets found restorative approaches to negative self-fashioning in their works. This formation represents the efforts of the discourse network of the thirties to construct and maintain a culture of American apartheid, which African Americans struggled to eradicate. Thus, the category itself is highly unstable; this instability generated voluntary and involuntary subject positions of the abject type. It is possible to assemble a long list of abject subject positions that were enthusiastically created, embraced, and transmitted through the national discourse network—a panoply of mammies, black fools, coons, jezebels, layabouts, thieves, rapists, and jigaboos that constituted the only visible African Americans in films, on radio broadcasts, and in newspapers and magazines. The instability of these subject positions was a prominent factor, as the example of Louis Armstrong demonstrates:

> Armstrong's film career began in the 30s, made possible by his well-known music of the last decade . . . but the roles he played were stereotyped, demeaning, and unimaginable to modern audiences. . . . On one side, he is the tuxedo-clad virtuoso, on the other a gruesome parody of blackness. . . . Sometimes he appears as a savage, others as a servile "Uncle Tom" type, but what is most disturbing is that every time he is clearly

Louis Armstrong. One of the most respected jazz musicians in history is transformed into a clown in these films, and one of the great puzzles of his life is how he could appear in such obviously degrading, even racist pictures. (Graham)

In her chapter on black modernist film criticism from 1930 to 1940, Anna Everett discusses how upwardly mobile African American responded to these images. According to Everett, Mrs. Carrie Pembrook—a college teacher "familiar with the viewing habits and preferences of black youth" (Everett 211)—wrote a letter in 1937 to respond to a "changing the movies" campaign:

> I believe that I speak for the race when I say that we feel personally affronted every time we see the coon hunting, dice-throwing scenes. We feel ashamed and disgusted when we see any stalwart man playing a frightened, cringing role. It is insulting to the race to show only the mammy type of woman. This type of woman is rarely given anything to do except hang clothes on a line in some rich lady's back yard, or chase small boys away from a dice game. . . . Will the general public ever get an idea of the "Souls of Black Folk" by the roles Negroes play in the movies? . . . We believe the present interpretation is faulty. (Everett 212)

And while it was not possible for African Americans to insert what Pembrook calls the "higher aspirations or sensibilities of the race" (Everett 212) into the mainstream Hollywood films of the era, it was possible to express them in formal poetry of a high caliber.

In general terms it is only possible for people living in modern societies to maintain the integrity of their identities at a minimal level. One of the salient supports for these fragile identities is race; thus, in the case of Louis Armstrong, whatever else he may indicate through his performances, blackness was his primary sign, and as such he marks the limits of whiteness. In the case of the construction of black identities, the starting place is with the rejected subject positions of the abject level—the slave and the coon. There is also a component of black identity that is a reaction to the positive processes, where (through the formulation of negative identity) individuals choose to rebelliously reject preferred or acceptable roles in favor of sociopathological roles, such as bohemians, gangsters, zoot-suiters, hipsters, criminals, and flagrant homosexuals. Abject subject positions serve the processes of identity formation in complex ways. It is not enough to simply reject abject subject positions, and in the case of the slave subject position it was neither desirable nor possible to dispense with that historical component of black reality. In the thirties many sonnets were written about the slaves, and the direct descendant of the slaves, the figure known as "the man farthest down,"[32] received attention as well.

My discussion of Henry Alexander Hunt shows that one of the most dynamic interventions in African American culture in the thirties was the attempt to uplift African American farmers in the South. Thus, under the tutelage of various intervening organizations such as the Share Croppers Union and the Southern Tenant Farmers Union, the oppressed black farmers of the South overcame some of the limitations of their former roles, claimed agency for themselves, and ultimately were empowered in new ways. For example, Hunt's efforts had measurable effects: "The agricultural instruction and demonstrations at the school and community outreach programs, in general, were deeply constructive forces. One white observer of Hunt's work noted that the 'work is being felt back on the plantations in a way that gives results that can be measured in cold dollars and cents as well as in good citizenship'"(Bellamy 472).

Indeed, the notion of progressive levels of black agency on the part of "the man farthest down" cannot be exaggerated. Something close to a war had broken out across the South as the Communist Party attempted to unionize sharecroppers, both black and white, and these efforts were met with violent resistance.[33] One of Marcus Christian's most poignant sonnets, "Southern Share-Cropper" (*Opportunity,* July 1937: 217), took up the subject of sharecropping, an economic practice that was rife with social and political implications at the time:

> A practice that emerged following the emancipation of African American slaves, sharecropping came to define the method of land lease that would eventually become a new form of slavery. Without land of their own, many blacks were drawn into schemes where they worked a portion of the land owned by whites for a share of the profit from the crops. They would get all the seeds, food, and equipment they needed from the company store, which allowed them to run a tab throughout the year and to settle up once the crops, usually cotton, were gathered. When accounting time came, the black farmer was always a few dollars short of what he owed the landowner, so he invariably began the new year with a deficit. As that deficit grew, he found it impossible to escape from his situation by legal means. The hard, backbreaking work led to stooped, physically destroyed, and mentally blighted black people who could seldom envision escape for themselves or their children; their lives were an endless round of poor diet, fickle weather, and the unbeatable figures at the company store. Those with courage to match their imaginations escaped under cover of darkness to the North, that fabled land of opportunity. (Harris "Sharecropping")

Marcus B. Christian's English sonnet, "Southern Share-Cropper" (1937), confronts this institution directly and contrives a deft balance of magisterial tone, objective observation, and outraged social protest:

SOUTHERN SHARE-CROPPER

He turns and tosses on his bed of moss;
The moon wheels high into the Southern sky;
He cannot sleep—production, gain, and loss
Harass him, while a question and a cry
Stir through the dim recesses of his soul
This slave to one-fourth, one-third, and one-half;
His sow will litter soon; his mare will foal;
His woman is with child; his cow, with calf.
Earth screams at him—beats clenched, insistent hands
Upon his brains—his labor and his health
He gives unceasingly to her demands;
She yields to him, but others grow in wealth
What nailed his soul upon the wrack of things—
That he must slave, while idlers live like kings?

Whatever there may have been of Christian's leftist politics has been filtered through a naturalist discourse so that the presentation is reminiscent of Communist short story writer Richard Wright's collection, *Uncle Tom's Children* (1936). (Christian's writings often show the influence of Oswald Spengler, a thinker whose ideas did not coincide with Marxism, though it is possible that Christian had some Marxist leanings.) Like many of Wright's characters, the sharecropper has been reduced to the status of an animal: he has lost the habits of a human being. In the poem, the sharecropper is lying sleeplessly outdoors on the ground. He is subject to natural forces, including the pull of the moon's gravity: "He turns and tosses on his bed of moss; / The moon wheels high into the Southern sky" (lines 1–2). Not only is he exposed to the natural world but also he suffers even more in the interplay of economic forces: "He cannot sleep—production, gain, and loss / Harass him, while a question and a cry / Stir through the dim recesses of his soul / This slave to one-fourth, one-third, and one-half" (lines 3–6). The figure's dehumanization is further emphasized by the comparison of his pregnant wife to farm animals—a pig, a horse, and a cow (lines 7–8). Christian again invokes nature's antagonistic forces: "Earth screams at him—beats clenched, insistent hands / Upon his brains—his labor and his health" (lines 8–10).

The verb *clenched* betrays the subtext of the poem, for *clenched* is a near rhyme with *lynched:* the narrator invokes the lynching theme as though saying it through gritted teeth. The lynching theme is a structured absence that is barely allowed to come to conscious utterance. The poem is reminiscent of McKay's "Harlem Dancer" in the way in which the remote/intimate subject position of McKay's narrator is infused with double-speaking. We can apply Beth Palatnik's gloss of McKay's poem to Christian's poem: Palatnik observes that "though the speaker wants to distance himself from the rest of the audience, he ends up identifying with them in that respect, both holding back from the objectification of the dancer and participating in it" ("Consumption"). To the extent that the narrator's lyric identity allows the dancer to reflect back to him his participatory identity as they are joined under the white gaze, he must take in the concrete form of his objectification of the black other—that in her embodiment as the black other, she is *always already lynched.* Thus, seeing and being seen have collided with "the chronic shame of being an African American in white America" (Bouson 208), and this collision has produced "the wish to 'disappear as the person' one has shown oneself to be, or 'to be seen as different' than one is" (Wurmser quoted in Bouson 208). Lacking the positive qualities of McKay's dancer, Christian's sharecropper brings little more into view than his shame.

It seems that in "Southern Share-Cropper" Christian resolves his sonnet's argument in the concluding couplet using the ironic resolution of a rhetorical question: "What nailed his soul upon the wrack of things— / That he must slave, while idlers live like kings?" (lines 13–14). On the surface, Christian seems to employ the sonnet form to carry one of the most highly regarded textual formations of the dominant culture into the depiction of the ordinarily invisible black peasant; in a sense, the peasant is framed within the most refined resources of bourgeois subjectivity. As if to emphasize this reading, Christian has resorted to what Sterner calls "sonnet diction" (xix). The thesis of the poem, at least as it is implied by the question asked in the couplet, is that economic injustice will bring about class war.

The word *slave* appears twice in the poem. The interests of the peasant, though, are opposed to those of the "idlers [who] live like kings"—an arrangement that bespeaks a medieval society, not the modern, agrarian South of the 1930s. This provisional reading of the sonnet is undercut by the inescapable sense of what the line does not say, since the peasant is not nailed to a *rack* (a framelike instrument of torture) but to a *wrack* (a wreckage, especially of a ship cast ashore). The unspoken torture of the rack, though, is shown by the torments that the peasant suffers. We do not see his torturers, for they are unrecognizable as the "idlers" that the poem blames for his condition. Wrack/rack, of course, refers to lynching, which was all too common in the black peasant's world. Christian's sharecropper has no agency: the southern peasant is depicted as a man/animal, powerless to alter his circumstances. The narrator seems content to observe with a remote, objective gaze the destruction of the man farthest down. Apparently, the speaker's distance is justified, since the peasant's condition is presented as a naturally occurring inevitability. In the concluding line of the poem, his oppressors are uncharacteristically identified as "idlers"—a group that is equally lacking in agency—and as such, Christian's handling of class is altogether a departure from leftist discourses of class. As Christian has it, *things* are in control of master and slave, and the narrator can do no more than pose questions that have no answers: any answers must come from beyond the limits of human knowledge.

There is, though, a definitive intertext supplied by the final line. The phrase "idlers live like kings" plays on the title of Alfred Tennyson's once canonical long poem, *Idylls of the King*. The epic intertext offers a number of possible readings for the poem. Christian brings under consideration Tennyson and the bourgeoisie. Tennyson was a prominent British romantic poet who used legendary narratives for his poems. He also condemned social injustice and attacked the moral degradation that he saw in Victorian society. The educated class of the South often used Tennyson's name to endorse the world of medieval chivalry. Thus, Tennyson's epic may be supposed to supply the answer to the "what?" posed by the narrator. Tennyson's Arthur is a virtuous ruler with a "selfless devotion to large social goals" (VS). Thus, Christian's sonnet uses Tennyson's Arthur to indict the owner class for its inability to live up to its own moral ideals. Through Christian's poem, the Southern landowners' hypocrisy becomes apparent. They condemn themselves with their own words.

In this way Christian's poem "Southern Share-Cropper" covertly indicts the owner class for creating a society that not only converts men into animals but also pretends to belong to the chivalric society that Tennyson's poems depict, despite Tennyson's advocacy of "the rights and moral worth of every individual" (VS). Christian's indirect treatment of Tennyson's poem is conceptually ironic: "Southern Share-Cropper" attacks the South's metadiscourse by stripping away its heroic illusions, all without naming the discourse that is under attack. The material that comes under direct treatment in the poem is the actual substance of the discourse under attack, but it is accessible only through the word play in the poem. However, Christian's sharecropper does come into sharp focus in relation to *The Negro a Beast* (1900), which played a key role in the discourse network of the period:

> While public opinion and the personal attitudes of whites concerning the Negroes were being formed by politicians and newspapers, there appeared

in 1900 a book entitled *The Negro a Beast*, published by the American Book and Bible House. The publishers of this book stated in the preface that if this book were "considered in an intelligent and prayerful manner, that it will be to the minds of the American people like unto the voice of God from the clouds appealing to Paul on his way to Damascus." In order that the American People might be convinced of the scientific nature of the "Biblical truths" presented in this book, the author included pictures of God and an idealized picture of a white man in order to prove that white people were made in the image of God, as stated in the Bible, and a caricature of the Negro showing that he could not have been made in the image of God. This book had a wide circulation, especially among the church-going whites, and helped to fix in their minds, as it was argued in the book, that the Negro was not the son of Ham or even the descendant of Adam and Eve, but "simply a beast without a soul." (Frazier 122–23)

By associating the sharecropper with animals, the narrator has linked the sharecropper to the South's racist/eugenicist/biblical discourse of *The Negro a Beast* but not *explicitly* to class war. At the same time, the sonnet has also revealed the mind and soul of the sharecropper—crucial elements that the racist discourse of *The Negro a Beast* denies in its insistence that the sharecropper is not a man but a soulless *thing*, as the penultimate line emphasizes: "What nailed his soul upon the wrack of *things*" (line 13; emphasis added), where the word *things* is a sign of the beast discourse.

Above all, we must account for the source of the narrational voice. As I have shown, the poem is a meticulously executed sonnet with a double subtext, through which the reader is confronted with the discourse of Southern chivalry and the practice of lynching. Christian's narrator is situated within a mastery of the official culture, and from that site the poem offers a measured, assured critique. The narrator is also intimately acquainted with the sharecropper's world, even to the point of entering the sharecropper's tormented psyche to give an account of the effects that the sharecropper suffers in his life of endless misery. While McKay's Harlem dancer is on display in a cabaret, we find Christian's peasant isolated in the rural South at night. McKay's speaker has a reason for his proximity to the dancer (for what the speaker does in consuming entertainment in a nightclub confers and confirms social status). Christian's speaker has no social pretext for intruding on the sharecropper, and the reader experiences some of the shock provided by Whitman's poetic access to private spaces in "The Sleepers"—"I stand in the dark with drooping eyes by the worst-suffering and most restless, / I pass my hands soothingly to and fro a few inches from them, / The restless sink in their beds, they fitfully sleep" ("The Sleepers" lines 23–25).

Christian's handling of the protest theme is rhetorically restrained throughout. He refuses to allow his sonnet to become a merely propagandistic exercise: the tension between the objectivity of the social realist gaze and the intimate and psychological details of the sharecropper's hard lot raises the poem to an effective emotional crescendo. The narrator refuses to descend into bathos or to offer the cliché of the pointed accusation. Posing a question at the conclusion is a device that allows a satisfactory reading of the sonnet, even when the reader has not registered the Tennysonian intertext. The subject position of Christian's narrator represents a complex, omniscient individuality, equally transcendent and immanent, who is able to penetrate time and space, but whose psychological insights allow the reader to arrive at the final revelation rather than contaminating the argument with reductive or didactic posturing. Christian's poem humanizes the peasant by supplying the genealogy of his socioeconomic predicament without sentimentalizing the depiction of his experiences. Christian has created a narrator who is complexly single-voiced.

Within the political theory of the Left, the role of the peasant was a matter of great importance, and beginning with Karl Marx, there had been a debate over the question of whether the peasant belonged within a revolutionary class or was, so to speak, outside of history. The debate surfaces in the discourses of the thirties in a number of places. The status of the black peasantry was also questioned in 1933 in Prinkipo, Turkey, during discussions between Trotsky and various members of the American Trotskyist movement (which, at the time of the first discussion, still regarded itself as the Communist League—an opposition group within the Communist Party) about its policy concerning the Negro question in America (Trotsky "On Black Nationalism"). B. A. Botkin referred to Constance Rourke's identification of the folk with the proletariat in a speech at the Second American Writers Conference in 1937 ("Regionalism and Culture" 141). Perhaps the most consequential discussion was the debate between W. E. B. Du Bois and the Communist Party following the publication of Du Bois's *Black Reconstruction* (1935). William Gorman describes the influence of Du Bois's study in this way:

> The main theme of *Black Reconstruction,* published in 1935, is not that "the Negro is an average, an ordinary human being." . . . In the chapter entitled "The General Strike," Du Bois presents the Negroes' physical movement from the Underground Railroad to the mass enlistment in the Union Amy, not as the flight of a broken people, but as a purposeful weakening and paralysis of Southern economy, as the necessary prelude to its fundamental reconstruction. This was part of a larger conception that the Negro in the South was not simply a long-suffering but essentially

a revolutionary laboring class which attempted "prematurely" to remake Southern society in its own image through land seizures and government based upon mass political participation. And if the prosperity of European imperialism was built on the massacre of the Paris Communards, America's rise as a participant and leader in world plunder was built on the unbridled deceit and terror which broke Black Reconstruction in the South. . . . This bold, new conception startled the bourgeois historical writers, petty-bourgeois radicals and Negro intellectuals. . . . Their attack on *Black Reconstruction* in a more concealed fashion has continued up to this day. (84–85)

In light of this debate, Marcus Christian's portrayal of the sharecropper seems to conform to the understanding of the black peasant as a weak element of society awaiting deliverance from the more organized component of the revolutionary class.

What Christian has presented through his sonnet "Southern Share-Cropper" is a version of the modern sublime, a metahistorical narrative from which seemingly unassailable and comprehensive assessments of individual and social performance can be delivered. Thus, the subject position of the narrator is defined by the suppression of any semblance of bourgeois subjectivity (possessive individualism, self-position, unity, self-control, and dominion over the future). The narrator is equally wary of the collective-revolutionary point of view that allows for the possibility of an revolution that intervenes in history. The poem avers that it was the bourgeoisie who effectively dehumanized the black peasant and profited from that process.

THE MODERNITY OF THE BLACK SONNET IN THE THIRTIES

H. A. Maxson has posited that Robert Frost's thirty-seven sonnets are organically composed reinventions of the sonnet: "The uniqueness of each is one reason they fit most definitions of a modernist poem, despite their 'sonnetness'" (5). There is little to be seen of formal experiment in the African American sonnet pantext of the 1930s, but the poems are no less modernist. Their modernism is situated in their embrace of radical individualism and the recontextualization of the individual within the fabric of a received social heritage, for "the deepest problems of modern life derive from the claim of the individual to preserve the autonomy and individuality of his existence in the face of overwhelming social forces, of historical heritage, of external culture, and of the technique of life" (Simmel). African American self-identity is exactly this self-same radical individualism, for it exists in the face of the institutional denial of individualism: "American collective identity is not only inclusionary but for a long time in its history was blatantly exclusionary toward certain groups. The case of African Americans is undoubtedly a prime example of the discriminatory and nonegalitarian aspect of American democracy and American collective identity" (Kook 158). The crucial contribution of African American poetry toward the sustenance of life under these hard conditions is difficult to frame, because in general terms there is little grasp of the psychological nature of human life in the materialist, consumerist, bottom-line, any-means-to-an-end, result-oriented, extroverted, competitive, and territorial American culture. Jay Parini addresses these factors directly when he states that "the world of the poet is largely an interior world of the intellect and the emotions—where we mostly live, in fact. And poetry bolsters that interior realm" (xiv).

The convention of the sonnet-as-body—the blazon that praises the various parts of the female anatomy—is by now quite familiar. However, except in the case of Shakespeare's disturbing antiblazon, there has been no canonical treatment of the black body in the sonnet tradition. Further, the disruptive presence of a black body in the Shakespeare sonnet is the very element that marks the poem as an antiblazon. During the thirties, poets composed an entire body of sonnets that present the African American individual in a kaleidoscope of fragmented attributes—attributes that I have categorized in connection with a theory of individuality, of self-in-process (eudaemonism, role models, and the expectations of others). It is not easy to recognize the modernist and subversive nature of the sonnets that seek to invent new subject positions for African Americans. For African Americans in the thirties, the sonnet pantext constructed a self-fashioning discourse in opposition to the many shame-inducing discourses that the American racist culture directed toward African Americans: eugenics, Jim Crow, the extraction of labor, biblical misreading, and so on. The sonnets oppose these activities with a counterdiscourse in which African Americans are newly endowed with many of the positive qualities that have been denied to them by the fundamentally racist construction of American society. By virtue of this literary discourse, the African American becomes refined, sensitive, reflective, quiet, elegant—in a word, lovable.

One of the most powerful subject positions adopted by the African American writers of sonnets in the thirties was that of the romantic lover. Though well within the framework of psychological normalcy and bourgeois subjectivity, the lover is often powerfully steadfast when others oppose the lover's choices (Waterman 29). Having succumbed to a dynamic form of agency, the lover is not necessarily aligned with conventional role models but instead uses romantic love to find the true self. While romantic love may generate knightly and courtly behavior, it may also lead to "misbehaviors" such as elopement, adultery, and miscegenation. The romantic lover's extreme impulses are aligned with the telic value of eudaemonism; such impulses bolster the ability to sustain directed action despite the obstacles and setbacks inevitably encountered in the pursuit of self-expression (Waterman 16). The crucial nature of the bourgeois erotic formation is evident when it is contrasted to the blues formation of romance, the latter of which may be designated "love from below" or "subordinate romance." Blues love combines the abject subject position with the expectations of others; thus, a typical lover who is portrayed in a blues song destructively and helplessly says, "I'm got a mind to ramble, a mind fo' to leave this town, / Got a mind my baby is goin' to turn me down" (Sterling Brown, "The Blues as Folk Poetry" 330) The love sonnet, as in the example below, combines the mediational subject position with the identity materials of self-discovery. It is the product of a more stable world.

In November of 1937, Mary T. Rauth published "Sonnet" in *The Crisis:*

SONNET

I love you, dear; so well, that should you leave
Your earthly garment, like a crumpled dress
Left fallen wearily; though I caress
Your lips forlornly, praying for reprieve,
Not yet aware, not ready to believe
That you were gone; though crowding years should press
Rudely against me—jostling years, whose stress
You kept at bay: I could not wholly grieve.
Death is a thief who steals my gleaming gold,
My jewels flashing in the firelight's play,
Silver and silks and furs, yet on his load
Heaps not my roses in their vase of gray.
My crimson roses! Death takes not away
Our love, whatever else his hands may hold.

Rauth's Millayan, neo-Petrarchan sonnet presents a series of dyads—soul/body, life/death, crime/security, and private/public. Above all the poem is a celebration of romantic love as a defense of individuality and interiority against the assaults of collective, consensual reality ("crowding years, . . . jostling years" [lines 6, 7]). Because the body is deemed insufficient, unable to defend the personal self from the bruises of reality, it is quickly dispensed with as "a crumpled dress" (line 2). Nevertheless, the poem remains haunted by the black female body through an antiblazon that simultaneously presents and absents the body through subtextual language play: *eye* ("I," line 1), *ear* ("dear," line 1; "earthly," line 2; "years," line 6), "lips" (line 4), "hand" (line 14), *arm* ("garment," line 2), and *rump* ("crumpled," line 2). So headlong is the progression of emotion and images that it is important to keep in mind that the speaker has not been abandoned by the lover to whom the poem is addressed. The crimes described—murder and theft—are fantasies, merely projected fears. The soul and the absent qualities ·of the lover are depicted as stolen wealth, while those qualities that could not be removed by death are "crimson roses"—thus, what remains is still subject to a "crime." Love, the sublime wealth that the speaker embezzles from the predations of time and death, is a paradoxical countercrime that drives the desperate fears of the guilty speaker of the poem. In the final analysis, the sonnet describes the speaker's struggle to preserve her true self: paradoxically, the speaker ultimately possesses herself by surrendering her lover.

Rauth's hysterical, diluted, and imitative sonnet takes on a completely new expressive scope in light of the following statement: "In the very year in which the first World War started, an advertised authority on the Negro stated that 'many animals below man manifest a far greater amount of real affection in their love-making than do negroes [*sic*]' and that it is very rare that 'we see two negroes kiss each other'" (Frazier 122–23). (Let us not suppose that by the thirties there had been a sufficient shift in race relations to cancel out the supposed veracity of this account.[34]) For an African American to assume the subject position of this deathless lover was to assume a radical and modernist identity. Rauth's speaker is derived from Edna St. Vincent Millay's *Fatal Interview*,[35] for Millay was one of the most influential American poets of the twenties and thirties. Though Millay wrote in traditional forms, she adopted the roles of bohemian and political dissenter. Nina Miller observes that "Countee Cullen, favorite son of the Harlem Renaissance, wrote his undergraduate thesis on Millay and pursued his professional career along distinctly lyrical and traditional lines." John Timberman Newcomb states that Millay demonstrates "the importance of alternative methods of constituting social identity through discourse, especially those which portray individuals as interdependent parts of an egalitarian collective rather than as masters of a hierarchical subject-object relationship" ("The Woman as Political Poet"). For African American poets and readers, association with a Millayan subject position was a foundational appropriation of autonomy, self-determination, and humanity.

In *Material Modernism: The Politics of the Page*, George Bornstein argues that

the literary text consists not only of words (its linguistic code) but also of the semantic features of its material instantiations (its bibliographic code). Such bibliographic codes might include cover design, page layout, or spacing, among other factors. They might also include the other contents of the book or periodical in which the work appears, as well as prefaces, notes, or dedications that affect the reception and interpretation of the work. Such material features correspond to Walter Benjamin's concept of the "aura" in his celebrated essay "The Work of Art in the Age of Mechanical Reproduction." (6)

Bornstein demonstrates that Yeats's "When You Are Old" "loses its original, courtly, medieval aura but still takes from its material instantiation a context both of love and of Irish nationalism, both of which disappear from contemporary collected editions and from anthologies" (2). According to Bornstein, "the 'aura' locates the work of art in time and space (that is, in history) . . . [and] the 'bibliographic code' as an important constituent of meanings, particularly of historical or political ones" (2). Thus, poems published in African American journals are embedded in a racialized social context and thereby assume a racialized aura that intervenes in the reception of the poem. The race of poets published in *The Crisis* and *Opportunity* was rarely disclosed, and race was only mentioned when the poets were African American.[36] At times the contents of the poems revealed the race of the poets, as in the sonnet "To a Negro Friend," in which it is obvious that the poet is white. In the case of the obscure poet Mary T. Rauth, her race is unknown, and there are no racial signifiers in her poem. However, Rauth's "Sonnet" was published along with poems titled "The Color Game," "To the Man Farthest Down," and "To One Sorrowing." Page 348 of the November 1937 number of *The Crisis* also carries advertisements for Merl R. Eppse's *A Guide to the Study of the Negro in American History* and for subscriptions to *The Woman's National Magazine.* In other words, Rauth's poem became a black poem by assuming a black aura, and in addition, the specific bibliographic code of the page on which it appeared further embedded the poem in more specific political and social contexts. Rauth's "Sonnet" was embedded in the politics of literary race in such a way that the universal, lyrical subjectivity that she had constructed applied to a racial objectivity, which it thereupon subjectivized, providing for the African American group identity an emotional resource that had been previously disallowed.

CONCLUSION

My project has been to assemble an account of how poets brought together those qualities that would form a new type of African American individuality, while keeping in mind the decentered nature of the selves that were being formulated. In fact, there is an inherent contradiction at the core of the African American sonnet pantext. On the one hand, the true self—the goal of self-fashioning—is singular, unitary, and not subject to change. On the other hand, the experiential processes of the self-in-process call into question the reality of a static self-identity. The new type of fully developed person never really emerges from the shifting colors, images, sounds, names, and shadows. But there are indications that may be taken as milestones along the route of self-in-process. In the thirties there were few role models available to African Americans. (Even now in the twenty-first century, African American role models are commonly drawn from athletes and vocalists; figures from the fields of law, politics, religion, television, and film have some application; while technology, medicine, science, and business do not really qualify as acceptable role models for the black masses.) In the thirties, the black discourse network was tenuous, the unfolding black culture was fragile, and there were few black figures that commanded all-embracing cultural power. Once Marian Anderson had sung on the steps of the Lincoln Memorial, a few poems, including sonnets, were directed toward her[37]—and here perhaps is the point at which powerful, positive role models came into play. In the thirties, poetry that addressed the self in relation to the requirements of others gained prominence, with many poetic calls for men and women to take on new responsibilities and new roles. Finally, the poets of the thirties were all too aware of the heritage of abjection; the black poetry of the thirties was pervasively haunted by slavery: the concluding couplet of Octave Lilly Jr.'s "Ex-slaves" mournfully observes that "for these old folks there is no freedom save / forgetfulness—fast in some welcome grave."

But the peasant was not so easily dismissed, and for many black poets in the thirties the black peasant was a site of great discursive interest. Owen Dodson's "Negro History" is informed by the positive pole of Spengler's thought. Dodson carries the peasant into the metropolis and bids him to align himself with the Caesarian strong men. By contrast, Marcus Christian's peasant is shown at the moment before he is relegated to the timeless village. Taking an even more objective view of society, Melvin B. Tolson intervened experimentally—hoping like Dr. Frankenstein to create a few superhuman individuals from the raw material of the masses of the black peasantry. These poets tended to reject the Marxist "transindividual conception of selfhood" (Foley) for the potentialities of the self-in-process. It is well known that even Richard Wright, who was accorded Communist Party celebrity because of his peasant origin, was finally unable to accept the erasure of his individuality at the hands of Third Period party discipline (Walker 70; Pells 232). If the ideas and methods of the black poets of the thirties now appear eccentric, limited, or anachronistic, we should keep in mind that in the thirties many nineteenth-century ideas (including Marxism) were in wide circulation, and esotericism, for example, was adopted by many of the most progressive writers and artists of the period. It was rare that an authentic modernism that broke with the past was broadly or consistently disseminated. Emerson's romantic modernism, Gurdjieff's esotericism, and Spengler's philosophy of history became prolific and regenerative resources out of which the black poets of the thirties were able to resist the discourses that enforced their inferior position in society.

3

"Race War"

AFRICAN AMERICAN POETRY ON THE ITALO-ETHIOPIAN WAR

> War is beautiful because it combines the gunfire, the cannonades, the cease-fire, the scents, and the stench of putrefaction into a symphony.
> —F. T. Marinetti, "Poesia, musica e architetture africane." *Manifesto Stile Futurista*, March 1935

> Oh, hang your heads, a voice accusing cries,
> And points a finger shaking in your face.
> —J. Harvey L. Baxter, "Oh, Hang Your Heads, A Voice Accusing Cries"

> But the greatest danger has not yet been even named. What if, one day, class war and race war joined forces to make an end of the white world?
> —Oswald Spengler, *Decline of the West*

The Italo-Ethiopian War (1935–36) was a notoriously unequal armed conflict that resulted in Ethiopia's subjection to Italian rule. According to Enzo Traverso's capsule history of the major armed conflicts that took place in the 1930s, the build-up to the Second World War began with the Italian imperial adventure: "Anti-fascism was also identified with the struggle for peace, in a continent where the wounds from the First World War were still open, and where the political balances seemed increasingly more precarious. The Italian attack on Ethiopia, the re-militarization of the Rhineland, the war in Spain, the Sino-Japanese war, then Munich and finally a new war: this escalation aroused an increasing anxiety whose echo was felt in art and culture" ("Intellectuals and Anti-Fascism"). Global technological warfare began with Italian fascism's predation of Ethiopia. Walter Benjamin theorized that such conflicts reflect the opposition between two discourses of aestheticized politics: Fascists claim that "war is beautiful," while Marxists say that "art is a weapon" (Griffin "Notes"). Another aspect of the Italian-Ethiopian conflict was its role in further establishing the centrality of warfare in modernity. Walter Benjamin pointed out that the human body could simply not absorb the speed and lethality of modern war (Kellner "Virilio"). Given that Italy was a highly regarded fascist state ruled by the dictator Mussolini while Ethiopia was a technologically primitive and politically feudal (though independent) African state, the conflict quickly came to symbolize Benjamin's observation about the nature of the human body, though inflected through a eugenic lens.

The particularly unusual feature of the conflict was the ten-month period between Mussolini's declaration of war and the beginning of the fighting. This delay allowed many questions to accrue. It reflected the impossibility of waging a modern war in Ethiopia until the Italians were able to make preparations to fight in a country with a harsh climate, forbidding terrain, and little infrastructure or natural resources. The hiatus of nearly a year between the announcement of hostilities and the actual invasion was filled with speculations about the nature of the conflict that would result. Strikingly, this period of military build-up was subject to a tense international drama fueled by conspiracies, betrayals, racism, and megalomania—all of which was reported by newspapers and on-the-scene radio correspondents, who reported each new development the moment it occurred.

In contrast to the Italians, the Ethiopians were virtually unarmed. Once fighting commenced, they fought with their bodies, relying on "human wave" assaults to overwhelm the machine guns of the Italians. Paul Virilio has further theorized the role of warfare in these terms:

> Logistics, the preparation for war, is the beginning of the modern industrial economy, fuelling development of a system of specialized and mechanized mass production. War and logistics require increased speed and efficiency, and technology provides instruments that create more lethal and effective instruments of war. The acceleration of speed and technology, in turn, create more dynamic industry, and an industrial system that obliterates distances in time and space through the development of technologies of transportation, communication, and information. The fate of the industrial system is thus bound up with the military system which provides . . . its origins and impetus. (Kellner "Virilio")

Inarguably, the war demonstrated the ineffectiveness of the League of Nations. League decisions were not supported by the great powers. Ethiopia

(Abyssinia), which Italy had unsuccessfully tried to conquer in the 1890s, was in 1934 one of the few independent states in a European-dominated Africa. A border incident between Ethiopia and Italian Somaliland that December gave Benito Mussolini an excuse to intervene. Rejecting all arbitration offers, the Italians invaded Ethiopia on October 3, 1935. Under Generals Rodolfo Graziani and Pietro Badoglio, the invading forces steadily pushed back the ill-armed and poorly trained Ethiopian army. The Italians won a major victory near Lake Ascianghi (Ashangi) on April 9, 1936, and took the capital, Addis Ababa, on May 5. Ethiopia's leader, Emperor Haile Selassie, went into exile. In Rome, Mussolini proclaimed Italy's king, Victor Emmanuel III, emperor of Ethiopia and appointed Badoglio to rule as viceroy. In response to Ethiopian appeals, the League of Nations had condemned the Italian invasion in 1935 and voted to impose economic sanctions on the aggressor. The sanctions remained ineffective because of a general lack of support. Although Mussolini's aggression was viewed with disfavor by the British, who had a stake in East Africa, the other major powers had no real interest in opposing him. The war, by giving substance to Italian imperialist claims, contributed to international tensions between the fascist states and the Western democracies ("Second Italo-Abyssinian War").

For African Americans, the impending Italo-Ethiopian War gave new focus to a wide range of social concerns. Because of the preexisting discourse of Ethiopianism,[1] African Americans understood the implications of a war between a European power and an independent African state. The international crisis captured African Americans' imaginations. Their interest in intervening in the conflict rapidly came into conflict with the American national policy of isolationism. Also, a small but influential cadre of African American leftist artists expressed Marxist antifascist opinions. The prospect of an African nation being overrun by a modern European nation appalled African Americans: reversing the situation would depend on Ethiopia's ability to marshal whatever forces that could be brought to bear on the Italian aggressors.

The African American reaction to the Ethiopian crisis was fueled by other factors as well. William R. Scott comments that

(1) "the concept of pan-Africanism, the belief in universal black solidarity and salvation, had forged in the postwar era important linkages among colonial Africans and American blacks, making scattered African peoples sensitive to the problems of blacks everywhere," (2) "[a] more militant Negro, deeply affected by the social changes produced by the black urban movement, the war experience, and disillusionment with both the traditional American system of justice and the established col-

ored leadership, had injected a fresh fighting spirit into the black American liberation struggle," (3) "during the Depression decade, the black American struggle for economic equity was expanded and transformed into a crusade for full equality fought 'on a scale, and with an intensity, unseen in any previous decade of the century,'" (4) "[t]he perception of an analogy between Italian imperialism and white racism in America also played an important part in provoking strong black reactions to the Abyssinian conflict. African American spokesmen consistently associated Fascist aggression in Ethiopia with racial injustice in the United States, pointing to the connections between the brutality of American anti-black violence and Italian militarism. The savage lynchings of blacks in the American South and the mass slaughter of Africans in Ethiopia seemed like parallel forms of oppression," and, finally, that "[a]n Ethiopianist tradition in African American thought was, however, identified by contemporaries as the central force generating the tremendous response of blacks in the United States to the East African conflict." (8–11)

Faced with an inevitable defeat at the hands of the Italian military, Haile Selassie seized the moral high ground in an attempt to persuade the European powers to take a stand against the Fascists, and he successfully maneuvered to convert Ethiopia's frail position from one of geopolitical irrelevance to some measure of consequence:

At the beginning of 1935 there was very little in the way of coherent opposition to fascism as a dangerous international force. Nazi Germany, however people felt about it, had so far committed depredations only against Germans. It was widely supposed that Italy and Germany were almost irreconcilably hostile to one another. The notion of fascism as monolithic, inescapably predatory, directed toward ideological world dominion in the same way that Communism was, had not yet been invented. It first began to take shape when the outrageous behavior of Mussolini in East Africa was brought, dramatically, to the forum of the League of Nations. The seismic effects of the crisis were not entirely due, of course, to the propriety of the Ethiopian position or the sympathy it evoked. That sympathy corresponded to deep ideals, illusions, hopes, and frustrations everywhere. And it owed something, too, to some coincidental and extraneous circumstances. Three circumstances in particular helped to convert Ethiopia into a martyr, a symbol, and in some ways a world power.

The first was climate. Walwal, coming at a time when Italy was still far from prepared for battle, took place six months before the beginning of the rainy season that would make battle unfeasible for another four. Ten months must intervene before Italy could get its war under way, ten months in which the Ethiopians could try to parry nemesis and the yeast of internationalism could work in western opinion. The second was the state of world press and radio news. Reporting had by now become big business. A need for news had developed, economic (for the proprietors of papers and broadcasting companies) and psychological (for readers and listeners). Lavish financing in the collection or even—in a certain sense—the creation of news was a very good investment. Newsmen began to assemble in Addis Ababa, and so provided the Ethiopians with a public. Third, the British were going to hold an election. It had, by law, to take place before September 1936, but the government could choose any date it pleased before that. Compelling political considerations made it desirable to hold one sooner. The date eventually chosen coincided, within weeks, with the ending of the rainy season and the beginning of the war. . . . Addis Ababa, by the summer of 1935, was becoming one of the world's major news capitals. (Dugan 118–19)

The effect on African Americans of the impending war between Italy and Ethiopia was complex and has to this day never been satisfactorily sorted out (W. R. Scott 165). A number of controversies arose at that time: debates over the Ethiopian's racial identity, antagonism between African Americans and Ethiopians, the treatment of black Americans who had come to Ethiopia, and the response of the Ethiopian elite to the African American defense and aid effort (W. R. Scott 165–66). As might be expected, the prolonged contemplation by the African American masses—whose sensibilities were overdetermined by racial oppression—of a European power methodically assembling a technological juggernaut for the sole purpose of overpowering and extinguishing an independent African nation produced a break with traditional habits of social protest, writing, stoicism, tolerance, passivity, and sublimation. The Italian threat to Ethiopia amplified nascent nationalistic stirrings in American blacks, but the general effect was to motivate African Americans to accept violence as the most appropriate response to the crisis. Whether it took the form of warfare, mob violence, riots, or the sport of boxing, the centrality of violence became a feature of the African American cultural formations in the 1930s.

William R. Scott states that "because of all the news, talk, and activity generated by the black media's coverage of the Abyssinian issue, the bulk of African Americans, even the young, probably knew of the Italian threat to remote Abyssinia and sympathized with its plight" (54). Given the centrality of this event, it is curious that the response by African American poets was not *more productive* than it was, and this aspect of the episode requires attention to the *negative presence* of the Ethiopian conflict. As might be expected, given his internationalism, leftist politics, and racial nationalism, Langston Hughes registered a number of poems in the campaign to defend Ethiopia. At the same time, such major poetic voices of the period as Sterling Brown and Frank Marshall Davis chose not to write on the topic, and it was left to new poets (Owen Dodson, Marcus B. Christian, and J. Harvey L. Baxter) and to what Eugene Redmond refers to as the magazine poets. Only one African American poet produced a volume dedicated to the war, J. Harvey L. Baxter's *Sonnets to the Ethiopians and Other Poems* (1936). This volume has consistently been overlooked in studies of this period, more than likely because Baxter has been consigned to the category of "romantic escapists" by the literary critics of the 1930s, who privileged social realist poets. Though information is lacking about the readership of Baxter's volume in the 1930s, he did advertise it prominently in *The Crisis,* and there is every reason to believe that it contributed to the various discourses of the period.

Poetry assumed an important role in the discourses that framed the African American reaction to the Italo-Ethiopian War. Kertzer states that

> modern wars depend on a sense of national allegiance, but the nation itself has no palpable existence outside the symbolism through which it is envisioned. As Walzer puts it, "The state is invisible; it must be personi-fied before it can be seen, symbolized before it can be loved, imagined before it can be conceived." People subscribe to the "master fiction" that the world is divided into a fixed number of mutually exclusive nations; they see these units as part of the nature of things, and assume an antiq-uity that the nations in fact lack. This symbolic conception of the universe leads people to believe that everyone "has" a nationality, in the same sense that everyone has a gender. It is in this light that Benedict Anderson defined a nation as "an imagined political community." Far from being window dressing on the reality that is the nation, symbolism is the stuff of which nations are made. Symbols instigate social action and define the individual's sense of self. They also furnish the means by which people make sense of the political process, which largely presents itself to people in symbolic form. (6)

Poems, then, compose the textual component of efforts that contribute to the personification of the state and affirm that black Americans participate in the "imagined political community" that the Ethiopians inhabit. Serving as a symbolic form that contributed to the sense of nationalism that African Americans directed toward the Ethiopian crisis, poetry allowed African

Americans to redefine their abject racial identities and to assume a more self-determined sense of purpose, power, and agency. Equally important is the conversion of the selfhood of African Americans into a new Ethiopian self, an activity best objectified by the formation of the Sons of Menelik clubs in Harlem once the nature of the Ethiopian crisis began to register on the African American imagination. The particular utility of poetry in such activities is suggested by Kertzer's discussion of the relationship between rhetorical forms of symbolism and emotion:

> Ritual can be seen as a form of rhetoric, the propagation of a message through a complex symbolic performance. Rhetoric follows certain culturally prescribed forms whose built-in logic makes the course of the argument predictable at the same time that it lends credence to the thesis advanced. . . . Of special relevance to an understanding of the political uses of ritual is the emotionally compelling structure of we/they imagery. . . .
>
> Successful ritual . . . creates an emotional state that makes the message uncontestable because it is framed in such a way as to be seen as inherent in the way things are. It presents a picture of the world that is so emotionally compelling that it is beyond debate. (101)

Two of the first poems published during the Ethiopian crisis attempt to construct new political identities for African Americans: Hughes's "Call of Ethiopia (*Opportunity,* September 1935) and Arthur N. Wright's "Ethiopia's Blacks" (*Baltimore Afro-American* August 3, 1935) are explicit examples of poetry used to formulate the new type of social solidarity through a participation mystique: "It is by uttering the same cry, pronouncing the same word, or performing the same gesture in regard to some object that they become to feel themselves to be in unison" (Durkheim qtd. in Kertzer 62). Hughes's poem is now an anthology piece.

CALL OF ETHIOPIA

Ethiopia,
Lift your night-dark face,
    Abyssinian
    Son of Sheba's race!
    Your palm trees tall
    And your mountains high
    Are shade and shelter

To men who die
For freedom's sake—
But in the wake of your sacrifice
May all Africa arise
With blazing eyes and night-dark face
In answer to the call of Sheba's race:

Ethiopia's free!
Be like me,
All of Africa,
Arise and be free!
All you black peoples,
Be free! Be free!
(Langston Hughes, *Opportunity,* September 1935)

For its part, A. N. Wright's long-forgotten anthem may best be described as versification.

ETHIOPIA'S BLACKS

Into the streets, Black Brothers,
Into the dust and rain,
Speak the word for freedom;
Shatter the torturer's brain

Up from our knees of prayer,
Up with our voices sing,
Brothers, Black, Brown and Yellow
Selassie's Emperor and king

Forward march, Black Brothers,
Break through the barricades
Guns and men and money
Mussolini must not prevail

Oh God of our Fathers
Thy People cry to Thee
To Ethiopia's millions
God, Give them liberty
(Arthur N. Wright, *Baltimore Afro-American*, August 3, 1935)

Wright's emotional plea is a call to arms, though it is unclear whether it is a call directed at African Americans, Ethiopians, or for both. Though the first, second, and third stanzas treat the conflict militarily, a matter of violently confronting a "torturer" to preserve freedom, the poem concludes with a religious turn, though in the final stanza prayer has been set aside so that the united black people "cry" (line 14) to God. We should also note that a demonized Mussolini in stanza three is opposed by an iconic Selassie in the fourth line of the preceding stanza. In the third stanza, Wright depicts a conventionalized revolutionary battle, with the confrontation between Italy and Ethiopia described in terms of barricades (imagery that perhaps suggests the urban warfare of the French Revolution). Of course, such imagery was anachronistic. The Italian protoblitzkrieg turned machine guns, bombs, and poison gas against the virtually unarmed Ethiopians. The imagery constructs a fantasy that equalizes the combatants.

The most striking aspect of the poems by Wright and Hughes is that they are both calls. For African Americans, the call is an activity freighted with cultural implications. The word *call* has several meanings, many of which apply to these poems. A call is a loud utterance, a demand, the characteristic sound produced by a bird, or a request (WordNet). Among the traditions of African American music are the traditions of song and chant associated with the world of men's work. These forms are variously referred to as field hollers, arhoolies, and calls. Imaginative call-and-response utterances were associated with whatever type of work was being performed. Agricultural workers created the evocative protoblues of cornfield hollers, ax and hoe songs, and songs to accompany plowing and cane cutting. Southern railroad crews used track-lining songs to synchronize the intricate operation of track lining. The call has many names and forms. The field holler has roots in the slavery era, but that musical form has persisted to this day (Judge). Langston Hughes had also been exposed to the peddler's calls that were a feature of Harlem street life in the 1930s. These highly original calls were the descendants of work songs. Fred McCormick discusses prison songs in the following passage, but his analysis serves as a more general description of what is believed to have been the social function of the call in traditional African American society:

> In all these verses you will not find the slightest iota of fantasy or escapism. If there were any would-be lottery winners in Parchman Farm or Angola they do not show up here. Instead the songs are vested with stark reality and sweat. They are the channeling of rage and resentment against the iniquity and brutality and rank injustice of a penal system which was nothing more than the legitimised extension of plantation slavery. All

folksongs involve catharsis but . . . song was the only voice which allowed prisoners to kick against the system. Shared songs did more than alleviate the work, they alleviated the misery. (McCormick)

Wright's poem clearly calls out to "Black brothers" (line 1), though the shifts from the objectified "Ethiopia's Blacks" of the title to "black brothers" (line 1) and "our knees" (line 1) obscures the subject position of the speaker who so vehemently calls upon the defenders of Ethiopia. Wright emphasizes the Ethiopians' potential to speak; in the first stanza they are asked to speak, in the second stanza to sing, and they are always already crying out in the final stanza. The third stanza urges them to march and to break down barricades, but the text as a whole seems to privilege speech—the response is not action, only more words. Clearly, the issue is agency, and the poet looks to the verbal response that presages yet another phase of action. Hughes's poem is also double-voiced: the poet's call is itself the subject of the poem. The speaker first calls to Ethiopia: "Ethiopia, / Lift your night-dark face" ("Call of Ethiopia" lines 1–2). The speaker first calls to Ethiopia, as the source of the call by addressing a call to Ethiopia, then iterates "the call of Sheba's race" (line 13) as direct discourse: "All you black peoples, / Be free! / Be free! (lines 18–19).

African Americans' newly rebellious spirit developed in many forms. Rather than deriving solely from the Ethiopian crisis, this rebellious spirit was also produced by "widespread black discontent in Harlem [that] contributed to intense pro-Ethiopian agitation" (W. R. Scott 104). The cultural atmosphere of this period is usually generalized in terms of what transpired in Harlem:

Frustrated by their inability to take up arms in defense of the Ethiopian "homeland," Abyssinian loyalists in Harlem charged collusion between Washington and Rome. New York's rabid race patriots concluded that U.S. government opposition to the volunteer movement was calculated to serve the interests of Italian imperialism rather than those of American neutrality. Many were suspicious that Italy was acting with the silent approval of their own government. Harlemites tended to agree with the reported observation of Robert L. Ephraim, president of the Negro World Alliance in Chicago, that Washington's stand against the volunteer effort and its refusal to act against Mussolini could only be taken as an indication that the white races of the world were lining up against the black. An international white conspiracy had been connived that would lead ultimately to *a war of the races.*

Whether or not most Harlemites foresaw a coming race war, fears of interracial struggle locally became rampant in the New York area during the summer of 1935 with a series of confrontations between Negroes

and Italian Americans. Preexisting antagonisms between the two groups,
albeit mild, had been greatly accentuated by the Italo-Ethiopian crisis and
began to assume the form of two conflicting nationalisms, one African
and the other Italian. (W. R. Scott 138; emphasis added)

Curiously, the Harlem riot of March 19–20, 1935, which was the first race
riot by a minority group in the North[2] (Puryear "Organized Crime"), has
not been attributed to influence from the Ethiopian crisis but to stimulation
by "deplorable social conditions" (W. R. Scott 104). Claude McKay's account
attributes the riot to interethnic tension that developed out of African
American protests against Harlem's Jewish merchants who refused to hire
black store clerks. The merchants eventually hired a small number of black
clerks, then let them go, claiming that business was suffering the effects of
the Depression. McKay concluded that "on Tuesday the crowds went crazy
like the remnants of a *defeated, abandoned, and hungry army.* Their rioting
was *the gesture of despair of a bewildered, baffled, and disillusioned people*"
("Harlem Runs Wild" 384; emphases added). McKay's language merges
the discourses of the military—the Harlemites constitute an *army*—and a
Marxist treatment of social identity. He presents the prescient reflection of
the defeated Ethiopian army superimposed on the massed instinctive aggression of an undirected, unscientific *class* that misidentifies itself as a *race.*
While McKay does not explicitly mention the Ethiopian crisis, he nevertheless manifests it in the paranoid imagery of race war and genocide.[3] McKay's
statement is dominated by the affective performance of the *gesture.* Though
many individuals are involved, their collective response is dreamlike, regres-
sive, and infantile in that they have lost the capacity for language. The riot is
incoherence made powerful, the cry at the collective level. The Harlem riot
may be thought of as a stage of the "identity work" (Snow 4) through which
African Americans constructed a revised collective identity that might serve
them in the traumatic conditions in which they found themselves. David
Snow comments that

> although there is no consensual definition of collective identity, discus-
> sions of the concept invariably suggest that its essence resides in a shared
> sense of "one-ness" or "we-ness" anchored in real or imagined shared
> attributes and experiences among those who comprise the collectivity
> and in relation or contrast to one or more actual or imagined sets of
> "others." (4)

A feature of the incoherence of the Harlem riot was not its displacement of
warfare in the sense that it was directed at the property of the Jewish mer-

chants and did not direct violence against persons considered the "other."
The Harlem riot was directed at the property, rather than the bodies, of
Jewish merchants. However, the event that set off the riot was the circulation of a rumor that the police had gunned down a young thief; this rumor
stimulated identity talk in the form of an "atrocity tale" (Snow 8). As I will
show in my discussion of the poems on the Ethiopian crisis, the atrocity tale
is an important element of the construction of the African American/Ethio-
pian collective identity.

It was the reaction to the Joe Louis–Primo Carnera boxing match on
June 26, 1935, that brought about direct conflict between African Americans
and Italian Americans. On Sunday, August 11, a fight broke out between the
two factions in Jersey City, and tensions remained high. William R. Scott
relates that

> violence soon flared anew in reaction to the long-anticipated Italian inva-
> sion of Ethiopia on October 3, 1935. This time the conflict occurred in
> New York, in the city's Brooklyn and Harlem sections. A local paper
> remarked that "the first shots of the Italo-Ethiopian War were echoed in
> New York City yesterday as Negroes and Italians battled in several patri-
> otic skirmishes," creating serious alarm in the two boroughs and causing
> anxious moments for metropolitan authorities. From the time paperboys
> first began to shout news through the streets of Harlem that Italian war
> planes had bombed Ethiopian towns, anger had mounted among the
> city's resident blacks. Outside the entrances to Italian fruit and vegetable
> markets in Harlem, fuming blacks scrawled chalk inscriptions reading
> "Italians, Keep Out." On streetcorners, where Harlemites often gathered
> to hear about and to discuss the Ethiopian crisis, soapbox orators berated
> Mussolini and demanded retaliation for the Italian attack on Africa, the
> black person's home. (140)

In the final stage of the "meaning making process,"[4] the black collective identity came to frame its existence within the bounds of an imminent global
race war. This polarization is a distinct feature of the second and third of
Hughes's three Ethiopian poems.

Langston Hughes took a plotted and episodic approach to the Ethiopian crisis in these three poems. They address the commencement of the
crisis ("Call of Ethiopia"), the Italian attack ("Air Raid over Harlem: Scenario
for a Little Black Movie"), and the defeat of the Ethiopian government with
the occupation of Addis Ababa by the Italians ("Broadcast on Ethiopia").
Though "Air Raid over Harlem" deals directly with the beginning of the
Italian invasion, the theme of the poem is not immediately apparent until

the twenty-third line: "Sure I know / The Ethiopian War broke out last night." The poem uses the pretext of the outbreak of fighting in Ethiopia to intervene in the formation of the Harlemites' race-war collective identity: Snow states that "in the absence of correspondence between personal identities and collective identities, some variety of identity work is necessary in order to facilitate their alignment" (10). Additionally, Snow observes that radical groups rely on the technique of identity construction (11).[5] Thus the "raid" is an exercise in "identity transformation," when a dramatic change in identity takes place and individuals see themselves as remarkably different than before (Snow 10). Questions of identity take precedence over the war crisis as the poem establishes a dialogue between social and personal identities: the Harlem social identity is on one side of the dialogue, and on the other side is the generalized black individual, who is slow to recognize the Harlem collectivity. In order to construct the new radical collective identity, Hughes must first install the Harlem individual in the Harlem collectivity. "Air Raid over Harlem"—the title shocks but does not divulge any historical context. Instead, the opening of "Air Raid" presents a speaker who is characterized by his palpable distress about his identity.

> AIR RAID OVER HARLEM
> (SCENARIO FOR A LITTLE BLACK MOVIE)
>
> Who you gonna put in it?
> Me.
> Who the hell are you?
> *Harlem.*
> Alright, then. (lines 1–5)

The speaker's voice is situated in the first-person subject position and couched in denial—"You're not talking about Harlem, are you?" (line 7). Presumably, the words of the title are a cry from a news vendor. As if to reassure himself and to restore the previous order of his world, the speaker identifies himself as an authentic Harlemite, through a catalog that testifies to his allegiance to his social identity as a black person:

> That's where my home is,
> My bed is my woman is, my kids is!
> Harlem, that's where I live!
> Look at my streets
> Full of black and brown and
> Yellow and high-yellow

Jokers like me.
Lenox, Seventh, Edgecombe, 145th.
Listen,
Hear 'em talkin' and laughin'?
Bombs over Harlem'd kill
People like me—
Kill ME! (lines 8–23)

He styles himself a joker—"Jokers like me" (line 14), yet, on the surface, his words demote his social identity, demonstrating its insufficiency and lack of agency. The implication is that initially Hughes's speaker intends "jokers" to be understood neutrally as *individuals*—as in "folks like me." *Joker*, however, suggests a complex range of semiotic-ethnic connotations, and Hughes's poem capitalizes on this polysemic word: a joker is a person who plays jokes, a thoughtless person, a person that is being disparaged, and a playing card that either is not used or is of high value, depending on the game. Thus the polarity of *joker* extends from nullity to potency. Buddy Moss recorded "Joker Man Blues" in 1933, so *joker* is also situated within the insubordinate discourse of blues subjectivity. In the context of the blues, the joker tends to be associated with the power to produce reversals. In the blues, the trickster, fooler, hoaxer, jilter, and startler are jokers. In "Come On in My Kitchen," bluesman Robert Johnson sings, "Took my woman from my best friend / Some *joker* got lucky, took her back again" (emphasis added). "Air Raid over Harlem" turns on the counterfeit nature of the Harlemites as jokers. Hughes's joker discourse constructs a joker/folk dyad, a sociopolitical dialectic on which his poem conjoins two familiar social identities. While the people of Harlem disparage themselves as jokers (the folk), they are also jokers who have the capacity for surprise and deception; they represent the unknown and unmanifested forces of resistance and transformation. As the poem proceeds, we realize that the speaker may even be aware of this duality of impotence/potency.

Hughes's treatment of the crisis is in keeping with the facts of the historical account insofar as he has situated his poem in the street, with his subject directly experiencing the conjunction of the Harlemites and the far-off Ethiopians, with whom they so closely identify. The innovation in Hughes's poem is the hyperbolic, Mayakovskian treatment of the danger. Through the avant-garde techniques of superimposition and simultaneity, Hughes cinematically fuses the occupations of Harlem and Brooklyn by twelve hundred police officers (W. R. Scott 141) with the Italian air war against Ethiopia. Hughes's poem achieves his transformational effects through two monumentalist intertexts, *King Kong* (1933) and Vladimir Mayakovsky's odes to the Soviet Union. In 1921, the cubo-futurist poet Mayakovsky produced the epic propaganda-art poem "150,000,000," an allegory of the decisive battle between 150,000,000 soviet workers and Woodrow Wilson's evil forces of capitalism. Ivan, the poem's hero, is a man with 150,000,000 heads and appears to be Mayakovsky's reification of mass man. In "Air Raid" Hughes presents the black masses as "a sleeping giant waking / To snatch bombs from the sky," a giant who "picks up the cop and lets him fly" (lines 112–14). Mayakovsky's transrational style also incorporates street slang, popular songs, satirical advertising jingles, grammatical deformations, bizarre grammatical inversions, neologisms, puns, and distorted rhymes (Blake 22–23). There are only dim reflections of Mayakovsky's avant-garde language arsenal in "Air Raid"; Hughes employs casual rhymes, black vernacular, anagrams (fits/ fist, planes/planted, air/raid), and capital letters. Shulman notices Hughes's "modernist disruptions of the text, surreal dreams and political juxtapositions, and the techniques of the Living Newspaper" (286). In the background of "Air Raid" are news reports from the radio, and continuing in a modernist vein, Hughes employs the technology of the film to establish his "scenario," though in comparison to Mayakovsky's poem, the monumental imagery in "Air Raid" is more realistic than transrational.[6] Foregoing Mayakovsky's grotesque image of the collective, Hughes shifts his poems into the context of the popular horror film *King Kong*, where gigantism is simultaneously familiar and defamiliarizing. Hughes recapitulates the suspenseful scene in which the gigantic ape, Kong, who has been rendered unconscious by the gas bombs of the moviemakers who have invaded Skull Island, begins to awaken: "A sleeping giant waking / To snatch bombs from the sky" (lines 103–4). Brought to New York, where he is displayed for profit, Kong escapes and defends himself by hurling his attackers and knocking airplanes out of the sky. Similarly, Hughes's monster awakens, but it awakens to political consciousness, which leads to the workers' revolution.

King Kong was one of the first mass spectacles of cinema's sound era. The movie garnered an unprecedented audience of fifty thousand people on its first day in two New York movie houses, Radio City Music Hall and the Roxy. The film was unabashedly racist, sexist, and antidemocratic. In "Air Raid," Hughes rearticulated[7] the semiotics of the film so that it operated entirely within an alternative register of black collective identity. Moreover, in the poem Hughes announces his project to rearticulate the film:

And someday
A sleeping giant waking
To snatch bombs from the sky
And push the sun up with a loud cry (lines 102–5)

In *Dreamworld and Catastrophe,* Susan Buck-Morss points out that the movie *King Kong* did more than provide a mass spectacle—it presented the mass to itself through the figure of the giant ape (Buck-Morss 176):

> Because Kong, too, falls in love with Ann [Darrow, played by Fay Wray], he is identified with the public that "loves a pretty face," precisely the mass audiences whom the director in the film and the directors of the film hope to attract. Descriptions of the masses as a giant animal, an instinctual, primitive force, were common at the time, an association in the film that intensifies when the director and his movie crew reach the mysterious Skull Island. King Kong is held back behind a giant gate from natives who have forgotten the more advanced civilization that built it. The native "primitives" worship Kong, providing for him the obligatory sacrifice of virgin girls. There is much in the movie that is racist. The dark-skinned villagers are as far removed from civilization as Kong himself. . . . Yet the connection between beasts and dangerously powerful masses (the working class during the Depression) is sustained in the staging of a boxing match between Kong and a dinosaur that mirrors the cuts and jabs of this quintessentially working-class sport. (177–78)

Hughes's rearticulation of "the big black giant" (line 107) as the monstrous ape King Kong constructs a narrative subtext in which the "big black giant"/King Kong is not *the masses* but is distinctly the *black masses*—simultaneously, the Ethiopians and the Harlemites. (Through its "boxing match," *King Kong* may also be thought to reinscribe the race war counternarrative: Hughes must be on guard lest the trope of the boxing matches between African and Italian Americans asserts itself.) The radical-collective counternarrative that Hughes develops begins with the trickster narrative set up by the first speaker in the poem: Harlem's joker constructs a linguistic continuum (what DuPlessis calls "lateral metonymic associations" and "vertical semantic coring" [*Genders* 18]) that elides and elevates the joker into a worker-giant that ultimately embodies pan-African unity and agency. In the scheme of Hughes's rearticulated "Little Black Movie" (line 113), the "primitives" of Skull Island are merely victims of the monster as the sign of their Galtonian regression and of the imperialistic movie makers who destroy their culture in the act of capturing Kong. The "primitives" are rearticulated as the Ethiopians, and Kong is Haile Selassie— literally "a king and god in his own world" (Buck-Morss 174). Up to this point in Hughes's reinscribed cinema-poem, King Kong is the polysemic sign of the atrocity tale: Kong may be understood as a monumentally and mutely suffering collective victim-figure, embodying the totality of the outrages against black peoples, whether American or Ethiopian.

The last three stanzas of "Air Raid" are a departure from the tragic outcome of the original *King Kong* film. In those final stanzas, Hughes further rearticulates his "Little Black Movie" as a Marxist comedy. Hayden White observes that "while Marx emplotted the history of the bourgeoisie as a Tragedy, that of the proletariat is set within the larger framework of a Comedy, the resolution of which consists of the dissolution of all classes and the transformation of humanity into an organic whole" (313). Hughes's scheme for this comedic transformation resides in yet another narrative countertext, the archracist text *The Story of Little Black Sambo*,[8] which Hughes evasively alludes to in the subtitle, "Scenario for a Little Black Movie." Just as Little Black Sambo's trickery melts the inimical tigers into butter, in Hughes's "Little Black Movie" the big black giant/King Kong survives despite the technological weapons of the elites. This fairy-tale victory is accomplished by the unification of the jokers into the heroic and triumphant "Sambo"-joker-worker-Kong of a new and omnipotent collective identity. The jokers become workers who then eat the butter of their magically homogenized class enemies:

Hey!
Scenario for a Little Black Movie,
You say?
A RED MOVIE TO MR. HEARST
Black and white workers united as one
In a city where
There'll never be
Air raids over Harlem
FOR THE WORKERS ARE FREE (lines 118–126)

"Air Raid" is driven by the tension between the impinging dangers of warfare and the childlike residents of Harlem. Hughes establishes the childish countertext not only by the "Little Black Sambo" subtext but also by the singsong, Mother Goose verse-form that surfaces in places along with its fearful content; one place where this usage is particularly effective occurs in the dreamlike metamorphoses that take place in the lines that parody the child's prayer, "Now I lay me down to sleep / I pray the Lord my soul to keep." Hughes renders this nighttime ritual as

Where the black millions sleep
Shepherds over Harlem
Their armed watch keep
Lest Harlem stirs in its sleep
And maybe remembers

And remembering forgets
To be peaceful and quiet
And has sudden fits
Of raising a black fist
Out of the dark
And that black fist
Becomes a red spark (lines 43–54)

The aggressive unification of the workers is specifically directed against a symbolic enemy: "A RED MOVIE TO MR. HEARST" (line 121). Snow's discussion of types of collective identity illuminates Hughes's incorporation of Hearst:

> Clearly a collective identity in which the boundaries between "us" and "them" are unambiguously drawn, in which there is strong feeling about those differences, and in which there is a sense of moral virtue associated with both the perceptions and feelings, should be a more potent collective identity than one in which either the emotional or moral dimensions are weakly developed. (11)

Hughes justifiably selected William Randolph Hearst as an American surrogate for Mussolini: "Hearst is known as one of the largest media moguls of all time. During the 1930s he worked with the Nazi party to help promote a positive image of the Nazi party in American media" ("American Supporters of the Fascists"). In the poem, Hearst localizes the fascist threat far more effectively than Hughes's depiction of the police as occupiers: even though the war has broken out on the other side of the world, there *can* be air raids over Harlem because there are Fascists like "MR. HEARST" in power in America.

In the final scene of "Air Raid," blackness has been effaced in the turn from ethnic conflict to class warfare. Anthony Dawahare states that Hughes often invoked a nationalist posture only to migrate to a final internationalist-utopian position, "a call to worker's multiracial unity" (96). In the last line, *"I'M HARLEM!"* (line 57), Hughes enunciates the joyous epiphany of the victorious giant, HARLEM. The HARLEM figure attains collective self-awareness through the individual/collective experience of remembering—"lest Harlem stirs in its sleep / and maybe remembers" (lines 42–43)—, a remembering so powerful that it instantly liberates the masses:

What workers are free?
THE BLACK AND WHITE WORKERS—

You and me!
Looky here, everybody!
Look at me!
I'M HARLEM! (lines 46–57)

While this transformation may sound magical, it is mediated by the technological discursive network of the film. Hughes invokes cinematic mediation through textually simulating the filmic vocabulary of montage in the structure of his poem (by using quick cuts, voiceovers, close-ups, flashbacks, and dream sequences), a method that appeals because of the presumed relationship of visibility to truth. Hughes's willingness to "show" the truth means that the author is willing to confront the public's gaze—to be seen and to see—a strategy that is an inescapable feature of cinema.[9] Thus, Hughes fuses seeing/being seen—the utopian-epiphanic gaze—and the comedic-revolutionary resolution in which the workers vanquish their oppressors by virtue of their ability to see their condition, to see who their enemies are, and to make the leap to effecting a revolutionary remedy.

The Italian attack against the Ethiopians, marked for the entire world the beginning of another long period of suspense, tension, and danger. The world had to wait ten months for the Italo-Ethiopian War to begin. The actual fighting went on from October of 1935 until May of 1936, when the Italians were able to occupy Addis Ababa—a period of eight months during which it was never clear how the war might end.

The most comprehensive response to the Italo-Ethiopian War by an African American poet was *Sonnets for the Ethiopians and Other Poems* (1936) by the prolific "magazine poet" J. Harvey L. Baxter. Baxter's forgotten volume stands out as the only collection of poetry dedicated to this seminal historical event. Baxter treated the Ethiopian crisis in a sequence of fifteen sonnets and another series of eleven poems titled "Lyrics (Ethiopian)." The preface to *Sonnets* is dated July 23, 1936, which was a mere two months after the fall of Ethiopia's government. It is possible to trace the events of the Ethiopian crisis through the sonnets. The poems titled "Lyrics (Ethiopian)" are more broadly thematic; in most cases, they do not speak directly to specific events.

The title of Baxter's volume betrays the reason why *Sonnets for the Ethiopians and Other Poems* is not considered a canonical[10] African American text from the thirties. For Sterling Brown (the pivotal black critic of the thirties), Baxter was beneath consideration. Brown considered Baxter yet another romantic escapist, an ideological and aesthetic failure. Given the valorization of experimental-modernist aesthetics centered on the documentary trend (calling above all for documentary sources and a detached delivery), and social-realist and secular-nationalist discourses, Baxter's *romantic* handling of the Italo-Ethiopian War branded him an irrelevant poet. Baxter's use of the sonnet and the irregularly rhymed lyric, his employment of a neo-Shakespearean diction reminiscent of Claude McKay's, his embrace of standard rhetorical archaisms, and his use of the Christian-Ethiopianist meta-narrative were all potential liabilities. As I have shown in chapter 2, such an absolutist dismissal of this poetry is itself based on unregistered forms of idealist literary theorizing. As Bornstein states, "The original sites of incarnation thus carry with them an aura placing the work in space and time, and constituting its authenticity as well as its contingency" (6). While "Air Raid over Harlem" is accorded a central position in contemporary discussions of 1930s poetry (in Smethurst, Nelson, Shulman, Dawahare, and Corbould), "Air Raid" was published in *New Theatre* in February 1936, a left-wing periodical with a small circulation and not available to a black readership. When Baxter's collection is restored to its material context and the sociology of the text is considered—factors that include the publisher, print run, price, and audience (Bornstein 7)—a profoundly altered sense of Baxter's Ethiopian poems is achieved. Baxter's volume had the distinction of being a discrete volume of poetry, in itself a rarity that accorded it notability at the time; moreover, *Sonnets* addressed a topic that, according to the *Chicago Defender,* had electrified the world. In "Books by Negro Authors in 1936," a two-page spread of "paragraph reviews for the guidance of *Crisis* readers," civil rights activist and bibliophile Arthur B. Spingarn endorsed Baxter's volume. Spingarn commented, "The author's second volume shows considerable advance over his first" (47). Three of the pamphlets on Spingarn's list concerned the Ethiopian crisis. Reviewed along with Baxter's volume were forthrightly political texts: George Padmore's *How Britain Rules Africa,* Lawrence Gellert's *Negro Songs of Protest,* Arna Bontemps's *Black Thunder,* and Mae V. Cowdery's *We Lift Our Voices.* James McGann has stated that "meaning is transmitted through bibliographical as well as linguistic codes" (Bornstein 7). This suggests a different narrative of reception for Baxter's *Sonnets for the Ethiopians* than that descending from an ideological and aesthetic analysis whereby *Sonnets for the Ethiopians* can be dismissed as "romantic escapism." Rather, the historicized and material association of Baxter's *Sonnets* with its printed context shifts its aura, utterance, and reception to a politically engaged meaning.

Other poets besides Baxter responded to the Italo-Ethiopian War with sonnets: Owen Dodson published "Desert in Ethiopia" in *Opportunity* in December 1935. Also in this category are P. J. White's "Vestis Virumque Cano" (*Opportunity,* January 1936), and Marcus B. Christian's "Selassie at Geneva" (*Opportunity,* June 1938). Like Baxter's *Sonnets,* these poems considered the Ethiopian crisis through the discourse of tragedy, a response advocated by Baxter in the opening sentence of his preface: "The world has currently observed the most wanton of the tragedies of the century, the gobbling up of Ethiopia by Italy." The treatment of the Ethiopian crisis through a tragic (and religious) narrative was the antithesis of Langston Hughes's comedic and transcendent Marxist-internationalist narrative, with its antecedent obligatory ridicule of Selassie. The sonnets that are situated in the tragic-romantic discourse lack realistic social details (such as urban atmospherics, vernacular language, and popular culture); however, they are more congruent with the historical record, as when Baxter compresses Haile Selassie's speech to the League of Nations into one of his sonnets. In comparison, Hughes's "Air Raid" may even be said to be antihistoric in that Hughes refused to record or to recognize the consequences of the factual present and instead grounded his poem in a fantastic futuristic vision of an unattainable industrial utopia.

Though Baxter speaks of the Ethiopian crisis as a tragedy, a distinction must be made between the tragic mood of his sonnets and the historic emplotment of his sonnet sequence as romance. Hayden White states that in tragedy there is a resignation to the inalterable and eternal conditions under which men must labor in the world (9). In Baxter's sequence there is no such reconciliation with "the limits on what may be aspired to" (White 9), so it is necessary to look to another form of historic emplotment, the romance:

> The romance is fundamentally a drama of self-identification symbolized by the hero's transcendence of the world of experience, his victory over it, and his final liberation from it—the sort of drama associated with the Grail legend or the story of the resurrection of Christ in Christian mythology. It is a drama of the triumph of good over evil, of virtue over vice, of light over darkness, and the ultimate transcendence of man over the world in which he was imprisoned by the Fall. (White 8–9)

"The World," which is the opening sonnet of Baxter's volume, addresses the amoral geopolitics that prevailed during the Ethiopian crisis, as France and England conspired with Italy to divide up Africa despite participation in the League of Nations. In an ironic departure from his reading of the events as tragedy, Baxter alludes in his first line to Shakespeare's As You Like It with his first line, for Baxter's "The world's a mummery of groggy lies / And we are victims of its undertow" (lines 1–2) is a labored variation on Shakespeare's "All the world's a stage / and all the men and women merely players" (AYL 2, 7). Not only is As You Like It a romantic comedy but also it presents the world as Christian romance, a struggle between good and evil in which good triumphs. (This development in Baxter's poetry is a noteworthy departure from the practice of Claude McKay, whose protest sonnets served as models for Baxter and other African American poets. McKay drew on Shakespeare but used the histories and tragedies as rhetorical resources. James R. Keller shows that "Look Within" (448–49) is based on *Hamlet* (2.5.154–56) and that the famous sonnet "If We Must Die" (450) is derived from the "St. Crispin Day" speech of *Henry V* (4.2.18–67). In *As You Like It*, a debate about the negative and positive aspects of life is carried out between Jaques, a chronically melancholy pessimist, and Rosalind, the play's Christian heroine. Baxter's "The World" is spoken in Jaques's voice, and the poem is drawn from his tirades against humanity. Baxter centers on the deceptions of the conspiratorial politicians that determined the course of the Ethiopian crisis so that the sonnet is an intricate catalog of disguises, avoidances, and misdirection. The catalog includes "mummery," "lies," "turn our backs," "close our eyes," "fallen low," "bewildered leaders," "ape the maniac," "dodge and shirk," "eat his words," "fog," and "chaff." The speaker addresses himself to God for redress, and this is the most salient feature of the sonnet—the power to end the depredations of the Europeans does not belong to men. Thus, even in the most thematically "realistic" sonnet of the sequence, realism has given way to romance.

In the next sonnet, "Africa," Baxter has abandoned the rhetorical and positional semblance of realism altogether, and he can state that

> I come a singer, yet a champion
> Of the undone, benighted folk, forgot;
> Of fleshy foot-stool, bleeding stepping-stone,
> Whom men beguiled in their despotic lot. (lines 5–8)

Baxter concludes the sonnet with an assertion of God's existence—"God is not *dead,* nor guarded in a *tomb!*" (line 14; emphases added). The word *victim* (line 2) appears in "Africa" and again in "The World." This echo suggests that at the heart of Baxter's concern is the question of the victimization of Africa, Africa that is an idealized abstraction not subject to the type of military intervention that I have discussed in connection with the call to action voiced by Arthur N. Wright and Langston Hughes. Nevertheless, Baxter's Africa is framed within an anti-imperialist discourse so that a stance of suitable political resistance is maintained.

Baxter's brand of social realism turns into historical nostalgia in the third sonnet:

WELL MAY I SING OF THE PROUD ETHIOPE

> Well may I sing of the proud Ethiope
> Who ruled before the will of Rome was born;

And did with Israel and Egypt cope
Ere pyramid or temple scanned the morn.
Well may I sing of his primeval speech,
And of his arts and obfuscated past,
Of priests who rose to prophesy and preach
That God was Soul, Almighty, First and Last.

Of how his blood seeped in the Arab-vein,
And Negrofied the skin of India.
Then leaped from Bosporus and colored Spain,
And mongreled up old Greece and Italia.
These men who wear the night upon their faces,
FOUGHT OFT WITH JEW AND NOMAD BIBLE RACES.

Here Baxter suggests that in the distant past the Ethiopians inhabited the other side of the victim/victor dyad. The sonnet's concluding line, "FOUGHT OFT WITH JEW AND NOMAD BIBLE RACES," is the only line in the entire volume that is printed in capital letters. It is the final line of the poem that asserts and recovers the biblical context of the Ethiopians, and the line plays upon the trope of reading the indecipherable writing on the wall that is rendered in Daniel 5:25—"MENE, MENE, TEKEL, UPHARSIN [PERES]." The book of Daniel relates the Persians' defeat of Belshazzar. The modern parallel with the Bible that the sonnet implies is the defeat of the Italians by the Ethiopians. Like the Babylonians, the Italians will be weighed and found wanting at the end of their days, and their kingdom will be divided and given to other rulers. In "Well May I Sing of the Proud Ethiope," Baxter has assumed the mantle of the prophet Daniel and invoked the destruction of the Fascists. Despite the semblance of unaffected directness afforded by the opening line of the poem, Baxter's appropriation of the prophetic books of the Bible is not direct but is instead mediated by Elizabeth Barrett Browning's prophetic novel in verse, *Aurora Leigh* (1856). Browning's epic-prophetic intertext has supplied the trope of wearing the night; Baxter's thirteenth line ("These men who wear the night upon their faces") echoes Barrett's "And last / I learnt cross-stitch, because she did not like / To see me wear the night with empty hands. / A-doing nothing" (book 1, lines 446–49). Moreover, the prophetic tenor of Baxter's *Sonnets for the Ethiopians* is derived from Browning's influence; this source is suggested by the allusion to the book of Revelation—"First and Last" (line 8)—which Baxter places at the end of the sonnet's octave to enforce the idea that the end is also the beginning. Browning aligned *Aurora Leigh* with the prophetic conventions of the Hebrews, Romans, and Greeks, and her epic's nine books may have alluded to the nine books of the Roman sibyls.[11] *Aurora Leigh* contains a plethora of biblical metaphors, and it concludes with allusions to the same Revelation 21:6, "[I am the] Alpha and [the] Omega," the beginning and the end that Baxter alludes to in line 8. Alison Booth (80) shows that Browning has converted Alpha and Omega into *first* and *last* in the final stanza of *Aurora Leigh*. Revelation 21:19 reads "the first was jasper" (*NRSV*) and Revelation 21:20 reads "the twelfth amethyst" (*NRSV*). In Browning's poetic version of this passage, she has substituted "last" for "twelfth."

> He stood a moment with erected brows,
> In silence, as a creature might who gazed,
> —Stood calm, and fed his blind, majestic eyes
> Upon the thought of perfect noon: and when
> I saw his soul saw,—"Jasper *first*" I said;
> "And second, sapphire; third, chalcedony;
> The rest in order:—*last*, an amethyst." (lines 984–90; emphases added)

Baxter has followed Browning's alterations in his sonnet, and he has further compressed the combination of Alpha and Omega and the vision of the jeweled city of God into the simplicity of "first and last" ("Well May I Sing" line 8)

To reinforce this prophetic discourse, Baxter has insinuated the original indecipherable text of the writing on the wall into the poem as a divine intertext, and he refers to this missing divine text in lines 5 and 6 as "primeval speech" and "obfuscated past," respectively. The words "MENE, MENE, TEKEL, UPHARSIN [also variously *parsin* and *peres*]," are written syllabically into Baxter's sonnet as "mongreled" (line 12), "men" (line 13), "temple" (line 4), "priests"/"prophesy"/"preach" (line 7), and "Bosporus" (line 11). Baxter has made significant alterations to the biblical narrative in order to cohere with the historical present. In the Bible, the prophet Daniel was confronted with a text ("MENE, MENE, TEKEL, UPHARSIN") that could be read ("measure, measure, count, divide") but could not be meaningfully interpreted. Daniel then produced an interpretation: *The king's deeds had been weighed and found deficient and his kingdom would therefore be divided.* "FOUGHT OFT WITH JEW AND NOMAD BIBLE RACES" is the writing on Baxter's contemporary wall. However, in Baxter's sonnet the writing on the wall is a trope that casts the Italians in the guise of the present-day Persians, while the Ethiopians are identified as JEW AND NOMAD BIBLE RACES. Thus, it is the Ethiopians themselves who are the unreadable text that the poet must interpret. This trope is inherent in the characteristics of the Ethiopians whom Baxter endows with "primeval speech" (line 5), an "obfuscated past" (line 6), and darkness ("These men who wear the night upon their faces" [line 13]), for their seeming obscurity indicates their divine protection. The concluding line, "FOUGHT OFT WITH JEW AND NOMAD BIBLE RACES," is not the text but is the interpretation, even though its presentation in capital letters suggests that in this modern context it is the indecipherable writing on the wall. Baxter sees himself as the incarnation of Daniel, but he revises Daniel's prophetic act. Speaking prophetically, he predicts an Ethiopian victory, because their powerful identity is not visible to their pagan opponents.

The antimodernist and romantic character of Baxter's antifascist discourse allows for no separation from the past. The Ethiopians of the 1930s are not distinguished from their biblical ancestors (as they are in Hill's poem on the Ethiopian fighter, for example). Such a separation would ensure the Nietzschean death of God alluded to in line fourteen of "Africa," where Baxter declares that "God is not *dead*" (Baxter's emphasis). Because the concluding line of "Well May I Sing" appears in capitals, it ordains a synchronous historical structure in opposition to the obliterative diachrony of fascist-modernist time. Baxter further advocates synchrony and synthesis in the substance of the sestet of "Well May I Sing," which (couched in the language of eugenic pseudoscience) addresses the seepage of "blood" (not genes) and makes a claim that the Italians' ancestors were the Ethiopians. In the sestet, Baxter advocates the view that the Ethiopians were the ancestors of the Italian Fascists, betraying through the black vernacular lilt of "Negrofied," "leaped," and "mongreled up" a malign pleasure derived from the aggressive assertion of a shared ancestry that must have seemed disagreeable to the Italians:

At issue here are competing notions about warfare. Paul Virilio has argued that Mussolini's mobilization against Ethiopia marked the beginning of a new age of history, military capitalism. Virilio theorizes modernity in terms of the effect of military capitalism on modern culture:

> For Virilio, logistics, the preparation for war, is the beginning of the modern industrial economy, fuelling development of a system of specialized and mechanized mass production. War and logistics require increased speed and efficiency, and technology provides instruments that create more lethal and effective instruments of war. The acceleration of speed and technology, in turn, create more dynamic industry, and an industrial system that obliterates distances in time and space through the development of technologies of transportation, communication, and information. The fate of the industrial system is thus bound up with the military system which provides, in Virilio's vision, its origins and impetus. (Kellner "Virilio")

It is exactly these unique conditions that Baxter confronts with his sonnet sequence. Baxter's *song* invoked in "I come a singer" ("Africa" line 5) and the title of "Well May I Sing of the Proud Ethiope" presents the Italian-Ethiopian conflict as a war between two competing modes of time—poetic time and linear time. Baxter's Italians are cut off from the past; they cannot recognize their genetic unity with the Ethiopians. Not only are they at war with their authentic selves but also they are violating their spiritual essence. The Fascists exist in the dromomatic, futuristic present in which time is always speeding up and running out.[12] Fascist time is linear, concrete, profane, and ahistorical; opposed to it is the sacred, mythical time of the prophetic and ritualistic mode of reality (Eliade 1965 20–21). Baxter's poetic time is paradoxical, circular, eternal, and transcendent. Mythical time places the poet in circular, prophetic time so that he joins the past to the future: what has been in the past will also exist in the future. Thus, the controlling figure of Baxter's entire sequence is, in a sense, the writing on the wall that tells of the intervention of a divine apportionment that measures, weighs, and divides.

For Baxter, the war is a matter of competing chronologies, a subject he confronts directly in "God Send Us Rains," the twelfth sonnet in the sequence. Baxter's sonnet constructs the opposition of fascist dromology by the natural order, in this case the seasonal Ethiopian rains that prevented the Italians from going on the offensive. While the sonnets are weak in addressing the concrete sequence of historical events, it is possible to temporally place this sonnet toward the end of the rainy season in the fall of 1935. "God Send Us Rains" is an appeal for a divine intervention by means of a natural cause: "For rains will snuff the breath of barking guns, / And form a Purgatory of the roads; / For rains will shield us from the greedy Huns" (lines 9–11). The Italians attacked when the rains no longer defended the Ethiopians:

> With the beginning of dry weather conducive to large-scale military operations, the long-awaited Italian invasion of Ethiopia began, just before dawn on the morning of October 3, 1935. From strategically located bases along the Eritrean border, one hundred thousand Italian troops advanced in three columns into Abyssinian territory. With banners flying and trumpets blaring, three columns of Il Duce's grand colonial army crossed the Mareb River, a muddy stream delineating the Ethiopian border, and advanced toward enemy military positions at Adigrat, Enticcio, and Adwa, scene of the great Italian disaster in Italy's first Ethiopian war. Although there was no official declaration of war, the fascist march for revenge and the glory of Rome was formally underway.
>
> News of the Italian assault on Ethiopia was flashed around the world. Cables from Addis Ababa broadcast to the international community that

Ethiopia's brave but meagerly armed warriors were pitted in fierce battle against a powerful invasion force of Italian troops equipped with modern combat rifles, aircraft, vehicles, and chemicals. Reports of the hostilities indicated that it was impossible to provide detailed accounts of the early fighting but stated that Mussolini's blackshirted legions had successfully penetrated northern Ethiopia and established a base there for an extensive attack on the rest of the country. (W. R. Scott 99)

Because they were not at the scenes of the fighting, African American poets could not incorporate their own first-hand observations of military combat into their writings. By contrast, the Italian futurist poet F. T. Marinetti, a veteran soldier who served with the invading Italian forces, gloried in effusive, experimental descriptions of the horror that resulted when modern armaments (dive bombers, mustard gas, machine guns) were directed at the ragtag Ethiopian forces. This futurist-fascist countertext was not available to African American writers—it was written in Italian and had not reached North America—though as I have shown, Langston Hughes did incorporate experimental techniques for some of his politically radical poetry in the thirties. The avant-garde techniques that allowed Marinetti to carry out his literary appropriation of the conflict were not generally a part of the African American repertoire of poetics. The culture of the 1930s was dominated by the documentary approach of poets such as Muriel Rukeyser, Charles Reznikoff, and Kay Boyle. Extraliterary materials[13] included through collage and montage techniques "to serve as direct, if fragmentary, representatives of the real social and historical world from which they emerged" (Dayton 65) represented intrusions in the lyric surface of those experimental documentary poems, so it was obvious that the poems were experimental. In contrast, documentary expression often was not an obvious feature of African American poetry.

This must not be taken at face value, however. Rather than relegate to another discussion the question of how else African American poets might have responded to the Italo-Ethiopian War, it is my intention to contextualize the documentary tendency and to retheorize the poetry that black poets composed in response to this conflict. Tim Dayton has summarized the documentary tendency of Muriel Rukeyser's *The Book of the Dead*, the most important documentary poem of the thirties:[14]

As William Stott argues in his seminal *Documentary Expression and Thirties America*, the 1930s were virtually dominated by the documentary mode of communication, in part because the seeming directness and factualness of the documentary suited it both to the traditional American

"cult of experience" (in the phrase of Philip Rahv) and to the more particular skepticism regarding the abstract and impalpable that was engen-
dered in the public by the Great Depression. Documentary in the 1930s,
Stott notes, was typically "social documentary," which "deals with facts
that are alterable. It has an intellectual dimension to make clear what
the facts are, why they came about, and how they can be changed for the
better. Its more important dimension, however, is usually the emotional:
feeling the fact may move the audience to wish to change it." (62–63)

What Stott broaches above as "emotion" is perhaps more usefully understood
as code for *propaganda:* in the thirties, photography was theorized as being
the closest approximation to the real, while in truth "the photographer's prej-
udices often entered into the creation of an image, making the photos part
enduring cultural record and part propaganda" (DP). The assumption that
documentary productions achieve ideological neutrality is entirely suspect;
ultimately, documentary productions do not provide more objective works
of art than do "romantic" aesthetics. But documentary theorists proceeded
as though they were making a verifiable departure from subjective aesthetics.
Tim Dayton has traced the formation of documentary poetry to Ezra Pound:

> The documentary trend found its first great poetic exemplar in Ezra
> Pound, eventual adherent of Italian fascism. Pound's *Cantos*, Michael
> Andre Bernstein argues, may be understood as an attempt to undo one
> of the major effects of nineteenth-century French poetics (an effect par-
> alleled less reputably and less brilliantly in the poetics of the Ameri-
> can Genteel Tradition), particularly as seen in Mallarmé: the sundering
> of poetic language from the things and events of this world. Mallarme
> wanted poetic language to confront a realm to which ordinary language
> had no access, where it was rendered silent. Pound, conversely, sought
> to reattach poetic language to the worldly concerns of men (as he would
> have put it). In his attempt to achieve this, Pound incorporated extralit-
> erary texts to serve as direct, if fragmentary, representatives of the real
> social and historical world from which they emerged. (64–65)

Dayton argues that Pound developed a documentary method for modern
poetry out of a reaction against "the extreme subjectiveness characteristic
of romanticism and powerfully expressed in the romantic lyric" (63). In the
final understanding of the romantic and postromantic,

> the subjective being that makes itself heard in lyric poetry is one which
> defines and expresses itself as something opposed to the collective and

the realm of objectivity. While its expressive gesture is directed toward, it is not intimately at one with nature. It has, so to speak, lost nature and seeks to recreate it through personification and through descent into the subjective being itself. (Theodor Adorno quoted by Dayton 66)

Through documentary, poets such as Rukeyser sought to intervene in the real and made it an "exterior" feature of their poems; thus, according to Dayton,

> the objective social content that Adorno finds latent within all lyric poetry does not, in *The Book of the Dead,* remain latent. Rukeyser does not permit objective content to remain merely implicit in the lyric; she renders it explicit in the documentary sections of the poem, which, as we have seen, are often edited and slightly revised versions of testimony offered before the House subcommittee investigating the construction of the tunnel at Gauley Mountain. (66)

However, Adorno has one final proviso that shifts the meaning of the African American lyric: "Adorno argues that despite this apparently asocial character of lyric expression, objective social content remains within it, though transformed by and enfolded within individual consciousness" (Dayton 66).

Following Adorno's lead, then, the task is to see by what means objective social content is documented under the methods with which the black poets wrote their sonnets in the thirties. The black subject position differs from that of white poets writing the modernist sonnet (for example, Millay and Cummings), because the black poets did not derive their personal and social identities from their sense of alienation.[15] The primary impetus of their sonnets is to express "the ideas of the human agent who is able to 'remake' himself [*sic*] by methodological and disciplined action" (Lupton 75). Even though the black sonneteers restricted themselves to the lyric mode, the objective social content of their work did not remain latent. In their work, one tangible aspect of the self-in-process is the form of the sonnet itself; the sonnet is discipline, and objective reality is a component of the refashioning of the self: as the self is remade, the world is remade. This is clarified if the sonnet is thought of as a speech act that reclaims a portion of the lost being of the slave; in the sonnet, the body of the bourgeois subject becomes a participant in resting, playing, using the senses, and reclaiming the "closed" body in an orderly manner. To arrive at this articulate, orderly leisure, the disorderly world (of the "open" body) that has imposed a pathological disciplinary regime must also be remade. For leftist or left-liberal writers, facts themselves were important in and of themselves, so "reportage seemed to offer a solution to problems both formal and political" (Dayton 64). The world of objective fact that Rukeyser introduces into her poem through documentary materials does not serve the needs of African Americans, since those "facts" (for example, the "facts" of blacks' imbecility, inarticulacy, hypersexuality, and subhumanity) are the source of the African American's social death. In order for the black bourgeois subject to exist at all, the "facts" that embody the African American's inferiority must be subordinated to the will for a refashioned self. The sonnet may be thought of as the sign of this will in operation; for a revolutionary Marxist poet like Hughes, who addresses the Italo-Ethiopian War in another register, parody in experimental form serves to some degree as a sign of his will, though in contrast to the precise self denoted by the sonnet, Hughes's will is directed toward revolutionary disorder

For formalist black poets who wrote about the Italo-Ethiopian War, the subjectivity of the poet was not opposed to the collective. This was African American poets' first departure from romantic and modernist procedures. Though the African American poet may in some cases be alienated from the authoritarian system that imposed racist, religious, social, and political regimes, the poet was part of the black collectivity, though the poet was also part of an idealized human collectivity. The second departure took place when the objective social content did not remain latent but instead became the directly perceived field of the poem—though this field was mediated by the consciousness of the poet and did not retain its own integrity as privileged *documents*. A third departure from modernist poetics by black poets was driven by the problem of poetic authority. In "Lyric Poetry and Society" Adorno observes the centrality and necessity of the lyric speaker who preserves both social and subjective experience—"all social experience being necessarily individual in character" (Dayton 2). Thus, there is an interplay between interiorized content and the outside world; specifically, the black bourgeois poet, rather than finding that he must exclude the world in order to achieve lyric expression, finds that he must encompass the Italo-Ethiopian War in order to voice his lyric, and the black lyricist strains to extend the capacity of the subjective mode into an intersubjective and transindividual mode. At the same time, while others situated more fortunately in society may take the possession of the "bourgeois" subjectivity as an inalienable right (and may reject subjectivity, or seek to alter or to destroy subjectivity), the black poet, as a self-in-process, may not make such a fortuitous claim. Instead, the black poet must struggle to forge his or her subjectivity from whatever materials may randomly come to hand. Analogues to the legendary example of Frederick Douglass's adventitious acquisition of the *Columbian Orator* include Owen Dodson's submission to a Keatsian disciplinary regime, Melvin B. Tolson's encounter with esotericism when his research on the Harlem school of Negro writers confronted him with Jean Toomer's disciples, and Sterling Brown's hoodwinked encounter with the black South.[16]

Four of the major African American social realist poets of the thirties—Frank Marshall Davis, Welborn Victor Jenkins, Fenton Johnson, and Sterling Brown—did not write poems on the Italo-Ethiopian War. Langston Hughes's three poems on the war contain documentary elements, but the poems also employ parody. Parody is a significant nonrealist departure from the mode of poems based on reportage. Rukeyser, for example, combined lyric, epic, and dramatic modes in *The Book of the Dead* through collage and montage. According to Shulman, the poem "can be seen as a series of documentary photographs" (183). In comparison to this mode of documentary seriousness, it may be observed that Hughes's poems are not addressed to the specifics of the military campaigns or to geopolitical developments. The war simply did not exist as a directly observed and unmediated historical event for Hughes. It was not until N. Jay Hill wrote "An Ethiope in Spain" (*The Crisis,* July 1937: 202) that a poem describes an Ethiopian soldier in combat:

> Silent man of the hour is he,
>> Hurling back the ejector,
>> Loading, firing grimly;
> Exchanging few words with his company,
> For he spoke neither Italian
>> Nor Spanish.
> Though little English
>> And some French,
> For the most part he spoke Amharic.
> And that was not necessary.
>> For language could not match
>> The eloquence of his silence. (lines 17–28)

Hill's Ethiopian rifleman is Ghvet, who fought with the International Brigade in Spain. Presumably, he escaped to Europe from Ethiopia along with Selassie and his court. Ghvet, the son of Ras Imru, is depicted as a grimly destructive antifascist fighter, "A prince, with no bright jewel in his ear," and "a victim of civilized barbarity." Hill dwells on Ghvet's surrendered "black majesty" so that Ghvet comes to symbolize the transformation of the fractured world of the past into a future classless humanity. In Hill's world, the Italo-Ethiopian War had little or no meaning.

Owen Dodson's magisterial and resignedly elegiac sonnet "Desert in Ethiopia" (*Opportunity,* December 1935: 375) came the closest to describing the fighting in documentary detail:

Desert, be prepared to blow your sand:
Be prepared to bury all the dead
Within the ripples of your burning hand
Where coins of gold should sparkle white instead.
O desert, your smooth bosom must receive
The lost, the silent agonizing eyes
Of men whose banners drooped, whose sires believe
That you must efface their fiendish lies.
I know that hope alone is not release
From scintillating swords that catch the sun;
I know that peace must some day bleed for peace
If stars in nights to come will shine again
Upon this husk inhabited by men.

Dodson's sonnet was published two months after the Italians invaded Ethiopia, but it is clear that the poem was written during the tense period between Mussolini's declaration of his intention to annex Ethiopia and the 1935 invasion. Dodson has advanced beyond the enthusiasm of the call to arms and composed a solemn contemplation of the outcome of battle: in the face of the massive build-up of military equipment by the Italians, Dodson foresees the tragic outcome that awaits the Ethiopian fighters. Through its intertextual reliance on Shelley's "Ozymandias of Egypt" (1817), "Desert in Ethiopia" originates from a remote perspective that refuses every attribute of modernity. Here is Shelley's sonnet:

I met a traveller from an antique land
Who said:—Two vast and trunkless legs of stone
Stand in the desert. Near them on the sand,
Half sunk, a shatter'd visage lies, whose frown
And wrinkled lip and sneer of cold command
Tell that its sculptor well those passions read
Which yet survive, stamp'd on these lifeless things,
The hand that mock'd them and the heart that fed.
And on the pedestal these words appear:
"My name is Ozymandias, king of kings:
Look on my works, ye mighty, and despair!"
Nothing beside remains: round the decay
Of that colossal wreck, boundless and bare,
The lone and level sands stretch far away.

Dodson's sonnet irrevocably recalls Baxter's similar handling of the war, namely, the shifting of the modern crisis into the opposition of egotistic, oedipal (fascist) time and cosmic-natural time. By implication, Dodson interrogates Mussolini through the intertext; we cannot read his poem without thinking of the arrogant Italian dictator in terms of what remains of Shelley's pharaoh—"a shatter'd visage lies, whose frown / And wrinkled lip and sneer of cold command" that is "half sunk" in the sand—who was destroyed by cosmic forces in the inevitable course of events on the planetary scale of history. And fortuitously, Shelley's sonnet has the word *stretch* in its final line, bringing to mind the prophecy that 'Ethiopia shall again stretch forth her hands unto God." Dodson capitalizes on this Ethiopianist association by building up *stretch* into a metonymy and apostrophizing the desert. Thus, the desert is the reification of naturalistic reality: in the desert, human will is illusory. By invading Ethiopia, the Italians have abandoned the industrial-modern scale of dromomatic time for the reaches of infinity, where they are always already defeated, disintegrated, and nullified. Dodson's treatment of the theme of temporal conflict is rooted in a skepticism that he derived from Shelley. Jennifer Ann Wagner has described Shelley's revision of the conventional sonnet's relation to time: "In 'Ozymandias,' Shelley revises his view of the sonnet function, seeing it not so much as that which memorializes but more importantly as that which forces one to look forward, since the poem teaches us that history—the progression of time forward—will not allow one to monumentalize any single instance and indeed will itself mock the mouth or the hand that thinks so" (73). Skepticism insists on closure, whereas in Baxter's romantic Ethiopianism there is no means to admit a limiting component of realism. Dodson's contemplation of the modern situation allows him to see not the end of an era but the end of human time and the requisite extinction of humanity. Dodson's Spenglerian historiography demotes humanity to mites who cling to a "husk" (line 14).

Addressing Waring Cuney's "'Ozimandias'-like [*sic*] reflections" in Cuney's poem "Dust," DuPlessis observes that "the critique by African American writers of the notions, and location, of the 'civilized' is one response to the plethora of 'primitivisms' in Euro-American work. In the 'civilization' trope, African American writers try to criticize and reconsider the locus of the 'primitive' against dominant discourse. Gail Bederman has argued that the hegemonic 'discourse of civilization' was, at root, a white-supremacist, male-supremacist set of ideas" (*Genders* 130). Since Mussolini characterized Ethiopia as "an African country universally branded as a country without the slightest shadow of civilization" (Mussolini 1935), Dodson's "Desert in Ethiopia" may best be read as his response to the fascist dictator's aggressive and specific investment in the "civilization" trope. After the defeat of Ethiopia, the "civilization" trope was again invoked by fascist apologists: the

Italians saw their victory as a conquest that "[opened] the doors to work and Italian civilization" (*Il Piccolo*). By reducing the Earth to a "husk," a worthless outer covering, Dodson mocks the Italian claim of possessing and disseminating civilization:

> I know that peace must some day bleed for peace
> If stars in nights to come will shine again
> Upon this husk inhabited by men. (lines 12–14)

"Desert in Ethiopia," however, is an irregular sonnet, having only thirteen lines. Dodson's model, Shelley's "Ozymandias," is also an irregular sonnet (*ababacdcedefef*), and Wagner speaks of its "Chinese box structure," its "complex narrative structure," its "resistance to closure," and its "resistance to the monumentality of the visionary moment in the Wordsworth sonnet" (70). Wagner links these effects to the questioning of lyric subjectivity (71). The failure of formal soundness in Dodson's sonnet underscores his downcast, resigned handling of the conflict between the Italian invaders and the Ethiopian defenders, a conflict that was almost certain to end in disaster for the Ethiopians. For Dodson, a racial component is at work: so long as the world is driven by "fiendish lies" (line 8) about race, the very existence of mankind will be threatened.

Italian and Ethiopian accounts of the cost of the war differ greatly:

> Italian approximate estimation of Ethiopian losses are 40 to 50 thousand men in the Northern front and 15 to 20 thousand in the Southern front. Conversely, the Ethiopian government claimed that 275,000 officers and soldiers had been killed in the war and 78,500 patriots during the five years of Italian occupation. In addition Ethiopia claimed another 477,800 civilians had died as a direct result of the Italian invasion and the ensuing years of guerilla warfare. (Sbacchi 91)

Despite the scale of the conflict, the specific battles of the Italo-Ethiopian War are nearly absent in African American poetry. Ada S. Woolfolk's two quatrains on the fighting in "Via Crucis" (*Opportunity*, January 1936: 23) broaches the subject but nevertheless confines her treatment to the passion-lynching trope. In her poem, each Ethiopian soldier is an analogue of Christ who must lift his own cross as he marches to Calvary:

VIA CRUCIS

Caesar has come again. No other's eyes

Or bitter lips could be so proud. Unfurled,
The flags of war, with shadows stain the skies,
And trail a pall of death across the world.

In Ethiopia the war drums moan,
And bare feet march. Each soldier's panoply
Of war, a cross that he must lift—his own—
His marching road, the slope of Calvary.

The treatment of the fighting as a *passion* is more often developed around the iconic figure of Haile Selassie; the actual fighting has been replaced by the trope of the passion of Haile Selassie. As the Italians closed in during the final phase of the invasion, Selassie fled Ethiopia, ultimately relocating to Bath, England. Selassie's removal to Europe was controversial. Langston Hughes implied in his poem "Broadcast" that Selassie was a coward. Others recognized that without Selassie's presence on the world stage, there would have been no voice that could have spoken adequately to the European powers on behalf of Ethiopia's survival as a nation.

For African American poets who were interested in using the passion trope, the speech that Selassie delivered to the League of Nations in 1936 was a signal event of the Italo-Ethiopian War. (As Selassie was not a role model for Hughes and other social-realist poets, their work composes the opposite side of the debate and does not recognize the relevance of Selassie's passion.) P. J. White Jr.'s "Vestis Virumque Cano" (*Opportunity*, January 1936: 10) puts the passion-lynching trope in perspective, though White's sonnet, which was published months before Selassie's transfiguring speech, is mired in an abject treatment of the entire race-war theme. Published in the same month as Haywood's "Via Crucis," White's poem constructs the opposite pole of the nigger/Christ dyad; in White's treatment of Selassie, there can be no transcendence. The white American's response to the Ethiopian "potentate" is inevitably, "Now, who the hell let these damned niggers in?" (line 14). Subsequent poems on Selassie's speech by Marcus B. Christian ("Selassie at Geneva") and by Violet G. Haywood ("Selassie") were published in 1938 and in 1939, respectively, well after Selassie's speech. These poems contextualize the historical drama surrounding Selassie in terms of a romantic-subjective religious discourse. In Christian's sonnet, the failure of the League initiates the end of the world, and the concluding couplet proclaims, "As weaker nations vanish, one by one . . . / Blow, bugles! Armageddon has begun!" (lines 13–14). In Haywood's poem Selassie's speech is equated (at the expense of all historical detail) with Christ's betrayal in Gethsemane—"He walked into a garden, too" (line 1).

After eight months of fighting, the Italians were able to bring their muddled campaign to a victorious conclusion. On May 5, 1936, Italy occupied Addis Abba and a few days later annexed all of Ethiopia. This catastrophic event met with little response from African American poets, the most significant exception being Langston Hughes. Hughes's programmatic attitude toward world events demanded a poem, so he supplied one. Hughes's response was "Broadcast on Ethiopia," a forty-seven-line send-up of T. S. Eliot's *The Waste Land*. Hughes's poem parodies the modernist document-poem, though it also takes aim at Ezra Pound's poetic sequence on the First World War, "Hugh Selwyn Mauberley." Where Pound's poem laments—

> There died a myriad,
> And of the best, among them,
> For an old bitch gone in the teeth,
> For a botched civilization (lines 98–101)

Hughes answers,

> Mussolini,
> Grit your teeth!
> Civilization's gone to hell!
> Major Bowes, ring your bell! (lines 31–35)

Hughes's poem is an example of the revolutionary impact of radio on the culture of the thirties: "Radio broke down what MacLeish called 'the superstition of distance': 'the superstition that what is done beyond three thousand miles of water is not really done at all; . . . that violence and lies and murder on another continent are not violence and lies and murder'" (Stott 137). While radio may generally have consolidated the collective identity of African Americans toward a closer association with the Ethiopian underdogs, in "Broadcast" Hughes responded to the occupation of Ethiopia with an eccentric mixture of irony, comedy, and ambiguity that emotionally distanced the reader from the catastrophe:

BROADCAST ON ETHIOPIA

> The little fox is still.
> > The dogs of war have made their kill.
> > Addis Ababa
> > Across the headlines all year long.
> > Ethiopia—

Tragi-song for the news reels.
Haile
With his slaves, his dusky wiles,
His second-hand planes like a child's,
But he has no gas—so he cannot last.
Poor little joker with no poison gas!
Thus his people now may learn
How Il Duce makes butter from an empty churn
To butter the bread
(If bread there be)
Of civilization's misery.

MISTER CHRISTOPHER COLUMBUS

DJIBOUTI, French Somaliland, May 4 (AP)—Emperor Haile Selassie and imperial family, in flight from his crumbling empire, reached the sanctuary of French soil and a British destroyer today. . . .

HE USED RHYTHM FOR HIS COMPASS

Hunter, hunter, running, too—
Look what's after you:

PARIS, May 4 (UP)—COMMUNIST STOP FRANCE'S SWEEP LEFT.
Minister of Colonies Defeated. Rise From 10 to 85 Seats.

France ain't Italy!

No, but Italy's cheated
When *any* Minister anywhere's
Defeated by Communists.
Goddamn! I swear! Hitler,
Tear your hair! Mussolini,
Grit your teeth!
Civilization's gone to hell!
Major Bowes, ring your bell!

(Gong!)

Station XYZW broadcasting:
MISTER CHRISTOPHER COLOMBO

Just made a splendid kill.
The British Legation stands solid on its hill
The natives run wild in the streets.
The fox is still.

Addis Ababa
In headlines all year long.
Ethiopia—tragi-song.

Hughes's poem, effecting an aleatory methodology, places the thirties reader within the modern experience of tuning back and forth across a radio dial: this familiar yet relatively exciting and novel activity brings in news, music, and a talent contest. The randomness of the assembled texts is illusory, for the mediating consciousness of the speaker (in Eliotic terms, Hughes's Tiresias[17]) has determined that the *broadcast* is *on Ethiopia*. More importantly, the speaker makes partisan comments, bringing up the issue of Ethiopian slavery in the eighth line.[18] When in line 36 the speaker says, "Major Bowes, ring your bell!" telling the host of the "Original Amateur Hour" to expel "Civilization" from the talent contest, it is understood that the intermittent shows are devices that comment on world politics. The speaker has inserted the war into the broadcast and has then assumed the role of the voting public and ousted the failed performance of bourgeois civilization.

Some of the questions raised by "Broadcast on Ethiopia" may be resolved by noting that the poem's venue was *American Spectator* (July–August 1936), a left-wing publication. The appearance of "Broadcast" in such a publication not only separated the poem from Hughes's African American readership but also placed the poem before a readership that consisted of radical sophisticates who would be familiar with the poetry of Ezra Pound and T. S. Eliot. For such a readership, Eliot was in particular the sign of everything that was culturally and politically objectionable. A straw man for leftist critics, Eliot was associated with fascism, elitism, and the enervation of bourgeois capitalism.[19] Hughes's appropriation and parody of the Eliotic style before such a readership was a sure sign that he knew his approach would be read as a send-up of *The Waste Land*, one of the major texts opposed to leftist aesthetic production in the 1930s. Hughes has incorporated and transformed some of Eliot's major motifs, such as the dog motif:

There I saw one I knew, and stopped him, crying "Stetson!
"You were with me in the ships at Mylae!
"That corpse you planted last year in your garden,
"Has it begun to sprout? Will it bloom this year?

"Or has the sudden frost disturbed its bed?
"Oh keep the Dog far hence, that's friend to men,
"Or with his nails he'll dig it up again!
"You! Hypocrite lecteur!—mon semblable,—mon frère!"
(*The Waste Land* lines 69–76)

The dog in "Broadcast" is cut from a different cloth than Eliot's dreadfully burrowing dog. The fox/dog dyad of "The little fox is still. / The dogs of war have made their kill" (lines 1–2) plays on the association of the packs of hounds used to hunt foxes, and thereby the lines achieve an unavoidable association with class privilege, so that for Hughes the Ethiopian fox has been dispatched by the ruling class. In the fourteen lines that follow the opening metaphor—the fascist dogs have killed the little fox—Hughes exhibits little sympathy for either the Ethiopian populace or the routinely iconic Haile Selassie. The first line demotes the lion of Judah to a fox, and the ninth line reduces Selassie to a child; in the eleventh line, he is a "poor little joker," and in the news broadcast of lines 18–20, he is a refugee "in flight from his crumbling empire." Having dismissed Selassie from serious consideration, the speaker reveals himself to be a Marxist concerned with a world revolution that will treat the present governments of Europe just as the fascists have treated Ethiopia: "Hunter, hunter, running, too— / Look what's after you" (lines 22–23). Hughes directs his efforts toward delineating a class-based collective identity in which Haile Selassie has been assigned to the "them" side of the us/them dyad.

The topical thrust of Hughes's poem changes at the fifteenth line, "MISTER CHRISTOPHER COLUMBUS," where Hughes has inserted three lines from the Fats Waller song "Mr. Christopher Columbus."[20] A hit in 1935, the comic jazz song would have been familiar to readers. Hughes's inclusion of a jazz lyric is an echo and parody of the improbable jazz lyric in *The Waste Land*:

O O O O that Shakespeherian Rag—
It's so elegant
So intelligent (lines 128–30)

The use of Waller's cartoonish song in a poem addressed to a major event in Western history erases a tragic interpretation of the war. Hughes's thesis is that only the capitalist-communist class war was real, so the Italian–Ethiopian race war was not to be taken seriously by revolutionaries. Through his reference to the newsreels (line 6)—newsreels were shown in newsreel houses all over Manhattan—Hughes's poem dismisses the war as profit-driven. By inference, sensationalized news was but one more form of entertainment and escape used by the masses during the Great Depression. Thus, he mocks the masses and the "news"—"Tragi-song for the news reels." Waller's complex song anarchically revises the historical discovery of the Americas: despite Waller's lyrics, Columbus did employ the compass on his voyages. Waller's song is itself a surrealistic heteroglossia in which Waller assumes a rapid succession of disparate personae: the American common man, the mock-authoritative academic, the Negro stereotype, and the aesthete. Layered on these layers is yet another level of wordplay, so that Waller declares the world "roundo" and their condition "soundo," a device that Hughes may have used to further connect Eliot's poem (with its "OOO") to his. Despite the apparent heteroglossia of Hughes's broadcast and its kaleidoscopic intertexts, the "Broadcast" is centered on the manifest occurrence of subjectivity, when the "I" who asserts that "Italy's cheated / when *any* minister anywhere's / Defeated by Communists. / Goddamn! I swear!" (lines 27–30) raises its voice to shout down the counterthesis, "France ain't Italy!" (line 26). The recorded version of Waller's song concludes with a sham history lesson recited in a stilted manner ("In the year 1492 / Columbus sailed the ocean blue"), and a final phrase is delivered as an ironically admonitory "What'd I say?" It was customary for Waller to close a recorded song by inserting a non sequitur, such as "One never knows do one?" at the end of "Your Feets Too Big." This signature device framed the completed song in a larger and consistent persona that was more authentic than the succession of voices that were assembled throughout his songs. In this way Waller asserted a final, authoritative, personal identity over all of his subvoices. With his "I swear" (line 30), Hughes's Marxist-revolutionary speaker, similarly, inserts his voice over and above the discourse network of the radio and "enthrone[s] the reflexive individual as the principal operator in history and human consciousness as the principal originator of messages" (Winthrop-Young 401). Despite the politics aired in the poem, Hughes's agitation-propaganda ultimately gives way to a speaker situated in bourgeois subjectivity.

With Selassie's flight from Ethiopia, "Broadcast" changes from a parody of high-modernist poetry to a Marxist comedy in which Hughes seeks to dismiss Selassie, Hitler, and Mussolini as a "tragi-song" (line 43), last season's hit song that no longer elicits emotions from the listener. Hughes's response to the end of the Italo-Ethiopian War did not address the war's human cost, nor did it take into account the effects of the war in destabilizing the League of Nations and the dire consequences for the world order. Though he generally avoided sentimentalizing Ethiopia and Haile Selassie, Hughes gave into this temptation in "Broadcast," a poem that propagandizes for inhumane regimes, so that Hughes produces a hollow, sentimental treatment of the technological world of mass communication, forcing the poem to confirm his belief in an inevitable "SWEEP LEFT" (line 24).

J. Harvey L. Baxter, like other poets writing on the Italo-Ethiopian War (with the exception of Hughes) resolved the problems raised by the uneven battles, the defeat of the Ethiopian army, and Italy's conquest of Ethiopia by iconizing Haile Selassie. Selassie's speech before the League of Nations came, rather as a last resort, to fulfill the meaning of the enigmatic phrase that stood prophetically at the center of African American Ethiopianism— "Ethiopia shall soon stretch forth her hands unto God" (*KJV* Psalms 68:31). In January 1936, many months before Selassie's speech, Rufus Gibson published his thirty-eight line poem "The Voice of Ethiopia" in *The Crisis*. The poem concludes,

> Long since have ravenous hordes despoiled our land,
> Long centuries did they our trust betray.
> *Now Ethiopia must stretch forth her hand*
> First unto God for refuge and for strength,
> That we may now our Native land reclaim
> And drive usurpers from its breadth and length.
> O sons and daughters mine, let not in shame
> Men rise to speak of Ethiopia's name. (lines 31–38; emphasis added)

Gibson's sonnet separates the emancipation of Ethiopia and the men rising to speak. However, the hurried and unrealistic compression of the military reclamation in two lines (lines 11–12) deemphasizes the war of liberation and subordinates fighting to speaking Ethiopia's name in the concluding couplet. This makes the speech-act, which is given emphasis by its place in the concluding line, synonymous with Ethiopia's emancipatory agency; Gibson seems to prepare the way for Baxter's Selassie-centered treatment of the Ethiopian crisis. In "Oh, Hang Your Heads, A Voice Accusing Cries," Baxter takes on the unique technical difficulties of reducing Selassie's climactic speech to the League of Nations to the thematic and formal limitations of an English sonnet—compressing nearly 4,000 words into 104 words. This literary exercise combines the documentary impulse with the need to enshrine and sublimate what was for many African Americans the emperor's most significant act—a redemptive speech-act (literally and figuratively). Baxter seeks to substitute Selassie's address to the League of Nations for victory on the battlefield. The sonnet thus attempts to transform the military defeat of the Ethiopians into the emperor's moral victory over Italy and the League. As we might expect, Baxter's romantic-documentary treatment of Selassie's contradicts what purported to be factual accounts of the event. *Time Maga-zine* described Selassie as "the bird-like little Ethiopian" who spoke while "Italian journalists in the press gallery . . . bellowed jeers and curses at the Emperor, screamed 'Viva Il Duce!'" (*Time Europe*, July 13, 1936).

Baxter's sonnet bypasses the subject of Italy's military atrocities, a sub-ject so near the heart of Selassie's speech that *Time* magazine was compelled to quote Selassie's harrowing account of Italian military tactics: "Groups of nine, 15 or 18 aircraft followed one another so that the fog issuing from them formed a continuous sheet. It was thus that, as from the end of January 1936, soldiers, women, children, cattle, rivers, lakes and pastures were drenched continually with this deadly rain. In order to kill off systematically all living creatures and in order more surely to poison the waters and pastures, the Italian command made its aircraft pass over and over again" (*Time Europe*, July 13, 1936). As the *Time* article indicated, Selassie's speech was simultane-ously factual and noble. Nothing of this tenor is projected by Baxter's sonnet, which narrates the event through exaggerated histrionics, as though it were a scene dramatized by Shakespeare; indeed, line 6—"And rid your ghastly togas of the stain"—may be interpreted as an allusion to the assassination in *Julius Caesar*. Baxter's poetic line is pseudo-Shakespearean pastiche: while *stain* and *ghastly* belong to the Shakespearean lexicon (47 and 8 usages, respectively, in Shakespeare's plays), in Shakespeare there are *robes* but no *togas*. Certainly, Baxter's lines "a voice accusing cries, /And points a finger shaking in your face" (lines 1–2) does not describe Selassie's actual speech; journalists believed that the emperor appeared to be "in total control and thus contempt and not anger was the emotion he felt" (Schwab 70–71).

Selassie's speech was also marked by factors of negative identity, for the Italian journalists (according to Selassie's autobiography) "started to whistle continuously with the intention of obstructing Our speech and rendering it inaudible" (Schwab 71). Moreover, the speech itself was delivered in an unknown language: "Ethiopia's Emperor read his speech in Amharic, a dig-nified language in which the syllables telescope into each other so closely that for minutes at a time His Majesty seemed to be uttering one enormous word" (*Time Europe*). Therefore, it is not surprising that the subtext of Bax-ter's sonnet is freighted with the trope of the passion-lynching,[21] which was already a familiar construct for the African American interpretation of the Italo-Ethiopian War. In Baxter's sonnet the lynching motif is announced by associating Selassie with Christ ("King of Kings"), by "oh hang" (line 1), and by the multiple readings that may be derived from "Don the ashy sackcloth, raid the hair" (line 5), with its implicit theme of death and mourning[22] and with its lexicon of lynching (*ash, hang,* and *raid*).

OH, HANG YOUR HEADS, A VOICE ACCUSING CRIES
(A KING OF KINGS BEFORE THE LEAGUE)

Oh, hang your heads, a voice accusing cries,
And points a finger shaking in your face.
Bewails of sickly treachery and lies,
Of noble oaths that welter in disgrace.
Don the ashy sackcloth, raid the hair
And rid your ghastly togas of the stain;
Albeit that your proffered words were fair,
Time has revealed your pompous speech was vain.
I did not ask for bounties of your blood,
Demand your sons for sacrifice supreme,
Yet I was led, believing that you would
Be succor and a shield to the extreme.
Bereft of friends, by evil foes beset,—
"God will remember, time will not forget."

While much of the sonnet is a paraphrase of Selassie's speech, Baxter has consistently shifted the meanings of the original words. The first seven lines have little to do with Selassie's original text, while the sestet paraphrases some of the words of the speech: "Albeit that your proffered words were fair, / Time has revealed your pompous speech, was vain" (lines 7–8) paraphrases Selassie's assertion that "all this was in vain: the arbitrators, two of whom were Italian officials, were forced to recognize unanimously that in the Walwal incident, as in the subsequent incidents, no international responsibility was to be attributed to Ethiopia" (Selassie "Appeal"). The weakened "I" that asserts itself in the sestet of "Oh, Hang Your Heads" characterizes Selassie's actions negatively—"I did not ask" (line 9)—and passively—"Yet I was led" (line 11), yet in the "Appeal" there is no hint of such a tendency toward self-cancellation:

> The Ethiopian Government never expected other Governments to shed their soldiers' blood to defend the Covenant when their own immediately personal interests were not at stake. Ethiopian warriors asked only for means to defend themselves. On many occasions I have asked for financial assistance for the purchase of arms. That assistance has been constantly refused me. What, then, in practice, is the meaning of Article 16 of the Covenant and of collective security? (Selassie "Appeal")

In "Oh, Hang Your Heads" the subject position differs between the octave and the sestet. The "Appeal" begins "I, Haile Selassie I, Emperor of

Ethiopia, am here today to claim that justice which is due to my people, and the assistance promised to it eight months ago, when fifty nations asserted that aggression had been committed in violation of international treaties." Why, then, has Baxter suppressed the first person in the octave in favor of a version of Selassie who cannot claim himself to be an "I" and must refer to his own disassociated *voice* and *finger* instead of enunciating himself as an "I," as he did in the "Appeal"? Baxter implies that Selassie's subject position as the racialized abject-Other has been conflated with an already assassinated Julius Caesar; although Baxter's version of Selassie delivers a funeral oration like Antony, he is also speaking from the grave about himself. For Baxter, Selassie is in effect a political corpse. As Kristeva observes, "The corpse, seen without God and outside of science, is the utmost of abjection. It is death infecting life. Abject." (1982 4). Indeed, in a reversal of subject and object, Baxter's Selassie invokes God in the last line of the sonnet and thereby confirms his political abjection (though the real Selassie did not invoke God in the "Appeal"). As may be seen in many other poems in the African American antilynching discourse, Baxter has consigned his victim, Selassie, to the consolation of eternal life in God's kingdom. Selassie presented himself to the League of Nations as an imperial figure and was able to maintain that identity even though his speech accomplished nothing directly. When Baxter at last allows Selassie to assert himself as "I" in the ninth and eleventh lines, Selassie is reduced to a figure separated from blues subjectivity only by the pseudo-Shakespearean cast of his lament—"Bereft of friends, by evil foes beset" (line 13)—which is not far from "My friends don't see me, no, they just pass me by, / I wouldn't mind it so much, but they hold their heads so high" (Oliver Paul 81).

The concluding line of the sonnet, "God will remember, time will not forget," is Baxter's stylistically deflated rendition of Selassie's "God and history will remember your judgment ("Appeal"). However, this was not the conclusion of Selassie's speech but only the end of the ninth section of his ten-part speech. Baxter surrenders the opportunity to depict the sense of defiant expectation that characterized the portentous conclusion of Selassie's "Appeal": "Representatives of the World I have come to Geneva to discharge in your midst the most painful of the duties of the head of a State. What reply shall I have to take back to my people?"

Race war is a topic distant from the twenty-first century. Yet the prospect of race war was an inescapable component of African American culture during the thirties. One factor that brought race war to wide attention in the thirties was the activity of George S. Schuyler, America's best-known black journalist. Schuyler was an iconoclastic social critic and a pioneering, prolific, and innovative genre writer who wrote fearlessly about the issues of his day. One such topic was Italy's invasion of Ethiopia. Outraged by the Fascists' takeover of the ancient, independent African kingdom and believing that African Americans should voice their objections and offer assistance to Ethiopia, Schuyler turned to fiction to arouse his public. Schuyler's serialized novels were published in the *Pittsburgh Courier,* a widely distributed publication that provided Schuyler's writings (and the idea of race war) a considerable audience of African American readers. In fact, while Schuyler was writing his story on the Italo-Ethiopian War, he lived in Mississippi, where he worked to increase the *Courier's* circulation. Printed as weekly serials, "Black Internationale" appeared in the *Courier* from November 1936 to July 1937, and "Black Empire" ran from October 1937 to April 1938. Reviews of Schuyler's serials and accounts of his career do not accurately describe these works. Most accounts are restricted to reporting that the serials narrate the exploits of the Black Internationale, a radical African American group equipped with scientific superweapons and led by a charismatic sociopath, Doctor Belsidus, who succeeds in creating an independent nation on the African continent. What is routinely omitted is that Belsidus was determined to exterminate the white race, and he would have ethnically cleansed the planet of the white race had his key agents been more fanatical. Doctor Belsidus did eradicate white people from the African continent.

Schuyler also published two other serials in the *Courier*—"Ethiopian Murder Mystery," set in Harlem and concerning the murder of an Ethiopian prince, and "Revolt in Ethiopia," concerning a plot to arm the Ethiopian fighters. In these fictions Schuyler sought to dispel commonly held misconceptions about Africa and the relationship of African Americans to Africans.

I have brought Schuyler into the discussion of Baxter's sonnets because I feel that such a comparison assists in the evaluation of Baxter's treatment of the Italo-Ethiopian War. It is clear that Schuyler chose serialized science fiction and detective fiction in order to communicate serious ideas to the African American populace during a time of crisis. Schuyler's Ethiopian serials are pulp fiction with no literary polish or psychological complexity; they are in the final analysis propaganda disguised as entertainments. While it is not at first obvious that there is a connection between Baxter's poems on Ethiopia and Schuyler's serialized stories, the suitability of Baxter's sonnets is put into perspective by Schuyler's success with popular forms. It is doubtful that Baxter would have done better in attempting to influence African Americans on behalf of Ethiopia with modernist-experimental, documentary-montage poems. It is also arguable that Baxter's inaccurate depiction of an emotional Haile Selassie (particularly, in his concluding sonnet) was a similarly apt choice. In an ideal world, Baxter would have retained Haile Selassie's composure in his rendering of the Emperor, but in communicating with African Americans in the thirties, such a strategy would no doubt have caused his poem to miss its mark. Baxter's accusatory posture carried the requisite emotional tenor that allowed his poems to reach his black audience. Like Schuyler's pulp serials, the sonnet was not culturally threatening to the African American reader,[23] and Baxter's familiar tone of passionate affront was in the range of attitudes that are commonly heard in African American sermons. As I have shown above, it is also an attitude commonly encountered in the blues.

During the Depression, African Americans gained an increased sense of participation in the creation of national identity even though there was at every level of American life a united effort to exclude them. As Alexander M. Bain has shown, Schuyler placed his prescient and corrective analysis of the ultimate meaning of the Italian fascist adventure in Africa at the disposal of his wide African American readership:

> In his July 1935 "Views and Reviews" column Schuyler asks *Courier* readers to balance the urge to "do or die for dear old Ethiopia" against the imperative to organize at home. "As an old soldier," Schuyler opines, "I would certainly like to participate in such an adventure and press a machine-gun trigger on the Italian hordes as they toiled over the Ethiopian terrain. . . . But it is all I can do to meet the exactions of the landlord, the butcher, the groceryman, the laundryman, the public utilities . . . and the other parasites that feed upon me." . . . Regardless of their identification with "dear old Ethiopia," Schuyler warns his readers that fantasy can only be validated through some correlation to meeting the demands of the home front. . . . But he ends the column by proclaiming that "the Ethiopian-Italian embroglio" [*sic*] will wreak worldwide violence on the "parasites," and that he is "frankly tickled at the prospect. All the great exploiting powers of the world who are squeezing and exploiting the colored brethren in Africa, Asia and America stand to lose everything by another world war." (950)

As the above passage demonstrates, Schuyler had an awareness of both domestic and international realities, which he effectively related to the troubles of the present and to the looming dangers of the future. In contrast with Schuyler's realistic grasp of the crisis as battle, poverty, and oppression, African American poets retained their interest in the person of Haile Selassie. Marcus Christian's sonnet "Selassie at Geneva," published in *Opportunity* in June of 1938, maintains the centrality of Selassie's passion until it reaches the thirteenth line, where its subject is finally made clear—the annexation of Austria by Germany in March of 1938.

SELASSIE AT GENEVA

They could have stayed the iron hand of might

And fought for right down to the earth's last man,
But louder voices brayed into the night,
So jackals ended what the League began.
Now suave-voiced diplomats drone on and on;
Geneva's air is rife with fear and hate,
While at the council-table fights alone
The fallen ruler of a member State.
Pile lies upon wrongs, bring the curtains down
Upon the closing scene of this last act;
The King of Kings now yields his ancient crown
To those who signed the Non-Aggression Pact,
As weaker nations vanish, one by one . . .
Blow, bugles! Armageddon has begun!

Here the documentary tendency has entered only to the degree that references to "member State" and the "Non-Aggression Pact" situate the poem as a recapitulation of Selassie's 1936 speech in Geneva. In Schuyler's terms, the sonnet is immersed in *fantasy:* there is biblical imagery ("iron hand," "jackals," "King of Kings," and "Armageddon"), dramatic imagery ("bring the curtains down / Upon the closing scene of this last act"), and unevenly applied quasi-Shakespearean rhetoric ("And fought for right down to the earth's last man"). Christian's sonnet obsessively connects the failure of nerve by the European powers during the Ethiopian crisis to the events that in 1938 were leading to world war. However, as compelling as the tragic-subjective reading of world history was for Christian and other Ethiopianists, the phase of identification with a black imperial subjectivity did open African Americans to new social identities invested with agency and autonomy that prepared the way for an even wider participation in the new social conditions that were soon to follow.

Schuyler was a complex and contradictory figure: he demanded much from his audience, while at the same time he disparaged not only African Americans but also the human race.[24] Schuyler hoped to mobilize his readers to directly assist the Ethiopian cause, a project that was far too difficult to be undertaken in the face of the United States government and the disorganization of African American institutions. There were too many intervening levels of myth, taboo, fear, and trauma that needed to be cleared away for African Americans to grapple with the distant, exotic, and horrifying war that simultaneously energized and enervated. What the Italo-Ethiopian War did, however, was bring to the attention of African Americans the dangerous nature of the modern world with its aggressive global fixations on race, a problem that had previously presented only intimate and local connotations.

Michael Kimmel observes that "the project of the self—of an identity that one 'works on' for one's entire life—is itself the cornerstone of modernity" (x). Thus, as African Americans were brought into the modernizing mainstream by travel, education, journalism, literature, film, and above all radio, individually and socially they rapidly evolved new and sophisticated psychological faculties. As I have stated above, "the preparation for war, is the beginning of the modern industrial economy" (Virilio). For African Americans, it was the beginning of a new form of subjectivity—one that was less self-alienated, more fluid, and more transparent. Pauli Murray described this new understanding of the participatory African American self in "Until the Final Man" in 1940:

> Oh, brown brothers, freedom is but to stand
> Erect from earth like stalwart trees
> That rear defiant heads against the wrath of storms,
> Roots wed with earth, deep-dwelling;
> To grow independently as leaves,
> Each from its own bough,
> Absorbing sunlight to itself;
> To rise in formless mists,
> All heaven to take shape in,
> And to return distinct and separate as raindrops;
> To know the vast equality of sands upon the shore,
> To each in time the wave returning. (lines 18–29)

Haunted by the threat of race war through the Depression, African Americans eventually recognized the nature of the even more complex and perilous actualities that faced them at the end of the decade, a situation given testimony by the militarized images on the covers of *The Crisis* throughout 1940 and by the caption that queried in December 1940—"When Do *We* Fly?" (emphasis in original). The NAACP organized a letter-writing campaign (*The Crisis*, November 1940, 357) to encourage African Americans to send letters to the president, to generals Marshall and Abrams, and to the commissioners in charge of hiring at defense plants. When the United States finally entered World War II, labor leader A. Philip Randolph threatened to organize a march on Washington to protest job discrimination in the military and other defense-related activities. In response, President Roosevelt issued Executive Order 8802, stating that all persons, regardless of race, creed, color, or national origin, would be allowed to participate fully in the defense of the United States.

A Concluding Note

The fluid nature of literary recovery (tied as it is to reception, reputation, publishing, prizes, cultural turns, and paradigm shifts) was reified for me recently when a postal clerk affixed a sixty-one-cent Richard Wright 2009 commemorative stamp to my envelope. Previously, the reconstruction of Robert Johnson's identity by the United States Postal Service had been inherent in the removal of the cigarette from a 1938 photobooth portrait of the great blues singer; the twenty-nine-cent Robert Johnson commemorative stamp of 1994 showed no cigarette, thereby shifting the discourse of the blues from despair, nihilism, hedonism, and intersubjective violence to a discourse of uplift—a discourse that romanticizes genius and endorses racial inclusion. In the case of Wright, it is the existence of the stamp itself that signals his rehabilitation, commodification, and neutralization. The United States Postal Service suggests that "Richard Wright used his pen to battle racism" (M. Jones, "Postal Service"). This rhetoric abolishes the systemic structure of the oppressions that Wright suffered and wrote about; the "abstract and disembodied racism" that Wright is said to have confronted is (to cite one example) disconnected from the lynch mobs and from the federal government that never passed an antilynching law. In explaining why I was surprised by the Richard Wright Stamp, I related to the clerk that Wright had been a member of the Communist Party, that he had lived for many years as an expatriate in France, and that some black intellectuals have suggested that he was murdered by the Central Intelligence Agency. In 1947, an expatriate Wright stated in an interview that "to be American in the United States means to be white, protestant, and very rich. This excludes almost entirely black people and anyone else who can be easily identified" (quoted in Tuhkanen 3). Richard Wright, the surrealist revolutionary poet, thus anchors the reclaiming discourse in extremes of thought, action, and emotion that characterized the black life-world (*Lebenswelt*) of the 1930s. Wright's example suggests what must be done constantly to reveal the other poets who have disappeared into contemporary social contexts that restrict and narrow the terms of their art.

Though this study examines black poetry through the crises of economic collapse, racial oppression, and race war, these catastrophes by no means exhaust the categorical horrors of the black life-world of the 1930s. Adam Gussow argues that the terrors of the lynching campaign that ran from the 1890s into the 1930s had a determining influence on black American culture—though subvocally, where lynching is the haunting, repressed contents of the blues: "Nor is the 'haunting' sound of early Mississippi blues merely [W. C.] Handy's unconscious projection of his own unresolved psychic conflicts onto unremarkable folk material. There is every reason to think that the 'agonizing strain' he describes may have been just that: the musical expression of a regionally inflected black social unconscious under grievous pressure" (73–74). An earlier version of this study contained a long chapter on the black antilynching poetry of the 1930s. There I concluded that the subject positions in the antilynching discourse had developed from first being centered on powerless witnesses (speaking trees), to being centered on a variety of victims (the lynched people and subsequently their children, who first are mute but then speak), and finally centering on militant children. Those imaginary politically engaged children were projections into the future. The discursive innovation in the black antilynching poetry of the 1930s ultimately positioned the child as a racial leader—a militant spokesperson and activist.

The culmination of the poetic antilynching discourse that centers on the motif of the black child—which used the black child so effectively that it was also the culmination of the poetic antilynching discourse—came in Esther Popel's "Flag Salute," published in *The Crisis* in 1934, 1936, 1938, and on the cover in 1940. Popel, a schoolteacher in Washington, D.C., was a minor figure in the Harlem Renaissance and was one of the poets characterized by Alain Locke as being "concerned with 'romantic escapes'" (Redmond 223), Popel is not mentioned in Eugene Redmond's *Drumvoices*, which was a critical historical account of African American poetry up until the 1970s. Though Popel did publish what can be described as "romantic" poems in journals during the 1930s, she was one of the many black poets writing in the 1930s who at times embraced social realism. The "new realist"/"romantic" rubric that left-leaning critics employed in the 1930s (and again in the 1970s, when critics in the black arts movement recovered their forerunners' work) did not prevent the so-called new realist poets from writing in the romantic mode, and it did not concede recognition when the so-called romantic poets wrote in the realist mode: to be ordained a "romantic" meant being cut off from serious consideration by the leading critics.

Popel's "Flag Salute" operates at the intersection of three *objective* texts that form a *meta-objective* text, endowing the poem with an unassailable moral judgment. "Flag Salute" anticipated what Gunnar Myrdal later defined as the American dilemma, the injustices that fly in the face of America's founding principles. In the poem, the flag salute indicts the report of the lynching. That Popel arrives at this effect through the deconstructive manipulation of texts by Negro students is the ultimate protest of racial injustice.

FLAG SALUTE

(Note: In a classroom in a Negro school a pupil gave as his news topic during the opening exercises of the morning, a report of the Princess Anne lynching of Oct. 18, 1933. A brief discussion of the facts of the case followed, after which the student in charge gave this direction: Pupils, rise, and give the flag salute! They did so without hesitation!)

"I PLEDGE ALLEGIANCE TO THE FLAG"—

They dragged him naked
Through the muddy streets,
A feeble-minded black boy!
And the charge? Supposed assault
Upon an aged woman!
"Of the United States of America"—
One mile they dragged him
Like a sack of meal,
A rope around his neck,
A bloody ear
Left dangling by the patriotic hand
Of Nordic youth! (A boy of seventeen!)
"And to the Republic for which it stands"—
And then they hanged his body to a tree
Below the window of the county judge
Whose pleadings for the battered human flesh
Were stifled by the brutish, raucous howls
Of men, and boys, and women with their babes,
Brought out to see the bloody spectacle

Of murder in the style of '33!
(Three thousand strong, they were!)
"One nation, Indivisible"—
To make the tale complete
They built a fire—
What matters that the stuff they burned
Was flesh—and bone—and hair—
And reeking gasoline!
"With Liberty—and Justice"—
They cut the rope in bits
And passed them out,
For souvenirs, among the men and boys!
The teeth no doubt, on golden chains
Will hang
About the favored necks of sweethearts, wives
And daughter, mother, sisters, babies, too!
"For All!"

Popel's "Flag Salute" framed a viable poetic response to lynching. Popel's poem is unique in the way that it presents a dissenting voice, for much of the antilynching poetry of the 1930s was protest poetry that did not rise above obligatory conceptions. At the same time, perhaps unavoidably, the poem was effective enough to stir up opposition to itself. The original publication in 1934 came in an issue dedicated to the theme of higher education. The issue promised news of the 1934 college graduates. The cover featured an illustration in the social realist style. It portrayed two oversized figures, one in chains with his arms around proportionally smaller figures (a laborer, a farmer, and a scrubwoman), while the second oversized figure holds a diploma, wears a mortarboard, and soars above two figures who watch and rejoice. Below the picture was a headline by Langston Hughes: "Cowards from the Colleges." Popel's poem appeared in the right-hand column of a complex page, which showed a picture of a crowd across the bottom—NAACP in Oklahoma City, Okla., June 27—July 1, 1934. The left-hand column contained a news story about recent NAACP events and "Persistent Quest," a sonnet by C. Faye Bennett. When the poem reappeared in May of 1936, it ran beneath a heading that proclaimed "School Officials Dislike This." The editor's note that followed stated that the poem was one of the items judged "objectionable" by a committee that reported to the Board of Education. The committee recommended against approving *The Crisis* for use in the District of Columbia's schools. The poem was printed below the headline and divided into two columns. The remainder of the page was occupied by the end of "'Objectionable Matter' in *The Crisis*," a story that began on the previous page. Apparently, the controversy continued, for the May 1938 issue carried as one of its headlines "*The Crisis* 'Not Approved,' A Ruling by the Board of Education in Washington, D.C." The end of the news story poses the question "of how a magazine could be published in the United States of America in the interest of Negroes and not be critical of the white race" ("*The Crisis* Is Not Approved"). The poem ran again in November of 1940, this time on the cover of the issue. The poem's visual appearance was striking. It appeared within a single-line border beneath the masthead, and the type size of the title was nearly as large as the type size of the magazine's name. The cover of the issue immediately preceding the number that featured Popel's poem had showed black men manning an anti-aircraft cannon, so the cover bearing a poem beneath the masthead of *The Crisis* would have seemed at once restrained and ominous. This time, Popel and the editors revised the poem's introductory note:

> (Note: In these days when armies are marching and there is much talk of loyalty and democracy on all fronts in America, it is being said that the strongest defense of democracy lies in the unity of all groups in the nation and a conviction that each has a stake in a democratic government. When it was announced in Washington on October 9, almost simultaneously, that the federal anti-lynching bill had been killed in the Senate and that Negro Americans would be segregated and discriminated against in the U. S. armed forces, THE CRISIS received several requests to reprint this poem. It was written after a lynching which occurred in Princess Anne, Maryland, October 18, 1933.)

The note had been revised so that it was politically and socially relevant to the threat of war and the failure of the government to address the continuing fact of racial violence. This relevance came at the expense of poetic meaning, for the crucial description of the school scene has been omitted. Given the urgency of the events described in the new note, it is possible to forgive the editors of *The Crisis* for their insensitivity to the text, but it must be pointed out that as it appeared in 1940, despite the grand appearance that it made on the cover, the poem had been rendered incoherent. Nevertheless, Esther Popel's disturbing poem "Flag Salute" was used to tie the continuation of racial terrorism to the promise that the African American would be expected to play a role in the imminent world war. The editor's note in the 1940 version of "Flag Salute" indicated that the poem was printed because of urgings from the readership. The note tangibly indicates that poetry in this vein was an important component of the black culture of the decade and that for many people it gave expression to crucial insights, feelings, and ideas that otherwise might have been lost to trauma, incoherence, and inarticulacy. Thus, far from being weak and irrelevant, in the 1930s poetry was a vital component of the complex and multifaceted African American struggle for identity, equality, and purpose.

In the second chapter, I have theorized that the sonnets written by black poets in the 1930s can be viewed as a metatext that frames the identity-work through which the poets constructed the subject positions that helped African Americans to adjust to the conditions of modernity, experimentally attuning their self-concepts to the performances of race. The aspirational modernity illuminated by reading the black poetry of the 1930s broached unanticipated realms. When Owen Dodson x-rayed Langston Hughes's mediational persona of the radical-left race man, he did so through Oswald Spengler's deduction that history was out of human control. With history no longer the progress-driven comic opera of Marxism or the equally comic opera of technological capitalism, Dodson posed the question of the meaning of race for the black man. These themes were further amplified by the Spengler-inflected poems of Victor Welborn Jenkins and Marcus Christian. In essence what emerges above all is what Gagnier calls "the tension between social role and desire that differentiates one's identity from one's self" (228). This theme emerges in the Harlem Renaissance and is never put to rest. As Eugene Holmes recognized, "The Negro has been imbued with the American Dream" (245). However, modernity demonstrates two phases. In one phase there is the emancipatory progress of speed, technology, urbanity, and mass communication over superstition, parochialism, and isolation; this allows for the admission of individuality, originality, genius, and masterpieces. On the other hand, there is in modernity the repressive phase of collectivity, productivity, public art, impersonality, and mechanical reproduction. When accounts are written about a poet of the second phase, like Frank Marshall Davis, the poet is described as an engaged social realist. However, a comprehensive view shows that there is a plurality of subject positions in play as expressed by the various modes of Davis's poetry, modes such as social realism, jazz poetry, social satire, and love poetry. Though it may be an overstatement to compare Davis's poetry with Orwell's *Nineteen Eighty-Four*, I cannot help but think of how the novel's totalitarian government used "newspeak" to control the characters' thoughts and rewrite history.

Various observers during the thirties claimed that a crucial body of black poetry written during a time of severe social and cultural trial did not exist or did not have substantive worth. When critics addressed these poems, they usually misrepresented the work through an impoverished selection of texts. My investigation is provisional and points the way to more detailed investigations. In an early phase of my research, I assembled a database of 563 poems published in black journals in the 1930s. By using this database, I was able to address in a preliminary manner some questions that otherwise would not have come up. I was mainly concerned with previous conceptions of the poetry of the 1930s. Future work could bring about new insights into the black poetry of the 1930s. However, the importance of the sonnet in the black poetry of the 1930s did not become apparent through the database, which was not set up to deal with form. This suggests that the data mining and computational linguistics used by Franco Moretti may be used with large groups of poems to address new kinds of questions. Had I been aware of methods like Moretti's, my investigation may have taken that direction, but I was not able to use my database beyond making concordances and counting motifs. Quantitative information may be useful in breaking down the habitual assumptions that have been made regarding African American poetry—from the start an insufficiently studied body of texts.

Appendix

POEMS

OWEN DODSON

NEGRO HISTORY: A SONNET SEQUENCE

ON THE SLAVE SHIP

We must not pray that death which now has passed
Too many times for fear will sleep again,
Or swim to other galleys till the last
Black exile dies or smites these pallid men,
Oh tears that fall like splinters from the stars
We would dry up your source, for salty tears
Will never wear away these iron bars
Or drown the ominous pounding of our fears.
Oh groaning men whose bodies sweat in pain,
Oh women with your infants on your breasts
Who chant your agonizing songs, the rain
Will come and wash these rancid nests,
The rain will come, be silent, we must wait
For time to change the destinies of fate.

PAST AND FUTURE

"You must not damn the future or the past;
That death will come in season and delay
The disillusion of this life (the last

Slow breath will come to cleanse the clay)
You know, yet knowing beat your dusky wings
And curse the men who made your blackness pain,
And chant your agonizing hymn that brings
An ointment in its notes to wash your stain."
This worshipper of dying is like a breath
Of hopeless resignation at the end
Of flaming autumn—forecasting death,
Blotting out the hope that we will mend
The patches of these transitory years
With swords, with hate, in spite of frequent tears.

POST EMANCIPATION

Rescind the hope that we may walk again
Without the heavy chains of servitude
That bind our flesh to soil and heartless men
Who mould our lives to fit each fickle mood.
Rescind the hope although it was decreed
That freedom would be ours to wear and keep
For centuries, aye, for eons till the seed
Of freedom died or earth was rocked to sleep.
The parchment that declared that we were free
Is now collecting dust in some dark spot,
Despite the promise and the certainty
We thought its words would give, but gave them not.
Distrust all words that echo to the stars
When earth is bound with unrelenting bars.

HARLEM

Harlem—deep, dark flower of the west
With girls for hollow stamens ribbed with joys,
Reject the easy sun, be wary lest
It shrivel up the pollen of your boys.
Together you must grow your flowers anew,
Not asking whose the gain or whose the gold;
Together you must silence winds that blew
Your fragrant copper petals to be sold
And not for beauty's dress or beauty's walls.
Remember that the ex-ray of the years

Reveals the rotting of the shallow halls
Within the petal's veins, reveals the fears
The copper must be conscious of
If they would hold their life. Grow strong or starve.

WELBORN VICTOR JENKINS

Almost nothing is known about Welborn Victor Jenkins (1879–?), a resident of Atlanta, Georgia. Aside from his volume of poems *Trumpet in the New Moon* (1934), his books are *The "Incident" at Monroe: A Requiem for the Victims of July 25th, 1944* (1948), a long Whitmanian protest poem; *We Also Serve: (Apologies to O. Henry)* (1920), a collection of short stories; and an essay, "Who Are the Thespians?" (ND).

TRUMPET IN THE NEW MOON

You have work to do, America—
You have work to be done.
The goal which was set for you in the dreams of your founders
Has not been realized.
You are off the trail, America—
You are wandering in the Wilderness like the Israelites of old.
You are worshipping strange gods, America—
You have lost your first love and fallen
From grace.

In your early garb, I thought you beautiful.
Your coon-skin cap, your leathern breeches, your brogans,
    your axe and your flintlock were beautiful to me, America,
Because your motives were pure.
Then was your Love boundless,
Then was your Hope boundless,
Then was your Enthusiasm boundless
Because
Your faith was boundless.
The clean wild air, the free new world seemed to animate
    you with a fraternal benevolence; and I even condone
    your questionable treatment of the Indians
Because
You were honor bright; and, at least, your heart was right.
And you have a rich heritage, America—

Your history reads like the songs of the bards
When the earth was young.
Remember the twilight years—
Remember the years of the dawn—
Sing of the heroic days of the Scandinavian Rovers
Who first saw your shores.
Sing of Cabot and Drake and Magellan and Balboa and De Soto
And Columbus, who gave you your song-name and
     started you on your way to Plymouth Rock and Yorktown!
Nay, sing of the slave-ships and Christopher Attucks.
Sing of the Declaration of Independence; there is
No grander human document.
I hear the opening lines which read like the cry of a
     new-born man-child—
lusty and defiant!
I hear the closing lines which read like a lover's sacred oath.
I see a young man riding out of Boston in the night;
I see a signal flashed to him from the belfry of a church;
And "embattled farmers firing the shot heard round the world."
I see suffering and sacrifice and trails of blood across
     the snows of Valley Forge;
And a dignified, Virginian gentleman looming to the
     stature of Hannibal, Alexander, Napoleon, Marlborough
Anon; and then I saw a mighty nation born into the world!
I saw that nation spreading toward the westward.
Horace Greely gave good advice to the young men—
St. Louis, Kansas City, Denver, San Francisco
Took form and grew like mushrooms in the night.
New Orleans, child of the Mississippi, basking in the
     rich cotton fields of the Delta,
Glanced proudly at the rising suns of Promise and Fulfillment.
Erelong I heard the boom of a cannon athwart the
     ramparts of Ft. Sumpter.
I saw Puritan and Cavalier come to grips over an idea:
Bull Run—Vicksburg—Missionary Ridge—
     Antietam—The Wilderness—
Lee—Grant—McClelland—Beauregard—Stone-wall Jackson—
And the finality of Appomattox!
Above all, I heard the peroration at Gettysburg:
"May not perish from the earth,"
Like a benediction

And a prayer . . . .
O you came from that fire like pure gold, America,
With high Purposes:
With noble Resolutions:
And lofty Aspirations.
I saw your write the "Fourteenth Amendment" in the Book
I saw you wish the Freedman :God speed"
As he launched his frail bark upon the sea of Emancipation.
I saw you "bind up the nation's wounds" while rebuilding
        your prosperity upon a sounder foundation.
Came now the matchless Grady
Wrapped in sunlit clouds of eloquence—
He of the silver tongue and the golden throat—
With the earnest hope for a new orientation;
With the hope that there should be "no further misunderstanding;"
With the hope North and South should make common
        cause to "consummate our great destiny."
I saw you build great railways; rear factories; dig mines.
I saw the black man patiently helping you to perform these miracles.
I saw you reorganize the Empire that was to amaze the world.
I saw your commerce begin to whiten every sea.
I saw you apply your mind to Experimental Science—
Sing, O Sing, of strange secrets wrested from nature—
Telegraph!—Telephone!—Phonograph!—Incandescent!
I saw mighty orators step forth into the arena of debate
With the winged words that challenged days of Ancient Greece.
I heard the voices of gifted poets rise in harmonious cadences,
Else in the dissonance of raw truth and highest art—
Emerson—Whittier—Whitman—Sandburg—Lindsay.
I saw you take on girth; your pockets bulge—
Astor—Vanderbilt—Harriman—Rockefeller—Ford—

And then I saw a great cloud overspread the sky.
I saw you mobilize, and shoulder gun and spade and march,
With hearts aflame, to "Make the World
Safe for Democracy!"
Sing of Submarines and Torpedoes! the mud of Brest!
        the blood of Verdun! the Fire of Chateau-Thierry!
Sing of "Flanders Fields!" and the "Rendezvous with
        Death!" of "Zeppelin Raids!" "Too Proud to Fight!"
        "Liberty Bonds!" "Victory!" "Versailles!"

But now I though I saw another shadow creeping
    over the epic canvass:
Unrest—The casting Adrift from the Moorings of Faith—
    "The Revolt of Youth"—Candor Run Riot—Morals Amuck—
A Break in conduct—A Loss of Respect for many of the Ancient Virtues.
So what have you? I ask you, America—
What have you done? ad what have you come upon?
Cynicism! Disillusionment! Night Clubs! "Legs" Diamond!
    "Speakies!" Capone! Joy Rides! "Whoopee!!!"
You have work to do America—
Your have work to be done.
Directly I thought I saw the bitter fruit of that "Disillusionment."
I saw you build a great colossus:
Intolerance!
I saw the zeal with which you fashioned your Idol.
I saw you offer up the incense of Prejudice;
And the smoke rise from the altars of Human Sacrifices!
Go hide your head in Shame, America,
And wrap yourself in Sack-Cloth and Ashes.
Erstwhile I heard your groan under your "white man's burden;"
Black men shivered while you wreaked vengeance at
    Tulsa, Atlanta, Washington, Chicago—
"O Masters, Lords and Rulers of the Land,"
Who are they who drove the shaft of hate between
    the working black and the working white?
Why can not a spirit of humane co-operation exist
    between these two?
You Masters who have exploited the black laborer for centuries,
Held us up as a constant threat to the white working-man,
Causing him to despise us,
Causing him to consider us a perennial menace to his well-being—
Is the light worth the candle?
Does the end justify the means?
Are all the years of the past forgotten?
Forgotten all the loyalties, the faithfulness, the tender
    care of your children, the genuflections, the service?
Sing of the service—
Remember the service:
"Come Susie, rock the baby—Go Hannah, get the
    dinner—Uncle Jim, go plough the new-ground—
    Here Sambo, grab my satchel and get to hell—"

Remember the service.
Remember the sweat, the cotton fields, the lumber
    logs, the brick yards, the saw mills and turpentine
        plantations—all black labor.
And in the field of Higher Service, Remember the immortal
    "Tenth Cavalry" and the "Hot Time in San Juan when they got there."
"—With regard to the Bravery in Action and the Exceptional
    Behavior (under the enemy's continuous fire) of the
    Negro Units in the 91st Division, American Expeditionary
    Forces, U. S. Army, I have the honor, Sir, to report—"
Remember the Service!
Remember, too, that black soldiers may be needed again.
Some day the Eagle may be wounded;
Some day the Flag may be insulted.
"Black-a-moors" make good cannon-fodder.
The World War seems not to have satisfied certain nations.
Every now and then there is a great rattling of sabers—
"Black-a-moors" make good cannon-fodder.
Black breasts can stop bullets like the Devil!
And Remember their 100% Loyalty—
President Wilson asked for a detail of "Black-a-moors"
to guard the Executive Mansion
In those days when everyman mistrusted every man.
Then, as now, a Black Face was badge of Loyalty no
    one doubted.
Remember the Service!
Remember, too, the Rocky Road, the "Deep Rivers"—
Sing of "Deep Rivers!"
Remember the silence and the patience—
Sing of the Patience!
You speak of the burdens—You speak of the "white man's burden!"
But you speak patronizingly,
And you boast overweeningly—
The "white man's burden!"
"A Negro should know his place"—
"A Negro should be taught his place"—
"A Negro should stay in his place"—
The "white man's burden!"
Listen, I shall tell you a true story, America:
There was a young Norseman came up from Obscurity
Upon wings.

Sing, O Sing, of wings—and the dark earth—and
    mountain crest—and stormy skies—
Sing of Wings!
He was intrepid; he was "American Youth Incarnate"
Sing of "Youth Incarnate!"
You saw him hover upon the shore of the Atlantic
Like some "Lone Eagle" poised above the rocky promontory;
And then you saw him point straight into the gloom
    of the ocean, America,
and the Night and a Silence like Death swallowed him up.
"Flying Fool!" said some;
"God keep his soul!" prayed some.
The World held its breath, America—
The World had one though, America:
Black water, angry—menacing—frightful—deep—
Black night, deep as all Eternity—
Loneliness sublime, infinite—
But Paris and Glory at least! America.
Glory for your Prowess, your Institutions,
Your undismayed and invincible Youth,
Your virile and intrepid Manhood,
Your courageous and Unquenchable Spirit!
Glory for the "Land of the Free and the Home of the Brave"—
A Land where a Rail-splitter may become a King!
Yet what have you Done, America—
How have you rewarded him who pawned his life for your Glory?
Gold you gave him—yes;
Fame you gave him—yes;
But the Dregs in the Cup you gave him to Drink—
Sing of the Bitterness, the Wormwood and the Gall!
Go hide your head in Shame, America.
You speak of burdens;
But you speak condescendingly,
And you boast unbecomingly.
Think, will you, of your underworld, America.
Ah! Here is the sore that is galling your back;
Here is the ulcer that is eating your vitals;
Here is the virus that is chilling your heart;
And the lethal fumes that are choking your spirit.
How can you denominate the black man Burden?
How be guilty of such Travesty upon Justice,

Or countenance such a Distortion of Truth,
Or heap such Humiliation upon him?
Stand forth before the Bar, America,
While I read from the Indictment;
While I enumerate your Transgressions;
While I prosecute before the Jury!
You have made of "Success" a fetish;
"Go-Getters" have been your high priests;
"Fail not" has been your watchword;
"Win out" has been your slogan.
You forgot Love and Justice,
You forgot Truth and Beauty:
You forgot Life and Humanity
In your mad race to "Win."
You trampled down the finer impulse of the soul
In a wild desire to "Compete"—
In a wild desire for "Riches"
And "Success' at all hazards.
And you worshipped Gold;
You idolized the Material;
You dwarfed the Spiritual—
Greed was your religion;
Gold was your God!
Vanity was your Raiment;
Prejudice, your Daily Bread;
Class hatred, your Life-Blood;
And Inconsistency, your Castle.
You hero-worshipped Jesse James;
You lionized Bandits—
You have been "Weighed in the Balances, America,
And found Wanting."
You have let rich murderers escape who had gold;
You have hanged poor wretches who had nothing
You have winked at injustice in high places,
And punished many unfortunates who may have been innocent.
You have Condoned the biting poverty of the many.
Racketeers infest your streets;
Dealers in "hot goods" lurk on every corner.
Kidnappers drive a thriving business;
"Come-on", men and Crooks consort with Ward-heelers
        and "Public Citizens."

Your children are abducted.
And you call high heaven to witness your sorrow;
But you shell out the "Spondulux."
Because the Underworld is so Powerful.

There was an eminent foreigner visited our Country
To observe and study our manners and customs.
Was told of certain Creeds and Laws and Restrictions
That held the two races in separate compartments.
Was told that the Noose and the Rack and Faggot
Are oftimes evoked to maintain these Restrictions.
The visitor listened in grave and respectful silence,
Then asked: "Whence so many octoroons and quadroons
        and mulattoes?"
Was told of a ship leaving port at a certain hour:
And that we were grieved he so soon must be going.

Wake up, America!
The black man is not your Real Burden.
Your inconsistence, your Selfishness, your Indifference, your
        materialism, your Intolerance, your descent from the Ancient Virtues,
Make up your Real Burden.
Buck up, America!
And "Come out of the Wilderness
Leaning on the Lord."
Drop some of your Prejudice—
Some of your Intolerance—
Some of your Disdain for the Common Man, the Forgotten
        Man, the Man Farthest Down.
Discard some of your Scorn for the Darker Races;
For the Darker Races will be living in their present habitat
When Chicago, London and Berlin are one
With Tyre, Sidon, Sodom, Gomorrah,
And all the buried cities of the past.
Gray beard Chinamen will be carrying burdens upon
        their backs in their native fields
When your civilization shall lie buried beneath the
        rust and dust of forgotten centuries.

Unless
You shall change your ways, America,

And get yourself a new Religion
Based on Humane Co-operation
And Brotherly Love twixt Man and Man;
And unless
You shall strip your hearts of Intolerance,
And turn unto the ways of Justice and Love,
The germs of decay will proceed unrestrained;
And your paths will lead down to Confusion and Death.

And now particularly to "white" America,
And the sovereign commonwealths of Georgia and Alabama—
I address myself to you:
You are direct descendants of the men
Who made the greatest contribution
To the conserving forces of civilization
This side of the crucified Jesus.
And it is not your science, nor your art, nor your citadels,
        nor your political power, nor your industrial efficiency,
(In all of which you have no peer
Under the smiling canopy of heaven);
But in your "Noble English Chivalry"
You have vouchsafed to mankind
The nearest approach to a redeeming perfection
Which has appeared upon this earth.
Emblazoned high in the blue field of your escutcheon
Is the historic, the immortal legend;
"LIBERTY—WISDOM—JUSTICE—MODERATION—"
The germ and essence of Chivalry.
You are really accountable to no higher tribunal;
And your own conscience need be your only guide.
You can therefore afford to be Tolerant;
You can therefore afford to be Just!
Chivalry bestows upon the lowliest man
An inalienable right to Justice;
And develops in him an pride to have privilege
To suffer, even die, for his country.
Look to "ATLANTA," America—
Have your been Tolerant?
Look to "SCOTTSBORO," America—
Have you been Just?
I am appealing to your Heart of Hearts, America—

You can afford to be Just.
I am appealing to the hearts of Georgians and Alabamians—
You can afford to be fair.

There is a classic example
Of High English Chivalry in action:
I see a ship leaving her berth at Southampton
Upon her maiden voyage
She is the ill-fated Titanic,
Largest and fastest boat in all the seven seas.
She points first for Cherbourgh,
Steams gracefully past the Isle of Wight,
Then drops anchor at Queenstown
Her port of last call,
At one-thirty P.M., April eleventh, Nineteen-twelve,
The Titanic stands out from Queenstown
With two and twenty hundred human souls aboard.
She ports her helm,
And signals her pilot,
While charting her course for New York
Where she is due in record time.
I see her as she begins her stately march
Across the storm-swept Atlantic,
Measuring her majestic tread to the muffled beat
Of her mighty turbines.
The great Titanic! Queen of the Ocean!
Mistress of the seas!
And "Monarch of all she surveys!"
At midnight all is calm and serene
Aboard the world's greatest ship,
Although the black water lay beneath her keel
Three thousand fathoms deep.
Suddenly a cry:
"Iceberg ahoy!"
As with the force of a falling mountain,
The ship plunges to her doom.
Panic and Horror!
Men and women crazed with fear!
A scramble for the life-boats!
It is now that Captain Smith
Walks coolly to the bridge

And gives voice to an expression
Which must go down in history:
"The law of the sea is women and children first;
Be British my men."
Erstwhile frantic men snapped to Attention
And saluted Captain Smith;
And after safely ensconcing what women and
    children they could
In what life-boats were available,
One thousand brave men (of the sixteen hundred humans lost)
Went down with Captain Smith to their doom!

What did Captain Smith mean: "Be British?"
That was the greatest compliment
Ever paid the British Empire
Upon whose flag the sun is said
Never to go down;
For it means that England sets a very high Standard
For the behavior of her Sons;
A Standard so high
That Mediocrity could never reach it
And none could attain to it
Save Gentlemen and Heroes!
God hasten the day when "Be American"
Shall carry the selfsame Inspiration
To call forth all the heroism and nobility
That lie dormant in the human spirit.
But how can it be thus, O my Countrymen,
While you are so Intolerant.
How can it be thus, O America,
While you are so Unjust.

As they entered into mortal combat
For the entertainment of the pampered patricians,
The gladiators of old used to shout:
"Caesar,
We who are about to die
Salute thee!"
But that was the homage of Despair
To the Iron Imperialism and Tyranny of Rome.
There's higher homage, deeper love for Country,

The grip of Faith, the Substance of Devotion,
The proper ring of unalloy'd Sincerity
Embodied in the Shout of Negro Soldiers:
"America,
Farewell! Goodbye!
You may not always have been kind to us;
We may have much to forgive;
But we'll return your Sacred Flag
In Honor,

Or else report to God the reason why."
Spirit of Truth and light, O Sacred Muse,
That didst inspire the Hebrew Harpist to declaim
In days of old:
"Blow up the Trumpet in the New Moon,
And the Appointed Time"—
Inspired by Thee,
Have I now Blown the Trumpet into the air,
That America may hear and well prepare
For the Joys of Rebirth and Regeneration
That shall come
At the solemn Love-Feast of Brotherhood and Democracy.

RICHARD WRIGHT

TRANSCONTINENTAL
(FOR LOUIS ARAGON, IN PRAISE OF RED FRONT)

Through trembling waves of roadside heat
We see the cool green of golf courses
Long red awnings catching the sunshine
Slender rainbows curved above the spirals of water
Swaying hammocks slung between trees—
Like in the movies . . .

America who built this dream

Above the ceaseless hiss of passing cars
We hear the tinkle of ice in tall glasses

Clacks of croquet balls scudding over the cropped lawns
Silvery crescendos of laughter—
Like in the movies
On Saturday nights
When we used to get our paychecks . . .

America who owns this wonderland

Lost
We hitch-hike down the hot highways
Looking for a ride home
Yanking tired thumbs at glazed faces
Behind the steering wheels of Packards Pierce Arrows
Lincolns La Salles Reos Chryslers—
Their lips are tight jaws set eyes straight ahead . . .

America America America why turn your face away

O for the minute
The joyous minute
The minute of the hour of the day
When the tumbling white ball of our anger
Rolling down the cold hill of our lives
Swelling like a moving mass of snow
Shall crash
Shall explode at the bottom of our patience Thundering
HALT
You shall not pass our begging thumbs
America is ours
This car is commandeered
America is ours
Take your ringed fingers from the steering wheel
Take your polished shoe off the gas
We'll drive and let you be the hitch-hiker
We'll show you how to pass 'em up
You say we're robbers
So what
We're bastards
So what
Sonofbitches
All right chop us into little pieces we don't care

Let the wind tousle your hair like ours have been tousled
Doesn't the sun's hot hate feel sweet on your back
Crook your thumbs and smudge the thin air
What kind of a growl does your gut make when meal-time comes
At night your hips can learn how soft the pavements are
Oh let's do it the good old American way
Sportsmanship Buddy Sportsmanship
But dear America's a free country
Sis you say Negroes
Oh I don't mean NEEEGROOOES
After all
Isn't there a limit to everything
You wouldn't want your daughter
And they say there's no GOD
And furthermore it's simply disgraceful how they're discriminating
against the
      Children of the rich in Soviet schools
PROLETARIAN CHILDREN
Good Lord
Why if we divided up everything today we'd be just where we are
inside of a year
The strong and the weak The quick and the slow You understand
But Lady even quivering lips can say
PLEASE COMRADE MY FATHER WAS A CARPENTER I SWEAR SWEAR
      HE WAS
I WAS NEVER AGAINST THE CUMMUNISTS REALLY
Fairplay Boys Fairplay
America America can every boy have the chance to rise from Wall Street
to the
      Commintern
America America can every boy have the chance to rise form Riverside
Drive to
      The General Secretaryship of the Communist Party
100% Justice
And Mister don't forget
Our hand shall be on the steering wheel
Our feet shall be on the gas
And you shall hear the grate of our gears
UNITEDFRONT—SSSTRIKE
The motor throbs with eager anger
UNITEDFRONT—SSSTRIKE

We're lurching toward the highway
UNITEDFRONT—SSSTRIKE
The pavement drops into the past The future smites our face
America is ours
10 15 20 30
America America
WOORKERSWOORKERS
Hop on the runningboard Pile in
We're leaving We're Leaving
Leaving the tired the timid the soft
Leaving the pimps idlers loungers
Leaving empty dinner-pails wage-cuts stretch-outs
Leaving the tight-lipped mother and the bare meal-can
Leaving the shamed girl and her bastard child
Leaving leaving the past leaving
The wind filled with leaflets leaflets of freedom
Millions and millions of leaflets fluttering
Like the wings of a million birds
AmericaAmericaAmerica

Scaling New England's stubborn hills Spanning the Hudson
Waving at Manhattan Waving at New Jersey
Throwing a Good Bye kiss to Way Down East
Through mine-pirred Pennsylvania Through Maryland Our Maryland
Careening over the Spinning the steering wheel
Taking the curves with determination
AmericaAmerica
SOFT SHOULDER AHEAD
AmericaAmerica
KEEP TO THE MIDDLE OF THE ROAD
AmericaAmerica
The telegraph poles are a solid wall
WASHINGTON—90 MILES
AmericaAmerica
The farms are a storm of green
Past rivers past towns
50 60 70 80
AmericaAmerica
CITY LIMITS
Vaulting Washington's Monument
Leaping desks of Senators Ending all bourgeois elections

Hurdling desks of Congressmen Fascist flesh sticking to our tires
Skidding into the White House Leaving a trail of carbon monoxide for the
    President
Roaring into the East Room Going straight through Lincoln's portrait
Letting
    the light of history through
AmericaAmerica
Swinging Southward Plunging the radiator into the lynch-mob Giving no
    warning
Slowing Slowing for the sharecroppers
Come on You Negroes Come on
There's room
Not in the back but front seat
We're heading for the highway of Self=Determination
UNITEDFRONT—SSSTRIKE
Dim your lights you Trotskyites
UNITEDFRONT—SSSTRIKE
Lenin's line is our stream line
UNITEDFRONT—SSSTRIKE
Through October's windshield we see the road Looping over the green
hills Dipping
    toward to-morrow

AmericaAmericaAmerica
Look back See the tiny thread of our tires leaving hammer and sickle
prints
    upon the pavement
See the tree-lined horizon turning slowly in our hearts
See the ripe fields Fields ripe as our love
See the eastern sky See the white clouds of our hope
See the blood-red afterglow in the west Our memory of October
See See See the pretty cottages the bungalows the sheltered homes
See the packing-box cities the jungles the huts
See See See the skyscrapers the clubs the pent-houses
See the bread-lines winding winding winding long as our road
AmericaAmericaAmerica

Tagging Kentucky Tagging Tennessee
Into Ohio Into the orchards of Michigan
Over the rising and falling dunes of Indiana
Across Illinois' glad fields of dancing corn

Slowing Comrades Slowing again
Slowing for the heart of proletarian America
CHICAGO—100 miles
WOORKERSWOORKERS
Steel and rail and stock All you sons of Haymarket
Swing on We're going your way America is ours
UNITEDFRONT—SSSTRIKE
The pressure of our tires is blood pounding in our hearts
UNITEDFRONT—SSSTRIKE
The steam of our courage blows from the radiator cap
UNITEDFRONT—SSSTRIKE
The wind screams red songs in our ears
60 70 80 90
AmericaAmericaAmerica

Listen Listen to the moans of those whose lives were laughter
Listen to the howls of the dogs of the dispossessed
Listen to bureaucratic insects spattering against the windshield
Listen to curses rebounding from fear-proof glass
Listen to the gravel of hate tingling on our fenders
Listen to the raindrops mumbling of yesterday
Listen to the wind whistling of to-morrow
Listen to our tires humming humming humming hymns of victory
AmericaAmericaAmerica

Coasting Comrades Coasting
Coasting on momentum of Revolution
Look Look at the village Like a lonesome egg in the nest of the hills
Soon Soon you shall fly over the hillsides Crowing the new dawn
Coasting Indulging in Lenin's dream

TUNE IN ON THE RADIO THE WORLD IS LAUGHING
Red Baseball
Great Day in the Morning

> *. . . the Leninites defeated the redbirds 3 to 0.*
> *Batteries for the Leninites: Kenji Sumarira and*
> *Boris Petrovsky. For the Redbirds: Wing Sing and*
> *Eddie O'Brien. Homeruns: Hugo Schmidt and Jack*
> *Ogletree. Umpires: Pierre Carpentier and Oswald Wallings . . .*

The world is laughing The world is laughing

> ... *Mike Gold's account of the revolution sells*
> *26 millions copies . . .*
> *26 million copies . . .*

The world is laughing The world is laughing

> ... *beginning May 1st the work day is limited to*
> *five hours . . .*

The world is laughing The world is laughing
> ... *last of the landlords liquidated*
> *in Texas . . .*

The world is laughing The world is laughing

Picking up speed to measure the Mississippi
AmericaAmericaAmerica
Plowing the richness of Iowa soil Into the Wheat Empire
Making Minnesota Taking the Dakotas Carrying Nebraska
On on toward the Badlands the Rockies the deserts the Golden Gate
Slowing once again Comrades Slowing to right a wrong
Say You Red Men You Forgotten Men
Come out of your tepees
Show us Pocahontas For we love her
Bring her from her hiding place Let the sun kiss her eyes
Drape her in a shawl of red wool Tuck her in beside us
Our arms shall thaw the long cold of her shoulders
The lights flash red Comrades let's go
UNITEDFRONT—SSSTRIKE
The future opens like an ever-widening V
UNITEDFRONT—SSSTRIKE
We're rolling over tiles of red logic
UNITEDFRONT—SSSTRIKE
We're speeding on wheels of revolution
AmericaAmerica
Mountain peaks are falling toward us
AmericaAmerica
Uphill and the earth rises and looms
AmericaAmerica
Downhill and the earth tilts and sways
AmericaAmerica
80 90 100
AmericaAmerica

Every factory is a fortress
Cities breed soviets
AmericaAmerica
Plains sprout collective farms
Ten thousand Units are meeting
AmericaAmerica
Resolutions passed unanimously
The Red Army is on the march
AmericaAmerica
Arise, ye prisoners . . .
AmericaAmerica
Speed Faster
Speed AmericaAmerica
Arise, ye wretched . . .
AmericaAmerica
Speed Faster
Ever Faster America America
For Justice America America Thunders
AmericaAmericaAmerica

JOAQUIN MILLER

IN CLASSIC SHADES

ALONE and sad I sat me down
To rest on Rousseau s narrow isle
Below Geneva. Mile on mile,
And set with many a shining town,.
Tow rd Dent du Midi danced the wave
Beneath the moon. Winds went and came
And fanned the stars into a flame.
I heard the far lake, dark and deep,
Rise up and talk as in its sleep;
I heard the laughing waters lave
And lap against the further shore,
An idle oar, and nothing more
Save that the isle had voice, and save
That round about its base of stone
There plashed and flashed the foamy
Rhone.

A stately man, as black as tan,
Kept up a stern and broken round
Among the strangers on the ground.
I named that awful African
A second Hannibal.

My elbows on the table sat
With chin in upturned palm to scan
His face, and contemplate the scene.
The moon rode by a crowned queen.
I was alone. Lo! not a man
To speak my mother tongue. Ah me!
How more than all alone can be
A man in crowds! Across the isle
My Hannibal strode on. The while
Diminished Rousseau sat his throne
Of books, unnoticed and unknown.
This strange, strong man, with fact
austere,
At last drew near. He bowed; he spake
In unknown tongues. I could but shake;
My head. Then half achill with fear,
Arose, and sought another place.
Again I mused. The kings of thought
Came by, and on that storied spot
I lifted up a tearful face.
The star-set Alps they sang a tune
Unheard by any soul save mine.
Mont Blanc, as lone and as divine
And white, seemed mated to the moon.
The past was mine ; strong-voiced and
Vast

Stern Calvin, strange Voltaire, and Tell,
And two whose names are known too well
To name, in grand procession passed.

And yet again came Hannibal;

King-like he came, and drawing near,
I saw his brow was now severe
And resolute.

In tongue unknown
Again he spake. I was alone,
Was all unarmed, was worn and sad;
But now, at last, my spirit had
Its old assertion.

I arose,

As startled from a dull repose;
With gathered strength I raised a hand
And cried, "I do not understand."

His black face brightened as I spake;
He bowed; he wagged his woolly head;
He showed his shining teeth, and said,
"Sah, if you please, dose tables heah
Am consecrate to lager beer;
And, sah, what will you have to take?"

Not that I loved that colored cuss
Nay! he had awed me all too much
But I sprang forth, and with a clutch
I grasped his hand, and holding thus,
Cried, "Bring my country' s drink for two!

For oh! that speech of Saxon sound
To me was as a fountain found
In wastes, and thrilled me through and
through.

On Rousseau s isle, in Rousseau s shade,
Two pink and spicy drinks were made,
In classic shades, on classic ground,
We stirred two cocktails round and round.

ISABEL FISKE CONANT

HAMPTON INSTITUTE
(REMEMBERING GENERAL ARMSTRONG)

There is more here than you can be aware of,
Even you who know it best, beyond the rules
Administered that you have the wise care of;
Something significant past other schools
Of learning or of actual education,
For here the movement of historic force
Is shaping the future of a forming nation
Into an altered but a destined course.

He builded even better than he knew
Working for those who gave our land their song,
Its rich, dark wine, the sunlight pouring through,
Cadence that now to all the States belong;
That haunting rhythm and that poignant metre
That make life more significant and sweeter.
Opportunity, Nov. 1937: 329

WILLIAM SHAKESPEARE

Sonnet 130 is addressed to a woman, sometimes called "the dark lady."
While there has been much speculation about her identity (most recently,
she has been identified as Aemilia Lanyer), there is nothing conclusive to
link any woman or man with the lovers Shakespeare addresses.

My mistress' eyes are nothing like the sun;
Coral is far more red than her lips' red;
If snow be white, why then her breasts are dun;
If hairs be wires, black wires grow on her head.
I have seen roses damasked, red and white,
But no such roses see I in her cheeks,
And in some perfumes is there more delight
Than in the breath that from my mistress reeks.
I love to hear her speak, yet well I know
That music hath a far more pleasing sound.
I grant I never saw a goddess go;

My mistress when she walks treads on the ground.
And yet, by heaven, I think my love as rare
As any she belied with false compare.

LANGSTON HUGHES

AIR RAID OVER HARLEM
(SCENARIO FOR A LITTLE BLACK MOVIE)

You're not talking 'bout Harlem, are you?
That's where my home is,
My bed is my woman is, my kids is!
Harlem, that's where I live!
Look at my streets
Full of black and brown and
Yellow and high-yellow
Jokers like me.
Lenox, Seventh, Edgecombe, 145th.
Listen,
Hear 'em talkin' and laughin'?
Bombs over Harlem'd kill
People like me—
Kill ME!
Sure, I know
The Ethiopian war broke out last night:
BOMBS OVER HARLEM
Cops on every corner
Most of 'em white
COPS IN HARLEM
Guns and billy-clubs
Double duty in Harlem
Walking in pairs
Under every light
Their faces
WHITE
In Harlem
And mixed in with 'em
A black cop or two
For the sake of the vote in Harlem
GUGSA A TRAITOR TOO

No, sir,
I ain't talkin' 'bout you,
Mister Policeman!
No, indeed!
I know we got to keep
ORDER OVER HARLEM
Where the black millions sleep
Shepherds over Harlem
Their armed watch keep
Lest Harlem stirs in its sleep
And maybe remembers
And remembering forgets
To be peaceful and quiet
And has sudden fits
Of raising a black fist
Out of the dark
And that black fist
Becomes a red spark
PLANES OVER HARLEM
BOMBS OVER Harlem
You're just making up
A fake funny picture, ain't you?
Not real, not real?
Did you ever taste blood
From an iron heel
Planted in your mouth
In the slavery-time South
Where to whip a nigger's
Easy as hell—
And not even a living nigger
Has a tale to tell
Lest the kick of the boot
Baring more blood to his mouth
In the slavery-time South
And a long billy-club
Split his head wide
And a white hand draw
A gun from its side
And send bullets splaying
Through the streets of Harlem
Where the dead're laying
Lest you stir in your sleep

And remember something
You'd best better keep
In the dark, in the dark
Where the ugly things hide
Under the white lights
With guns by their side
In Harlem?

Say what are yuh tryin' to do?
Start a riot?
You keep quiet!
You niggers keep quiet!

BLACK WORLD
Never wake up
Lest you knock over the cup
Of gold that the men who
Keep order guard so well
And then—well, then
There'd be hell
To pay
And bombs over Harlem

AIR RAID OVER HARLEM

Bullets through Harlem
And someday
A sleeping giant waking
To snatch bombs from the sky
And push the sun up with a loud cry
Off to hell with the cops on the corners at night
Armed to the teeth under the light
Lest Harlem see red
And suddenly sit on the edge of its bed
And shake the whole world with a new dream
As the squad cars come and the sirens scream
And the big black giant snatches bombs from the sky
And picks up the cop and lets him fly
Into the dust of the Jimcrow past
And laughs and Hollers
Kiss my
!x!&!

Hey!
Scenario for a Little Black Movie,
You say?
A RED MOVIE TO MR. HEARST
Black and white workers united as one
In a city where
There'll never be
Air raids over Harlem
FOR THE WORKERS ARE FREE
What workers are free?
THE BLACK AND WHITE WORKERS—
You and me!
Looky here, everybody!
Look at me!
I'M HARLEM!

JAY N. HILL

ETHIOPE IN SPAIN

(This verse was inspired by the activities of Ghvet son of Ras Imru of
Ethiopia who is now fighting for the International Brigade in Spain.)

No jewel shone in this Ethiope's ear,
No gay cloth draped his form.
  Dust bespattered his dusky limbs,
  Sweat covered his stern face,
  Determination furrowed his brow,
As he stood, half-erect half-crouching
  On Spanish soil,
  Fighting his old enemy.

Silent man of the past, he seemed heroic,
  Through disillusion and forced exile,
  Through faded visions of Adowa,
  Of ancient streets in Addis Ababa,
  Of mountains and muddy roads in Abyssinia,
Where barefoot men
  Trudged their way through centuries
  Of peace, and calmly roamed the hills.

Silent man of the hour is he,
  Hurling back the ejector,
  Loading, firing grimly;
Exchanging few words with his company,
  For he spoke neither Italian
  Nor Spanish.
Though little English
  And some French,
For the most part he spoke Amharic.
And that was not necessary.
  For language could not match
  The eloquence of his silence.

A distant radiance shines in his eye—
A kindred light, that some men claim
  Set the flame
    At Runnymede
      At the Bastille
      At Boston
        At Moscow
          At Madrid.

Civil conflagration
Sweeps the hills of Guadalajara,
The halls at University City
Tell frightful tales of direst tragedy.
As "Frenchman's Bridge" becomes a
bridge of sighs—
Manzares turns a sanguine hue.
Bilboa chants Niobe's fateful strain—
As children's feet—
Beat out a terrified retreat,
Before the roar and scream
Of planes that fleck the sky.

Spain writhes in pain.
Her gates—humanity's gates—
Withhold a devastating horde,
A pack of 'hireling wolves'. . . .

At one gate, in silence, fights this Ethiope,
Goaded by the rape
Of motherland, of sisterland—
Yesterday, a symbol of black majesty,
Today a victim of civilized barbarity,
A prince, with no bright jewel in his ear

The Crisis. July 1937: 202.

RUFUS GIBSON

THE VOICE OF ETHIOPIA

What voice this be
That strangely calls to me
From out the maze of dreams my slumbers bring?
Ah, no this seems no captive's cry to be;
For yesternight I heard its clarion ring
Within my thoughts dense wilderness, when sleep
Her somniferous breath upon my eyes
Had blown, bidding my soul its tryst to keep.
I heard it say
"Children arise! arise!
Now gather to me out of every land
To which the four-winds bore you long ago,
Come you to me again, a motley band,
Come children all that from my loins did grow,
Bring borrowed jewels from the strangers' camps
Yet while in sleep upon their beds they lie,
Bring to your Motherland oil for her lamps
To light the path on which your brethren ply
Through centuries of deep and dark con- tent.
O come I but not as prodigals to me,
Or wayward children seeking to repent
Your sins; for from all guilt are you made free.
Gird well your loins, take up both sword and shield
And forthwith march. As warriors, meet the foe
As did your sires who ne'er to tyrants yield;
But by their righteous might gave blow for blow
Until the foes of peace were driven back

Beyond the hills from whence sweet waters flow.
O! sons of mine of regal bronze and black—My queenly daughters, hither
come I pray!
Long since have ravenous hordes despoiled our land,
Long centuries did they our trust betray.
Now Ethiopia must stretch forth her hand
First unto God for refuge and for strength,
That we may now our Native land reclaim
And drive usurpers from its breadth and length.
O sons and daughters mine, let not in shame
Men rise to speak of Ethiopia's name."
Crisis, January 1936: 13

J. HARVEY L. BAXTER

SONNETS (ETHIOPIAN)

THE WORLD

The world's a mummery of groggy lies,
And we are victims of its undertow.
We turn our backs to Heaven, close our eyes
To probity. Ah! Lord, we've fallen low.
Bed-fellows with the filth of gutter trash,
Maggots of slime that know not foot or head;
Bewildered leaders, wary of a crash,
Base minions of the slough of fear and dead.

No more the parliaments of justice work!
Their flaccid pivots ape the maniac;
Man's bounded duty, now's to dodge and shirk
And eat his words, postpone each noble act
Great God! this fog, this chaff, must pass away
Ere Thy poor mortals flounder in decay.

AFRICA

For you, long raped and baited, trammeled down,
Black harried Victim of the heels of woe

I forge this thunder-bolt to blast around
Each chain and pillory that bows you low.
I come a singer, yet a champion
Of the undone, benighted folk, forgot;
Of fleshy foot-stool, bleeding stepping-stone,
Whom men beguiled in their despotic lot.

Oh, natal Mother, how your heart bewails!
Bereft of vineyards and of freedom too;
Kissed and betrayed, rifled, rent of sails
By Godless thugs that care not what they do.
Brood no despair, this hell is not your doom,
God is not *dead,* nor guarded in a *tomb!*

WELL MAY I SING OF THE PROUD ETHIOPE

Well may I sing of the proud Ethiope
Who ruled before the will of Rome was born;
And did with Israel and Egypt cope
Ere pyramid or temple scanned the morn.
Well may I sing of his primeval speech,
And of his arts and obfuscated past,
Of priests who rose to prophesy and preach
That God Was Soul, Almighty, First and Last.

Of how his blood seeped in the Arab-vein,
And Negrofied the skin of India.
Then leaped from Bosporus and colored Spain,
And mongreled up old Greece and Italia.
These men who wear the night upon their faces,
FOUGHT OFT WITH JEW AND NOMAD
    BIBLE RACES.

TO ETHIOPIA

If you must go the way of fallen states
Outnumbered and outbullied by your foes,
If you must quaff the drugs of vengeful fates
Forced by the heavy fist of Fascist blows;
If peace doth cower, and forsake your plight,
And war must break, as likely war's to be,
Up like the Greeks, a bloody Marathon fight

Or die as Spartans at Thermopylae.

Know well the battle-dice are loaded, cast,
And cheating hands, the toss in blood may win;
Yet to the bloody end, war to the last,
Be not debased, nor serve as chattel-men;
Oh, Ethiopia, Now's the Great Command,
God bids you as of old to stretch your hand.

ITALY TO ETHIOPIA

Salute my flag, make me Protector, Lord,
Or I will smite your kingdom, house by house;
No Nero's heart, no Caesar's will as hard
As this great hand, ordained to rule alld oust.
Negate the vested power I maintain,—
And I will bait you foul, speak you base
Crush each sphere and realm of your domain
And swear you hit me first within the face.

Come forth and close embrace me Ethiope
And make me heir of your inviting clime;
Can such as you, outlandish mortals hope
To keep that which for long was counted mine?
Like wolfish hordes along a mountain way
Rome goads itself to fall upon its prey.

ETHIOPIA TO ITALY

Long have I watched world-empires rise and fall,
Defeated foe and foemen at my gate,
Uprooted odds, and triumphed over all
The petty states, and those renowned and great.
I felled the arms of Egypt and the Greek,
I thwarted the order and the might of Rome,
The wanted spoil and wealth they came to seek,
Became no alien's loot to carry home.

Age on age I dealt them blow for blow,
Age on age I gave them Hell for Hell,
Not then I bowed to ancient spear and bow,
Not now I yield to modern shot and shell.

Be moved these hills and mountains in retreat
Ere I salute your flag, or kiss your feet.

IL DUCE'S CHALLENGE

Away to savage bounds of Ethiope,
Oh, legions, I challenge you to war;
Revenge our noble dead of Audowa!
My every rhythm war; my heart I stoke
With fiery slogans of our people's hope.
Now, on to Africa, to make or mar
The rising power of the Fascist STAR;
To glory, or to death, for King and Pope!

Imperial realm, great of ancient fame,
Our Caesars ruled as gods of many states,
And kings and monarchs trembled at their name
Ere Vandals felled our mighty doors and gates.
Ah! such did Rome into her whirl and spin
Swallow up a Carthage now and then.

THE EMPEROR'S VOICE

His Thor-like voice shook chancelleries
And rocked each mighty forum, awed each
        throne,
With flash of lightning, and of thunder's tone.
It marshalled allies, stirred auxiliaries
Against the iron-clad yoke of tyrannies;
Its moving tremors shook dry land and foam
And broke volcano-like on hostile Rome,
It rumbled to and fro through Italy's skies.

The Lion's roar did echo round the earth,
It rang with pity in Geneva's ears;
This ancient speech, made modern willed new
        birth
To epochs on the horizon of years.
Today I raise my head, to God rejoice,
I've heard the thunder of the NEGUS-VOICE.

DIE FREE

Your king's behest, my countrymen, die free!
Die with the spirit that your fathers kept,
While pagan Europe and godless Egypt slept.
Your sires were lords of lands as well as sea,
Ere Sheba rose to guide their destiny.
Over this mountain fastness they have swept
As peer to any foes in war adept.
Arise and strike! This is our God's decree!

We shall not wear this curse of alien chains!
We bid for freedom, otherwise for death;
For it we'll cash our blood, will drain our veins
And die as men; fight to the fatal breath;
Let him who will the scourge of nations spread
Proclaim him *Conqueror, when we are dead!*

FRANCE, ENGLAND

Oh, I am startled, stripped of all belief,
As France and England's tardy hand and pulse
Feed Haile gall, and mad II Duce mulse.
The eyes of peace are loaded with a grief
As sad and sere as any autumn leaf;
Now, crafty Romans will the League *divulse—*
Refrigerate its blood, and RIGHT repulse,
Ah! now I know the victim pays the fief.

My hate is one indignant world of fire,
My anger all the madness of a tide;
Yet, over might and its cohorts of war,
I cling to RIGHT, though on the weaker side.
O, God, is Justice only soot and ash,
And all Thy people filthy rags and trash?

TO THE ASKARIS

How could I fight, if I were you, my brother?
I'd rather dodge, be yellow, dally, shirk;

And let the cannon's breath, the Romans smother,
And put their healthy vitals out of work.
I would be dumb to every Fascist trumpet
And swell at each old epithet of race;
I'd swing a carcass; die no motley puppet
Bearing the Stigma of the World's disgrace.

I'd play the role of traitor, of the traitors,
And fight as friend of my old hated foe,
My soul would be a thorn to foreign baiters,
A grim defiance grained from head to toe.
Now, such would be my way if I were you,
Though I were servant, slave and soldier too.

GOD SEND US RAINS

God send us rains, draft every sky and cloud,
And bid them into torrents rise and spill
And plunge below to drown the foemen's will;
Parade the elements, all heaven crowd,
With raging blast in storm and whirlwind loud,
God send us rain, flood every vale and hill,
And turn each parching glade into a rill;
Drop wanton seas and make Thy people proud.

For rains will snuff the breath of barking guns,
And form a Purgatory of the roads;
For rains will shield us from the greedy Huns
And foil the coming of their bloody hordes.
O, Father, God, have pity, send us rains,
Grant us great bounties from Thy high domains!

HAILE SELASSIE

Call up the dead from mute, immortal shade
Name L 'Ouverture, Cromwell, Washington;
Great men who led and flashed the bloody blade,
And left their deathless glory in the sun.
Point out in archives of the musty times
Arch-god or spear-god of the.olden days,
Whose ancient prowess into epic chimes

Into old Homer, or old Virgil's lays.

Yet ere you shelve your volumes of the great
    Of Israel, of Gentiles of renown,
Name Haile of the Ethiopes and rate
Him King and man; above those whom you
    crown.
This man to Jove or unto Arthur's Rings,
Would too have been a master, King of Kings.

FOR A KING AT THE SEPULCHRE

Alas, O, God, the fallen look to Thee!
A kingdom sacked of freedom and her crown;
Alone she prays, as in Gethsemane,
And treads a ruthless Calvary baited down.
Here is the Cross, and there the place of Skull;
Hark! she can hear the pounding hammers ring,
And taste the gall, and see the flow of love
From gory sides of earth's Messiah spring.

This royal group invades the Sepulchre,
The rocks of holy Zion, and the Birth;
They seek a Saviour, ask a Comforter,
Who reigned, and still must reign upon the
    earth.
Before Thy face and at Thy tomb of old,
God, hear their prayers, tragic stories told.

OH, HANG YOUR HEADS, A VOICE ACCUSING CRIES
(A King of Kings before the League)

Oh, hang your heads, a voice accusing cries,
And points a finger shaking in your face.
Bewails of sickly treachery and lies,
Of noble oaths that welter in disgrace.
Don the ashy sackcloth, raid the hair
And rid your ghastly togas of the stain;
Albeit that your proffered words were fair,
Time has revealed your pompous speech was vain.

I did not ask for bounties of your blood,
Demand your sons for sacrifice supreme,
Yet I was led, believing that you would
Be succor and a shield to the extreme.
Bereft of friends, by evil foes beset,—
"God will remember, time will not forget."

P. J. WHITE, JR.

VESTIS VIRUMQUE CANO
A Sonnet on American Officials Greeting
An Ethiopian Potentate

I SEE you bow in state humility,
Welcoming, with the dignity and grace
Due noble sons of distinguished race,
These swarthy men from Afric's sun-baked lea.
And the Imperial son-in-law I see
Acknowledging your greeting, as his face
Glows with a Pleasure nothing can efface,—
A man of color—and authority.

Ah, Potentate! How greatly do I fear
(Knowing my Nordic brother and his way)
That, should that beard remove from off thy chin,
Thy rich dress change to occidental gear,
Some of those with thee might be heard to say,
"Now, who the hell let these damned niggers in?"
Opportunity, January, 1936: 10

Notes

INTRODUCTION

1. Cary Nelson, *Revolutionary Memory: Recovering the Poetry of the American Left* (New York: Routledge, 2001); Mark W. Van Wienen, *Partisans and Poets: The Political Work of American Poetry in the Great War* (Cambridge: Cambridge University Press, 1997); William J. Maxwell, *New Negro, Old Left: African American Writing and Communism Between the Wars* (New York: Columbia University Press, 1999); Nancy Berke, *Women Poets on the Left: Lola Ridge, Genevieve Taggard, Margaret Walker* (Gainesville: University Press of Florida, 2001); Paula Bernat Bennett, *Poets in the Public Sphere: The Emancipatory Project of American Women's Poetry, 1800–1900* (Princeton: Princeton University Press, 2003); Michael Thurston, *Making Something Happen: American Political Poetry Between the World Wars* (Chapel Hill: University of North Carolina Press, 2001); Joseph Harrington, *Poetry and the Public: The Social Form of Modern U.S. Poetics* (Middletown, CT: Wesleyan University Press, 2002).

2. "A social philology claims that social materials (both specific and general politics, attitudes, subjectivities, ideologies, discourses, debates) are activated and situated within the deepest texture of the sharpest specificities of the poetic text: on the level of word choice, crypt word, impacted etymologies, segmentivity and line break, the stanza, the image, diction, sound, genre, the 'events' and speakers selected inside the work (enounced), and the rhetorical tactics of the thing on the page (enunciation). All the materials of the signifier are susceptible of a topical/topographic reading in a social philology. The attentiveness that poetry excites is a productive way to engage ideologies and contradictions in texts, while honoring the depth and complexity of poetry as an intensive genre. So by a social philology; I mean an application of the techniques of close reading to reveal social discourses, subjectivities negotiated, and ideological debates in a poetic text." (DuPlessis 12)

3. For the New Critic, the text's relationship to a world that extends beyond it is of little interest: the poem is not a cultural or biographical artifact but rather

an autonomous and self-determinant (i.e. "autotelic") art object. The meaning of literature is not dependent upon its reflection of an external cultural reality; instead, literary meaning is an intrinsic attribute of the work and therefore publicly accessible and verifiable.

CHAPTER ONE

1. According to Marteinson, "The formal structure of comedy may be seen as a sequence of five epistemological states. 1. Situation: a conflict is posited between a hero's plans and society's conventions; 2. Invention: by design or through another's error, the hero's identity is fragmented into a 'true' and one or more 'mistaken' interpretations; 3. Illusion: the 'competing truths' form the basis on which two opposed camps view the hero in different terms—generating interpretative disjunctions whose cognitive and ontological incongruity provokes laughter and mocks those 'duped.' 4. Discovery: the hero's true identity is revealed, and the play's comic mechanism is thus brought to an end; 5. Denouement: the audience is delighted the hero's plans have succeeded, despite his underdog status, by means of *social opportunities obtained through the false identity,* a fact which compromises the plot's authority figures, who represent *deformed norms destroyed in effigy*" (1; emphases in original).

2. The discourse of narrative muralism in the United States during the 1930s was an extension of the activist iconographic program of the mural renaissance in Mexico (Mello 65). During the late 1920s, three Mexican muralists, José Clemente Orozco, Diego Rivera, and David Alfaro Siqueiros, came to the United States and began to paint murals. Their aesthetic prescribed that "not only should [a mural] express some form of ethical, political, and social commitment, but its composition should be programmatic" (Mello 65). Originally, the muralistic discourse had been formulated specifically to express the social ideals of the Mexican Revolution. However, once the painters began to work in the United States, they adopted "a continental perspective, seeking universality and moving counter to the European experience, which had been seen as the only valid one until then" (Mello 225). Working in this way, the painters reframed discourses of identity and origin myths for the entire region (Mello 225). Influenced by the Mexican muralists, Thomas Hart Benton's murals gave him a leading role in American art. After Benton successfully completed other commissions, *Time* magazine featured his self-portrait on its cover in 1934. Benton's nine vignettes of American life, *America Today* (1929) (*Indiana Murals* [1933]), bore such titles as *Cotton Loading; Lumber, Corn, and Wheat; Steel;* and *City Building*. Benton's controversial mural stirred up interest in mural painting and was one of the key factors in motivating the government to support artists through the Federal Art Project.

3. Thus, in "*On the Slave Ship,*" which is the opening sonnet in the sequence, the trope of time foreshadows an inevitable but essentially illusory and undelineated outcome. In Marxist dialectical materialism, time is not an abstraction and does not smite anything: Eddie Clynes states that "if change (motion) is to be conceived as qualitative change resulting from quantitative changes arising from contradictions within matter, then allowing for an ultimate (indivisible) unit of matter, or opening the door to a first impulse defy dialectical materialism. . . . In my understanding of Marxism, time and space are not abstract concepts in the sense of having an exis-

tence divorced from matter, and vice-versa!" ("Time and Teleology").

4. Nowhere in *Decline* is Spengler's scheme presented as concisely as in this summary: "The central theme in *The Decline of the West* is that all higher cultures go through a life cycle analogous to that of an organic evolution, from birth to maturation, and to inevitable decline. Spengler also used the analogy of four seasons: the spring (birth and infancy), summer (youth), fall (maturity), and winter (old age and decay)" (Liukkonen).

5. Eleanor Cook comments: "the decline of Western civilization and the parallel between Roman and modern civilization: this suggests Spengler. We tend to associate *The Waste Land* with Spengler, in general because of this sense of the decline of civilization, and in particular because Spengler's seasonal cycle so neatly fits Eliot's allusions to English literature in Parts I to IV of the poem" (344). "Spengler maintained that every culture passes a life cycle from youth through maturity and old age to death" (*Columbia Encyclopedia*).

6. The word *work* occurs sixty-five times in the 1891–1892 version of Whitman's *Leaves of Grass*.

7. "Seventy years after its initial release, Josef von Sternberg's *Underworld*, based on a taut story by Ben Hecht (who received the first Oscar for the story in 1927) has not lost any of its style and luster. While this film has been erroneously credited as the first 'gangster film,' it is arguably the most important. (In 1927, *Underworld* was on the N.Y. Times 'Top 10 Film List.') The central character, Bull Weed, the self-proclaimed king of the underworld (played by George Bancroft), is a complex monarch. He is not pure evil. He isn't even a pure opportunist. He is a burly bank robber who fancies himself a businessman and philanthropist. He has the ego of a king, but also has a benevolent air. He admires class and crudely attempts to socially elevate his moll, Feathers (played by Evelyn Brent), with stolen jewels and purchased votes" (McIntyre).

8. The controversial sex-racism discourse has barely been researched and formulated by authoritative academics. It remains the subject of amateur psychologists and radical theorists, such as Calvin Hernton (*Sex and Racism in America*), Eldridge Cleaver (*Soul on Ice*), and Orlando Patterson (*Rituals of Blood*). Carl Jung referred to the energy propelling this communal sex-racism complex as the "shadow" (repressed psychological elements) projected onto the black victim. Jung states that "shadows can also be collective, an entire cultural *zeitgeist* shadowed by its antithesis as the Nazi's Triumph of the Will was shadowed by a mass annihilation of wills in the Gotterdammerung" (Hampden-Turner 46).

9. "The community, too, evolves a super-ego under whose influence cultural development proceeds. The super-ego of an epoch of civilization has an origin similar to that of an individual. It is based on the impression left behind by the personalities of great leaders—men of overwhelming force of mind in whom one of the human impulsions has found its strongest and purest, and therefore often its most one-sided, expression" (Freud 141).

10. Paul Roazen states that "there is a well-known irony in the ease and extent of Freud's American triumph. For he had the utmost disdain and contempt for American life. 'America,' he joked, 'is a mistake; a gigantic mistake, but a mistake.' He denied 'hating' America; he merely 'regretted' it. His reasons for his difficulties in adjusting to American customs on his trip in 1909 ranged from the absence of public toilets, the quality of the water and food, to the more common complaints about

America—the manners, the sexual hypocrisy, the general lack of culture, the brash wealth" (97).

11. Numbers 9:1 reads, "And the Lord spake unto Moses in the wilderness of Sinai, in the first month of the second year after they were come out of the land of Egypt, saying. . . . " John 13:23 reads, "Now there was leaning on Jesus' bosom one of his disciples, whom Jesus loved" (KJV).

12. Spengler's *Untergang den Abenlandes* (1918), which presents his organicist philosophy of history, was available in English in the United States after 1928. The volume was rapidly disseminated and was influential in many circles.

13. James Longenbach calls *The Waste Land* the ultimate "poem including history produced in the twentieth century" (237). Rather than operating within the framework of professional historians, the poem is hallucinatory, mystical, and ahistorical in approach. Though Eliot's handling of history viewed in terms of the development of cultures is often compared to Spengler, Vico, and Toynbee, Longenbach points out that Spengler and Toynbee recapitulated nineteenth-century historiography and were considered old-fashioned and naïve by their contemporaries (6). Ross in *The Failure of Modernism* suggests that modernist historical poems were poets' attempts to allow history to articulate itself; thus, length and inclusivity were the formal means by which poetry was endowed with the capacity for self-articulation (212–213).

CHAPTER TWO

1. The reported number of lynchings of African Americans rose from seven in 1929 to twenty in 1930, and to twenty-four in 1933, the worst year of the economic collapse (*EA*).

2. For example, Véronique Tadjo and Werewere Liking, who are quoted in Michael Syotinski's *Singular Performances*.

3. Juan Suárez provides this detailed evaluation of Kittler's theory:

The term "discourse network" (English translation of *Aufschreibesystem*) was coined by German historian and theorist Friedrich A. Kittler to designate the material and ideological substratum of discourse and textuality—the web of "technologies and institutions that allow a given culture to select, store and produce relevant data." A discourse network is, then, a sort of unconscious, or *impensé*, of signification. In a way, the concept combines Michel Foucault's concept of the "archive," which had been applied mostly to print culture, with Marshall McLuhan's insights on the influence of media technologies on thought and cultural processes. In Kittler's work the term has a materialistic thrust. It seeks to deflect the interiorizing, psychologizing tendency of traditional literary hermeneutics by exploring how the material support, or hardware, of signification shapes textuality. This hardware connects abstract meanings to real, tangible bodies, and bodies to regimes of power, information channels, and institutions. . . . [In] his description of "the discourse network of 1900" (where "1900" stands for the period stretching from the media revolution of the 1880s to the 1920s), to which modernism belongs, Kittler traces the traffic of ideologies, forms of discourse, and inscription mechanisms through the fields of psychophysics, psychoanalysis, the electronic recording media, and literature." (74–75)

4. Kelly Oliver states that "as subjects-in-process we are always negotiating the other within, that is to say, the return of the repressed. . . . Some feminists have found Kristeva's notion of a subject-in-process a useful alternative to traditional notions of an autonomous unified (masculine) subject" ("Kristeva and Feminism").

5. The source text that Redmond uses here is Sterling Brown's *Negro Poetry and Drama* (1937). This text has afforded a degree of confusion. Redmond does not cite it clearly in *Drumvoices*, while Gabbin attributes it to the Carnegie-Myrdal research (*Sterling A. Brown* 5), and Wintz (*Remembering the Harlem Renaissance* 108–31) cites it as an Atheneum publication of 1969. The text was the seventh Bronze Booklet in the adult education pamphlet series edited by Alain Locke and commissioned by his Associates in Negro Folk Education. Interestingly, Locke approaches Brown's views in one of his columns: in *Opportunity* in 1937, Locke addresses the subject of escape ("the escapist mode of compensation" [11]) and comments on some of the poets in Redmond's catalog—Lynn, Cuthbert, and Cowdery.

6. Under the title "Negro Songs of Protest," Lawrence Gellert published, as a regular feature in *New Masses* between 1931 and 1934, some of the three hundred songs that he collected during his travels through Georgia, the Carolinas, Mississippi, and Louisiana. The selections that appeared in 1931 were included in the *Profile Anthology* published by *New Masses* in 1932. A digest of the "Negro Songs of Protest" articles from *New Masses* were included in Nancy Cunard's anthology, *Negro* (1934). Some of the songs also were included in *Proletarian Literature in the United States* (1935). In 1936 after years of failing to find a publisher for this material, the American Music League published twenty-four of the songs in a book, *Negro Songs of Protest*. The songs were arranged for voice and piano. Sterling Brown, Alain Locke, and Guy Johnson contributed an extensive section on blues to the 1930 volume of *Folk-Say: A Regional Miscellany*, edited by B. A. Botkin, a 473-page book published by the University of Oklahoma Press. "Seven Negro Convict Songs" and "Twenty-one Negro Spirituals" were published in the Federal Writers' Project's collection, *American Stuff: An Anthology of Prose and Verse by Members of the Federal Writers' Project with Sixteen Prints by the Federal Arts Project*, edited by Jim Thompson (New York: Viking, 1937).

7. Robert Appelbaum has characterized the poststructuralist treatment of interiority:

> The Renaissance has been associated with the development of a newly intensified, individualized experience of subjectivity since the early nineteenth century. No more decisive evidence for that development has been found than the appearance of the character of Shakespeare's Hamlet, brooding over the dilemmas posed by his sense of his own "conscience," and telling his fellow characters and audience that he has "that within which passes show." Nevertheless, a number of recent critics of English Renaissance literature have come to call the traditional model of the rise of Renaissance individualism into question. Some have argued that the very "interiority" of characters like Hamlet is an illusion, an invention of anachronistic, liberal humanistic criticism. Critics like Barker and Belsey have argued that the "bourgeois subject," transparent to himself as an internally driven source of autonomous behavior, doesn't come into his own at least until the Restoration. Hamlet wasn't Samuel Pepys—Barker's model for the new bourgeois subject—and had no way of being Samuel Pepys. Hamlet's interiority, Barker argues, is

entirely "gestural"; beneath Hamlet's theatrical display of interiority and their mystery there is ultimately "nothing." . . . (1)

8. John Paul Russo has provided an extensive critique of this approach in the "Disappearance of the Self" chapter of *The Future without a Past*. His account is based on the assumption, which is held by many disciplines, that "the sovereign self—the subjectivity ideal—has become impoverished and sickly; for some it has died" (190).

9. Susan Schweik provides some notion of what word counts might reveal about meanings in poetry:

> So, for instance, when [Josephine] Miles read [Sylvia] Plath's *Ariel*, her notes counted the number of nouns and verbs in each poem and compared the count to her quantitative analyses of the distribution of vocabulary in poems by Plath's contemporaries. The point was not, as Burr notes, to obscure individual poetic choices but to illuminate the context in which those choices occurred and by which they were constrained. Discussions of individual poetic style could then ensue, with a technical and impersonal kind of grounding, as in Miles's addendum to her word-count of Plath: "The very high number of frequently used nouns calls for further discussion. Miss Plath not only allows certain nouns to carry a very intense, repetitive symbolic reference, but *she tends to distort the semantic value some words carry, with consistency. . . .* Thus to Miss Plath, *certain words are associated with horror:* these include, in the majority of cases, the adjectives *pure, little, beautiful;* the nouns *face, man, foot, blood, baby, veil, cry, hair, finger, sin, walls, Jew, skin* and *smile.*" (59; emphases added)

10. "When an adolescent is confronted by role confusion, Erikson says he or she is suffering from an identity crisis. In fact, a common question adolescents in our society ask is a straight-forward question of identity: 'Who am I?'" (Boeree "Erik Erikson").

11. "Foregather," "Search," "The Wine of Ecstasy," "Desert in Ethiopia," "Interview," "Museum Portrait," "Pennsylvania Station," "Spring in the South," "Thoughts from a Train Window," "Carnival Torch-Bearer," "The Octaroon," "Song of the Mulatto," "Torches."

12. "Cross Bearer," "Hampton Institute: (Remembering General Armstrong)," "Henry Alexander Hunt," "To a Fallen Leader," "Vestis Virumque Cano," "Ex-Slaves," "Ph.D."

13. "Achievement," "To France," "McDonogh Day," "Muse," "Ode" [Dodson], "Similies," "Sonnet" [Lilly], "Sonnet" [Prendergast], "Sonnet in Black," "St. Charles Ave.," "This Is the Dream America," "Jesters," "Southern Share-Cropper."

14. Insubordination bolsters a fundamental, lived ethical system that is clearly expressed in the blues but has been overlooked. Like many commentators, Sterling Brown addresses this foundational ethos piecemeal. He writes of "longing for a far country" (*Folk-Say* 332) when confronted with a verse like "I'm got a mind to ramble, a mind fo' to leave this town, / Got a mind my baby is goin' to turn me down." The verse frames the consistently encountered refusal to submit to authority, an attitude that often in life brings about catastrophe for the individual.

15. Religious mysticism includes a number of activities, including alchemy, yoga,

gnosticism, and Kabbalah. Jung referred to alchemy as the yoga of the Gnostics, and this formula serves as a useful definition for mysticism. The cabala code that Tolson uses in his sonnet was a traditional linguistic disguise used by the alchemists to write arcane texts. Many authorities believe that the alchemists were mystics and that their "attempts" to change lead to gold were merely a ruse, a metaphor, or a joke. Yoga is a mystical discipline—a system of meditation—and it is comparable to the meditative practices of the Kabbalists (so Jung might have also correctly said that alchemy is the Kabbalah of the Gnostics, though fewer readers might have understood). Thus, when Tolson invokes Kabbalah in his sonnet and hides within the language of the phonetic cabala to do so, he places himself within the mainstream of mysticism. Finally, Gurdjieff, the most important modern occultist, is often described as a Gnostic.

16. On Tolson and Marxism: Marianne Russell ascribes Tolson a Marxist-Christian position that Raymond Nelson reiterates: "The Tolson of *Harlem Gallery* wrote as a proponent of neither of the systems of belief, Marxism or Christianity, he had once espoused, although he still drew ethical strength and direction from both of them." Raymond Nelson, *"Harlem Gallery: An Advertisement," Virginia Quarterly Review* (Summer 1999). 25 June 2007 <http://www.vqronline.org/articles/1999/summer/nelson-harlem-gallery/>.

On Tolson and the black arts movement: The account of Tolson's confrontation with Robert Hayden at Fisk University's First Black Writers' Conference during a panel discussion—which included Tolson, Arna Bontemps, and Margaret Walker—appears in a number of places; see Coniff (1999). See also Flasch 134–50. Tolson purportedly denounced Hayden as follows: "'When a man writes, he tells me which way he went in society.' 'I'm a black poet,' he continued, 'an African American poet, a Negro poet. I'm no accident—and I don't give a tinker's damn what you think'" (Coniff 487). Commentators have not appreciated Tolson's intellectual resources and his motivations for deception. In Gurdjieff's teaching, ordinary man is governed by the Law of Accident, and it is this law that is behind Tolson's declaration that he is not an accident. Gurdjieff taught that man changes at each moment. These changes are produced by exterior shocks, which he can never foresee, as he can never foresee his own interior changes. Thus, he is helplessly carried along by the streams of life and by his own mood fluctuations. To escape from the influence of exterior and interior changes, Gurdjieff suggests specific methods, such as self-observation, working on oneself (individually and in groups), and performing exercises and movements—so that man can become master of himself. One of those exercises calls for the subject to assume disguises, as Tolson did in posing as a black cultural nationalist.

17. "Dark Symphony" won the National Poetry Prize in a contest sponsored by the American Negro Exposition in Chicago in 1940.

18. A. E. Waite was a member of the Order of the Golden Dawn. W. B. Yeats was also a member. Waite worked with Pamela Coleman-Smith on a deck of tarot cards ("The Waite deck") and wrote *The Key to the Tarot* (1910). T. S. Eliot refers to specific cards in the Waite tarot pack in *The Waste Land*.

19. "More sublime than any language on earth, Hebrew is the Divine language of the Torah and the Jewish Nation and the code and the conduit through which God created and re-creates everything that is. . . . According to the celebrated Jewish Sage Rabbi Shimon bar Yochai, author of the Zohar, the masterwork of the Mystical Tradition [Kabbalah], it was through and by means of the Hebrew letters of Torah that God actually conceived, formed, and created the world" ("On Hebrew").

20. In "Contribution to the Critique of Hegel's *Philosophy of Right,*" Karl Marx stated that "religious suffering is, at one and the same time, the expression of real suffering and a protest against real suffering. Religion is the sigh of the oppressed creature, the heart of a heartless world, and the soul of soulless conditions. It is the opium of the people."

21. Joy Flasch refers to the Zulu Club, the basement room in which Tolson wrote in his house in Langston, Oklahoma (44). There is, however, no record of the contents of Tolson's personal library. This is dismaying. For instance, in his *Libretto* (see the note to line 572) Tolson alludes to Jonathan Swift's awareness of the cabala and to Swift's use of that code in writing *Gulliver's Travels,* a subject discussed by the alchemist Eugene Canseliet in his volume *L'Hermetisme dans la vie de Swift et dans ses voyages* (Editions Fata Morgana 1983). How was Tolson able to come by this information in Langston, Oklahoma, in the late 1940s and early 1950s? Victoria Arana suggests that the required esoteric books may have been in circulation among Tolson's circle, and this seems likely. (See http://www.levity.com/alchemy/afrm0250.html.)

22. See also note 15 above. Cabala was the code in which European alchemical-hermetic texts were written. Tolson's sonnet, in its most interior level, uses cabala to sound out the word *alchemy* by means of the end sounds in the upward direction using lines 11 and 9 (*all*), 5 (*came*), 3 (*became*), and 3 and 1 (*y*). In the sonnet's cabala, words or lettters may be reversed. Other names and words that appear in Tolson's cabala are [Jean] *Toomer, C. Daly King, yayin,* and *Gurdjieff.* Gleb Butuzov states that

> the fourth important issue I would like to discuss relates to what we normally call punning and wordplay and, in the Hermetic context, mostly concerns French sources. Play on words, or phonetic cabala, represents another level of reading in a Hermetic text, and this level of the hierarchy of terms has been in use in French literature from the Middle Ages until the present day. Of course, the term cabala itself is a sort of pun. We have to admit that its understanding in a modern context refers to the Renaissance and is undoubtedly connected with Jewish Kabbalah which gained authority among Christian mystics and Western esoteric schools mainly owing to the efforts of Giovanni Pico della Mirandola in the end of [the] XV century. However, the history of European cabala began much earlier, hundreds of years before the dissemination of Judaic esoteric teachings in Europe. The abovementioned pun lies in the fact that cabala has the same Latin root as caballus, which means "horse," and, therefore, it refers to cabaliero and chevalier, i.e. "knight." . . . Thus, Jewish Kabbalah implies, besides the obvious meaning of the word, its numeric value on the one hand, and, on the other, possible words, contained in its letters that would allow a commentator to expand interpretation of the word up to several pages. In the case of the Hermetic cabala numerology also plays some role, but most important is the fact that the phrases, read aloud must be understood not just in the sense they have on paper, but also in that elusive sense they acquire on being "misheard" (where, in common speech, we would ask our interlocutor to repeat the sentence, because we had heard something that seemed to be inappropriate to the context of the conversation). *This second—really esoteric—meaning is often irrelevant to the first, and people who neglect this level of the information-exchange actually read a very different book.*

Phonetic cabala is thoroughly enough analyzed in the case of many French sources, especially in the works by Claude-Sosthène Grasset d'Orcet, Fulcanelli, Canseliet and others, but one comes across this type of coding in other languages too, in certain Greek, Italian and *English* sources for instance. (emphases added)

23. See Woodson 1999. Two recent critical studies (George Hutchinson, 2006 [541] and Cherene-Sherrard Johnson, 2007 [200]) assert that I have "overstated" the influence of Jean Toomer and George I. Gurdjieff on Harlem Renaissance writers of the 1920s and 1930s. Having taken no position, I have followed, as best as I could, where the research led since I first began to explicate Tolson's long poems, which turned out to be presentations of Gurdjieff's entire occult system by means of cabalistic coding. Given the importance of Carl Van Vechten to the Harlem Renaissance and my demonstration that Van Vechten was a member of the New York Gurdjieff group, I do not see that I have overstated my argument. Through further research, I now know that at least one major classic of American modernism *outside of the Harlem school* was written in the phonetic cabala (C. Daly King's cipher), namely, James Agee's *Let Us Now Praise Famous Men.* I have already shown King's cipher to have been used by such Harlem writers as Hurston, Larsen, Thurman, Fisher, and Schuyler, though my recent research shows that this is not a complete list. The problem here is not my treatment of occultism but the general resistance to and inability of critics and scholars to ascertain the influence of occultism on modern literature.

24. For example, "Jesse Seegar" barely manages to hide *Gurdjieff*'s name once the table of contents is read as code; for the sake of clarity, I will point out that this *cabala* assigns the phonetic syllables to other locations so that *Gurdjieff* is heard in gar-Jesse. Some names are intended to reveal the code itself, like "Bella Scaritt"—*be scared.* Similarly, "Etchings Uriah Houze" offers the phrase *at your house.* Other names present information about the Gurdjieff groups, so that "Margaret Levy" comments that *A. R. [Orage] leaves G. [Gurdjieff];* by this means, Tolson referred to the split between Orage and Gurdjieff, an event so crucial to the American Gurdjieff circle that several books address the meaning of this crisis that took place in 1931. See, for example, Paul Beekman Taylor's *Gurdjieff and Orage.*

25. Emerson's piece on Shakespeare begins with "Great men are more distinguished by *range* and tent than by originality" (Emerson "Shakespeare"; my emphasis). Range is also central to his description of Plato: "This *range* of Plato instructs us what to think of the vexed question concerning his reputed works,—what are genuine, what spurious" (Emerson "Plato"; my emphasis).

26. In "Representative Men" Emerson writes that "the *search* after the great man is the dream of youth and the most serious occupation of manhood" and that "we have hope to *search* out what might be the very self of everything" (Emerson "Representative Men"; my emphasis).

27. "Fundamental to every philosophy of history is the concept of historical time. . . . In *The Decline of the West* [Spengler] portrayed world history as being virtually eternal. Cultures rose and declined in an apparently endless, grand procession" (Farrenkopf 202). These vast expanses of time seem to threaten the idea of human freedom. "The various cultures express the arbitrariness of nature in the sense that their emergence in a particular place and time is accidental" (Farrenkopf 30).

28. Russell Anderson, "To Marian Anderson," *Crisis* (August 1939): 246. Marcus

Christian, "Selassie at Geneva," *Opportunity* (June 1938): 213.

29. William Banks has clarified the compositions of the African American groups that were closest to Franklin D. Roosevelt's White House:

> In 1934 Foreman and Weaver helped establish an interagency advisory group that would monitor "Negro Affairs." The group was led by Robert Vann, editor of the popular black weekly newspaper the *Pittsburgh Courier* and assistant to the U.S. attorney general. Vann's group included Eugene Jones, formerly with the Urban League, and Henry A. Hunt, president of Fort Valley State College. In most respects this formal group of highly educated blacks was eclipsed by the informal black cabinet or "brain trust" led by Mary McCleod Bethune, president of Bethune-Cookman College in Florida, and director of the Negro division of the New Deal's National Youth Administration. (*Black Intellectuals* 116)

30. Joaquin Miller (1837?–1913) "was the pen name of the American eccentric and poet, Cincinnatus Heine (or Hiner) Miller. . . . A 2004 conference on Miller referred to him as 'Poet of the Sierras,' the founder of California's Arbor Day, prose stylist extraordinaire, horse thief, judge, Pony Express rider, newspaper editor, critic, gold miner, successful playwright, champion of Native American rights, Indian fighter, rogue and hero." Miller was "more of a celebrity in Europe than in his native United States. . . . 'His adventures through Oregon, Idaho, and Northern California brought him fame in England, notoriety in America and provided fodder for much of his poetry and prose.' However, some literary critics felt that he was a first-class self-promoter, but a second-rate poet" (Sierra Nevada Virtual Museum "Joaquin Miller").

31. Though he repudiated Adolf Hitler and would have nothing to do with the Nazis, Oswald Spengler did invent the concept of National Socialism. I mention this to demonstrate the compelling nature of the role models in his world history. The following is one of his comments on the "force-men" that arise in the final phase of the history of a civilization: "So we find by the side of Michael III (842–61) Bardas, and by Constantine VII (912–959) Romanos the latter even formally Co-Emperor. In 867 the ex-groom Basileios, a Napoleonic figure, overthrew Bardas and founded the sword-dynasty of the Armenians (to 1081), in which generals instead of Emperors mostly ruled—*force-men* like Romanos, Nicephorus, and Bardas Phocas. The greatest amongst them was John Tzimisces (969–976) in Armenian Kiur Zan" (Spengler *Decline vol.* 2 426; emphasis added).

32. The man farthest down was not originally the African American peasant. Booker T. Washington traveled to Italy and wrote a book, *The Man Farthest Down: A Record of Observation and Study in Europe* (1912), advancing the thesis that the African American was better off than the depressed classes of Europe. His thesis was that "the cruelties to which the child slaves of Sicily have been subjected are as bad as anything reported of the cruelties of Negro slavery."

33. Robin D. G. Kelley states:

> A predominantly black underground organization of sharecroppers, tenant farmers, and agricultural laborers, the Share Croppers Union (SCU) was the largest Communist-led mass organization in the Deep South. Founded in Alabama in the spring of 1931, the organization was first initiated by black tenant farmers in Tallapoosa County. . . . Union. Based mainly in Tallapoosa and Lee counties, Alabama, under Coad's leadership the union built up an estimated membership of eight hundred

within a two-month period. In July 1931, the union faced its first in a series of violent confrontations with local authorities. . . . Once the union was reconstructed, it adopted the name SCU. By the summer of 1932, the reconstituted SCU claimed six hundred members and a new secretary was appointed. Al Murphy, a black Birmingham Communist originally from McRae, Georgia, transformed the SCU into a secret, underground organization. SCU militants were armed for self-defense and met under the auspices of "Bible meetings" and "sewing clubs." Under Murphy's leadership, the union spread into the "black belt" counties of Alabama and into a few areas on the Georgia-Alabama border. In December 1932, another shootout occurred near Reeltown, Alabama (not far from Camp Hill), which resulted in the deaths of SCU members Clifford James, John McMullen, and Milo Bentley, and the wounding of several others. . . . Faced with large-scale evictions resulting from New Deal acreage reduction policies, sharecroppers flocked to the union. Its growth was by no means hindered by the gun battle. By June 1933, Murphy claimed nearly two thousand members, and by the fall of 1934 the official figures skyrocketed to eight thousand. . . . Throughout 1935, despite the union's push for legal status in the black belt, SCU activists faced severe repression during a cotton choppers' strike in the spring and a cotton pickers' strike between August and September. In Lowndes and Dallas counties in particular, dozens of strikers were jailed and beaten, and at least six people were killed. In 1936 the SCU, claiming between ten thousand and twelve thousand members, spread into Louisiana and Mississippi. It opened its first public headquarters in New Orleans and, in an attempt to transform the SCU into a trade union, officially abandoned its underground structure. . . . Failing to solve the problems created by the New Deal and the mechanization of agriculture in the cotton South, the Party's decision to divide the organization "by tenure" in 1937 marked the end of the SCU. Nevertheless, a few SCU locals in Alabama and Louisiana chose not to affiliate with any other organization and maintained an autonomous existence well into World War II. ("Share Croppers Union")

34. The following statement by Robert C. Liberman indicates the general state of race relations in the 1930s: "All of the policies in the Social Security Act carried race-laden exclusion, features that inherently, whether by accident or design, excluded African Americans from full participation in their benefits. Given the status of African Americans in American society in the 1930s, it is not surprising to find that the social policy innovations of that period largely excluded them, and scholars have often noted the racial disparities that resulted from the Social Security Act" (23). In a more specific example, Anna Everett states that the decency taboo was elastic with respect to the Hays production code: "On one hand, the Code's morality clause shielded nude white bodies from the prurient gaze, while on the other, the fetishized 'native' black body, positioned outside the code of human morality and decency, was at once made an acceptable site for sexual titillation and sanctioned racial degradation" (244).

35. Natasha Distiller describes Millay's status as a poet as follows:

Edna St Vincent Millay was, at the height of her popularity, America's most celebrated woman poet. She was the first woman to win the Pulitzer Prize for her poetry, which she did in 1923. In 1925, Genevieve Taggard

(1993: 137) wrote of Millay that she "is really the first woman poet to take herself seriously as an artist." Locating Millay in a trajectory that begins with Sappho, Taggard finds "the meager list in our own tongue [to comprise] Emily Brontë, Christina Rossetti and Elizabeth Barrett— none of them very adequate to our desire. And then—suddenly, quite dazzlingly, in America, . . . Edna St. Vincent Millay." She was also well-known for her independence and unconventionality; this has translated into a reputation for feminist activism. As John Timberman Newcomb puts it, "Millay . . . was seen by many as a prototype of the 'modern woman,' especially in her assertion of the right to and need for female self-determination of body, mind, pocketbook, and voice." . . . Amongst the many sonnets that she wrote, Millay wrote two extended sonnet sequences. . . . *Fatal Interview*, first published in 1931, is a sequence of 52 sonnets which charts the course of a heterosexual love affair from the point of view of the female lover. It was extremely popular in its own time. Issued during the Depression, it sold 33,000 copies in its first ten weeks. (Disteller 153–54).

36. In the issue for December of 1931, the editor of *Opportunity* describes Helene Johnson as "one of the younger Negro poets."

37. Charles Edward Russell, 'To Marian Anderson," *Crisis* (August 1939): 6; Milton Bright, "Lines for Marian Anderson," *Opportunity* (May 1939): 136.

CHAPTER THREE

1. John Cullen Gruesser defines Ethiopianism as follows:

The excerpt from Stewart's 1833 "Address" provides a vivid illustration of four key Ethiopianist elements. First, it asserts a common heritage shared by African Americans and Africans: "We sprung from one of the most learned nations of the whole earth." Second, the passage adopts the biblical notion of a Supreme Being who raises and punishes nations, leading to a belief in a cyclical view of history in which the fortunes of peoples rise and fall: "But it was our gross sins and abominations that provoked the Almighty to frown thus heavily upon us, and give our glory to others. Sin and prodigality have caused the downfall of nations, kings, and emperors." Third, it predicts a bright future for peoples of African descent: "a promise is left us; 'Ethiopia shall again stretch forth her hands unto God.'" Fourth, Stewart's statement exhibits monumentalism, which Wilson Moses defines, in an essay entitled "More Stately Mansions," as "an expression of the desire to associate black Americans with symbols of wealth, intelligence, stability, and power such as those of ancient Egypt and Ethiopia." (*Black on Black* 4)

William R. Scott contextualizes these beliefs:

Legally free and lawfully enslaved American blacks first began to acclaim and assert identity with an African state called Ethiopia in colonial times, in the years preceding and following the war between Great Britain and its North American colonies. It was then that African American converts to Christianity discovered Ethiopia of the Bible and forged from the Scriptures an inspiriting myth of Ethiopian peoplehood and ordained resurgence. That myth, expanded and embellished between the time of the American Revolution and the era of the Great Depression, was deeply embedded in the U.S. black psyche when war erupted in 1935 between Italy and Ethiopia. (11)

2. "March 19, 1935. Sixteen-year-old Lino Rivera was caught stealing a penknife from a white-owned shop in Harlem. When the police were called, a group formed around the shop, and fearing the crowd the police officer and shop owner let the boy go. However, rumors spread that the boy had been lynched, instigating pickets followed by full-blown violent riots of over 3,000 people continuing over two days. By the time the riot was quelled, 125 people had been arrested, 100 injured and three killed" (Puryear).

3. This is not surprising given the persistence and centrality of the idea of race war in the African American community. For instance, in 1923 Marcus Garvey stated that "I feel that it is only a question of a few more years before our program will be accepted not only by the few statesmen of America who are now interested in it, but by the strong statesmen of the world, as the only solution to the great race problem. *There is no other way to avoid the threatening war of the races that is bound to engulf all mankind, which has been prophesied by the world's greatest thinkers;* there is no better method than by apportioning every race to its own habitat" ("Africa for Africans"; emphasis added). Garvey is no doubt referring to Oswald Spengler as an authority on this topic.

4. Though *Cultural Trauma and Collective Identity* by Alexander et al. is about "the meaning making process," this convenient phrase appears in abstracts but not in the study; see, for example, page 62, where "meaning struggle" is discussed. In their discussion of African American identity, the volume's contributors align black collective identity with the Harlem Renaissance and Garveyism: "In the 1920s, after the first wave of what has come to be called the 'great migration' in the context of a newly forming black public sphere, two distinct frameworks for narrating and giving meaning to the past took form, one progressive and the other tragic. These narrative frame works were articulated by activists in two social movements, the Harlem renaissance [progressive meaning] and Garveyism [tragic meaning], both of which were directed primarily inward, toward the transformation of racially based collective identity" (78). They advocate that "carrier groups" (62)—in their study, intellectuals (and in this study, poets)—play a significant role in the "trauma process" (62) when there is a crisis of meaning and identity. However, the study does not take in what appears to be the adjustments made to the collective identity between the 1920s and the next major phase when slavery moved outside group memory and become part of America's collective memory (78).

5. Snow observes that the alignment created by identity work "can vary significantly, ranging from the elevation of the salience of a particular identity to a fairly dramatic change in one's sense of self. Four identity construction processes have been identified that capture this variation: identity amplification, identity consolidation, identity extension, and identity transformation (Snow and McAdam 2000)" (11).

6. It is tempting to describe Wright's imagery as *surrealistic*, but that term is not useful when Wright's surrealism is being distinguished from Mayakovsky's *zaumnyi iazyk* (transreason poetry). In the quotation below, Anna Lawton (facing the limi-

tations of the critical vocabulary for dreamlike effects) does describe Mayakovsky's effects as surrealist. Mayakovsky's cubo-futurism precipitated "transreason" or "transrational" effects that today might superficially resemble the effects of surrealism, but they were not derived from the same aesthetics. Cubo-futurism was a vibrant and influential movement in its own right. Anna Lawton states that

> "in general terms, the Cubo-Futurists proposed to treat the poetic word as an object in itself devoid of any referent. Transrational language, rich in sound but devoid of conventional meaning, was organized by phonetic analogy and rhythm rather than by grammar and syntax. . . . Mayakovsky, the most popular and charismatic figure in the group, created his own strikingly original poetic language by using conventional words in a nonconventional way. . . . The basic trait that distinguished the Cubo-Futurists from the Italians [the Futurists who followed Marinetti] was an underlying archaism, a leaning toward a primitivism of forms and often of themes (water nymphs, bogeymen, and other figures of Slavic folklore . . .), . . . where the word in its pristine purity created myth; and where the human being, in a prelogical state of mind, through the word discovered the universe. . . . Mayakovsky's urban landscapes are often nightmarish settings (the Gogol and Dostoevsky models were not after all 'thrown overboard from the Ship of Modernity') in which animated and surrealistically misplaced objects threaten to subvert the hierarchical order based on human supremacy." (12–18)

7. Rearticulate: "Discursive reorganization or reinterpretation of ideological themes and interests already present in the subject's consciousness, such that these elements obtain new meanings or coherence" (Omi and Winant 195 n. 11).

8. *The Story of Little Black Sambo*, a children's book by Helen Bannerman, a Scot living in India, was first published in London in 1899. In the tale, an Indian boy named Sambo prevails over a group of hungry tigers. The little boy has to give his colorful new clothes, shoes, and umbrella to four tigers so they will not eat him. Sambo recovers the clothes when the jealous, conceited tigers chase each other around a tree until they are reduced to a pool of delicious melted butter. The story was a children's favorite for half a century but became controversial due to the use of the word *sambo*, a racial slur in some countries. In 1932 Langston Hughes said *Little Black Sambo* exemplified the "pickaninny variety" of storybook, "amusing undoubtedly to the white child, but like an unkind word to one who has known too many hurts to enjoy the additional pain of being laughed at" (Pilgrim).

9. In film theory, the cinematic suture involves three easy steps of telling the truth via visual contact between subject and observer. In every way, the suture is a dialectical existential contract between an author, a reader, and a work of art—*I see you, therefore I am. You see me, therefore you are. We see one another, therefore we seem to exist.* In film theory, the suture is evident when slowing down the frames to observe how dialogue works: actors and the camera look at something (step 1), the camera shows another angle to reveal the reaction of the viewed subject/object (step 2), and a secondary camera pulls back for a long shot so that viewers can judge the relationship themselves (step 3) (Bialik 1).

10. I mean *canonical* in the limited sense of anthologized poems, since Hughes's radical poetry from this decade has not been accorded critical attention (Shulman 286; writing in 2000), and Hughes is the major figure of this period. Problemati-

cally, Hughes is considered a canonical poet even though his radical poems from the thirties are not considered canonical. If the black poets of the thirties are ranked by importance, Hughes is followed by Sterling Brown, Frank Marshall Davis, and perhaps by Fenton Johnson, all of whom by virtue of their inclusion in anthologies are canonical.

11. Julia Bolton Holloway observes that "*Aurora Leigh* . . . published in 1856, is a male epic and a woman's novel, written in nine books, echoing the nine books of the prophetic Cumaean Sibyl and the nine months of a woman's pregnancy. It quarries the Bible and the Classics, Homer, Aeschylus, Sophocles, Virgil, Apuleius, Dante, Langland, Shakespeare, Milton, and Byron, while it also uses contemporary women's writings, Madame de Staël (1776–1817), George Sand (1804–76) and Charlotte Brontë (1816–55), and discusses Brook Farm's communism (1841–6), Ireland's Great Famine (1846–7), and the working conditions of women and children. [Elizabeth Barrett Browning] read the Bible's scriptures in Hebrew, Chaldean and Greek, the other texts in their original Greek, Latin, Italian, French and English; yet she filled her learning with life. Across [*Aurora Leigh's*] pages we hear dialectic and reconciliation, the voices of women and men, of poor and rich, and in its epic similes genders are generally reversed" (Holloway).

12. "In *Speed and Politics* (1986 [1977]), Virilio undertakes his first sustained attempt to delineate the importance of accelerated speed, of the impact of technologies of motion, of types of mobility and their effects in the contemporary era. Subtitled 'Essay on Dromology,' Virilio proposes what he calls a 'dromomatics' which interrogates the role of speed in history and its important functions in urban and social life, warfare, the economy, transportation and communication, and other aspects of everyday life. 'Dromology' comes from the Latin term, dromos, signifying race, and dromology studies how innovations in speed influence social and political life. The 'dromocratic revolution' for Virilio involves means of fabricating speed with the steam engine, then the combustion engine, and in our day nuclear energy and instantaneous forms of warfare and communication" (Paul Kellner, "Virilio").

13. "In noting her sources, Rukeyser mentions 'other documents, including the Egyptian Book of the Dead (in various translations), magazine and newspaper articles on Gauley Bridge, letters and photographs.' . . . Her understatement conceals a complex of bold literary and political commitments. Rukeyser fuses the immediacy of the Gauley dead with the timelessness of the *Egyptian Book of the Dead* and that in turn with the documentary language of congressional hearings and 'magazine and newspaper articles on Gauley Bridge, letters and photographs.' She has assimilated, subverted, and turned to her own politically radical uses the modernist techniques of poems like Eliot's 'The Waste Land'" (Shulman 182).

14. Robert Shulman locates Muriel Rukeyser in the documentary trend as follows:

> In *U.S. 1* and *The Book of the Dead*, Rukeyser also shares with other left artists a concern with the documentary. Among the achievements of Popular Front culture is the documentary, in film, photography, and reportage. In *The Book of the Dead* Rukeyser takes her place along with Joris Ivens and Leo Hurwitz, Meridel Le Sueur and Josephine Herbst. As Rukeyser puts it in *The Life of Poetry*, "the work of Joris Ivens, Paul Rotha, Grierson, Legge, Lerner, Steiner, Van Dyke, Strand, Hurwitz, Ferno, Kline, Flaherty, and the groups that formed behind such productions as *Spanish Earth, Crisis, Native Land, The City*, and *Heart of Spain*

sent an impulse through the other arts" [159]. Rukeyser responded to that impulse. In *US. 1* and especially in *The Book of the Dead*, she shows her belief that "poetry can extend the document" (*U.S. 1*, p. 146). Like others in the tradition she emerges from and contributes to, Rukeyser says of her intentions that "I wish to make my poems exist in the quick images that arrive crowding on us now (most familiarly from the screen), in the lives of Americans who are unpraised and vivid and indicative, in my own 'documents.'"

Beyond the films, *The Book of the Dead* also needs to be seen as one in a series of works by 1930s documentary photographers, collections of photographs with accompanying text: Margaret Bourke-White and Erskine Caldwell's *You Have Seen Their Faces* (1937), Archibald MacLeish's *Land of the Free* (1938), Walker Evans's *American Photographs* (1938), Dorothea Lange and Paul Schuster Taylor's *An American Exodus* (1939), Berenice Abbott's *Changing New York* (1939), Richard Wright and Edwin Rosskam's *12 Million Black Voices* (1941), and Walker Evans and James Agee's *Let Us Now Praise Famous Men* (1941). These collections are closely related to the large, ongoing Farm Security Administration (FSA) photography project." (183)

15. "The sonnets of Edna St. Vincent Millay and E. E. Cummings work, each by inverse subversions regarding, respectively, subject matter and aesthetic sensibility, simultaneously to identify with the British sonnet tradition, and, in identifying with the tradition but palpably subverting its conventions, to work to contradict the tenets which are connotatively central to British sonneteering. In doing so, these sonneteers worked in opposition to and in the embrace of Modernist poetic dogma in order to assert, deliberately or not, the dawn of an American literary theoretical and aesthetic consciousness, and to democratize the sonnet as a form available to any mode of formal experimentation, and any variety of subject matter" (Cairns).

16. Sterling A. Brown's poetic maturity resulted from a well-known dialectical engagement with the aesthetics of African American folk traditions. As Brown recounted so often, these experiential and imaginative encounters derived from a benevolent conspiracy between his theologian father (the Reverend Sterling Nelson Brown) and the eminent historian Carter G. Woodson, who sent the younger Brown to the South so that he would learn something about his people (Tidwell).

17. In *The Waste Land*, Tiresias, a blind prophet, serves as the poem's organizing consciousness. Eliot's note to line 218 states that "What Tiresias *sees*, in fact, is the substance of the poem."

18. "There were approximately 2 million Ethiopian slaves in the early 1930s, out of an estimated population of between 8 [million] and 16 million. Slavery continued in Ethiopia until the Italian invasion in October 1935, when it was abolished by order of the Italian occupying forces. In response to pressure by Western Allies of World War II. Ethiopia officially abolished slavery and involuntary servitude after regaining its independence in 1942. On August 26, 1942, Haile Selassie issued a proclamation outlawing slavery" ("African Slave Trade." Wikipedia. Web. 20 July 2010).

19. To indicate Eliot's reception in leftist circles, I will point out that V. F. Calverton, editor of the leftist journal *Modern Quarterly*, wrote and published "T. S. Eliot: Leisure Class Laureate" (February 1933), while a subsequent article was titled "T. S. Eliot—An Inverted Marxian" (July 1934).

20. Mr. Christopher Columbus
Sailed the sea without a compass
Well, when his men began a rumpus
Up spoke Christopher Columbus

He said, "There is land somewhere
So until we get there we will not go wrong
If we sing a swing song
Since the world is round[o] we'll be safe and sound[o]
'Till our goal is found we'll just keep the rhythm bound"

Soon the crew was makin' merry
Then came a yell, let's drink to Isabella
Bring on the rum
A music in that all the rumpus
A wise old Christopher Columbus

Soon the crew was makin' merry and Mary got mad
Then came a yell, let's drink to Isabel
So bring on the rum
A music in that all of the rumpus
A wise old Christopher Columbus

Christopher Columbus
Christopher Columbus
Christopher Columbus

21. Christ was unjustly accused, put on trial, crucified, and ultimately rose again.

22. Part 2, act 1, scene 2 of *Henry IV* supplies the source of Baxter's line, though not the sense." Falstaff says, "I have chequed him for it, and the young lion repents; marry, not in ashes and sackcloth, but in new silk and old sack" (2.1. lines 189–91).

23. Danny Cairns states that "In spite of its reputation being partly the product of historical, revisionist (mis)construction, the sonnet's connotation as lifeless and aristocratic was, by the dawn of Modernism, nonetheless entrenched irrevocably into literary culture, and this (mis)construction impacted to a considerable degree the ways in which the poetry and reputations of Cummings and Millay were received and perceived in their era, and the eras which followed. The sonnet's stultifying connotation lives on even today, and continues to influence our perception of these poets' reputations, as evidenced by the back flap of *The Collected Poems of Edna St. Vincent Millay*, [whose] précis seems to anticipate that the modern reader, informed by some kind of enlightened literary consciousness, should and will be repelled by the notion of a sonnet, as if any sonnet represented a dead and exhausted tradition regardless of its content, and insists, optimistically and apologetically that "Millay lost none of her vitality when she turned to sonnets" (Norma Millay, back flap). And so the sonnet as Millay and Cummings knew it . . . was rigid, regal, masculine, and rule-based. And it was these undertones with which Modernist sonneteers approach and subverted the form of the sonnet—and, in particular, how these American sonneteers approached the sonnet as a distinctly, historically British device" (6–7). Yet I must point out that in the face of these conditions, the sonnet was *poetry* for many African Americans in

the thirties, and they wrote and read sonnets despite these purported barriers, though I suspect that in most cases the attraction of the sonnet was the perceived difficulties of the form.

24. "I have been greatly amused by the public enthusiasm for 'The Black Internationale,' which is hokum and hack work of the purest vein. I deliberately set out to crowd as much race chauvinism and sheer improbability into it as my fertile imagination could conjure. The result vindicates my low opinion of the human race" (George S. Schuyler, from a letter to P. L. Prattis, April 4, 1937).

Works Cited

PRIMARY WORKS

Alexander, Jeffrey C., et al. *Cultural Trauma and Collective Identity*. Berkeley: University of California Press, 2004.

Aragon, Louis. "The Red Front." Translated by E. E. Cummings. Chapel Hill, NC: Contempo Publishers, 1933.

Auld, Carmen. "Interview." *Opportunity* (August 1935): 249.

Baxter, J. Harvey L. *Sonnets for the Ethiopians and Other Poems*. Roanoke, VA: The Magic City Press, 1936.

Bennet, Faye C. "Achievement." *The Crisis* (Feb. 1934): 38.

Brooks, Jonathan Henderson. "Muse in Late November." *Opportunity* (Nov. 1935): 338.

Brown, Sterling, Arthur P. Davis, and Ulysses Lee, eds. *The Negro Caravan: Writings by American Negroes*. Sterling A. Brown. New York: Dryden Press, 1941.

Brown, Sterling. *The Collected Poems of Sterling Brown*. Selected by Michael S. Harper. Chicago, Il.: Another Chicago Press, 1989.

———. Brown, Sterling A. *Collected Poems*. Evanston: Northwestern University Press, 1996.

Browning, Elizabeth Barrett. *Aurora Leigh*. 1865.

Cannon, David Wadsworth, Jr. *Black Labor Chant and Other Poems*. New York: Association Press, 1939.

Chittick, Conrad. "Torches." *Opportunity* (April 1935): 118.

———. "Museum Portrait." *Opportunity* (Feb. 1937): 50.

Christian, Marcus. "Southern Share-Cropper" *Opportunity* (July 1937): 217.

———. "Carnival Torch Bearer." *Opportunity* (Feb. 1938): 45.

———. "The Slave." *Opportunity* (Sept. 1937): 26.

———. "Selassie at Genva." *Opportunity* (June 1938): 213.

———. "McDonogh Day in New Orleans." *Opportunity* (June 1934): 171.

———. "Spring in the South." *Opportunity* (July 1934): 201.

———. "Martyrs of the Rope Brigade." *Opportunity* (Dec. 1934): 135.

Conant, Isabel Fiske. "Hampton Institute (*Remembering General Armstrong*)." *Opportunity* (Nov. 1937): 329.

Cowdery, Mae. *We Lift Our Voices and Other Poems*. Philadelphia: Alpress, 1936.

Cullen, Countee. "To France." *Opportunity* (August 1935): 242.

Davis, Frank Marshall. *Black Man's Verse*. Chicago: Black Cat, 1935.

Dodson, Owen. "Negro History: A Sonnet Sequence" *New Masses* 14 (April 1936): 21.

———."Metaphor for Negroes." *Opportunity* (July 1937): 213

———. "Desert in Ethiopia." *Opportunity* (Dec. 1935): 375.

———. "*Similies For Negroes*." *Opportunity* (November 1934): 335.

———. "Ode to the Class of 1936 Everywhere." *Opportunity* (August 1936): 238.

Drake, J.G. St. Clair. "Dedication in Time of Crisis." *Crisis* (July 1937): 207.

Du Bois, W. E. B. *The Souls of Black Folk* 1903. NY: Dodd, 1979.

———. *Black reconstruction in America : an essay toward a history of the part which Black folk played in the attempt to reconstruct democracy in America, 1860–1920.* New York : Russell & Russell c1935, 1962 1935.

Eliot, T. S. "The Waste Land. *Anthology of Modern American Poetry*. Ed. Cary Nelson. New York: Oxford University Press, 2000: 285–301.

Gibson, Rufus. "The Voice of Ethiopia" *The Crisis* (January 1936): 13.

Haywood, Violet G. "Selassie." *The Crisis* (October 1939): 293.

Henegan, Herbert. "The Negro Speaks to America." *The Crisis* (September 1931): 306.

Hill. N. Jay. "An Ethiope in Spain." *The Crisis*. (July 1937): 202.

House, Homer."Lyncher's Rally Song." *Crisis* (January 1935): 29

Hughes, Langston. *The Big Sea. An Autobiography*. Hill and Wang, 1940, 1963; 2nd ed. 1993. New York: Hill and Wang.

———. *The Negro Mother, and Other Dramatic Recitations*. With decorations by Prentiss Taylor. New York: Golden Stair Press, 1931.

———. *The Big Sea. Voices from the Harlem Renaissance*. Ed. Nathan Huggins. New York: Oxford University Press, 1976. 370–381.

———. "The Negro Speaks of Rivers." *The Collected Poems of Langston Hughes*. Ed. Arnold Rampersad. New York: Knopf, 1994. 23.

———. "The Negro Artist and the Racial Mountain." *Voices from the Harlem Renaissance*. Ed. Nathan I. Huggins. New York: Oxford University Press, 1976. 305–9.

———. "I, Too." The Collected Poems of Langston Hughes. Ed. Arnold Rampersad. New York: Knopf, 1994. 46

———. "Pennsylvania Station." ["Terminal"]. *Opportunity* (Feb. 1932): 52.

———. "Search" *Opportunity* (July 1937): 207.

———. "Ph.D." *Opportunity* (Aug. 1932): 249.

Illich, Ijvan. *ABC: The Alphabetization of the Popular Mind*. San Francisco: North Point Press, 1988.

Jenkins, Welborn Victor. *Trumpet in the New Moon and Other Poems*. Boston: The Peabody Press, 1934.

Johnson, Georgia Douglas. "Foregather." *Opportunity* (Jan. 1935): 20

Lilly, Octave. "Saint Charles Avenue." *Opportunity* (Sept. 1938): 264.

———. "Song of the Mulatto." *Opportunity* (Nov. 1938): 333.

———. "Ex-Slaves." *Opportunity* (Dec. 1939): 364.

———. "Sonnet." *Opportunity* (June 1934): 178.

Masters, Edgar Lee. *Spoon River Anthology*. New York: Dover Publications, 1992.

Mayakovsky, Vladimir. *The Bedbug and Selected Poetry*. Ed. Patricia Blake. Bloomington: Indiana University Press, 1975.

McKay, Claude. "I Know My Soul." New York: Harcourt, Brace and Company, 1922.

———. "Harlem Runs Wild." *Voices from the Harlem Renaissance*. Ed. Nathan I. Huggins. New York: Oxford University Press, 1976.

Murray, Pauli. "Until the Final Man." *The Crisis*. (September 1940): 297.

Popel, Esther. "Flag Salute." *The Crisis* (August 1934): 342.

———. "Flag Salute." *The Crisis* (May 1936): 137.

———. "Flag Salute." *The Crisis* (May 1938): 146.

———. "Flag Salute." *The Crisis* (November 1940): Cover.

Pound, Ezra. "Hugh Selwyn Mauberley." November 18, 2007 [EBook #23538] 8 August 2008. www.gutenberg.org.

Prendergast, Marcia. "Sonnet." *Opportunity* (April 1937): 117.

Rauth, Mary T. "Sonnet." *The Crisis* (November 1937): 348.

Rowe, Sawney. "To A Fallen Leader." *Opportunity* (March 1936): 87.

———. "This is the Dream, America." *Opportunity* (Dec. 1935): 373.

Sandburg, Carl. "Chicago." *Anthology of Modern American Poetry*. Ed. Cary Nelson. New York: Oxford, 2000. 107–8.

Selassie, Haile. "Appeal to the League of Nations." Geneva, June, 1936. 7 November 2004 http://www.mtholyoke.edu/acad/interwar.htm.

Shakespeare, William. *Julius Caesar*. 8 October 2004 http://etext.lib.virginia.edu/shakespeare.

———. *As You Like It*. Web. 2 July 2010.

Shelley. P. B. "Mont Blanc: Lines Written in the Vale of Chamouni" (1817). 8 October 2004 http://eir.library.utoronto.ca/rpo/display/poem1898.html.

———. "Ozymandias of Egypt." Palgrave, Francis T. *The Golden Treasury*. London: Macmillan, 1875; Bartleby.com, 1999. 24 August 2008. www.bartleby.com/106/.

Smalls, Frank. "The Octaroon." *Opportunity* (March 1938): 78.

Tolson, Melvin. "The Wine of Ecstasy." *Negro Voices*. Ed. Beatrice Murphy. New York: Henry Harrison, 1938. 153.

———. *Harlem Gallery*. New York: Twayne, 1965.

Thurman, Wallace. *Infants of the Spring*. Boston: Northeastern University Press, 1992.

Toussaint, Irma. "Jesters." *Opportunity* (May 1936): 153.

Townes, George A. "*Henry Alexander* Hunt." *Opportunity* (Dec. 1938): 358.

Twynham, Leonard. "Cross Bearer." *Opportunity* (April 1938): 109.

———. "Thoughts from a Train Window." *Opportunity* September 1935: 278.

Walker, Margaret. "Sorrow Home." *Opportunity* (January 1935): 139.

Waller, Fats. "Mister Christopher Columbus." 8 August 2008 http://music.yahoo.com/Fats-Waller/Christopher-Columbus/lyrics/57670851

Washington, Haines J. "Sonnet in Black." *Opportunity* (May 1934): 135.

White, Jr., P. J. "Vestis Virumque Cano." *Opportunity* (Jan. 1936): 10.

Whitman, Walt. *Leaves of Grass. Bartleby on line, great books on line*. 22 October 2004 http://www.bartleby.com/142/.

———. "The Sleepers." *Leaves of Grass and Selected Prose*. Ed Sculley Bradley. New York: Holt, Rinehart and Winston: 1965: 349–357.

Williamson, Harvey M. "From the Delta's Unmarked Graves." *The Crisis* (May 1934): 129.

Woolfolk, Ada F. "Via Crucis." *Opportunity* January 1936: 23

Wright, Arthur N. "Ethiopia's Blacks." *Baltimore Afro-American.* August 3, 1935.

Wright, Richard. "The Ethics of Living Jim Crow." *American Stuff*, New York: The Viking Press,1937: 39–52.

——. "Transcontinental." *International Literature* (January 1936): 52–57.

SECONDARY WORKS

Adams, Don, and Arlene Goldbarb. "New Deal Cultural Programs: Experiments in Cultural Democracy." 29 December 2003 http://www.wwcd.org/plicy/US/Newdeal.html#TREAS.

Adamson, Joseph and Hilary Clark, "Introduction: Shame, Affect, Writing." In *Scenes of Shame: Psychoanalysis, Shame, and Writing.* Albany: State University of New York Press, 1999.

Adler, Alfred. *Understanding Human Nature.* New York: Premier, 1959.

"African Slave Trade." Wikipedia. Web. 20 July 2010.

Alexander, Elizabeth. *The Black Interior.* Saint Paul, MN: Graywolf Press, 2004.

Appelbaum, Robert. "Review of Katharine Eisman Maus. *Inwardness and Theater in the English Renaissance. Early Modern Literary Studies*" 1.2 (1995):101–8.

Arbor, J. Edward. "Upon this Rock." *The Crisis* (April 1935) 110.

Armed Conflicts Events Data. "Second Italo-Abyssinian War, 1935–1936." 8 November 2004 http://www.onwar.com/aced/nation/eat/ethiopia/fitalyethiopia1935.htm.

Atwater, Deborah F. "History of the *Pittsburgh Courier.*" 15 June 2005. http://newpittsburghcourier.com/?article+9951.

Aughterson, Kate, ed. *Renaissance Women: Constructions of Femininity in England.* New York: Routledge, 1995.

Bain, Alexander M. "Shocks Americana!: George Schuyler Serializes Black Internationalism." *American Literary History* 19.4 (2007):937–63.

Baker, Houston, Jr. *A Many-colored Coat of Dreams: the Poetry of Countee Cullen.* Detroit: Broadside Press, 1974.

Baker, Moira. "'The Uncanny Stranger on Display': The Female Body in Sixteenth- and Seventeenth-Century Love Poetry." *The South-Atlantic Review* 56.2 (1991): 7–25.

Barnard, Rita. *The Great Depression and the Culture of Abundance: Kenneth Fearing, Nathanael West, and Mass Culture in the 1930s.* New York: Cambridge University Press, 1995.

Barnes, Deborah. "'The Elephant and the Race Problem': Sterling A. Brown and Arthur P. Davis as Cultural Conservators." *Callaloo.* 21. 4. (Fall 1998): 985–97.

Banks, William M. *Black Intellectuals: Race and Responsibility in American Life.* New York: Norton, 1998.

Bellamy, Donnie D. "Henry A. Hunt and Black Agricultural Leadership in the New South." *The Journal of Negro History* 60, no. 4 (Oct., 1975): 464–79.

Berardi, Marianne. "Thomas Hart Benton." Owen Gallery. New York. 30 December 2003 http://www.tfaaoi.com/aa/2aa/2aa573.htm.

Bercovitch, Sacvan. *The American Jeremiad.* Madison: University of Wisconsin Press, 1978.

Berg, Philip S. *The Zohar*. Vol. 1. New York: Research Center of Kabbalah Press, 1986.

Berry, Faith. *Langston Hughes: Before and Beyond Harlem*. Westport, CN: L. Hill, 1983.

Besser, Howard. "Elements of Modern Consciousness." 7 October 2004 http://www.usyd.edu.au/su/social/papers/besser.html.

Bialik, Louise. "I Can't Believe My Eyes: Thoughts on Literary Suturism." Gart Pages. 8 November 2004 //hergart.tripod.com/172a/index.html.

Blake, Patricia. "Introduction: The Two Deaths of Vladamir Mayakovsky." *The Bedbug and Selected Poetry*. Bloomington: Indiana University Press, 1975: 9–50.

Blue Letter Bible. Dictionary and Word Search for smite. *Blue Letter Bible*. 1996–2002. 29 October 2003 http://www.blueletterbible.org/cgi-bin/words.pl?word=smite&page=1.

Boeree, George C. "Erik Erikson." *Personality Theories*. 2006. Web. 12 July 2010.

Bontemps, Arna Wendell. Introduction. *Black Thunder*. Boston: Beacon Press, 1968, 1992. xxi–xxix.

Booth, Alison. *Famous Last Words: Changes in Gender and Narrative Closure*. Charlottesville: University of Virginia Press, 1993.

Bornstein, George. *Material Modernism: The Politics of the Page*. New York: Cambridge University Press, 2000.

Botkin, B. A. "Regionalism and Culture." *The Writer in a Changing World*. New York: League of American Writers. 140–58.

Bouson, J. Brooks. "'Quiet As It's Kept': Shame and Trauma in Toni Morrison's *The Bluest Eye*." *Scenes of Shame: Psychoanalysis, Shame, and Writing*. Eds. Joseph Adamson and Hillary Clark. Albany: State University of New York Press, 1999. 207–36.

Braddock, Jeremy. "The Poetics of Conjecture: Countee Cullen's Subversive Exemplarity." *Callaloo* 25.4 (2002): 1250–71.

Bremer, Sidney H. "Home in Harlem, New York: Lesson from the Harlem Writers." *Analysis and Assessment, 1980–1994 (The Harlem Renaissance, 1920–1940)*. Ed. Cary D. Wintz. New York: Routledge, 1996. 47–56.

Bronowski, Jacob. *The Identity of Man*. Amherst, NY: Prometheus Books, 2002.

Browder, Earl. "The Writer and Politics." in *The Writer in a Changing World: American Writers' Congress*. 2nd ed. Edited by Henry Hart. New York: Equinox Cooperative Press, 1937. 48–55.

Brown, Norman O. *Life against Death: The Psychoanalytical Meaning of History*. New York: Vintage, 1959.

Brown, Sterling. "The Blues as Folk Poetry." *Folk-Say: A Regional Miscellany, 1930*. Ed. B. A. Botkin. Norman: University of Oklahoma Press, 1930. 324–39.

———. "Folk Values in a New Medium." Co-author, Alain Locke. *Folk-Say, 2*. Ed. Benjamin A. Botkin. Norman: University of Oklahoma Press, 1930. 340–45.

———. "A Romantic Defense." *Opportunity* 9 (April 1931): 118. [Review of *I'll Take My Stand*, a collection of essays by Twelve Southerners.]

———. "Two Negro Poets." *Opportunity* 14 (July 1936): 216–20. [Review of *Black Thunder*, a historical novel by Arna Bontemps, and *Black Man's Verse*, a collection of poems by Frank Marshall Davis.]

———. Excerpt From *Negro Poetry and Drama*. *Remembering the Harlem Renaissance*. Ed. Cary Wintz. New York: Routledge, 1996. 108–30.

Brown, Sterling, Arthur P. Davis, and Ulysses Lee, eds. *The Negro Caravan: Writings by American Negroes.* New York: Dryden Press, 1941.

Bruce, Jr. Dickson D. "W.E.B. Du Bois and the Idea of Double Consciousness." *American Literature* 64 2 (1992): 295–309.

Brudson, Charlotte. "What Is the 'Television' of Television Studies?" *The Television Studes Book.* Ed. Christine Geraghty and David Lusted. London: Edward Arnold, 1988. 95–113.

Buck-Morss, Susan. *Dreamworld and Catastrophe: The Passing of Mrs Utopia in East and West.* Cambridge, MA: MIT Press, 2000.

Bulwer-Lytton, Edward. *Richelieu; Or the Conspiracy: A Play in Five Acts.* 2nd ed. London: Saunders and Otley, Conduit St., 1839.

Butuzov, Gleb. "Some Traits of Hermetic Language." The Alchemy website. 20 July 2008 http://www.levity.com/alchemy/butuzov_hermetic_language.html.

Cairns, Danny. "[mis]Signification, Subversion, and Americanism in the Sonnets of Edna St. Vincent Millay and E. E. Cummings." 11 July 2009 http://www.lagrange.edu/resources/pdf/citations/2007/english/english%20-%20Cairns%20paper.pdf.

Calo, Mary Ann. "African American Art and Critical Discourse between World Wars." *American Quarterly* 51, no. 3 (September 1999): 580–621.

Carby, Hazel V. "Ideologies of Black Folk: The Historical Novel of Slavery." *Slavery and the Literary Imagination.* Ed. Deborah E. McDowell and Arnold Rampersad. Baltimore: Johns Hopkins University Press, 1989. 125–43.

Caudwell, Christopher. *Studies and Further Studies in a Dying Culture.* New York: Monthly Review Press, 1938, 1971.

———. *The Crisis in Physics.* Edited with an introduction by Hyman Levy. London: John Lane, Bodley Head, 1939.

Caws, Mary Ann. *The Poetry of Dada and Surrealism.* Princeton: Princeton University Press, 1970.

Chasar, Mike. "A Full Nelson? Getting a Grip on Cultural Criticism of Modern American Poetry." *Word For/Word* #9: Winter 2006.

Cleaver, Eldridge. *Soul on Ice.* With an introduction by Maxwell Geismar. New York: McGraw-Hill, 1967.

Clynes, Eddie. "Time and Teleology: Order in the Universe." *Australian Marxist Review* (April 1999). Web. 10 July 2010.

Cober. "Hello, I must be going." 24 June 2008 http://xroads.virginia.edu/~MA01/Cober/marx/identity.html

Collier, Eugenia, "I Do Not Marvel, Countee Cullen." *College Language Association Journal* 11.1 (1967): 73–87.

Columbia Encyclopedia. "Oswald Spengler." Web. 10 July 2010.

Connif, Brian. "Answering 'The Waste Land': Robert Hayden and the Rise of the African American Poetic Sequence." *African American Review* 33.3 (Fall 1999): 487–506.

Cook, Eleanor. "T. S. Eliot and the Carthaginian Peace." *ELH* 46.2 (Summer 1970): 341–55.

Corbould, Clare. *Becoming African Americans: Black Public Life in Harlem, 1919–1939.* Boston: Harvard University Press, 2009.

"*The Crisis* 'Is Not Approved.'" *Crisis* 45 (May 1938): 40.

Cubitt, Sean. "The Materiality of the Text." *Digital Aesthetic,* 14 February 2004 http://www.ucl.ac.uk/slade/digita/materiality.html .

Culler, Jonathan. *Structuralist Poetics: structuralism, linguistics, and the study of literature.* Ithaca: Cornell University Press, 1975.

Curtin, Maureen Francis. *Out of Touch: Skin Tropes and Identities in Woolf, Ellison, Pynchon, and Acker.* New York: Routledge, 2003.

Damon, Maria. "Review of *Genders, Races and Religious Cultures in Modern American Poetry, 1908–1934.* Rachel Blau DuPlessis." *Modernism/Modernity* 8.4 (2001):687–89.

Davey, Elizabeth. "Building a Black Audience in the 1930s: Langston Hughes, Poetry Readings, and the Golden Stair Press." *Print Culture in a Diverse America.* Ed. James P. Danky and Wayne A. Wiegand. Urbana: University of Illinois Press, 1998. 223–43.

Dawahare, Anthony. *Nationalism, Marxism, and African American Literature between Wars: A New Pandora's Box.* Jackson: University Press of Mississippi, 2003.

Dayton, Tim. *Muriel Rukeyser's The Book of the Dead.* Columbia, MO: University of Missouri Press, 2003.

Deleuze, Gilles, and Felix Guattari. *Anti-Oedipus: Capitalism and Schizophrenia.* Trans. Robert Hurley, Mark Seem, and Helen Lane. Minneapolis: University of Minnesota Press, 1983.

Derrida, Jacques. *Politics of Friendship.* Trans. George Collins. New York: Verso, 1997.

Dewarto, Nirwan. "Periphery—Lost and Found." Web. 6 June 2010.

Dewey, John. *Individualism Old and New.* New York, 1930.

Dickson-Carr, Darryl. *African American Satire.* Columbia: University of Missouri Press, 2001.

Dickstein, Morris. *Partisan Review* 38 (Winter 1971–72): 376–95.

Didier, Eribon. *Insult and the Making of the Gay Self.* Durham, NC: Duke University Press, 2004.

Distiller, Natasha. *Desire and Gender in the Sonnet Tradition.* New York: Palgrave MacMillan, 2008.

"Documentary Photography as a Medium." May 10, 1999. 8 4 2008 http://xroads.virginia.edu/~UG99/brady/doc.html.

Douglas, Mary. "The Social Control of Cognition: Some Factors in Joke Perception." *Man* 3.3 (1968): 361–76.

Dragstra, Henk; Sheila Ottway; and Helen Wilcox, eds. *Betraying Our Selves: Forms of Self-Representation in Early Modern English Texts.* London: Macmillan, 2000.

Duffy, Susan. ed. *The Political Plays of Langston Hughes.* Carbondale: Southern Illinois University Press, 2000.

Dugan, James, and Laurence Lafore. *Days of Emperor and Clown: The Italo-Ethiopian War 1936–1936.* Garden City, NY: Doubleday & Company, Inc., 1973.

DuPlessis, Rachel Blau. *Genders, Races and Religious Cultures in Modern American Poetry, 1908–1934.* New York: Cambridge University Press, 2001.

Dyche, Nathon. *Self-Fashioning in Frankenstein.* 7 July 2003 http://www.chakabraka.com/resources/frankenstein-self-fashioning.doc.

Earnest, Ernest. "The Popularity of *Spoon River Anthology*." ["*Spoon River* Revisited."] *Western Humanities Review* 21 (1967): 59–65. 16 November 2003 http://www.english.uiuc.edu/masps/poets/m_r/masters/masters.htm.

Eckhardt, Joshua. "On 'The Lynching.'" *Modern American Poetry.* 8 January 2004 http://www.english.uiuc.edu/maps/poets/m_r/mckay/lynching.htm.

Eliade, Mircea . *Myth and Reality.* Trans. W. Trask. New York: Harper and Row, 1963.

———. *The Myth of the Eternal Return or, Cosmos and History*. Princeton, N.J.: Princeton University Press, 1965.

Eliot, T. S. *The Waste Land and Other Poems*. New York: Dover Publications, 1998.

Emerson, Ralph Waldo. "Shakespeare, or, The Poet." 15 July 2003 http://www.textfiles.com/etext/AUTHORS/EMERSONemerson-representative-238.txt .

———. "Representative Men." 15 July 2003 http://www.textfiles.com/etext/AUTHORS/EMERSONemerson-representative-238.txt.

———. "Plato." 15 July 2003 http://www.textfiles.com/etext/AUTHORS/EMERSONemerson-representative-238.txtEngels, Friedrich. "Socialism: Utopian and Scientific." In Lewis S. Feuer, ed., *Marx and Engels: Basic Writings on Politics and Philosophy*. London: Collins, 1959. 68–111.

Encyclopedia Africana. "Blacks in the Great Depression." 30 October 2003 http://www.africana.com/articles/tt-644.htm.

Encyclopedia of Marxism. "Depression." 30 October 2003 http://www.marxists.org/glossary/events/d/e.htm#depression

Erikson, E. H. *Young Man Luther*. New York: Norton, 1958.

———. *Identity: Youth and Crisis*. New York: Norton, 1968.

Everett, Anna. *Returning the Gaze: A Genealogy of Black Film Criticism, 1909–1949*. Durham: Duke University Press, 2001.

Fabre, Michel. *The Unfinished Quest of Richard Wright*. New York: Morrow, 1973.

Fand, Roxanne J. *The Dialogic Self: Reconstructing Subjectivity in Woolf, Lessing, and Atwood*. Cranbury: Associated University Press, 1999.

Farrenkopf, John. *Prophet of Decline. Spengler on World History and Politics*. Baton Rouge: Louisiana State University Press, 2001.

Favor, J. Martin. *Authentic Blackness*. Durham: Duke University Press, 1999.

Fennelly, John F. *Twilight of the Evening Lands: Oswald Spengler a Half Century Later*. New York: Brookdale Press, 1972.

Feuer, Lewis S., ed. *Marx and Engels: Basic Writings on Politics and Philosophy*. London, Collins, 1959.

Flasch, Joy. *Melvin B. Tolson*. New York: Twayne, 1972.

Foley, Barbara. "Renarrating the Thirties in the Forties and Fifties." 13 July 2009 http://victorian.fortunecity.com/holbein/439/bf/foleyfifties.html.

Frazier, E. Franklin. *Black Bourgeoisie*. New York: Collier Books, 1962.

Freud, Sigmund. *Civilization and Its Discontents*. Trans. J. Strachey. New York: W.W. Norton, 1961.

Fromm, Erich. *Marx's Concept of Man*. New York: Frederick Ungar Publishing Co., 1966.

———. "What Does It Mean To Be Human?" [*The Revolution of Hope*. Vol. 38, World Perspectives Series, Ed. Ruth Nanda Anshen. 1968] *Significance: The Struggle We Share*. Ed. J. H. Brennecke and R. G. Amick. Encino, CA: Glencoe Pub. Co., 1980. 42–44.

Frye, Northrop. *The Great Code: The Bible and Literature*. New York: Harcourt Brace Jovanovich, 1982.

Gabbin, Joanne V. *Sterling A. Brown: Building the Black Aesthetic Tradition*. Charlottesville: University of Virginia Press, 1985.

Gagnier, Regenia. *Subjectivities: A History of Self-Representation in Britain, 1832–1920*. New York: Oxford University Press, 1991.

Garvey, Marcus. "Africa for the Africans." Gates, Henry Louis, et al., eds. *The Norton*

Anthology of African American Literature. 1st ed. New York: Norton, 1997. 976–77.

Gates, Henry Louis, et al., eds. *The Norton Anthology of African American Literature*. 1st ed. New York: Norton, 1997.

Gergen, Kenneth J. "Warranting Voice and the Elaboration of the Self." *Texts of Identity*. Ed. John Shotter and K. J. Gergen. Newbury Park, CA: Sage Publications, 1990. 70–81.

Gandhi, Nilay. "On 'The Lynching.'" *Modern American Poetry*. 18 November 2004 http://www.english.uiuc.edu/maps/poets/m_r/mckay/lynching.htm.

Gorman, William. "W.E.B. Du Bois and His Work." *Fourth International* 11.3 (May-June 1950): 80–86. 7 October 2004 http://www.clrjamesinstitute.org/gorman1.html.

Graham. "Armstrong's Film Roles" 6 25 2008 http://xroads.virginia.edu/~ug99/graham/biography.html.

Greene, Thomas M. "The Flexibility of the Self in Renaissance Literature." In *The Disciplines of Criticism: Essays in Literary Theory, Interpretation, and History*. Eds. Peter Demetz, Thomas Greene, and Lowry Nelson, Jr. New Haven: Yale University Press, 1968

Greenblatt, Stephen. *Renaissance Self-Fashioning: From More to Shakespeare*. Chicago: Chicago University Press, 1980.

Gordon, Eugene. "Blacks Turn Red." *Negro*. Ed. Nancy Cunard (1931–33). 236–40.

Griffin, Roger. "Notes towards the definition of fascist culture: the prospects for synergy between Marxist and liberal heuristics." *Renaissance and Modern Studies* 42 (Autumn 2001): 95–115. 8 August 2004 http://ah.brookes.ac.uk/history/staff/griffin/fasaesthetics.pdf.

Gruesser, John Cullen. *Black on Black: Twentieth-Century African American Writing about Africa*. Lexington, KY: University Press of Kentucky, 2000.

Gurdjieff, G. I. *Beelzebub's Tales to His Grandson*. New York: E. P. D. Dutton & Co., Inc., 1973.

Gussow, Adam. *Seems Like Murder Here: Southern Violence and the Blues Tradition*. Chicago: University of Chicago Press, 2002.

———. "Racial Violence, 'Primitive' Music, and the Blues Entrepreneur W. C. Handy's Mississippi Problem." *Southern Cultures*. 8.3 (2002): 56–77.

Hakutani, Yoshinobu. *Richard Wright and Radical Discourse*. Columbia: University of Missouri Press, 1996.

Halevi, Z'ev Ben Shimoln. *Kabbalah: Tradition of Hidden Knowledge*. New York: Thames & Hudson, 1985.

Hampden-Turner, Charles. "The Dynamic Unities of Carl Jung." *Maps of the Mind*. New York: Macmillan, 1981.

Hanson, Marilee. "Selected Letters of John Keats." EnglishHistory.net. 2003 13 July 2007 http://englishhistory.net/keats/bykeats.html.

Harris, David. *A Society of Signs?* London: Routledge: 1996.

Harris, Trudier. "About Sharecropping." [*The Oxford Companion to Women's Writing in the United States*.] 21 July 2008 http://www.english.uiuc.edu/maps/poets/a_f/brown/sharecropping.htm.

Hatch, James V. *Sorrow Is the Only Faithful One: The Life of Owen Dodson*. Champaign: University of Illinois Press, 1993.

Herder, Johann Gottfried. *Materials for the Philosophy of Mankind*. 11 November

2004 http://www.forham.edu/halsall.mod/1784herder-mankind.html.

Hernton, Calvin. *Sex and Racism in America*. New York: Doubleday & Co., 1965.

Hill, Herbert, ed. "Reflections on Richard Wright: A Symposium on an Exiled Native Son, with Horace Cayton, Arna Bontemps, Saunders Redding." *Anger and Beyond: The Negro Writer in the United States*. New York: Harper and Row, 1966. 196–203.

Hillman, James. *The Soul's Code*. New York: Warner, 1997.

Hollier, Denis. Introduction. *Against Architecture: The Writings of Georges Bataille*. Trans. Betsy Wing. Berkeley: Zone, 1992.

Holloway, Julia Bolton. Florin Website. [The Elizabeth Barrett Browning Website 16 June 2009 http://www.florin.ms/ebb.html] http://www.florin.ms/.

Holmes, Eugene. "A Writer's Social Obligations." In *The Writer in a Changing World: American Writers' Congress*. 2nd ed. Edited by Henry Hart. New York: Equinox Cooperative Press, 1937. 172–79.

Horne, Gerald. "Reformers Faced Tough Job in Stopping Black Lynching." [Editorial. No. 348.] *Baltimore Sun* 16 April 1998. 29 October 2004. htttp://www.unc.edu/news/archives/apr98/horne.html.

Howard-Pitney, David. *The Afro-American Jeremiad: Appeals for Justice in America*. Philadelphia: Temple University Press, 1990.

Howe, Irving. Review of *Invisible Man*. 21 June 2004 http://www.honors.umd.edu/HONR269J/archive/howeReview.html.

Huggins, Nathan Irvin, ed. *Voices from the Harlem Renaissance*. New York: Oxford University Press, 1976.

Hutchinson, George. *In Search of Nella Larsen: A Biography of the Color Line*. Cambridge: Harvard University Press, 2006.

Il Piccolo. Trieste, 6 May 1936. 27 August 2004 http://www.library.wisc.edu/libraries/dpf/Fascism/Foreign.html.

Jakobson, R., and Halle, M. *Fundamentals of Language*. The Hague: Mouton Publishers: 1980.

James, Allen. *Without Sanctuary: Lynching Photographs in America*. Santa Fe, NM: Twin Palms Publishers, 2000.

Johnson, James Weldon. "Preface to the First Edition." *The Book of American Negro Poetry*. *Voices from the Harlem* Renaissance. Ed. Nathan I. Huggins. New York: Oxford, 1976. 281.

Jones, Amerlia. *Irrational Modernism: A Neurasthenic History of New York Dada*. Cambridge, MA: The MIT Press, 2004.

Jones, Marilyn. "Postal Service Honors American Author." *FedSmith*. 7 April 2009. Web. 10 July 2010.

Jordan, Jennifer. *Arthur P. Davis: Forging the Way for the Formation of the Canon*. *Callaloo* 20. 2 (1997): 450–60.

Judge, Chris. "Blues Genres." 11 July 2007   http://www.wordofmouthproductions.org/genres.htm.

Keegan, Bridget. "'Ode on a Grecian Urn': Hypercanonicity and Pedagogy—Teaching Like an Urn." Crieighton University. Rolmantic circles Praxis Series. Web. 15 March 2007.

Keller, James R. "A Chafing Savage Down the Decent Street": The Politics of Compromise in Claude McKay's Protest Sonnets." *African American Review* 28.3 (1994): 447–56.

Keller, Lynn. *Forms of Expansion: Recent Long Poems by Women*. Chicago: University of Chicago Press, 1997.

Kelley, Robin D. G. Foreword. Lin Shi Khan and Tony Perez, Eds. *Scottsboro, Alabama: A Story in Linoleum Cuts*. Andrew H. Lee. New York: New York University Press. 2002. vii–xviii.

Kellner, Bruce, ed. *The Harlem Renaissance: A Historical Dictionary for the Era*. Westport, CN: Greenwood Press, 1984.

Kellner, Paul. "Virilio, War, and Technology: Some Critical Reflections." 11 July 2004 http://www.gseis.ucla.edu/faculty/kellner/kellner.html .

——. "Share Croppers Union." [*Hammer and Hoe: Alabama Communists during the Great Depression. Chapel Hill: University of North Carolina Press, 1990.*] 21 July 2008 http://www.english.uiuc.edu/maps/poets/a_f/brown/sharecropping.htm.

Kertzer, David I. *Ritual, Politics, and Power*. New Haven: Yale University Press, 1989.

Kimmel, Michael, ed. Introduction. *The Sexual Self: The Construction of Sexual Scripts*. Nashville, Tennessee: Vanderbilt University Press, 2003.

Koethe, John. "The Romance of Realism." *New Literary History* 28.4 (Autumn 1997): 723–37.

Kook, Rebecca. "The Shifting Status of African Americans in the American Collective Identity." *Journal of Black Studies* 29.2 (1998): 154–78.

Kristeva, Julia. *Desire in Language: A Semiotic Approach to Literature and Art*. New York: Columbia University Press, 1980.

——. *Powers of Horror: An Essay on Abjection*. New York: Columbia University Press, 1982.

Lawton, Anna. "Introduction." *Words in Revolution: Russian Futurism through Its Manifestoes, 1912–1928*. Washington, D.C.: New Academia Press, 2005. 1–33.

Leithart, Peter J. "Caesar's Reviving Blood: Shakespeare and the Religion of Revolution." 7 October 2004 http://www.leithart.com/archives/000799.php.

Lendering, Jona. "Hannibal." Web. 7 July 2010. Livius.org

Lever, J. W. *The Elizabethan Love Sonnet*. London: Methuen, 1966.

Lewis, David Levering. *When Harlem Was in Vogue*. New York: Oxford University Press, 1979.

Liberman, Robert C. *Shifting the Color Line: Race and the American Welfare State*. Cambridge: Harvard University Press, 1998.

Liukkonen, Petri. "Oswald Arnold Gottfried Spengler (1880–1936)." 12 July 2009 http://www.kirjasto.sci.fi/spengle.htm.

Locke, Alain. "Art or Propaganda?" *Voices from the Harlem* Renaissance. Ed. Nathan I. Huggins. New York: Oxford, 1976. 312.

——. Foreword. *The New Negro*. Ed. Alain Locke. New York: Atheneum, 1969. xv–xvii.

——. "Jingo, Counter-Jingo and Us, Part 1. Retrospective Review of the Literature of the Negro: 1937." *Opportunity* (Jan. 1938): 7–11, 27.

——. "We Turn to Prose: A Retrospective Review of the Literature of the Negro for 1931." *Opportunity* 10 (1931): 40–43.

——. "Black Truth and Black Beauty: A Retrospective Review of the Literature of the Negro for 1932." *Opportunity* 10 (1932).

——. "The Eleventh Hour of Nordicism: Retrospective Review of the Literature of the Negro for 1934." *Opportunity* 12 (1935): 8–12.

——. "Deep River: Deeper Sea: Retrospective Review of the Literature of the Negro for 1935." *Opportunity* 13 (1935): 7–10.

———. "The Negro: 'New' and Newer: A Retrospective Review of the Literature of the Negro for 1938." *Opportunity* 17 (1939): 8–10.

Longenbach, James. *Modernist Poetics of History: Pound, Eliot, and a Sense of the Past.* Princeton, NJ: Princeton University Press, 1987.

Lubiano, Wahneema. "Constructing and Reconstructing Afro-American Texts: The Critic as Ambassador and Referee." *American Literary History* 1 (1989): 432–47.

Lucky, Crystal T. "Black Women Writers of the Harlem Renaissance." *Challenging Boundaries: Gender and Periodization.* Ed. Joyce W. Warren and Margaret Dickie. Athens: University of Georgia Press, 2000. 91–106.

Lupton, Deborah. *The Emotional Self: A Sociocultural Exploration.* London; Thousand Oaks, CA: Sage, 1998.

Makovsky, Paul. "Growing Up Modern." *Metropolis* 20.7 (March 2001): 146–49.

Maltby, Richard. "Tragic Heroes? Al Capone and the Spectacle of Criminality, 1927–1931." In John Benson, Ken Berryman, and Wayne Levy, eds., *Screening the Past: The Sixth Australian History and Film Conference.* Melbourne: Le Trobe University Press, 1995. October 30 2003 http://www.klc.ac.uk/humanities/cch/film-studies/course/mobculture/.

Marinetti, F. T. "Poesia, musica, e architetture africane." *Manifesto Stile Futurista.* March 1935. Web. 10 July 2010.

Marling, Kara Ann. *American Post Office Murals in the Great Depression.* Minneapolis: University of Minneapolis Press, 1982.

Marotti, Arthur F. "'Love Is Not Love': Elizabethan Sonnet Sequences and the Social Order." *ELH* 49 (October 8 2004) http://www2.arts.gla.ac.uk/SESLL/EngLit/ugrad/hons/theory/CultMaterialism.htm.

Marteinson, Peter. "Semiotics of the Comic." October 22, 2004 http://www.chass.uto-ronto.ca/french/as-sa/editors/Thesis.html .

Marx, Karl. "Contribution to the Critique of Hegel's *Philosophy of Right*." 25 June 2007 http://www.baylor.edu/~Scott_Moore/texts/Marx_Contr_Crit.html.

Marzorati, Gerald. "All By Himself." *The New York Times Magazine,* March 17, 2002: 32–37, 68–70.

Matthews, J. H. *Surrealist Poetry in France.* Syracuse, NY: Syracuse University Press, 1969.

Maxson, H. A. *On the Sonnets of Robert Frost: A Critical Examination of the 37 Poems.* Jefferson, NC and London: McFarland & Co., Publishers, 1997.

Maxwell, William J. *From New Negro, Old Left: African-American Writing and Communism between the Wars.* New York: Columbia University Press, 1999. 8 January 2004 http://www.english.uiuc.edu/maps/poets/m_r/mckay/lynching.htm.

McCall, Dan. *The Example of Richard Wright.* New York: Harcourt, Brace, 1969.

McCormick, Fred. "Review of "Prison Songs." Musical Traditions Web Services 7 November 2004 http://www.mustrad.org.uk/reviews/prison.htm.

McDonogh Neighborhood Snapshot. 23 June 2008 http://www.gnocd.org/index.html.

McInnes, Neil. "Oswald Spengler Reconsidered." *The National Interest.* 1997. Web. 14 July 2010.

McIntyre, Diane. Review of *Underworld.* online.

Mead, Rebecca "The Marx Brother" [Žižek]. *The New Yorker,* May 5, 2003, 40.

Mello, Gonzalez, and Diane Miliotes, eds. *Jose Clemente Orozco in the United States,*

1927–1934. [Hood Museum of Art, Dartmouth College] New York: W.W. Norton, 2002.

Mikics, David. *The Romance of Individualism in Emerson and Nietzsche*. Athens: Ohio University Press, 2003.

Miller, Eugene. *Voice of a Native Son: The Poetics of Richard Wright*. Jackson, MS: University Press of Mississippi, 1990.

Miller, Nina. *MAPS* "Millay's Poetry in a Greenwich Village Context." 2 July 2008 http://www.english.illinois.edu/maps/poets/m_r/millay/ninamiller.htm.

Miller, R. Baxter, ed. *Black American Poets between Worlds, 1940–1960*. Knoxville: University of Tennessee Press, 1986.

Miller, William Ian. Quoted in Scott McCleme, "Getting Emotional." *Chronicle of Higher Education*, Feb. 21, 2003, 15.

Morgan, Stacy I. *Rethinking Social Realism: African American Art and Literature, 1930–1953*. Athens: University of Georgia Press, 2004.

Morson, Gary Saul, and Caryl Emerson. *Mikhail Bakhtin: Creation of a Prosaics*. Stanford: Stanford University Press, 1990.

Mussolini, Benito. Speech 1935. 27 August 2004 http://www.dickinson.edu/~rhyne/232/EthiopiaSpeech.html.

Nelson, Cary. *MAPS*. From *Revolutionary Memory: Recovering the Poetry of the American Left*. New York: Routledge, 2001. August 8 2004. http://www.english.uiuc.edu/maps/poets/m_r/mckay/lynching.htm.

Nelson, Raymond. "*Harlem Gallery*: An Advertisement and User's Manual." *Virginia Quarterly Review* (Summer 1999). Web. 25 June 2007.

Newcomb, John Timberman. "The Woman as Political Poet: Edna St. Vincent Millay and the Mid-Century Canon." *Criticism* 37.2 (Spring 1995): 261–64.

Ng, Janet. *The Experience of Modernity: Chinese Autobiography of the Early Twentieth Century*. Ann Arbor: University of Michigan Press, 2003.

Oliver, Kelly. "Kristeva and Feminism." 1998. 21 July 2008 http://www.cddc.vt.edu/feminism/kristeva.html.

Oliver, Paul. *The Meaning of the Blues*. Toronto: Collier Books, 1960.

O'Meally, Robert G. "An Annotated Bibliography of the Works of Sterling A. Brown." *Callaloo* 21, no. 4. Sterling A. Brown: A Special Issue (Autumn 1998): 822–35.

Omi, Michael, and Howard Winant. *Racial Formation in the United States*. New York: Routledge, 1994.

"On Hebrew." Hebrew eTutorGlobal Navigation 2008/5768. 20 July 2008 Jewish Language Institute http://hebrewetutor.com/on_hebrew.html.

Palatnik, Beth. "Consumption: Devouring 'The Harlem Dancer.'" *Modern American Poetry*. MAPS. Web. 7 October 2004. http://www.english.uiuc.edu/maps/poets/m_r/mckay/harlemdancer.htm.

Parini, Jay. *Why Poetry Matters*. New Haven: Yale University Press, 2008.

Parker, Ian. "Discourse and Power." *Texts of Identity*. Ed. John Shotter and K. J. Gergen. Newbury Park, CA: Sage Publications, 1990. 56–69.

Pells, Radical. *Visions and American Dreams: Culture and Social Thought in the Depression Years*. New York: Harper & Row, 1973.

Pereira, Mario. "Racialized Bodies in Murals of the 1930s." 19 July 2007 http://www.brown.edu/courses/HA0293/racialized bodies.html.

Perry, Bliss. *Emerson Today. The Louis Clark Vanuxem Foundation Lectures*. Princeton, NJ: Princeton University Press, 1931.

Pieroth, Doris H. *Their Day in the Sun: Women of the 1932 Olympics*. Seattle: University of Washington Press, 1996.

Pilgrim, David. "The Picaninny Caricature." Jim Crow Museum of Racist Memorabilia. 11 August 2008. 2008 http://www.ferris.edu/news/jimcrow/picaninny/.htm.

Pinkus, Jenny. "Subject Positions and Positioning." August 1996. 13 June 2008 http://www.massey.ac.nz/~alock/theory/subpos.htm.

Pizzitola, Louis. *Hearst over Hollywood: Power, Passion and Propaganda in the Movies*. New York: Columbia University Press, 2001. 394–95.

Poggi, Christine. *Modernism/Modernity* 4.3 (1997):19–43.

Potter, Chris. "You Had to Ask" [Boardman Robinson Mural]. *Pittsburg City Paper—online*. 19 July 2007 http://www.pittsburgcitypapaper.ws/prev/archives/news-arch/ask/ask00/ya11800.html.

Powell, Richard. "Harlem Renaissance." Online NewsHour (February 20, 1998) 5 July 2003 http://www.pbs.org/newshour/forum/february98/harlem5.html.

Powers, Ron. "The Apocalypse of Adolescence." *The Atlantic Monthly* (March 2002): 58–74.

Puryear, Susan C. "Eunice Roberta Hunton Carter: 1889–1970, Prosecuting Organized Crime." 11 August 2004 http://www.law.stanford.edu/library/wlhbp/papers0203/eunice.2002.pd .

Randall, Dudley. "The Black Aesthetic in the Thirties, Forties, and Fifties." *The Black Aesthetic*. Ed. Addison Gayle, Jr. Garden City, NY: Anchor Books, 1971. 211–16.

Rationalrevolution.net. "American Supporters of the European Fascists." Web. 11 July 2010.

Redmond, Eugene. *Drumvoices: The Mission of Afro-American Poetry: A Critical History*. Garden City, NY: Anchor Books, 1976.

Reed, Brian. "Carl Sandburg's The People, Yes, Thirties Modernism, and the Problem of Bad Political Poetry." *Texas Studies in Literature and Language* 46.2 (2004): 181–212.

Reed, T. V. *Fifteen Jugglers, Five Believers: Literary Politics and the Poetics of American Social Movements*. Berkeley: University of California Press, 1992.

The Reflector, "Anti-Lynching Efforts." Issue No. 24, January 20, 1934. 12 March 2007 http://www.vcdh.virginia.edu/afam/reflector/historicalb.html.

Rice, John Steadman. "Romantic Modernism and the Self." *Hedgehog Review*. Institute for Advanced Studies in Culture. 10 July 2004 http://religionanddemocracy.lib.virginia.edu/hh/ThrTocs1–1.html.

Robertson, Ritchie. "Roth's *Hiob* and the Traditions of Ghetto Fiction." *Joseph Roth in Retrospect: Co-Existent Contradictions*. Ed. Helen Chambers. Riverside, CA: Ariadne Press, 1991.

Robinson, Marilyn. "Collins to Grisham: A Brief History of the Legal Thriller." [A web-enhanced version of 22 *Legal Studies Forum* 21 (1998).] 11 August 2004 http://www.law.utexas.edu/lpop/legstud.htm

Rock, P. *The Making of Symbolic Interactionism*. London: Macmillan, 1979.

Ross, Andrew. *The Failure of Modernism: Symptoms of American Poetry*. New York: Columbia University Press, 1986.

Roth, Joseph. *Job: The Story of a Simple Man*. New York: Viking, 1931.

Rotman, Brian. *Becoming Beside Ourselves: The Alphabet, Ghosts, and Distributed Human Beings*. Durham: Duke University Press, 2008.

Rotenberg, C. T., and Francene Rotenberg. "Idealization and Disillusionment in the Dramas of Henrik Ibsen." *Journal of American Academy of Psychoanalysis* 24.1 (January 1996): 137–61.

Rudy, Jason R."On Cultural Neoformalism, Spasmodic Poetry, and the Victorian Ballad." *Victorian Poetry* 41. 4 (2003): 590–96.

Ruhle, Jurgen. *Literature and Revolution: A Critical Study of the Writer and Communism in the Twentieth Century*. New York: Praeger, 1969.

Russo, John Paul. *The Future without a Past: The Humanities in a Technological Society*. Columbia: University of Missouri Press, 2005.

Sanders, Mark A. *Afro-Modernist Aesthetics and the Poetry of Sterling A. Brown*. Athens: University of Georgia Press, 1999.

Sbacchi, Alberto. *Legacy of Bitterness: Ethiopia and Fascist Italy, 1935–1941*. Lawrenceville, NJ: Red Sea Press, 1997.

Schatz, Thomas. *Hollywood Genres*. Mexico: McGraw-Hill, 1981.

Schmidt, Alfred. *History and Structure: An Essay on Hegelian-Marxist and Structuralist Theories of History*. Cambridge: MIT Press, 1981.

Schwab, Peter. *Haile Selassie I: Ethiopia's Lion of Judah*. Chicago: Nelson Hall, 1979.

Schweik, Susan. "Josephine Miles's Crip(t) Words: Gender, Disability, 'Doll.'" *Journal of Literary Disability* 1.1 (2008): 49–60.

Scott, Nathan. "African American Poetry." *The New Princeton Encyclopedia of Poetry and Poetics*. Ed. Alex Preminger and T. V. F. Brogan. Princeton, NJ: Princeton University Press, 1994. 23–25

Scott, William R. *The Sons of Sheba's Race: African-Americans and the Italo-Ethiopian War, 1935–1941*. Bloomington: Indiana University Press, 1993.

Scully, James. *Line Break: Poetry as Social Practice*. Seattle: Bay Press, 1988.

Shepherd, Reginald. "Revised Thoughts on the Long Poem." 19 July 2007 http://reginaldshepherd.blogspot.com/2007/06/revised-thoughts-on-long-poem.html.

Sherrard-Johnson, Cherene. *Portraits of the New Negro Woman: Visual and Literary Culture in the Harlem Renaissance*. New Brunswick: Rutgers, 2007.

Shulman, Robert. *The Power of Political Art: The 1930's Political Left Reconsidered*. Chapel Hill: The University of North Carolina Press, 2000.

Sierra Nevada Virtual Museum. "Joaquin Miller." Web. 20 July 2010.

Simmel, Georg "The Metropolis and Mental Life" (1903). 25 July 2008 http://en.wikipedia.org/w/index.php?title=Modernist_literature&printable=yes—cite_note-2

Simmons, Hortense E. "Sterling A. Brown's 'Literary Chronicles.'" *African American Review* 31.3 (Fall 1997): 443–49.

Sklar, Robert. *Movie-Made America*. New York, Random House, 1975.

Smethurst, James Edward. *The New Red Negro: The Literary Left and African American Poetry, 1930–1946*. New York: Oxford University Press, 1999.

Smith, Katherine Capshaw. "Introduction: The Landscape of Ethnic American Children's Literature." *MELUS* (Summer 2002). 19 July 2007 http://www.findarticles.com/cf_)/m2278/2_27/92589722/pl/article.jhtml.

Smylie, James H. "Countee Cullen's 'The Black Christ.'" *Theology Today* 38, no. 2 (July 1981): 160–65.

Snow, David. "Collective Identity and Expressive Forms." (October 1, 2001). Center for the Study of Democracy. Paper 01–07. 14 August 2008 http://repositories.cdlib.org/csd/01–07.

Spengler, Oswald. *The Decline of The West*, 2 vols. Trans. Charles Francis Atkinson, New York: Alfred A. Knopf, 1922. *Internet Modern History Sourcebook*. 8 October 2004 http://www.fordham.edu/halsall/mod/spengler-decline.html.

Spillers, Hortense. "Changing the Letter: the yokes, the jokes, of discourse, or, Mrs. Stowe, Mr. Reed." in *Slavery and the Literary Imagination*. Ed. Deborah E. McDowell and Arnold Rampersad. Baltimore: Johns Hopkins University Press, 1989. 25–61.

Spingern, Arthur B. "Books by Negro Authors in 1930." *The Crisis* (February 1937): 47.

Staples, Shelley. "Negotiating the Racial Mountain: The Depression Era Murals of Aaron Douglas." American Studies Program. University of Virginia. 2003. 27 October 04 http://xroads.virginia.edu/~MA03/staples/douglas/usable.html.

Steinsaltz, Adin. "After the Bright Light of Revelation." *Parabola* 14.2 (1989): 95–102.

Sterner, Lewis. G. "The Sonnet in American Literature." MA Thesis, University of Pennsylvania,1930.

Stimely, Keith. "Oswald Spengler: An Introduction to His Life and Ideas." Institute for Historical Review. Web. 14 July 2010.

Stott, William. *Documentary Expression and Thirties America*. New York: Oxford University Press, 1973.

Strathausen, Carsten. *The Book of Things: Poetry and Vision around 1900*. Chapel Hill: The University of North Carolina Press, 2007.

Suárez, Juan A. "T. S. Eliot's *The Waste Land*, the Gramophone, and the Modernist Discourse Network." *New Literary History* 32.3 (2001): 747–68.

Sullivan, Nancy. *The Treasury of American Poetry*. Garden City, NY: Doubleday, 1978.

Sunić, Tomislav. "History and Decadence: Spengler's Cultural Pessimism Today." *CLIO* (A Journal of Literature, History and the Philosophy of History) 19, no 1 (Fall 1989): 51–62.

Sutton, Walter. *Modern American Criticism*. Englewood Cliffs, NJ: Prentice-Hall, Inc., 1963.

Syrotinski, Michael. *Singular Performances: Reinscribing the Subject in Francophone African Writing*. Charlottesville: University of Virginia Press, 2002.

Szalay, Thomas. *New Deal Modernism: American Literature and the Invention of the Welfare State* Durham, NC: Duke University Press, 2000.

Tennyson, Alfred. *Idylls of the King*: Project Gutenberg. 8 October 2004 http://www.gutenberg.net/etext/610.

Thurston, Michael. *Making Something Happen: American Poetry between the World Wars*. Chapel Hill: University of North Carolina Press, 2001.

———. MAPS. From "Black Christ, Red Flag: Langston Hughes on Scottsboro." 28 January 2004 [*College Literature*, 1995.] http://www.english.uiuc.edu/maps.

Tidwell, John Edgar, and Ted Genoways. "Two Lost Sonnets by Sterling A. Brown." *Callaloo* 21.4 (1998): 741–44.

Tiffany, Daniel. *Radio Corpse: Imagism and the Cryptaesthetic of Ezra Pound*. Cambridge, MA: Harvard University Press, 1995.

Time Europe Magazine. "The League: Answering Ethiopia." July 13, 1936. 11 September 2004 http://www.time.com/time/europe/index.html.

Toynbee, Arnold J. *A Study of History*. London: Oxford University Press, 1948.

Traverso, Enzo. "Intellectuals and Anti-Fascism: For a Critical Historization." *New Politics* 9.4 [new series]. Whole number 36 (Winter 2004). 5 June 2004 http://

www.wpunj.edu/~newpol/issue36/Travers036.htm.

Trotsky, Leon. "On Black Nationalism." *International Socialism* 43, April/May 1970, UKM 8 October 2004 http://www.marxists.org/archive/trotsky/works/1940/negr01.htm.

Tuhkanen, Mikko. *The American Optic: Psychoanalysis, Critical Race Theory, and Richard Wright.* Albany: State University of New York Press, 2009.

Ullman, Robert, and J. Reichenberg-Ullman. *Mystics, Masters, Saints, and Sages.* Berkeley: Conari Press, 2001.

Verdelle, A. J. "The Largesse of Zora Neale Hurston." *Village Voice* (April 17–23, 2002). 11 November 2004 http://www.villagevoice.com/issues/0216/verdelle.php.

———. "The Truth of the Picnic: Writing about American Slavery." *Representing Slavery: A Roundtable Discussion. Common Place* 1.4 (July 2001). 11 November 2004 http://www.common-place.org.

Wagner, Jennifer Ann. *A Moment's Monument: Revisionary Poetics and the Nineteenth-Century Sonnet.* Madison, PA: Fairleigh Dickinson University Press, 1996.

Waite, A. E. *The Holy Kabbalah: A Study of the Secret Tradition in Israel.* London: Westfriar's Press, 1924.

Walker, Margaret. *Richard Wright, Daemonic Genius: A Portrait of the Man, a Critical Look at His Work.* New York: Warner Books, 1988.

Wallace, Maurice Orlando. *Constructing the Black Masculine: Identity and Ideality in African American Men's Literature and Culture, 1775–1995.* Durham, NC: Duke University Press, 2003.

Warren, Joyce W. "Challenge of Women's Periods" [Introduction]. *Challenging Boundaries: Gender and Periodization.* Ed. Joyce W. Warren and Margaret Dickie. Athens: University of Georgia Press, 2000. ix–xxiv.

Waterman, Alan S. *The Psychology of Individualism.* New York : Praeger, 1984.

Weatherly, Tom. "Black Oral Poetry in America: An Open Letter." *Alcheringa/Ethnopoetics* (Winter 1971): 94–95.

Weinroth, Michelle. "Kant, Sendak, and the Limits of Modern Subjectivity." 8 October 04 http://www.uqtr.uquebec.ca/AE/Vol_5/Weinroth/Weinroth.htm.

Werhane, Patricia H. "Community and Individuality." *New Literary History* 27.1 (1996):15–24.

White, Hayden. *Metahistory: The Historical Imagination in Nineteenth-Century Europe.* Baltimore: Johns Hopkins University Press, 1973.

Whitman, Walt. "Democratic Vistas." *Leaves of Grass and Selected Prose.* Ed. Sculley Bradley. New York: Holt, Rhinehart and Winston, 1965. 489–546.

Whittier, Gayle. "The Sonnet's Body and the Body Sonnetized in *Romeo and Juliet*." *Shakespeare Quarterly* 40 (Spring, 1989): 27–41.

Willett, Cynthia, John Lysaker, and Michael Sullivan. "Individualism Bold and New: A Panel Proposal." HTML Document. Web. 28 July 2003.

Winthrop-Young, Geoffrey. "Silicon Sociology, or, Two Kings on Hegel's Throne? Kittler, Luhmann, and the Posthuman Merger of German Media Theory." *The Yale Journal of Criticism* 13.2 (2000):391–420.

Woodson, Jon. *To Make a New Race: Gurdjieff, Toomer, and the Harlem Renaissance.* Jackson: University Press of Mississippi, 1999.

Woodward, C. Van. *The Strange Career of Jim Crow.* New York: Oxford University Press, 1966.

WordNet—Online Dictionary. Web. 10 July 2010.

Wright, Richard. "A Tale of Folk courage." Review of Arna Bontemps, *Black Thunder*. *Partisan Review* and *Anvil* 3.3 (1936): 31.

Wurmser, Leon. *The Mask of Shame*. Baltimore: Johns Hopkins University Press, 1981.

Young, James O. *Black Writers of the Thirties*. Baton Rouge: Louisiana State University Press, 1973.

Žižek, Miroslav. *The Sublime Object of Ideology*. London: Verso, 1989.

Index